Understanding, Implementing, and Evaluating Knowledge Management in Business Settings

Tereza Raquel Merlo
University of North Texas, USA

A volume in the Advances in Knowledge Acquisition, Transfer, and Management (AKATM) Book Series

IGI Global
PUBLISHER of TIMELY KNOWLEDGE

Published in the United States of America by
IGI Global
Business Science Reference (an imprint of IGI Global)
701 E. Chocolate Avenue
Hershey PA, USA 17033
Tel: 717-533-8845
Fax: 717-533-8661
E-mail: cust@igi-global.com
Web site: http://www.igi-global.com

Library of Congress Cataloging-in-Publication Data

Name: Merlo, Tereza Raquel, 1972- editor.
Title: Understanding, implementing, and evaluating knowledge management in business settings / Tereza Raquel Merlo, editor.
Description: Hershey, PA : Business Science Reference, [2022] | Includes bibliographical references and index. | Summary: "This edited book presents a comprehensive approach to knowledge management, from concepts to practices, in corporations of different segments, particularly in high tech, impacting the way KM is understood and implemented, and even evaluated"-- Provided by publisher.
Identifiers: LCCN 2022001282 (print) | LCCN 2022001283 (ebook) | ISBN 9781668444313 (hardcover) | ISBN 9781668444320 (paperback) | ISBN 9781668444337 (ebook)
Subjects: LCSH: Knowledge management.
Classification: LCC HD30.2 .U525 2022 (print) | LCC HD30.2 (ebook) | DDC 658.4/038--dc23/eng/20220113
LC record available at https://lccn.loc.gov/2022001282
LC ebook record available at https://lccn.loc.gov/2022001283

This book is published in the IGI Global book series Advances in Knowledge Acquisition, Transfer, and Management (AKATM) (ISSN: 2326-7607; eISSN: 2326-7615)

British Cataloguing in Publication Data
A Cataloguing in Publication record for this book is available from the British Library.

Advances in Knowledge Acquisition, Transfer, and Management (AKATM) Book Series

Murray E. Jennex
San Diego State University, USA

ISSN:2326-7607
EISSN:2326-7615

MISSION

Organizations and businesses continue to utilize knowledge management practices in order to streamline processes and procedures. The emergence of web technologies has provided new methods of information usage and knowledge sharing.

The **Advances in Knowledge Acquisition, Transfer, and Management (AKATM) Book Series** brings together research on emerging technologies and their effect on information systems as well as the knowledge society. **AKATM** will provide researchers, students, practitioners, and industry leaders with research highlights surrounding the knowledge management discipline, including technology support issues and knowledge representation.

COVERAGE

- Cognitive Theories
- Cultural Impacts
- Information and Communication Systems
- Knowledge Acquisition and Transfer Processes
- Knowledge Management Strategy
- Knowledge Sharing
- Organizational Learning
- Organizational Memory
- Small and Medium Enterprises
- Virtual Communities

The Advances in Knowledge Acquisition, Transfer, and Management (AKATM) Book Series (ISSN 2326-7607) is published by IGI Global, 701 E. Chocolate Avenue, Hershey, PA 17033-1240, USA, www.igi-global.com. This series is composed of titles available for purchase individually; each title is edited to be contextually exclusive from any other title within the series. For pricing and ordering information please visit http://www.igi-global.com/book-series/advances-knowledge-acquisition-transfer-management/37159. Postmaster: Send all address changes to above address.

Titles in this Series

For a list of additional titles in this series, please visit: http://www.igi-global.com/book-series/

Handbook of Research on the Global View of Open Access and Scholarly Communications
Daniel Gelaw Alemneh (University of North Texas, USA)
Information Science Reference • © 2022 • 432pp • H/C (ISBN: 9781799898054) • US $150.00

Knowledge Management and Big Data Analytics for Strategic Decision Making
Abdalmuttaleb M.A. Musleh Al-Sartawi (Ahlia University, Bahrain) Anjum Razzaque (Ahlia University, Bahrain) Mukhtar Alhashimi (Ahlia University, Bahrain) and Allam Hamdan (Ahlia University, Bahrain)
Engineering Science Reference • © 2022 • 325pp • H/C (ISBN: 9781799855521) • US $245.00

Handbook of Research on Mixed Methods Research in Information Science
Patrick Ngulube (University of South Africa, South Africa)
Information Science Reference • © 2022 • 737pp • H/C (ISBN: 9781799888444) • US $345.00

Methodological Innovations in Research and Academic Writing
Aaron Samuel Zimmerman (Texas Tech University, USA)
Information Science Reference • © 2022 • 377pp • H/C (ISBN: 9781799882831) • US $195.00

Handbook of Research on Advanced Research Methodologies for a Digital Society
Gabriella Punziano (University of Naples Federico II, Italy) and Angela Delli Paoli (University of Salerno, Italy)
Information Science Reference • © 2022 • 919pp • H/C (ISBN: 9781799884736) • US $495.00

Handbook of Research on Organizational Culture Strategies for Effective Knowledge Management and Performance
Dana Tessier (Independent Researcher, Canada)
Business Science Reference • © 2021 • 394pp • H/C (ISBN: 9781799874225) • US $295.00

IGI Global
PUBLISHER of TIMELY KNOWLEDGE

701 East Chocolate Avenue, Hershey, PA 17033, USA
Tel: 717-533-8845 x100 • Fax: 717-533-8661
E-Mail: cust@igi-global.com • www.igi-global.com

This book is dedicated to my loving husband, Jason Merlo, whose unshakable support for my academic endeavors has served as a source of strength, not only during the process of creating this book, but throughout my career. Special recognition also goes to my former mentors, professors, students, colleagues, and managers, who, in one way or another, inspired the concept for this book. Finally, this book is for science and the limitless possibilities for knowledge management in business settings.

Editorial Advisory Board

List of Reviewers

Table of Contents

Section 2
Knowledge Sharing and Innovation: Knowledge Systems and the Empowerment of Collective Wisdom

Section 3
Data Analytics, Visualization, Cybersecurity, and Knowledge Management Systems in KM Governance

Detailed Table of Contents

of social groups and work tribes that cause an opportunity for firms to identify and understand how the work tribe plays a role in the knowledge management system. A case study of flight attendants with a U.S.-based international carrier provides a practical example of how firms can learn from work tribes. Understanding work tribes enables a company to identify the factors that impact knowledge management systems so companies can empower work tribes to propel knowledge forward.

Knowledge sharing (KS) is one method for businesses to build knowledge within their walls and create a learning environment. It enables the achievement of common goals, which improves organisational performance and competitiveness. The willingness to contribute and participate in knowledge-sharing activities are the most important issues that must be addressed and for which a management solution is required. This chapter will investigate the factors that influence Halal food organisation staff to participate in and contribute to the organization's knowledge sharing activities. A phenomenology approach was used to investigate employees' attitudes or levels of adoption toward knowledge sharing in a case study of one Halal food organisation in Malaysia. The enhanced adoption model for Halal organisations is established using the TOE framework as the theoretical lens and the concept of knowledge sharing from an Islamic perspective.

Wisdom, both personal and collective, is largely missing in both information science and knowledge management literature. Workplace culture and shared vision impact every level of organizations in a positive or negative direction. A healthy culture and optimistic shared vision can provide a climate for knowledge sharing and provide opportunity for rich transfer of collective wisdom in our workplace communities. Wisdom is evolved from knowledge and can be cultivated by knowledge and learning specialists. This chapter places wisdom as the desired result of successful knowledge management and provides an opportunity for scholars, students, and practitioners to leverage this rich resource in organizations and extends the models, processes, and theories.

Some of the tasks of organizations in the digital age include information formation, coding and increasing value, data mining, and encoding information to make it accessible to others. As disruptive technology permeates all aspects of social life, new threats and vulnerabilities emerge. Cyber threats and cyber-security incidents may affect organizations, whether public or private, individuals, and all social network actors. The idea of a system that must defend against all possible attacks has given rise to the cyber resilience phenomenon. In public organizations, cyber resilience is obtained in various ways such as storing private classified data assets and records on independent backup platforms. Regardless of whether one platform is in danger, the other can provide a copy of missing or maliciously encrypted data immediately. Given the preceding discussion, this chapter focuses on agility, which is now regarded as a core competency in organizations in terms of cyber management, cyber resilience, knowledge management, and artificial intelligence in the cyber cosmos.

Knowledge management is a consolidation of various endeavours and disciplines. This chapter assesses the space of knowledge management and examines the significance of running a successful business with an efficient management system. To have a smooth management in a company, all the employees in the company need to access all the required information, which may be comprised of documents, collaboration of teams, policies in various departments, etc. All of these require an efficient knowledge management system. A framework for characterising the various tools and techniques available to knowledge management practitioners are well explored in the chapter.

Foreword

As this book with its collected chapters by experts in knowledge management and data analytics underscores, now is a great time in history to apply knowledge management (KM) concepts and practices to business systems and organizational challenges. Establishing a culture of sharing requires understanding across a community, implementation at all levels, and evaluation practices to keep knowledge growing.

The editor, Dr. Tereza Raquel Merlo, has assembled for you findings by international authors with experience, practical advice, and scholarly evidence from India to Turkey, and South Africa to the United States. If you are new to KM, Section 1 by global leader and researcher Dr. Suliman Hawamdeh (University of North Texas) will provide a starting place for you to explore the foundations of knowledge and systems management. How can you convert data to information to knowledge today and tomorrow? The potential impact on society makes this chapter worth reading for everyone.

Supporting the theme of idea evolution and a natural desire to know in humans throughout history introduced by Dr. Merlo, the editor, Chapters 2 through 6 show you the path to building a workplace culture that supports innovation in an evolving world. For example, Chapter 3 "Knowledge Flows through Unbounded Innovation," by two authors from Turkey, describes a case study of KM at work guiding staff in an organization to build communities of practice (CoP) that truly supports knowledge sharing and effective decision making. They describe an intra-firm process worth your investigation to learn how to describe the social/cognitive aspects of a business, and they illustrate the process that includes increasing communication among Muslim scholars. More issues, such as context, relations among "tribes" in a company, and collective wisdom, are presented in Section 2. It is a great place to learn how to encourage knowledge sharing in any culture.

Today's emphasis on data science may mean digging deeper into the data that leads to knowledge and even "wisdom" in business strategies. Finding answers in a world of fast-changing technology and consumer demands, Section 3 will guide you to check on your cybersecurity challenges, to apply tools and technology for effective governance of KM, and to use analytics and visualizations of data to understand the various types of data driving your business. From healthcare data for patients and providers to supply chains and customer databases in marketing, this book can help you plan and evolve into an efficient business no matter the domain and variety of databases where you work. There can be collective wisdom even in world of ever accelerating change and you do not need to abandon efficient management; in fact, KM can help with measuring and utilizing intellectual capital, one of your most valuable resources. Evidence from surveys will show you how to map your KM processes and change.

If you are new to KM or if you have applied KM in business management for many years, you will want to support the learning model that evaluation provides. What should you measure? Learn in Section 4 about defining key performance indicators based on well-designed records management systems. The examples come from Africa and the USA. How to have KM success starts with defining and preparing metrics for regular measuring. Growth and success for your educational institution or your profit-making business seem unlimited in a world of artificial intelligence and machine learning. However, this book, *Understanding, Implementing, and Evaluating Knowledge Management in Business Settings,* will introduce you to managing knowledge based on the ever-increasing digital data of the 21st century and to learning from scholars and business managers how you can apply knowledge to your decision making and wisdom to any business strategies.

I encourage you to read selectively but to touch each chapter to discover those nuggets of knowledge that might best help you and your business to thrive in a global market.

Deborah Swain
NC Central University, Durham, USA

Preface

In *Meditationes Sacrae* (1597), Sir Francis Bacon wrote the words *Ipsa Scientia Potestas,* a Latin phrase meaning Knowledge Itself is Power, which describes the core principle that inspired the concept of this book. Although centuries have passed since its publication, this quote is just as relevant today as it was then. Throughout history, philosophers have wondered about the science of knowledge and the many theories examining logic, perception, belief, and opinion, conceptualizing its meaning in an epistemological journey to know the truth and examine the essence of humanity. Many layers of knowledge theories and the complexity of human behaviors and minds have been at the center of centuries of studies undertaken by influential scientists and thinkers seeking to contribute not only to the general improvement of human existence, but the evolution of theories, principles, and methodologies for the analysis and comprehension of knowledge. Aristotle (c. 384 B.C.E.), considered one of the greatest thinkers and scientists in the history of humankind, used the Greek term *Telos* to explain that the inherent intent of human existence is to have a purpose. Contained within this concept is the belief that knowing signifies being able to identify things and what they mean. His claim asserts that men have the natural desire to know, *Episteme*.

The term knowledge embodies a multitude of concepts, evolving over time. Historically, theorists have conceptualized and created models discussing diverse aspects of knowledge, from theories based on perceptions, opinions, and experiences, to the Kantian philosophy. Propose by Immanuel Kant in the eighteenth century, it reversed the metaphysical construct defended by classical predecessors while defending that knowledge is based on epistemology, empiricism (*posteriori),* and rationale (*a priori).* Kantian theory seeks not only to understand but to criticize knowledge itself, claiming that knowledge is a form of judgment. Following the ancient Greek theories on knowledge, Kant's inquires differentiate between sensibility and perceptions of things that are seen and the theory of thought that investigates logic and the consolidation of concepts, knowingly using the expression G*edanken ohne Inhalt sind leereauschawwngen ohne bergriffe sind blind,* meaning "Thoughts without contents are empty; intuitions without concepts are blind." In his studies about the concepts and approaches to evolutionary epistemology, Wuketits (1983) concluded that: "in the course of evolution living systems increasingly accumulated information about their environment, so that evolution itself can also be described as information-processing, i.e., a universal process of learning and cognition." (p. 16).

Numerous historical constructs have provided a rich roadmap of information and knowledge theory evolution, from rudimentary transcripts to the creation of the Gutenberg Bible in 1455, the first printed book in the history of humanity. In conjunction with the proliferation of information access, including the world wide web and other technological advances, we now live in a society that is complex, interconnected, and, some would argue, dangerously misinformed. It was defined by Castells (2000) as Network Society, placing information as a key means of production and technology as the transformative advent that brought a societal change where information is the determinant economic productivity factor. Castells claims that the expansion of information and communication technologies (ICTs), particularly the internet, imposes a need for the decentralization of business operations processes with a focus on a reallocation of resources from a horizontal corporation structure that is project-oriented rather than capability-oriented. Expanding on the discussions about a networked society, Castells (2004) examines the interconnectedness of individuals and social structures, defining the increase in the importance of information and technologies in a globalized society as informationalism. The author correlates network possibilities with cooperation, claiming that:

Cooperation is based on the ability to communicate between networks. This ability depends on the existence of codes of translation and inter-operability between the networks (protocols of communication), and on access to connection points (switches). Competition depends on the ability to outperform other networks by superior efficiency in performance or in cooperation capacity. Competition may also take a destructive form by disrupting the switches of competing networks and/ or interfering with their communication protocols. (p. 3)

The definition of informationalism provided by Castells (2004) is based on a networked environment resulting from three major features: flexibility, scalability, and survivability, all of which define organizational efficiency. Where capitalist and post-capitalist systems are reexamined, some researchers would argue that it places too much emphasis on technology, although the author states that technology enables competitiveness, it does not determine it.

The complex computer network systems Castells (2004) investigated are the basis for the expansion of artificial intelligence (AI), nanotechnologies, machine learning, and robotics, which enable limitless new possibilities to experience and process information and knowledge. Whether on-premises or in the cloud, and despite the remaining security concerns, information management and access have been radically transformed. AI is defined by John McCarthy, its "father," as "the science and engineering of making intelligent machines, especially intelligent computer programs" (2019, pp. 1–2). Based on his theory, AI is computer science and human intelligence combined in order to create intelligent machines that will mirror human behaviors and perceptions in processing data and information at a fast pace. AI is designed to simulate and replicate humans' experiences and intelligence through complex computer systems for faster reasoning, learning, problem-solving, and decision making in organizations.

The transition from an economy centered around physical labor to a knowledge-based economy began with the industrial revolution in the 1800s, which fundamentally changed the means of production that has affected every facet of life in society. The new emerging industry, defined as Industry 4.0 (Patil and Surwade, 2018), focuses on interconnectivity, automation, digitalization of data, the Internet of Things (IoT), and interactive access to information online. Amidst the phenomenon of Big Data and analytics, businesses are facing a challenge to remain competitive and effectively use knowledge and technologies in such a way that knowledge workers will be attracted, valued, engaged, and have their knowledge assets incorporated as part of an organizational culture that will foster constant learning and innovation through a neural network system that utilizes AI and its subsets of machine and deep learning.

A much-debated question among modern theorists, researchers, and practitioners of data sciences, knowledge management is whether knowledge is tangible and how it can be measured, reproduced, stored, shared, and converted. In business, the conversion of knowledge and its effective use is at the core of its existence, where individuals and their knowledge are as important, or more important than, technological apparatuses and systems. Whether machines will ever replace humans in organizations is a recurring topic in the field of nanorobotics and AI, with growth in machine learning operating large datasets and defining data patterns that replace, in many instances, the need for human interference beyond programming. This new technological revolution is inspiring innovative ways to think of, understand, use, share, process, store, and manage information and knowledge. Most importantly, it raises questions about how to effectively design, manage, and measure knowledge and define realistic evaluation metrics that will result in successful and profitable organizations.

In a number of studies and existing literature, the importance of knowledge management (KM) in organizations has been discussed, investigating the roles and responsibilities of leaders in the adoption and consolidation of a KM system that is effective and competitive. Currently there is a gap in the literature investigating data visualization in business and the aspects of data overload that impact the business intelligence process. Enough studies have demonstrated the relevance of knowledge in organizations, however, the gap in investigations about the adoption and use of those new technologies and how they impact employees' perceptions, use, performance, and metrics remains limited. Aspects of information overload, the importance of data visualization, the impact of AI, the importance of knowledge workers, knowledge management and sharing in organizations, collective intelligence and knowledge use and competitive intelligence are some of the topics discussed in this book. The design and implementation of realistic key performance indicators (KPIs) are also lacking in most of the existing literature, impacting perceptions of KM and an accurate assessment of its importance and application in business strategies and practices.

After more than twenty years as a practitioner and professor teaching classes in business and technology and information science, with a particular interest in studies and practices in knowledge management technologies and business performance, the persistent question about the effectiveness of knowledge management and impact in business practices permeates most of what I do professionally, both academically and in the corporate world, and the pursuit of answers has directed my commitment to a lifelong knowledge acquisition and the investigation of the many complex aspects of knowledge management systems and business. I have observed, examined, written, read, and presented content on knowledge management in organizations and finally I have invited inquisitive and knowledgeable colleagues in the field to come together and create this book, which we hope will present valuable information about KM theories and practices to help both students and practitioners better understand some of the factors involved in designing, implementing, and evaluating knowledge management in business settings. This book intends to inspire the development of further work in the field, thereby expanding the area of knowledge as well as practices for business effectiveness.

This book can be read on two different levels. First, researchers of information sciences, data analytics and visualization, knowledge management, business and systems management, and information technologies project managers should find the work contained here to be of particular interest. Second, it should serve as reference to professionals in the aforementioned fields, as well as leaders and managers in multiple sectors of business including CEOs, CFOs, CIOs, and startup entrepreneurs. The book has been written with this audience in mind.

Additionally, this book was inspired by my experience dealing with talented, passionate, and knowledgeable professors and mentors, colleagues in academia and corporate, and my students. It was structured with the purpose of allowing readers to easily navigate through the pages and chapters with a straightforward approach to the topics. It presents a comprehensive approach to KM, from concepts to practices in businesses of different segments, including case studies discussing organizational learning, knowledge sharing, information technologies, knowledge issues, processes, and metrics.

ORGANIZATION OF THE BOOK

In order to shape the contributions from the authors, the book was organized in a coherent scheme presented in four sections, with a structure that flows from information about the foundations of knowledge management and organizational culture to an analysis of how to design and evaluate KPIs to measure knowledge in organizations, as follows:

Section 1: Foundations of Knowledge Management and Organizational Culture

Chapter 1: The book opens with a chapter that introduces fundamental concepts about knowledge management and discusses the importance of knowledge in the development of society and how societal transformation recontextualizes the accumulation of knowledge, leading to innovation. The author elaborates on the process of acquisition, processing, creation, dissemination, and applied knowledge efficiently, so it is deemed essential to the survival of organizations and competitiveness. It is argued that technological advances ignited the quest for knowledge and that the ability of individuals to efficiently process information, big data, and the knowledge discovery process in a digital format redefine the need for data analytics tools and applications for connectiveness. In this chapter the complex nature of knowledge is discussed and the relationship between data and information are explained. The author stresses knowledge management and its relevance to the information and knowledge profession.

Chapter 2: An investigation on Intra-Firm Knowledge Sharing (KS) evaluating the roles of contextual and socio-cognitive factors. The authors stress that knowledge is an asset to organizations and that managing it is a key to organizational competence and should be the main priority for leaders. Various theoretical assumptions are analyzed and theories on intra-organizational KS are reviewed. The authors examine four categories in investigating KS: individual, motivational, environmental (organizational), and perceptual; stressing the problematic nature of those contextualized concepts, particularly in the category of interpersonal trust as a dimension of motivational factors. This study has identified three distinct areas of emphasis in KS research: contextual (organizational), relational, and perceptual (socio-cognitive). Three organizational factors were detailed since they have been studied quite often: 1. organizational structure, 2. communication climate, and 3. technology infrastructure. This study scrutinized these three relational factors extensively. Lastly, perceived reciprocity and perceived value were emphasized by researchers. This review contributes to the body of knowledge by discussing emerging concepts and directing future KS research.

Chapter 3: Discusses the theories of Thomas Kuhn related to science and technology arguing that a new paradigm of knowledge management promotes a scientific revolution. This study maintains that innovative technologies provide an unrivalled competitive advantage, allowing companies to gain control over their own data, information, and knowledge; therefore, guaranteeing the management of knowledge and the tools for increasing agility, adequacy and disruptive evolution in organizations. In the light of all this, this chapter is designed to be a roadmap for organizations and decision makers in the digital transformation journey, which starts with the flow of information and takes organizations toward innovation that has no boundaries. For this reason, the kind of relationship that exists between knowledge flow and open innovation is the research question. This chapter aims to illustrate the importance of knowledge flow through unbounded innovation, particularly the correspondence between aspects of knowledge management and open innovation.

Section 2: Knowledge Sharing and Innovation – Knowledge Systems and the Empowerment of Collective Wisdom

Chapter 4: An investigation of work tribes, the practical impact that they have on knowledge management systems, and the implication to further research the topic, is presented. It is argued that the study of work tribes within knowledge management systems benefit companies so that they better understand how to align the values and goals of the knowledge management system with those of the work tribe to maximize outcomes. The definition of work tribes is discussed within the practice of culture and knowledge. It is identified that work tribes have a level of loyalty and membership that does not require a one-on-one social interaction, where members are connected through association to the tribe itself, rather than connected to each other. Exemplifications of work tribes are provided, and the authors conclude that unpredictability and constant changes in work activities impose changes in individuals' lifestyle that are reflected outside of the workplace.

Chapter 5: Examines a case study of knowledge processes and sharing in the Halal food organization systems, a leading Islamic organization in Malaysia. It is demonstrated that although knowledge management and sharing are the central focus of the business strategies and goals it is being strongly affected by cultural boundaries and the misinterpretation of policies and procedures by managers and stakeholders across different countries. Inconsistencies in the implementation of KM policies are found to affect the overall organizational performance and management approach to solutions. The author concludes that the way that individuals interpret regulations and the differences in compliances standards leads to ineffective coordination among stakeholders and failure in the transfer of information and knowledge. The results of this empirical research seek to identify the practices of knowledge sharing and the factors impacting knowledge sharing in Halal food organization.

Chapter 6: In this analysis, an extension of the scholarship offered in "Fostering Wisdom at Work" is presented and is catered for knowledge management scholars and practitioners. The purpose of the chapter is to open the field of wisdom to knowledge management scholars so that, as a field, we can further our understanding of individual and collective wisdom to impact organization culture. It begins by describing the relationship of wisdom to information science and provides an overview of wisdom from a knowledge management and learning perspective. An understanding of classical individual wisdom provides a solid theoretical foundation to explore the cultivation of collective wisdom in organizations. Finally, the researchers explore collective wisdom as it applies to workplace communities and organizations. Wisdom is highly prized yet remains a largely untapped resource in knowledge organizations.

Section 3: Data Analytics, Visualization, Cybersecurity, and Knowledge Management Systems in KM Governance

Chapter 7: The disruptive impact of technological advances which defines the knowledge-based society is discussed in this chapter. It is argued that cyber threats and cyber security incidents affect organizations (whether public or private), individuals, and all social network actors. As the interconnectedness of cyberspace enables large organizations to become more agile, flexible, and adaptive, organizations that want to capitalize on innovation may be vulnerable to cyber threats while using a variety of technology tools for knowledge management. In the face of cyber threats, the learning and adaptation process of public organizations are at the center of studies. This illustrates how cyber space offerings have accelerated the adoption of agility, which was previously regarded as slow in the public sector, and how big data, artificial intelligence, the internet of things, robots, quantum technologies, and distributed registry systems all play a role in knowledge management with digital technologies. In the face of cyber threats, the learning and adaptation process of public organizations with more central and hierarchical structures which are likely to resist change will be explained. This chapter focuses on digital transformation and agility in terms of cyber management, cyber resilience, and knowledge management in cyberspace, which is currently considered a core competency in public organizations.

Chapter 8: In this examination of knowledge management and organization alignment maintains that there are a few knowledge management techniques that are followed in the market, but these are inadequate to match the requirements of current organizational needs. Modern trends which change the face of knowledge management are discussed as a response to meet our demands and challenges. It is defended that in order to run a successful business, an efficient management system is mandatory, and that management must ensure that all employees in the company have access to all the required information. The claim that the collaboration of teams and policies in various departments are necessary for an efficient knowledge management system, and it is argued that the process of accessing, managing, and sharing information within an organization is the core principle of KM. KM strategies help manage documentation, guidelines, lists, databases, memos, files, and staff management, resulting in the enhancement of organizational goals. This chapter details the KM tools and technologies used to devise a good KMS for organizational knowledge dissemination and the reuse of data for a firm's competitiveness, detailing the two major trends in KM: developing measurement indexes for the intellectual capital of an organization and using information technology to map knowledge. The crux of this approach outlines a core development of knowledge with a smart engine that consolidates information to disparate locations with differing databases.

Chapter 9: Findings of a survey study examining information overload and data visualization in organizations are presented in this examination. The purpose of this study is to present insight into the problematic emerging topic of information overload and the value of data. This chapter examines information overload and its impact on organizational performance and productivity, the level of use of data analytics tools by organizations to address the information overload problem, and reports on the results from some of the data collected from online survey about the use of visual analytics tools in organizations. The survey was aimed at gathering users' experiences in dealing with information overload and their level of exposure to data analytics tools. The results from the survey show that email is still the most time-consuming application, with a reported increase in remote access via handheld devices. A relevant percentage of respondents (65%) confirmed having knowledge and experience using some sort of data analytic tools, while 69.23% stated that exposure to large amounts of information at work causes stress and anxiety. Analysis from the literature combined with the online survey findings confirmed the original assumption that information overload is a growing and pervasive phenomenon that impacts to performance and productivity level within the organization.

The benefits of this research will be to advance the field of study among practitioners, consequently contributing to business processes improvement and business performance and pipeline success management. The field of Information Science will benefit from the perspective of data management insights, and the business field will benefit from research work that will allow a clear and fresh perspective on business processes improvement, data management, and information systems adoption, use/application, and evaluation. This is a particularly relevant topic for those in computer science that are responsible for the design of software in an era driven by data and digital data consumption with spectacular human-interface dimensions.

Section 4: Metrics in Knowledge Management

Chapter 10: The assessment of the practices of mechanisms, policies, rules, procedures, legislation, and standards that are in place for managing records are discussed in this chapter. It is argued that effective records management is a key element of good governance. This study established that the National Archives and Records Service Act 43 of 1996 is the legal framework for the management of university records in South Africa. The challenges facing South African universities are ineffective records management, the availability of policies, rules, procedures for managing records, and the availability of records management standards. After introducing the research problem and approach, this chapter reviewed the literature to allow the researcher to understand the records and archives management program in South Africa. Studies were then reviewed and evaluations were made that attempted to examine the effectiveness of records management systems. This chapter intends to answer the following research questions:

- What are the current practices of managing the records?
- What are the mechanisms, policies, rules, procedures, and legislation in place for managing records?
- Which records management standards are in place for managing records?

The literature review shows that research has been conducted on records and archives management programs, especially in the corporate world. Less explored, however, is the integration of records management programs into the organization's strategy. Furthermore, the records management division frequently contends with intangible value, which is a challenge to define and measure records management programs. As a result, records managers emphasize tangible outputs that do not reflect the value presented by this discipline. Finally, challenges to organizations' records management are detailed and conclusions are presented.

Chapter 11: The book concludes with a work examining the exponential growth of digital data generation and consumption in the past decade and how it has ignited new discussions about the relevance and impact of knowledge management (KM) on individuals and businesses. It is claimed that successful management of data and knowledge is no longer an option for organizations aiming to be innovative, dynamic, and profitable, it is now compulsory for competitiveness and business intelligence. Organizations are increasingly relying on artificial intelligence tools to build a knowledge base, improve processes and operations, and minimize financial losses while focusing on the optimization of the use of knowledge systems resources. In the midst of such a dynamic data production and consumption environment and with the recognition of knowledge as a valuable asset in organizations, the question becomes:

how is knowledge measured and quantified? This chapter will discuss knowledge management and systems of learning and some of the critical factors in the design, implementation, and evaluation of metrics for KM success. It highlights the roles of leadership and knowledge workers for effective KM and KMS, the design of KPIs that are aligned with businesses' needs and strategies, and the need to adapt to Web 4.0 data processing in a competitive global market. This chapter will discuss critical factors for successful knowledge management implementation and metrics, from conceptualizing knowledge management and knowledge management systems to how an organizational culture focused on effective learning innovation will enable the use of performance metrics to track and measure the value of knowledge to organizations that increasingly demand the promotion of a knowledge-based approach to productivity.

Aude sapere.

Tereza Raquel Merlo
University of North Texas, USA

REFERENCES

Aristotle. (1976). *The Nicomachean Ethics*. Penguin.

Bacon, Francis (1597). *Meditationes Sacrae*. Londini: Excusum impensis Humfredi Hooper.

Castells, M. (2000). *The rise of the network society* (2nd ed.). Blackwell Publishing.

Castells, M. (Ed.). (2004). *The network society: A cross-cultural perspective*. Edward Elgar. doi:10.4337/9781845421663

McCarthy, J. (2019). *Artificial Intelligence Tutorial – It's your time to innovate the future*. Dataflair Team. https://data-flair.training/blogs/artificial-intelligence-ai-tutorial

Patil, H., & Surwade, Y. (2018). Web Technologies from web 2.0 to Web 4.0. *International Journal for Science and Advance Research in Technology, 8*(5), 810-814. Retrieved from: https://www.researchgate.net/publication/324537592_Web_Technologies_From_Web_20_To_Web_40

Wuketits, F. (Ed.). (1983). Concept and Approaches in evolutionary epistemology: towards an evolutionary theory of knowledge. Boston: Lancaster.

Acknowledgment

The editor would like to acknowledge the hard work and critique of the editorial advisory board and reviewers whose contributions were critical to the consolidation of this book. In addition, my appreciation to all authors that so enthusiastically shared their experiences and studies in the many aspects of knowledge management in business that were included in this book; and the IGI-Global team for the valuable guidance throughout the book development process.

Section 1

Foundations of Knowledge Management and Organizational Culture

Chapter 1
Foundations of Knowledge Management

Suliman Hawamdeh
https://orcid.org/0000-0001-7018-6945
University of North Texas, USA

ABSTRACT

Knowledge played an important role in the development of society including the transformation from agrarian society to industrial society and then to the information and knowledge society. Societal transformation in the context of knowledge management involved the accumulation of knowledge over a long period of time that led to more innovations and human development. Today, the ability to acquire, process, create, disseminate, and apply knowledge effectively and efficiently is deemed essential to the survival of the organization. In this chapter, the author discusses the complex nature of knowledge and its relationship to data and information as well as the concept of knowledge management and its relevance to the information and knowledge profession.

INTRODUCTION

Knowledge played an important role in the development of mankind, society, and civilizations. The societal transformation from agrarian society to industrial society to information and knowledge society were driven by knowledge creation and innovation. Today, the ability to acquire, process, create, disseminate, and apply knowledge effectively and efficiently is essential to the survival of any organization (Dima, et. al., 2018; Eliasson, 2000; Castro and Laszlo, 2002). The transition from the industrial society to the information and knowledge society has been characterized

DOI: 10.4018/978-1-6684-4431-3.ch001

by technological advances such as the invention of computers, handheld devices, Internet, and the World Wide Web. Rapid technological advances ignited the social discourse and lead to exponential growth in digital information. Data and information are no longer in short supply, however, the quest for knowledge has increased. Massive data stored in digital format on organizational servers and devices is not considered useful unless this information can be processed and turned into active information and actionable knowledge.

Knowledge discovery from big data has grown in importance over the last two decades. Newly emerging knowledge discovery disciplines such as data science and advanced data analytics are signs of the growing importance of data and its use in artificial intelligence applications such as smart cities, Internet of Things (IoT), autonomous vehicles, and augmented reality. Recognizing the importance of knowledge management processes and practices, organizations are rethinking their knowledge management strategies and taking measures to increase the return on their knowledge capital.

Figure 1. The utilization pyramid (Source: Al-Hawamdeh, 2003)

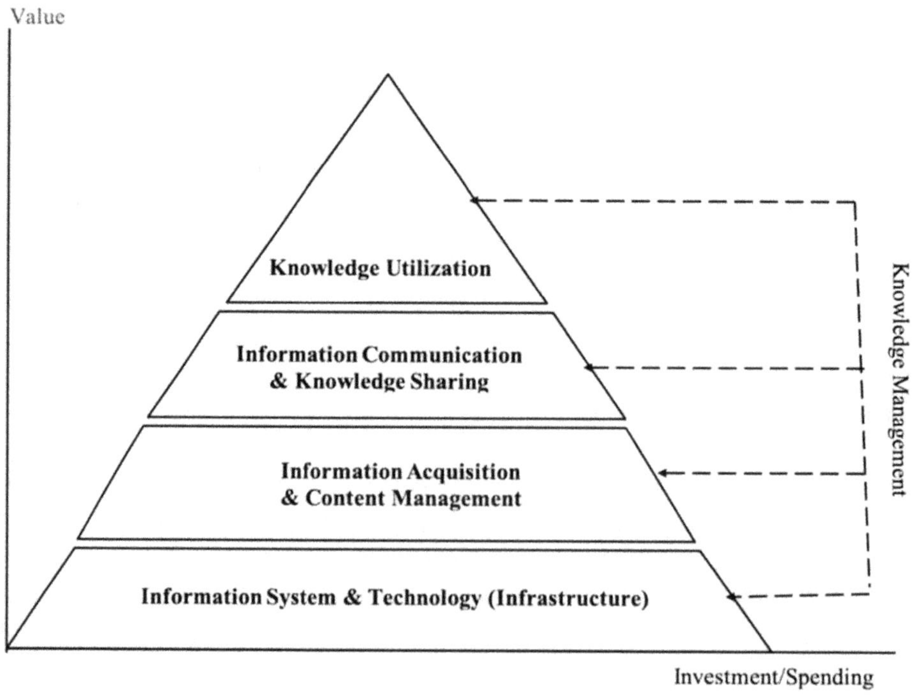

Traditionally organizations spent more money on tangibles and physical good compared to intangible good such knowledge sharing or knowledge utilization processes. From a management perspective, it easier to justify buying a new computer for the employees compared to sending them to a benchmarking? field trip, a conference, or a workshop. Figure 1 illustrates the point about return on investment where organizations tend to spend more at the bottom of the pyramid (that has less return on investment) compared to areas at the top of the pyramid which has much higher value. While it is important to invest in areas such as infrastructure and content, it is equally important to invest in areas such as communication, knowledge sharing and knowledge utilization. Knowledge utilization is concerned with the ability to turn innovation and knowledge creation into product and services.

Knowledge sharing activities such as building communities of practice, joining different interest groups, attending workshops, seminars and conferences enhances the organization innovation and product development. Most of the time, small organization are nimbler and better at allocating resources to enhance innovation and productivity.

THE COMPLEX NATURE OF KNOWLEDGE

Knowledge as a concept has been discussed and studied extensively in the literature (Robinson, 1971; Ayer and Maric, 1956; Sowell, 2022). From a philosophical perspective, scholars and philosophers viewed knowledge as the state of knowing, perception of the truth or justified true beliefs. According to Merriam Webster Dictionary, knowledge is the fact or condition of knowing something with familiarity gained through experience or association. Macquarie Concise Dictionary defines knowledge as the state of knowing. Clear and certain mental apprehension. According to Allen (2022) "Knowledge is the depth and breadth of information and skills acquired through interaction, participation, observation integrated with an individual's comprehension of connected experiences" (p. 118).

The philosophical approach to knowledge implies that knowledge is personal. It is the state of knowing, justified true beliefs gained normally by interacting with the environment and with other people. Zagzebski (2017) referred to knowledge as the state of true belief arising from the acts of intellectual virtue. Unlike moral virtue that defines the characteristics of good people, intellectual virtue emphasizes people ability to succeed and achieve their goals. According to Aristotle, intellectual virtues include scientific and technical knowledge, intuitive and practical wisdom as well as philosophical wisdom (Annas, 2010; Deslauriers, 2002).

From business perspective, knowledge is power. It is a key economic development factor. Drucker (1994), implied that knowledge will become the main source of wealth and the knowledge society inevitably will be far more competitive that any society that we have known. According to Davenport & Prusak, (1998), "Knowledge is a fluid mix of framed experience, values, contextual information, and expert insight that provides a framework for evaluating and incorporating new experiences and information. It originates in the minds of knower. In organizations, it often becomes embedded not only in documents or repositories but also in organizational routines, processes, practices, and norms" (p .5). Knowledge is not only a property of the individual, but it also held by people working together that makes up the organization collective memory (Brown and Druguid, 1998).

From a technology perspective, knowledge involves knowledge embodies in systems, machines, mobile devices, algorithms, artificial intelligence, deep learning, natural language processing and others. In the last two decades key Internet technologies such as Internet of Things (IoT), smart city applications, social media, and others have emerged giving momentum to knowledge discovery from data generated using advance AI applications. The increased importance of data and its use in AI applications have led to the emergence of new disciplines such as big data analytics, data mining and data science.

Understand the relationships between concepts such as data, information, knowledge, and wisdom, is not only important from philosophical point of view, but also from the practical consideration of designing academic programs, building information systems, and creating training effective and useful training material. The DIKW model which stands for Data, Information, Knowledge, and Wisdom is one of the first attempt to explain how these concepts relate to each other. The DIKW model attributed to Ackoff, (1989) is a hierarchical relationship in the form of a pyramid that shows a linear relationship between these four concepts. In the DIKW model (Figure 2), data is placed at the base of the pyramid indicating abundance whereas wisdom is placed at the top of the pyramid indicating scarcity. The four steps of the pyramid show linear progression in which data is processed into information, information is conceptualized as knowledge, and knowledge is then turned into enlightenment that can be elevated to highest level in the pyramid as wisdom.

While the DIKW model is a good visual to explain a simple progression and is easily understood, it has been criticized as an attempt to oversimplify rather a complex problem. According to David Weinberger (2010), the real problem with DIKW is the fact that it is a pyramid and paints the wrong picture by viewing knowledge as the results of applying finer-grained filters to information. In fact, knowledge is more creative, messier, and far more discontinuous. Frick´e (2019) highlighted the point by stating that tacit knowledge is more elusive and subjective and could not be simply obtained by induction and empirical reasoning.

Figure 2. DIKW model

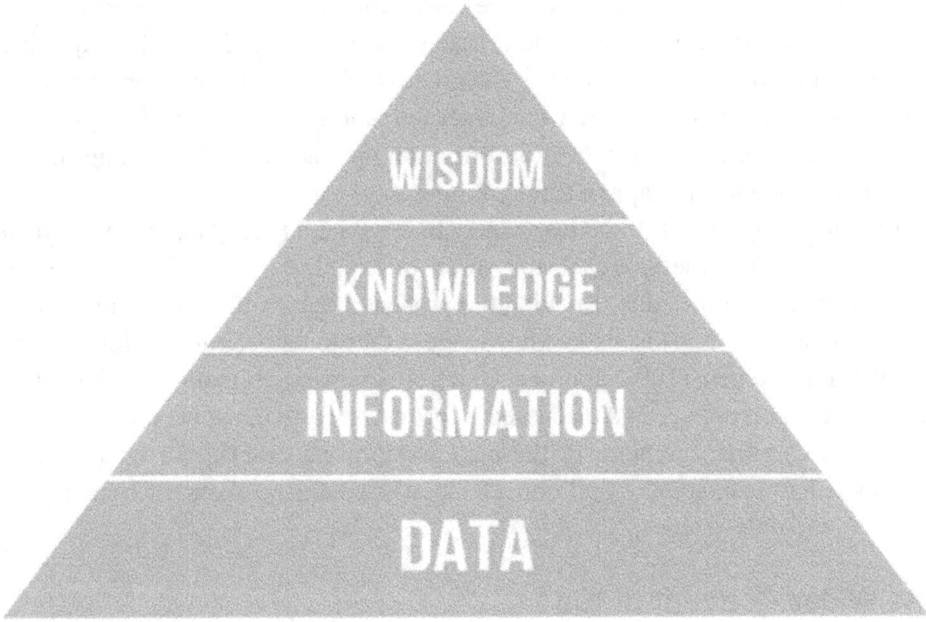

In a paper published in 1991 in the Journal of the American Society for Information Science under the title "Information as a Thing". Michael Buckland conceptualized information into three different categories: Information-as-thing, information-as-knowledge, and information-as-process. He described information-as-thing to be made of data, text, documents, objects, and events. He referred to information-as-knowledge as the intangible made of ideas, beliefs, and opinion. His description of information-as-process reflect the activity takes place between a sender and a receiver. He also referred to it as the "the act of inform".

A few years later, Nonaka and Takeuchi (1995) conceptualized knowledge as made of explicit knowledge and tacit knowledge. They described knowledge creation as a spiraling process resulting from the interaction between explicit knowledge and tacit knowledge. While explicit knowledge refers to documented knowledge in the form of data and information, Tacit knowledge is described as highly personal and most of the time we are not aware of its existence. In his work the "Tacit Dimension", Polanyi (1966) stated the famously, "we can know more than we can tell" (Polanyi, 1966, p. 4). This implies that there is more to knowledge than what we can articulate and document. Nonaka and Takeuchi (1995) then conceptualized the SECI model which stands for socialization, externalization, combination, and internalization. Socialization is described as the process of sharing tacit knowledge in the form of skills, competencies, and experiences using in person communications such as mentoring, shadowing, and observing. Externalization is described as the process of articulating tacit knowledge into explicit knowledge (information) in the form of reports, documents, and artifacts. Combination deals with explicit-to-explicit conversion and described as the process of synthesizing information from multiple sources and create a new one. Internalization is described as the process of transforming explicit knowledge or information into tacit knowledge. Internalizing explicit knowledge can happen through doing.

An interesting aspect of the two papers by Buckland (1991) and by Nonaka and Takeuchi (1995) is the approach they used in explaining the difference between information and knowledge. Buckland approached the problem from information science perspective and discussed knowledge in the context of information. Whereas Nonaka and Takeuchi (1995) approached it from knowledge creation and knowledge management perspective and discussed information from the context of knowledge and knowledge management. In the next section, we discuss the wider concept of knowledge management and consider newly emerging areas such as big data analytics and data science.

The Wider Concept of KM

Several scholars and practitioners over the years questioned the wisdom of using of the term knowledge management given the notion that tacit knowledge as articulated by Polanyi (1966) can only exist in the minds of the knowers and cannot be managed in the traditional sense (Sutton, 2001; Wilson, 2002; Wallace, 2007). In an article titled the “nonsense of knowledge management”, Wilson (2002) viewed knowledge management as a consultancy strategy and referred to it as a management fad. Wilson criticized the paper by Marwick (2001) as flawed for accepting, uncritically Nonaka’s mistaken understanding of Polanyi’s tacit knowledge. In his view, since technology is not able to support the use of tacit knowledge, he concluded that ‘knowledge management’ is more of an umbrella term for a variety of organizational activities, none of which are concerned with the real management of knowledge.

However, a study by Ponzi and Koenig (2002) carried out at the same time and published in the *Information Research Journal*, examined the KM literature, and concluded that management fads or fashions normally reveal themselves within five years. They added, this is not the case with knowledge management that did not seems to fit the pattern and continued to grow over the years. Davenport and Prusak (1998) acknowledged the complex nature of knowledge stating that when dealing with people, knowledge is a mix of experiences, contextual information, and insights. However, when dealing with organizations, knowledge is embedded not only in documents or repositories but also in organizational routines, processes, norms, and practices.

Peter Drucker (2012) emphasized the importance of information and knowledge. He highlighted the close relationship between information and knowledge by stating that information can only become knowledge in the hands of someone who knows what to do with it. As a management guru he understood the importance of knowledge as a resource. He went on to say that knowledge is not just another resource, it is the only meaningful resource in the knowledge economy.

There are plenty of definitions in the literature for knowledge management. We highlight here some of the definitions that illustrate the wider and broader concept of KM. One of these definitions is by Karl Wiig (1999) who described knowledge management as the systematic, explicit, and deliberate building, renewal, and application of knowledge with the objective of maximizing the enterprise's knowledge-related effectiveness and returns from its knowledge assets. Along the same line, Sveiby (1990) viewed knowledge management as consisting of an IT-Track (management of data and information) and a People-Track (management of people). The IT-Track involves the construction of information systems, artificial intelligence, reengineering, and groupware etc. The People-Track involves people development, training, learning, skills, and competencies, rewards, and recognition. Sveiby (1997) also described knowledge management as the art of creating value to organizations by leveraging intangible assets.

Davenport (1994) defined knowledge management as the process of capturing, distributing and effectively using knowledge management. This leaves out process such as knowledge creation, discovery, and retention. We on the other hand, define knowledge management as an interdisciplinary approach to dealing with knowledge processes (creation, capture, distribution, discovery, retention, and utilization) and knowledge practices (best practice, communities of practice, lessons learned, mentoring, apprenticeship and learning organization). It is the amalgamation of people, technology, and processes.

While knowledge management is not about technology, recent advances in technology elevated the importance of knowledge management where KM key drivers are more obvious than ever before. Al-Hawamdeh, (2002) viewed knowledge management as people centric and rather than focusing on developing intelligent systems to replace people. We should focus on developing tools to be placed in the hand of intelligent and knowledgeable people. Computers have proven to be good at automating functions and can be trained to perform complex tasks. However, people remain the final arbitrator to what can be done using machines.

The emergence of data science and data analytics as fields of study has once again shined the spotlight on our understanding of how data, information and knowledge interrelate. Data science is viewed as part of the knowledge discovery process. Knowledge discovery from databases or big data (KDD) is a systematic process of identifying patterns and trends in large data using advance tools and technologies such as machine learning, neural networks, and deep learning. Big data is generated from various application such as social media, Internet of Things (IoT) applications, and smart city applications. The data exist in various formats including text, business transactions, images, and video.

To better understand the relationship between the three related disciplines information science, knowledge management, and data science, we view data as made of numbers, symbols, text, images, graphics, and video. Data can be described as anything that can be documented in the form of an object. Information should not be confused with data as information is not an object. Instead, information is an activity that takes place between a sender and a receiver. For example, signal processing, storytelling, and messaging. Information derived from term *inform* is an activity that implies telling someone something or an activity that keeps the information system alive and functioning. Information is dynamic and once it loses this characteristic it ceases to exit.

Knowledge is more personal than information. It is the state of mind. It can be described as an action or the act of doing. Every time data, in the form of an object, is conceptualized and communicated using information as an activity, knowledge is created in the form of action or judgment made based on previous experience and insights accumulated over time. Actions and judgements over times are transformed into accumulated rich experiences and insights. Accumulated rich experiences and insights could be framed as wisdom if necessary.

Knowledge and information are closely related entities. One cannot exist without the other. Therefore, the inseparable relationship between information and knowledge should make us rethink our approach to what constitute the information and knowledge professions. Are there fundamental difference between information science and knowledge management? Are we talking about the two sides of the same coin?

THE KEY DRIVERS OF KM

As discussed earlier, knowledge management is not new and most knowledge management processes and practices exist in organizations, but not necessarily under the title or labeled as knowledge management. Recent advances in information communication technologies, the advent of the Internet, and the Web have achieved interest in knowledge management practices to achieve organizational efficiency, maximize organizational potential, protect intellectual capital, minimize the knowledge loss and building a learning, agile and adaptable organizations. The followings are description of these key drivers.

Achieving Organizational Efficiency

Organization efficiency examines how organization are utilizing their resources to increase output and enhance productivity. Knowledge management practices such as best practices, lessons learned, knowledge audit enables organizations to achieve organizational efficiency and operational effectiveness. Timely, accurate, and relevant information is important not only for decision-making purposes but also for tailoring products and services to the needs of their customers. In the knowledge economy speed and responsiveness are key elements in attracting and retaining customers (Dima, et. al., 2018; Eliasson, 2000). Especially when your competitors are just a click away. To stay ahead of the competition, organizations must examine their knowledge management practices from time to time, conduct, assess and make improvement in areas such as time-to-market, time-to-solution, and time-to-delivery.

Maximizing Organizational Potential

In an environment with increased competition, organizations must innovate and maximize their knowledge potential. The ability of an organization to improve product and services is critical to its survival and ability to stay ahead of the competition. The Continuous improvement process is an example of an ongoing strategy and effort to assess, evaluate and improve organizational products and services. Knowledge management processes such as knowledge creation and knowledge utilization do not happen in vacuum or by accident. These processes must be governed by KM strategies in the form of a continuous improvement process providing organizations the opportunity to see the big picture and the importance of the parts to the whole.

Managing Intellectual Capital

The knowledge economy has changed the way organizations account for their intellectual asset and market valuations. The value of an organization can be largely measured by the value of its knowledge resources in the form of intangible assets. Intellectual capital consists of human capital, customer capital, structural capital. Steward (1997) defined intellectual capital as the total stocks of the collective knowledge, information, technologies, intellectual property rights, experience, organization learning and competence, team communication systems, customer relations, and brands that can create values for a firm. Drucker (1993) highlighted both the importance of intellectual capital and the importance of the knowledge workers to the organization.

Minimizing Knowledge Loss and Brain Drain

Knowledge loss is a common problem organizations must deal with when employees leave the organization. Knowledge retention is one of the critical knowledge management processes. Organizations may underestimate its impact on organizational efficiency and productivity. Organizations have the tendency to place more emphasis on recruiting the best talents but not on retaining them. Knowledge loss and brain drain can happen for various reasons such as lack of recognition, undesirable organizational culture, poor economic situation, and unsatisfactory political environment.

Knowledge loss can have lasting impact on organizations and communities. It can affect the organization business bottom line and jeopardize its survivability. Small and medium size organizations sometime rely on key people as the source of innovation and growth. Having these people leave and join competitors might not only slow down the operation, but also jeopardies the organization chances of future success.

Building a Learning Organization

Learning organization is defined as the ability to gain insights and understanding from experience through experimentation, observation, analysis, and application of lessons learned. It is also the ability and willingness of the organization to learn from failures and successes. According to Senge (1990), a learning organization is one that continually transforms itself to survive and excel in a rapidly changing business environment. Senge outlined five different areas that distinguish a learning organization from a traditional bureaucratic one: personal mastery, mental models, shared vision, team learning and system thinking. System thinking represents the heart of the learning organization model that integrates the other four disciplines to fusing them in a coherent body of theory and practice. It provides the organization the ability to understand the big picture by looking at the interrelatedness of the parts to the whole.

While every organization strives to be a learning organization, achieving a learning organization status is not an uneasy task. Garvin (2003) noted that the progress toward achieving learning organization status is rather slow. Learning and knowledge sharing are important activities in any learning organization. According Liebowitz and Beckman, 2020), learning must result in change behavior, thoughts, and beliefs necessary to improve performance. Learning within the organization takes place in many different forms including single loop learning, double loop learning, triple loop, or Deutero-learning (Tosey, et. al., 2012). Deutero-learning is a type of learning where inquiry goes beyond the root causes and outcomes to involve the examination of the whole learning process.

CONCLUSION

Technology and innovation have given rise to intellectual capital, the knowledge-based economy, and the concept of knowledge management. Despite the growing body of knowledge and expanded research activities in this area, knowledge management as a discipline has not found its footing yet. This can be attributed to many reasons one of which could be the lack of clarity about the relationships between basic concepts such as data, information, and knowledge. The discussion in this chapter about the complex nature of knowledge, the DIKW model and the inseparable relationship between information and knowledge is important to understanding the foundations of knowledge management. A fresh examination of these concepts in the wider context of knowledge management could bring us a step closer to understand the close relationship between knowledge management and information science. The emergence of data science as a field of study concerned mainly with knowledge discovery could also add clarity to what constitute the information and knowledge profession.

REFERENCES

Ackoff, R. L. (1989). From data to wisdom. *Journal of Applied Systems Analysis*, *16*(1), 3–9.

Al-Hawamdeh, S. (2002). Knowledge management: Re-thinking information management and facing the challenge of managing tacit knowledge. *Information Research*, *8*(1), 8–1.

Allen, J. (2022). *Fostering Wisdom at Work*. Rutledge Taylor & Francis Group., doi:10.4324/9781003018759

Annas, J. (2010). The structure of virtue. In *Intellectual virtue: Perspectives from ethics and epistemology*. Oxford University Press.

Ayer, A. J., & Marić, S. (1956). *The problem of knowledge*. Penguin books.

Brown, J. S., & Duguid, P. (1998). Organizing knowledge. *California Management Review*, *40*(3), 90–111. doi:10.2307/41165945

Buckland, M. K. (1991). Information as thing. *Journal of the American Society for Information Science*, *42*(5), 351–360. doi:10.1002/(SICI)1097-4571(199106)42:5<351::AID-ASI5>3.0.CO;2-3

Castro Laszlo, K., & Laszlo, A. (2002). Evolving knowledge for development: The role of knowledge management in a changing world. *Journal of Knowledge Management, 6*(4), 400–412. doi:10.1108/13673270210440893

Davenport, T. H., & Prusak, L. (1998). *Working knowledge: How organizations manage what they know*. Harvard Business Press.

Davenport, T. M. (1994). Saving IT's soul: Human-centered information management. *Harvard Business Review, 72*(2), 119–131.

Deslauriers, M. (2002). How to distinguish Aristotle's virtues. *Phronesis (Barcelona, Spain), 47*(2), 101–126.

Dima, A. M., Begu, L., Vasilescu, M. D., & Maassen, M. A. (2018). The relationship between the knowledge economy and global competitiveness in the European Union. *Sustainability, 10*(6), 1706. doi:10.3390u10061706

Drucker, P. (1994, November). The age of social transformation. *Atlantic Monthly*, 53–80.

Drucker, P. (2000). Knowledge work. *Executive Excellence, 17*(4), 11–11.

Drucker, P. (2012). *Managing in a time of great change*. Routledge. doi:10.4324/9780080938752

Drucker, P. F. (1993). The rise of the knowledge society. *The Wilson Quarterly, 17*(2), 52–72.

Eliasson, G. (2000). *The role of knowledge in economic growth*. Royal Institute of Technology.

Frick'e, M. (2019). The Knowledge Pyramid: The DIKW Hierarchy. *Knowledge Organization, 46*(1), 33–46. doi:10.5771/0943-7444-2019-1-33

Garvin, D. A. (2003). *Learning in action: A guide to putting the learning organization to work*. Harvard Business Review Press.

Liebowitz, J., & Beckman, T. (2020). *Knowledge organizations: What every manager should know*. CRC press. doi:10.4324/9781003076001

Marwick, A. D. (2001). Knowledge management technology. *IBM Systems Journal, 40*(4), 814–830. doi:10.1147j.404.0814

Nonaka, I. (1995). *The Knowledge-Creating Company. How Japanese Companies Create the Dynamics of Innovation*. Harvard Business Review Classics.

Polanyi, M. (1966). *The Tacit Dimension*. University of Chicago Press.

Ponzi, L., & Koenig, M. (2002). Knowledge management: Another management fad. *Information Research*, *8*(1), 8–1.

Robinson, R. (1971). The concept of knowledge. *Mind*, *80*(317), 17–28. doi:10.1093/mind/LXXX.317.17

Senge, P. (1990). *The Fifth Discipline: The Art and Practice of the Learning Organization*. Doubleday/Currency.

Sowell, T. (2022). *Knowledge and decisions*. Basic Books.

Sutton, D. C. (2001). What is knowledge and can it be managed? *European Journal of Information Systems*, *10*(2), 80–88. doi:10.1057/palgrave.ejis.3000397

Sveiby, K. E. (1990). *Kunskapsledning: 101 råd till ledare i kunskapsintensiva organisationer*. Affärsvärlden.

Sveiby, K. E. (1997). *The new organizational wealth: Managing & measuring knowledge-based assets*. Berrett-Koehler Publishers.

Tosey, P., Visser, M., & Saunders, M. N. (2012). The origins and conceptualizations of 'triple-loop 'learning: A critical review. *Management Learning*, *43*(3), 291–307. doi:10.1177/1350507611426239

Wallace, D. P. (2007). *Knowledge Management-Historical and Cross-Disciplinary Themes*. Academic Press.

Weinberger, D. (2010). The problem with the data-information-knowledge-wisdom hierarchy. *Harvard Business Review*, 2.

Wiig, K. M. (1999). What future knowledge management users may expect. *Journal of Knowledge Management*, *3*(2), 155–166. doi:10.1108/13673279910275611

Wilson, T.D. (2002). The nonsense of 'knowledge management'. *Information Research*, 8(1). Available at http://InformationR.net/ir/8-1/paper144.html]

Zagzebski, L. (2017). What is knowledge? *The Blackwell guide to epistemology*, 92-116.

Chapter 2
A Theoretical Investigation on Intra-Firm Knowledge Sharing:
The Roles of Contextual, Relational, and Socio-Cognitive Factors

Umut Uyan
https://orcid.org/0000-0002-8466-2903
Munzur University, Turkey

Musa Şanal
Çukurova University, Turkey

Adil Ibin
Mersin University, Turkey

ABSTRACT

Considering that knowledge management is a multifaceted process, studies that examine a limited number of factors individually may not explain the process sufficiently. This chapter set out to advance our knowledge on intra-organizational knowledge sharing (KS) by addressing multiple factors (relational, organizational, and socio-cognitive factors) holistically. This would also lead to an explicit discussion of various organizational theories towards intra-firm KS. The study, which is designed as a conceptual one, compiles and synthesizes previous studies. Unlike previous research, the current one is encouraging as it develops a holistic perspective towards intra-organizational KS.

DOI: 10.4018/978-1-6684-4431-3.ch002

INTRODUCTION

Since knowledge is treated as one of the most valuable assets for organizations, managing it has become a key competence that organizations should possess. In this sense, the effective dissemination of knowledge within organizations is one of the main concerns managers should accentuate. By referring to various theoretical assumptions, previous studies have examined different factors either enhance or inhibit intra-organizational KS. Wang & Noe (2010) reviewed those studies and organized examined factors under four distinct categories: individual, motivational, environmental (organizational), and perceptual. Yet, the contextualization of the concepts discussed seems problematic, for instance, as they categorized interpersonal trust as a dimension of motivational factors. Therefore, a more accurate and clear contextualization is required.

This study, on the other hand, has identified three distinct areas of emphasis in KS research: contextual (organizational), relational, and perceptual (socio-cognitive). Three organizational factors were detailed since they have been studied quite often: [1]*organizational structure* (Tsai, 2002; Kim & Lee, 2006; Chen & Huang, 2007; Lin, 2008), [2]*communication climate* (Zboralski, 2009; Hoegl & Gemuenden, 2001; De Vries, Van den Hooff & De Ridder, 2006; Salis & Williams, 2010; Ali, Pascoe & Warne, 2002), and [3]*technology infrastructure* (Alavi & Leidner, 2001; Choi, Lee & Yoo, 2010; Huysman & Wulf, 2006; Yuan et al., 2013; Davison, Ou & Martinsons, 2013; Kim & Lee, 2006; Lin, 2007). Among the relational factors studied, [1]*interpersonal trust* (Renzl, 2008; Sankowska, 2013; Politis, 2003; Rutten, Blaas-Franken & Martin, 2016; Bakker et al., 2006), [2]*affiliation* (Chennamaneni, 2007; Yu, Lu & Liu, 2010; Jeon, Kim & Koh, 2011; Xue, Bradley & Liang, 2011; Fullwood, Rowley & Delbridge, 2013; Jain, Sandhu & Goh, 2015; Killingsworth, Xue & Liu, 2016), and [3]*subjective norms* (Lin & Lee, 2004; Ryu et al., 2003; Chau & Hu, 2001; Jolaee et al., 2014) have been mostly addressed concepts. Therefore, this study scrutinized these three relational factors extensively. Lastly, two perceptual factors upon social exchange among individuals, [1]*perceived reciprocity* (Ipe, 2003; Kankanhalli et al., 2005; Bock et al., 2005) and [2]*perceived value of knowledge* (Chennamaneni, 2007; Hsu & Chang, 2014; Joia & Lemos, 2010; Kankanhalli et al., 2005; Han & Anantatmula, 2007), were emphasized by researchers. This review contributes to the body of knowledge by discussing emerging concepts and directs future KS research.

RESEARCH METHODOLOGY

This study is designed as a systematic review that compiles and synthesizes prior academic endeavors in the field of KS. Klassen, Jahad & Moher (1998, p. 700) defined this specific type of review as *'a review in which there is a comprehensive search for relevant studies on a specific topic, and those identified are then appraised and synthesized according to a pre-determined explicit method'*. As the initial step, a number of questions were framed to address the research problem explicitly: What are both human and non-human factors that enhance or inhibit individual KS? How might these predictors be categorized under different constructs? Are those differently contextualized factors affecting each other? Do the factors vary according to national or organizational cultures? Subsequently, several key terms were identified based on the research questions and were looked for in various databases. Since the primary focus was gaining insight on KS, studies developing a model or testing measurement instruments were excluded deliberately. Finally, possible articles meeting the inclusion criteria were identified and evaluated by examining the bibliographies of resources identified through the screening process.

CONCEPTUAL FRAMEWORK

Intra-Organizational Knowledge Sharing

Integration of KS practices into organizational routines has been agreed as a critical success factor since it provides the link between individuals, where knowledge reside, and the organization where knowledge gains its (e.g. economic) value (Hendriks, 1999). Yet, there is no consensus towards the definition of the concept since researchers deal with it from different angles. Ipe (2003) simply defined the term KS as *'the act of making knowledge available to others within the organization'*. Van Wijk, Jansen & Lyles (2008), on the other hand, defined the concept as *'the process through which organizational actors, (e.g. teams, units) exchange, receive and are influenced by the experience and knowledge of others'*. From the assumption that *'knowledge is not what people have, but what people do'*, Swan et al., (2016, p. 2) defined KS as *'a proactive process that involves efforts to transform practices through the circulation of knowledge across practice domains'*. This definition argues that organizations are composed of multiple collective mind-lines that can legitimize knowledge dissimilarly.

A considerable amount of literature has been published in the field of intra-organizational knowledge sharing (KS). The majority of those studies have been dominated by *technology-driven perspectives* (Gourlay, 2001) much the same as

KM research. Many of those have argued that the intended intra-organizational KS level could be achieved through advancing the information technology capacity (Alavi & Leidner, 2001; Lee & Kim, 2001; Pan & Leidner, 2003; Kim & Lee, 2006; Davison et al., 2013; Chen & Liang, 2016). In a sense, researchers emphasized the necessity of strategies for coding and storing knowledge (Choi & Lee, 2002). Yet, this school of thought has been criticized as it underestimates *'interpretative flexibility'* (Weick, 1995) of technology which implies technologies can be interpreted and used differently by different actors (Newell et al., 2009, p. 58).

Recently, however, researchers have begun to acknowledge that KS between entities is a complex process due to the nature of knowledge (Ipe, 2003) and the being multifaceted of the process itself (Voelpel & Han, 2005; Swan et al., 2016, p. 230). Beyond the technology, the *human-oriented account* (Choi & Lee, 2002) treats knowledge as a socially-situated phenomenon (Swan et al., 2016, p. 7) and therefore prioritizes to understand human-specific factors and social dynamics to facilitate KS practices within organizations. In other words, individuals' motivation to share (i.e. perceived power of knowledge, reciprocity) (Ipe, 2003; Kankanhalli et al., 2005; Bock et al., 2005) and the characteristics of social context (i.e. trust, communication climate) (Nahapiet & Ghoshal, 1998; Widén-Wulff & Ginman, 2004; Wu et al., 2009; Xue et al., 2011) play a crucial role in KS. Considering this perspective, it can be suggested that KS occurs as a result of interactions between individuals and groups through both formal and informal channels.

Yet, several researchers claim that KS does not simply occur even if organizations ensure the enabling contexts for formal and informal interactions between individuals and groups. This freshly minted theoretical framework called *'ecological view'* (Swan et al., 2016) suggests that intra-organizational knowledge sharing can be fully understood only if the considerations of distinct groups within an organization are addressed. Those considerations (i.e. political, contextual, social) held by distinct communities largely legitimize what knowledge is to be shared and how (McGivern et al., 2016). So, the circulation of knowledge within an organization is possible by the help of human agents (e.g. managers) who operates across multiple domains. This view provides relevant arguments to explain KS practices in organizations especially those that shelter multiple professionals (e.g. healthcare institutions, consultant firms) and therefore different *'epistemic stances'* (McGivern et al., 2016).

The current literature is flooded with a great volume of studies examining different factors that are thought to influence intra-organizational KS practices. Some researchers address contextual elements of organizations such as culture (De Long & Fahey, 2000; Al-Alawi et al., 2007; Jones, Cline & Ryan, 2006), structure (Kim & Lee, 2006; Chen, & Huang, 2007; Willem & Buelens, 2009), management support (Connelly & Kevin Kelloway; 2003; Chen, & Huang, 2007; Gopalakrishnan & Santoro, 2004), rewards and incentives (Kankanhalli et al., 2005; Cabrera et al.,

2006) as an antecedent of KS. While some emphasized the role of relational factors such as interpersonal trust (Nahapiet & Ghoshal, 1998, Bock et al., 2005, Mooradian et al., 2006), affiliation (Wu & Sukoco, 2010; Jeon, Kim & Koh, 2011). Apart from those, several studies focus on the cognitive domain such as perceived reciprocity (Kankanhalli et al., 2005; Ganguly, Talukdar & Chatterjee, 2019; Wasko & Faraj, 2005; Ipe, 2003), perceived power of knowledge (Ipe, 2003) and also individual characteristics such as self-efficacy, personality (Wang & Noe, 2010). Those and many other factors have been scrutinized at different levels (e.g. individual, group) and in different organizational contexts (e.g. online, face to face). Based on the current literature, this study will organize determinants of KS under three categories: cognitive domain, relational domain, and contextual domain.

Relational Side of Intra-Firm Knowledge Sharing

One major issue that has dominated organization studies for many years is how these entities gain advantages over their rivals. According to research adopting the *resource-based perspective*, gaining a distinctive organizational advantage is closely related to the creation and enhancement of intellectual capital. At this point, the question is what actually constitutes intellectual capital. Based on the assumption of the social embeddedness of intellectual capital, Nahapiet and Ghoshal (1998) introduced the *social capital theory* as a basis for understanding the formation of intellectual capital. The theory suggests that social capital facilitates the development of intellectual capital through building favorable conditions for knowledge exchange and combination. *Table 1* summarizes the construct and its three sub-dimensions.

Table 1. Social capital - Source: Nahapiet & Ghoshal (1998)

Structural Dimensions	Cognitive Dimensions	Relational Dimensions
Network ties Network configuration Appropriable organization	Shared codes and language Shared narratives	Trust Norms Obligations Identification

More recent studies have frequently consulted Nahapiet & Ghoshal's (1998) theoretical framework while addressing intra-organizational knowledge sharing (e.g. Inkpen & Tsang, 2005; Chiu, et al., 2006; Chow & Chan, 2008; Maurer, Bartsch & Ebers, 2011; Chang & Chuang, 2011; Mura, et al., 2013; Bharati, Zhang & Chaudhury, 2015). Unlike the original theory, many of those studies dealt with the different dimensions of social capital separately and designated alternative sub-dimensions by combining several theoretical stances. For instance, Chang & Chuang (2011) identified trust, identification, and reciprocity as the sub-dimensions of the relational dimension by merging theories of social capital and individual motivation.

Trust has been treated as the key relational aspect of social capital and is also the most studied concept of social capital in the field of KS (Widén-Wulff & Ginman, 2004). Although the term is defined in different ways, two issues emerged as the central concern: *trust is about accepting vulnerability*; and second, *trust is about dealing with uncertainty and risk* (Newell et al., 2009, p.94). Since knowledge sharing may pose risks such as being subjected to exploitation by others (Holste & Fields, 2010; Lam & Lambermont-Ford, 2010), the interpersonal trust could be expected to diminish the probability of opportunism and minimize the need for costly monitoring processes (Nahapiet & Ghoshal, 1998). In this sense, ensuring high-level trust among individuals encourages them to engage in social exchanges (Nahapiet & Ghoshal, 1998; Staples & Webster, 2008) which are also decisive for achieving the intended KS level within an organization (Nonaka, 1994). Hence, KS literature is flooded with studies examining the role of trust as an antecedent or mediator/moderator of KS (Wang & Noe, 2010).

Renzl (2008) suggested that trust in management is a strong predictor of knowledge sharing between and within teams as it reduces fear. Sankowska (2013), on the other hand, evaluated the concept at the organizational level and indicated that trust is substantial for knowledge creation and articulation and therefore organizational innovativeness. By referring to Cook & Wall's (1980) study, Politis (2003) examined the role of two different components of trust (faith & confidence) in KS practices separately and resulted that faith in peers facilitates knowledge dissemination whereas confidence in colleagues harms knowledge sharing in self-managing teams. Rutten, Blaas-Franken & Martin (2016) attempted to understand the impact of a low level of trust in KS and concluded that a lower level of trust leads to a lower level of knowledge sharing.

Bakker et al. (2006) reached interesting results in their study conducted to understand the roles of both individual and team level trust in KS. The study indicated that without the team effect, trust does not explain knowledge sharing at a statistically significant level. In other words, individual-level trust does not explain KS without team effect (sense of the membership of a team). Another important finding in their study was that cognition-based trust inhibits explicit knowledge sharing in teams. Since the high level of cognition-based trust implies that a colleague is believed to be quite qualified in a certain area (Rutten, Blaas-Franken & Martin, 2016) and they are already assumed to possess the knowledge to be shared, individuals may be reluctant to share knowledge with those co-workers (Bakker et al., 2006).

Some previous studies, on the other hand, have acknowledged that trust is a multidimensional construct and must be dealt with according to its source (McAllister, 1995; Levin, et al., 2002). Correspondingly, several researchers have pursued to elucidate the relationship between different types of trust (i.e. *affect-based, cognition-based*) and knowledge sharing practices. In their study, Holste & Fields (2010) demonstrated that while affect-based trust significantly influences tacit knowledge sharing; cognition-based trust positively affects knowledge use. Similarly, Pangil & Moi Chan's (2014) study suggests that personal-based trust and institutional-based trust were significantly related to knowledge sharing, whereas cognitive-based trust does not a predictor of KS in virtual teams. These results are understandable to a certain degree since cognitive-based trust is difficult to develop within virtual teams (absence of physical interaction) (Newell et al., 2009, p. 62; Pangil & Moi Chan's, 2014). The results mentioned herein are consistent with Rutten, Blaas-Franken & Martin (2016); Swift & Hwang's (2013); Casimir, Lee & Loon (2012) as they suggest the affect-based trust accelerates knowledge sharing activities (but not cognition-based).

On the contrary, Chowdhury's (2005) findings indicated that cognition-based trust has a stronger influence on complex knowledge sharing than affect-based trust. Chowdhury's findings overlap with Levin & Cross's (2004) results that suggest cognitive-based trust facilitates implicit knowledge sharing. As the explanation, O'Neill & Adya (2007) argued that individuals consider the knowledge they have accumulated in their job as a valuable asset and they are only willing to share with coworkers who have a good reputation about decent performance. A serious weakness with this argument, however, is that individuals may well perceive these competent co-workers as a rival and therefore refrain from sharing valuable knowledge they possessed.

Drawing previous discussions together, it can be concluded that the role of various types of trust (e.g. cognition-based, affect-based) and its components (e.g. faith, confidence) on knowledge sharing have been investigated extensively. Only a limited number of those studies in the literature reported that there is no relationship between trust and KS (e.g. Chow & Chan; 2008; Li, 2005). Rather, the majority of those have emphasized the facilitating role of trust in intra-organizational knowledge exchange.

As the second relational factor to be scrutinized in this study, the term *affiliation* implies the intrinsic motivation towards engaging warm, close, intimate personal relationships as a part of socialization (Baker, 1979). Jeon, Kim & Koh (2011) have argued that individuals, as social beings, tend to affiliate themselves with others for certain reasons such as ensuring personal safety. Similarly, J. R. Greenberg & P. J. Greenberg (1991, p. 120) have argued that affiliation is closely related to safety needs and these needs stimulate the formation of intimate relations within a social network. Since sharing knowledge with other members involves a certain degree of uncertainty (Holste & Fields, 2010) and therefore, requires personal sacrifice (Wasko & Faraj, 2000), the sense of *'togetherness'* (Bock et al., 2005) may facilitate knowledge sharing by eliminating the sense of insecurity.

There is a large volume of published studies describing the role of affiliation in knowledge sharing within CoPs (Bock et al, 2005; Chennamaneni, 2007; Yu, Lu & Liu, 2010; Jeon, Kim & Koh, 2011; Xue, Bradley & Liang, 2011; Fullwood, Rowley & Delbridge, 2013; Jain, Sandhu & Goh, 2015; Killingsworth, Xue & Liu, 2016). Jeon, Kim & Koh (2011) treated affiliation as an aspect of intrinsic motivation, and their findings suggested that affiliation exert a significant impact on knowledge sharing attitudes. Nevertheless, the study was conducted where collective culture prevails, and in such cultures, it would be already expected that affiliation tends to shape social attitudes. Therefore, the results may not be generalized to individualistic cultures. On the other hand, Xue, Bradley & Liang (2011) discussed affiliation as a part of the perceived organizational climate. Their findings are consistent with others that suggest the sense of affiliation has a positive impact on subjective norms towards knowledge sharing behavior (Wu & Zhu, 2012). From a slightly different perspective, Jain, Sandhu & Goh (2015) indicated that affiliation is positively related to both *knowledge donating (KD)* and *knowledge collecting (KC).*

These results are understandable since the presence of strong affiliation in an organization encourages individuals to go beyond their responsibility and to help others further (Bock and Kim, 2002). Yet, inconsistent results have emerged in the sense of understanding the role of affiliation among knowledge sharing studies conducted in virtual communities. Lee, Reid & Kim (2012) argued that affiliation strengthens community identification and therefore the intention to knowledge sharing in online travel communities. Yet, Killingsworth, Xue & Liu (2016) analyzed KS practices among global virtual teams and concluded that affiliation does not significantly influence knowledge sharing attitudes. The scholars explicated these results based on the idea that affiliation may be perceived and acted upon dissimilarly in different cultures.

Several studies have argued that *subjective norms* guide individuals' behavioral intention to KS (Nahapiet & Ghoshal, 1998; Chau & Hu, 2001; Bock et al., 2005; Chow & Chan, 2008; Jeon, Kim & Koh, 2011). Based on the theory of reasoned action (TRA), Cabrera & Cabrera (2005) described the term as *'beliefs as to the existence of social expectations regarding behavior'*. In other words, the term implies that the pressure posed by socially-constructed norms has an impact on whether to perform or not perform a behavior (Ajzen, 1991). Similar to TRA, the social identity perspective suggested that individuals tend to comply with norms to preserve in-group identity (Christensen et al., 2004). In this sense, the greater social pressure to exchange knowledge may constitute a more favorable attitude toward it within an organization (Chow & Chan, 2008).

Bock et al. (2005) considered subjective norms as a constituent of institutional structure and demonstrated that these norms affect behavioral intention towards knowledge sharing, especially within cultural contexts characterized by strong collectivist orientation. In a different context (within both formal and informal CoPs in a globally known electronic company), Jeon, Kim & Koh (2011) examined the linkages between subjective norms and intention of individuals towards KS, and their findings confirmed Bock and his colleagues' results. Lin & Lee (2004) assessed the role of senior managers' subjective norms and these norms were found to be a major effect on the intention to KS. Consistent with those, Ryu et al. (2003) applied a model based on the theory of planned behavior (TPB) and concluded that subjective norms are one of the influential factors in behavioral intention to share knowledge among healthcare professionals. Tohidinia & Mosakhani (2010) claimed that facilitative organizational climate towards knowledge sharing can be established through the presence of collectively accepted norms.

Yet, Chau & Hu (2001) concluded that subjective norms do not have a significant impact on physicians' behavioral intention since they perform a highly autonomous profession. The researchers' findings are understandable since healthcare institutions operate in an environment where strict legislative regulations limit sharing of certain knowledge types. Similarly, Jolaee et al. (2014) demonstrated that there is no significant relationship between subjective norms and KS intention of academic staff. They also explained these results with the type of profession individuals perform. Huang, Davison & Gu (2008) reached intriguing results within the Chinese context where personal relationships are mostly shaped by Guanxi orientation. The results indicated that there is no significant relationship between norms and KS intention. The researchers have attempted to interpret these results in terms of the undesirable consequences of excessive social pressure triggered by subjective norms.

Despite the certain inconsistencies in empirical findings, relational factors have remained to be one of the most addressed issues in KS studies. The main assumption of those studies is that sharing is a voluntary act (Davenport, 1997, p.87), and thus the quality of interpersonal relations is decisive in the constitution of behavioral intention towards KS. Yet, other research has indicated that transferring knowledge through social processes within an organization may require more than ensuring good relationships between parties involved. Understanding the complex nature of the process is possible by tackling multiple issues (i.e. political, cultural, and institutional factors) simultaneously.

Contextual Side of Intra-Firm Knowledge Sharing

Recent theoretical approaches have tended to portray organizational behavior from a holistic perspective. One of those, the social cognitive theory (SCT) suggests that individuals' behaviors are molded as a result of continuous reciprocal interaction between cognitive, behavioral, and environmental influences (Tsai & Cheng, 2010). Similar to this, Pan & Scarbrough (1998) suggested that organizational practices are mainly constituted as a result of complex interactions which take place between the subjective perceptions of individuals and the objective characteristics of work processes. Drawing on these theoretical perspectives, Fernie et al. (2003) defined organizations as a product of their own politics, economics, and social factors that contribute to the formation of processes, practices, and philosophies. Fernie and his colleagues, in fact, have laid stress on the inseparability of contexts and practices.

Prior studies have frequently addressed the characteristics of the environment in which organizations operate while explaining organizational behavior, and more specifically, KS behavior (i.e. De Long and Fahey, 2000; Kim & Lee, 2006; Bock et al., 2005; Kankanhalli et al., 2005; Lee, Kim & Kim, 2006; Connelly & Kelloway, 2003; Davison, Ou, & Martinsons, 2013). Drawing on the fact that contextual conditions may differ regarding the organization itself (Fernie et al., 2003) or the industry in which the organization operates or even national cultures (Ford & Chan, 2003), academic efforts have steered to address a great variety of different aspect of organizational contexts. Yet, confusion has arisen about the definition of the term organizational context and boundaries of it. Porter & McLaughlin (2006) examined related studies and identified seven major components of organizational context: *Culture/climate, goals/purposes, people/composition, processes, state/ condition, structure, and time.* In this study, three components of organizational context (structural properties, communication climate, and IT infrastructure) are examined in connection with the behavioral intention to KS.

Since KS has been treated as a form of communication (Van Den Hooff & De Ridder, 2004), institutional communication climate is highly valued in the field of knowledge management. Therefore, researchers dwelled on the different aspects of communication concerning knowledge sharing: *interaction frequency & interaction quality* (Zboralski, 2009); *team communication* (Hoegl & Gemuenden, 2001; De Vries, Van den Hooff & De Ridder, 2006); *the quality of face-to-face interaction, use of common language and teamwork collaboration* (Al-Alawi, Al-Marzooqi & Mohammed, 2007); *vertical and horizontal interactions* (De Long & Fahey, 2000); *leadership communication styles* (De Vries, Bakker-Pieper & Oostenveld, 2010); *HRM practices toward face-to-face communication* (Salis & Williams, 2010), *formal and informal communication channels* (Ipe, 2003) and *overall communication climate* (Ali, Pascoe & Warne, 2002; Van Den Hooff & de Ridder, 2004).

Van Den Hooff & de Ridder's (2004) results revealed that the presence of a constructive communication climate is central for organizations in terms of creating affective commitment which is crucial for knowledge donation in particular. Yet, the study results did not indicate any direct or indirect relationship between communication climate and knowledge collecting. By referring to Granovetter's (1992) concept of *relational embeddedness*, Ipe (2003) emphasized the role of informal communication channels as a facilitator of knowledge sharing. As the explanation, the researcher suggests that informal communication opportunities allow for the genesis of interpersonal trust and therefore facilitate KS. Zboralski's (2009) findings, on the other hand, indicate that the frequency and the quality of communication positively related to individual motivation to share knowledge within CoPs.

De Vries, Van den Hooff & De Ridder's (2006) study differs from other studies in terms of associating certain communication styles of teams to KS practices. The study results indicate a positive relationship between the agreeable (i.e. friendliness & empathy) and extravert (i.e. talkativeness & enthusiasm) communication style with the willingness of employees to share knowledge. Al-Alawi, Al-Marzooqi & Mohammed (2007) suggested three components for building a constructive communication climate (the quality of face-to-face interaction, use of common language, and collaboration) and demonstrated that each component is strongly related to KS. Al-Alawi and colleagues' findings have been partially confirmed (regarding face-to-face communication) by Salis & Williams (2010) as they concluded that long-term HRM practices toward face-to-face interactions facilitate knowledge articulation within a work environment. Last but not least, De Vries, Bakker-Pieper & Oostenveld, (2010) assessed the communication features of certain leadership styles (i.e. charismatic, human-oriented & task-oriented), and supportiveness and preciseness of leaders were found significant as regards collecting and donating knowledge.

Unsurprisingly, communication has received strong literature support in the field of knowledge sharing. Yet, there has been little discussion about the differentiation in communication practices of distinct subcultures within a single organization and also its effects on KS. Additionally, most of the studies were carried out without considering legislative boundaries that closely concern organizational communication. For instance, there are several legislations in healthcare organizations to limit the communication of certain information, including patients' information, among practitioners. In this sense, external factors also must be considered while examining the internal communication climate concerning KS practices in certain organizational forms.

Parallel to the rapid advancement in the technology itself, *information technologies (IT)* has been begun to be studied quite extensively in knowledge sharing literature. Although contradictory findings emerge, the majority of researchers have emphasized the critical role of IT technologies in the sense of improving collaborative endeavors (Alavi & Leidner, 2001; Choi, Lee & Yoo, 2010) and creating opportunities for KS. (Connelly & Kelloway, 2003; Huysman & Wulf, 2006; Yuan et al., 2013; Davison, Ou & Martinsons, 2013). Choi, Lee & Yoo (2010) reached a conclusion that suggests along with the mediation role of transactive memory systems (TMS), IT has a positive impact on KS. Davison, Ou & Martinsons (2013) reported that interactive IT applications do play a critical role in the effective communication needed for informal KS. Similar to those, Kim & Lee's (2006) results revealed that IT systems significantly affect the KS capabilities of individuals in both public and private organizations. Lin (2007), on the other hand, found that there is a meaningful relationship between IT usage and knowledge collecting, yet reported no significant relationship between IT and knowledge donating. In contrast, the study results of Connelly & Kelloway (2003) revealed that technology does not significantly conducive to the prediction of positive knowledge sharing culture.

However, some commentators advised that one should be careful about the significance attributed to IT technologies. Various rationales have been asserted to explain this situation. One of those argued that the technologies introduced can only be beneficial if long-standing organizational values associated with KS are supportive (De Long & Fahey, 2000). In this sense, the interactions of individuals with technology are largely molded by the cultural components of an organization (i.e. values, norms, practices). Similar to those researchers, Cabrera, Collins & Salgado (2006) and Chennamaneni, Teng & Raja (2012) suggest that technology alone cannot guarantee individual willingness to share knowledge. Newell et al. (2009, p.20) took this a step further and argued that the relationship between the organization and IT systems is complex, as the outcomes are difficult to predict.

Within the current literature, several reasons were indicated that likely to be undermined possible benefits of technological tools. The first one is the technology used itself. Wasko & Faraj (2005) suggested that contributions to such systems are voluntary and it is irrational that individuals donate their time, effort, and knowledge toward the collective benefit instead of free-riding on the efforts of others. Hence, the technology acquired must be well-designed and user-friendly (Chennamaneni, Teng & Raja, 2012; Kim & Lee; 2006) to ensure personal beliefs that using such systems would be free of excessive effort (Davis, 1989). Secondly, Newell et al. (2009, p.20-21) claimed that technologies are mainly *'open-ended'* (Orlikowski, 2000) in nature and therefore the same technology can be interpreted and used in different ways by different actors. Yet more, the authors argued that people may pretend to use technologies, but in fact, they may sustain their old-fashioned work practices. Such behavioral patterns can be explained by the difficulties posed by the fact that *'getting individuals out of their comfort zones by having them operate in unfamiliar settings and deal with unfamiliar problems'* (Dilworth, 2010). In other words, Ignoring IT technologies or using them minimally can be explained by the resistance to change about the work habits of individuals (McDermott, 1999).

Apart from the technology adopted, the nature of knowledge to be shared has been discussed as a challenge while sharing knowledge through such technologies. Huysman & Wulf (2006) stressed that knowledge in an organizational setting is mainly tacit and appears to be difficult to be shared or stored in a system. Rather, they suggest social networks are more promising in supporting the exchange of individual knowledge. Similarly, Yuan et al. (2013) highlighted the socially-situated side of knowledge while sharing tacit expertise rather than formal technological systems. Similarly, Swan et al. (2016, p. 7) characterized knowledge as a contextually embedded phenomenon and stressed the key role of informal communication channels while sharing tacit expertise rather than formal IT tools. Contrary to those, Choi, Lee & Yoo (2010) argued that IT allows tacit knowledge to be shared in a more standardized format.

The overall tendency in the current literature is that technology-based tools will maintain their key role as an intermediary for KS (Panahi, Watson & Partridge, 2013). Yet, motivational factors toward the acceptance and usage of these technologies are needed to be studied further. The literature also suggests that the socio-cultural environment of organizations should be considered while evaluating the role of such systems. Although IT is assumed to enhance KS by lowering temporal and spatial barriers between workers (Hendriks, 1999), by itself, it may fail to constitute individual willingness to share knowledge. Rather, knowledge sharing involves social and human interaction (Lin, 2007). Considering all, there is a need for further studies investigating socio-cognitive factors which may enhance or inhibit the role of IT regarding particularly tacit KS.

Beyond these, the studies conducted have accentuated the role of *structural characteristics* of firms insistently while explaining KS practices within entities. The majority of those studies have focus on certain properties of the organizational structure, which are thought to either foster or impair KS activities: The level of centralization (Tsai, 2002); The level of hierarchy (Sharratt & Usoro, 2003); the level of formalization and centralization (Kim & Lee, 2006); participative decision-making, ease of information flow, cross-functional teams (less hierarchical structures) (Al-Alawi, Al-Marzooqi & Mohammed, 2007); the level of formalization, centralization, and integration (Chen & Huang, 2007); the level of formalization, centralization, and complication (Lin, 2008); the level of formalization, specialization and centralization (Willem & Buelens, 2009); Hierarchy (Friesl, Sackmann & Kremser, 2011); centralization (Lee, Gon Kim, & Kim, 2012); the level of centralization, and formalization (Amayah, 2013).

A great number of empirical studies have evidenced that highly formalized, centralized and hierarchical structures are likely to create barriers for KS activities (Tsai, 2002; Sharratt & Usoro, 2003; Kim & Lee, 2006; Al-Alawi, Al-Marzooqi & Mohammed, 2007; Chen & Huang, 2007). For instance, Sharratt & Usoro (2003) reported that a highly centralized and bureaucratic structure poses challenges for the dissemination of knowledge throughout the organization. Similarly, Al-Alawi, Al-Marzooqi & Mohammed (2007) found that participative decision-making processes, mechanisms to ease of information flow, cross-functional teams facilitate KS activities Chen & Huang (2007) suggested that more integrated (less formalized and less centralized) organizational structures may naturally lead to more favorable social interactions among organizational members and then the levels of KS would be more enhanced. To some extent, these findings are understandable as such structural characteristics hinder interactions between individuals, participatory decision-making processes, interdependence and collaborative works (Lin, 2008). These findings are also consistent with Newell and colleagues' (2009, pp.35-36) proposal towards the creation of facilitating context for knowledge practices. As the most appropriate configuration, they proposed *'adhocracy'* that represents minimum hierarchy, few or no formal rules and decentralized decision-making processes.

However, contradictory findings emerged in the studies conducted by Willem & Buelens (2009), Amayah (2013) and Lin (2008) (partially). In their comparative study, Willem & Buelens (2009) reported that less formalized, specialized and centralized structures do not necessarily lead to more knowledge sharing. In fact, they suggested that structural characteristics affect the processes of knowledge sharing in only cooperative episodes. The result also confirms the idea that knowledge and knowledge sharing are context-dependent. Similarly, Amayah (2013) concluded that centralization and formalization do not have any significant impact on KS in public organizations as they are bureaucratic in nature. In Lin's (2008) study, on the other hand, KS was found in a significant reverse relationship with formalized and complicated organizational structure, while no relationship was reported between centralization.

To summarize, the vast majority of research indicates that certain structural characteristics of organizations are related to KS either directly or indirectly. Yet, others argue that structure, by itself, may not facilitate KS practices but it well may create obstacles (Kim & Lee, 2006; Tsai, 2002). The underlying reason is that sharing is a complex and multifaceted act (Nonaka, 1994). Therefore, those studies examined the complexity level of knowledge to be shared (Willem & Buelens, 2009), the interpersonal interaction level (between and within units) (Tsai, 2002; Al-Alawi, Al-Marzooqi & Mohammed, 2007; Lin, 2008) and motivational factors (Amayah, 2013) along with structural dimensions. The current study interrogates two structural features of the organization regarding KS: *Formalization* refers to the degree to which jobs within the organization are standardized by rules and procedures (Rapert & Wren, 1998), and *Hierarchy* implies the centralization of authority relations where coordination is realized through vertically imposed bureaucratic processes (Tsai, 2002).

Socio-Cognitive Side of Intra-Firm Knowledge Sharing

By referring to the assumptions of cognitive psychology, some researchers have suggested that individuals' mental processes are closely related to their behavior towards KS. The majority of those efforts have strived to explain the role of *perceptions*, which is a constituent of the cognitive domain, in the knowledge exchange between provider and seeker. Ferguson & Bargh (2004) stressed that individuals' perceptions towards a stimulus in the environment can influence people's judgments, and so their behavior. Inspired by this assumption, it can be suggested that individual perceptions towards social facts determine their social behaviors. In other words, perceptual and behavioral representations are closely interconnected with each other (Dijksterhuis & Bargh, 2001). In this respect, it is not surprising to suggest that individuals' perceptions may play a crucial role in either fostering or inhibiting knowledge sharing activities.

In his study examining the impact of knowledge repositories on the distribution of power, Gray (2001) revealed that such systems cause shifts in power balances within the organization. He suggests that those systems lead to a shift of power away from employees to managers and, this can cause reluctance about engaging in KS activities. Similarly, Chennamaneni (2007) demonstrated that the more the individuals perceive that sharing knowledge reduces their power within the organization, the less likely they engage in KS activities. Hsu & Chang (2014) indicated that fear of losing knowledge power significantly boosts the feeling of uncertainty that is assumed to create barriers to intra-organizational KS activities. Consistent with those, Joia & Lemos (2010) confirmed that perceived loss of power impedes tacit knowledge transfer. In contrast, Kankanhalli et al. (2005), Han & Anantatmula (2007) suggested that there is no significant relationship between perceived loss of power and KS activities.

SOLUTION AND RECOMMENDATIONS

One of the fundamental processes of knowledge management, knowledge dissemination, is a complex and multifaceted process. As reported in this study, at least three main predictors affect the individual KS process: organizational, relational, and socio-cognitive. First of all, since knowledge is a context-dependent phenomenon (Swan et al., 2016, p. 7), the institutional context (i.e. culture, structure, network ties, and technology infrastructure) must be scrutinized and reorganized if necessary. In particular, communication channels (both formal & informal) must be varied to establish enabling context for KS practices. Yet, creating a facilitating organizational setting may not necessarily boost individual willingness to share knowledge. Therefore, the nature of social context needs to be considered carefully. Practitioners must focus on building mutual trust that individuals are able to express their ideas and be open to those of others. Considering all, to establish an effective knowledge dissemination strategy, managers should critically evaluate the set of factors suggested.

FUTURE RESEARCH DIRECTIONS

KS studies to date depict organizations as entities that contain a single culture. However, certain organizational forms may well contain multiple subcultures with different KS practices. Further studies, therefore, should evaluate KS dynamics specific to these communities carefully. It would also be interesting to conduct comparative studies on the factors affecting KS practices among these sub-groups. Further studies that investigate KS barriers among these distinct groups are also highly recommended. Beyond these, creating a knowledge culture is crucial and is only possible with the genesis of appropriate organizational culture (Oliver & Kandadi, 2006). Further research, therefore, is required to examine the elements of organizational culture and whether the national culture in which shapes it. Since organizations shelter workers from multiple generations, it would also be worth understanding possible differences in KS practices among generations.

CONCLUSION

This chapter has synthesized the research dealing with multiple factors that influence KS practices. Considering all, a set of organizational, relational, and socio-cognitive factors discussed seem decisive in shaping KS practices in organizations. It can be suggested several implications for both scholars and practitioners. First of all, since trust is a prerequisite for interactions among individuals, establishing an organizational culture that emphasizes interpersonal trust is crucial. Beyond simply focusing on interpersonal trust, institutional-based trust must be dealt with to strengthen ties between workers and organizations. The other relational factor scrutinized, affiliation, is also essential since it encourages workers to go beyond their responsibilities and help others (Bock and Kim, 2002). In a sense, affiliation is expected to stimulate knowledge donation. Subjective norms are the most controversial among relational factors investigated since the effect of these norms on KS practices varied according to the level of job-related autonomy.

Second, institutional context must be emphasized since knowledge dissemination is a complex interaction among agents that requires facilitating conditions. In particular, those organizational structures characterized as highly formalized, centralized, and hierarchical structures are likely to create barriers for KS practices (Chen & Huang, 2007). These structural characteristics may well deteriorate communication climate & organizational integration. The role of technology in improving collaborative endeavors and mediating KS practices has been emphasized by many scholars (Alavi & Leidner, 2001; Choi, Lee & Yoo, 2010). Yet, only well-designed and integrated IT systems have the potential to facilitate KS practices (Chennamaneni, Teng & Raja, 2012). Nevertheless, putting too much emphasis on technologies can lead to undermining the central role of the human agent.

Third, individuals' perceptions towards their social interactions have also become decisive in sharing or hiding the knowledge they possess. Considering reciprocity as a norm and supported by organizational culture can make individuals are more willing to do everything on behalf of the other (Tamjidyamcholo et al., 2013). Besides, power relations and legitimacy-seeking that are assumed to shape ones' perception towards the communities must be analyzed critically by both scholars and practitioners.

To sum up, evaluation of these predictors individually may be lacking in explaining KS practices. Since knowledge articulation takes place in a variety of organizational settings and is justified by multiple actors (Swan et al., 2016, p.11), a more holistic perspective is required to be built by both scholars and practitioners.

ACKNOWLEDGMENT

The current study was funded by Çukurova University Scientific Research Projects Unit with the project number SDK-2020-12662.

REFERENCES

Ajzen, I. (1991). The theory of planned behavior. *Organizational Behavior and Human Decision Processes*, *50*(2), 179–211. doi:10.1016/0749-5978(91)90020-T

Al-Alawi, A. I., Al-Marzooqi, N. Y., & Mohammed, Y. F. (2007). Organizational culture and knowledge sharing: Critical success factors. *Journal of Knowledge Management.*

Alavi, M., & Leidner, D. E. (2001). Knowledge management and knowledge management systems: Conceptual foundations and research issues. *Management Information Systems Quarterly*, *25*(1), 107–136. doi:10.2307/3250961

Ali, I. M., Pascoe, C., & Warne, L. (2002). Interactions of organizational culture and collaboration in working and learning. *Journal of Educational Technology & Society*, *5*(2), 60–68.

Amayah, A. T. (2013). Determinants of knowledge sharing in a public sector organization. *Journal of Knowledge Management*, *17*(3), 454–471. doi:10.1108/JKM-11-2012-0369

Baker, C. R. (1979). Defining and measuring affiliation motivation. *European Journal of Social Psychology*, *9*(1), 97–99. doi:10.1002/ejsp.2420090108

Bakker, M., Leenders, R. T. A., Gabbay, S. M., Kratzer, J., & Van Engelen, J. M. (2006). Is trust really social capital? Knowledge sharing in product development projects. *The Learning Organization*, *13*(6), 594–605. doi:10.1108/09696470610705479

Bharati, P., Zhang, W., & Chaudhury, A. (2015). Better knowledge with social media? Exploring the roles of social capital and organizational knowledge management. *Journal of Knowledge Management*, *19*(3), 456–475. doi:10.1108/JKM-11-2014-0467

Bock, G. W., & Kim, Y. G. (2002). Breaking the myths of rewards: An exploratory study of attitudes about knowledge sharing. *Information Resources Management Journal*, *15*(2), 14–21. doi:10.4018/irmj.2002040102

Bock, G. W., Zmud, R. W., Kim, Y. G., & Lee, J. N. (2005). Behavioral intention formation in knowledge sharing: Examining the roles of extrinsic motivators, social-psychological factors, and organizational climate. *Management Information Systems Quarterly*, *29*(1), 87–111. doi:10.2307/25148669

Cabrera, A., Collins, W. C., & Salgado, J. F. (2006). Determinants of individual engagement in knowledge sharing. *International Journal of Human Resource Management*, *17*(2), 245–264. doi:10.1080/09585190500404614

Cabrera, E. F., & Cabrera, A. (2005). Fostering knowledge sharing through people management practices. *International Journal of Human Resource Management*, *16*(5), 720–735. doi:10.1080/09585190500083020

Casimir, G., Lee, K., & Loon, M. (2012). Knowledge sharing: Influences of trust, commitment and cost. *Journal of Knowledge Management*, *16*(5), 740–753. doi:10.1108/13673271211262781

Chang, H. H., & Chuang, S. S. (2011). Social capital and individual motivations on knowledge sharing: Participant involvement as a moderator. *Information & Management*, *48*(1), 9–18. doi:10.1016/j.im.2010.11.001

Chau, P. Y., & Hu, P. J. H. (2001). Information technology acceptance by individual professionals: A model comparison approach. *Decision Sciences*, *32*(4), 699–719. doi:10.1111/j.1540-5915.2001.tb00978.x

Chen, C. J., & Huang, J. W. (2007). How organizational climate and structure affect knowledge management—The social interaction perspective. *International Journal of Information Management*, *27*(2), 104–118. doi:10.1016/j.ijinfomgt.2006.11.001

Chen, D. N., & Liang, T. P. (2016). Knowledge diversity and firm performance: An ecological view. *Journal of Knowledge Management*, *20*(4), 671–686. doi:10.1108/JKM-10-2015-0377

Chennamaneni, A. (2007). *Determinants of knowledge sharing behaviors: Developing and testing an integrated theoretical model* (Doctoral dissertation). The University of Texas at Arlington.

Chennamaneni, A., Teng, J. T., & Raja, M. K. (2012). A unified model of knowledge sharing behaviours: Theoretical development and empirical test. *Behaviour & Information Technology*, *31*(11), 1097–1115. doi:10.1080/0144929X.2011.624637

Chiu, C. M., Hsu, M. H., & Wang, E. T. (2006). Understanding knowledge sharing in virtual communities: An integration of social capital and social cognitive theories. *Decision Support Systems*, *42*(3), 1872–1888. doi:10.1016/j.dss.2006.04.001

Choi, B., & Lee, H. (2002). Knowledge management strategy and its link to knowledge creation process. *Expert Systems with Applications*, *23*(3), 173–187. doi:10.1016/S0957-4174(02)00038-6

Choi, S. Y., Lee, H., & Yoo, Y. (2010). The impact of information technology and transactive memory systems on knowledge sharing, application, and team performance: A field study. *Management Information Systems Quarterly*, *34*(4), 855–870. doi:10.2307/25750708

Chow, W. S., & Chan, L. S. (2008). Social network, social trust and shared goals in organizational knowledge sharing. *Information & Management*, *45*(7), 458–465. doi:10.1016/j.im.2008.06.007

Chowdhury, S. (2005). The role of affect-and cognition-based trust in complex knowledge sharing. *Journal of Managerial Issues*, 310–326.

Christensen, P. N., Rothgerber, H., Wood, W., & Matz, D. C. (2004). Social norms and identity relevance: A motivational approach to normative behavior. *Personality and Social Psychology Bulletin*, *30*(10), 1295–1309. doi:10.1177/0146167204264480 PMID:15466602

Connelly, C. E., & Kevin Kelloway, E. (2003). Predictors of employees' perceptions of knowledge sharing cultures. *Leadership and Organization Development Journal*, *24*(5), 294–301. doi:10.1108/01437730310485815

Cook, J., & Wall, T. (1980). New work attitude measures of trust, organizational commitment and personal need non-fulfilment. *Journal of Occupational Psychology*, *53*(1), 39–52. doi:10.1111/j.2044-8325.1980.tb00005.x

Davenport, T. H. (1997). *Information ecology: Mastering the information and knowledge environment*. Oxford University Press on Demand.

Davis, F. D. (1989). Perceived usefulness, perceived ease of use, and user acceptance of information technology. *Management Information Systems Quarterly*, *13*(3), 319–340. doi:10.2307/249008

Davison, R. M., Ou, C. X., & Martinsons, M. G. (2013). Information technology to support informal knowledge sharing. *Information Systems Journal*, *23*(1), 89–109. doi:10.1111/j.1365-2575.2012.00400.x

De Long, D. W., & Fahey, L. (2000). Diagnosing cultural barriers to knowledge management. *The Academy of Management Perspectives*, *14*(4), 113–127. doi:10.5465/ame.2000.3979820

De Vries, R. E., Bakker-Pieper, A., & Oostenveld, W. (2010). Leadership= communication? The relations of leaders' communication styles with leadership styles, knowledge sharing and leadership outcomes. *Journal of Business and Psychology*, *25*(3), 367–380. doi:10.100710869-009-9140-2 PMID:20700375

De Vries, R. E., Van den Hooff, B., & de Ridder, J. A. (2006). Explaining knowledge sharing: The role of team communication styles, job satisfaction, and performance beliefs. *Communication Research*, *33*(2), 115–135. doi:10.1177/0093650205285366

Dijksterhuis, A., & Bargh, J. A. (2001). The perception-behavior expressway: Automatic effects of social perception on social behavior. In Advances in experimental social psychology (Vol. 33, pp. 1–40). Academic Press. doi:10.1016/S0065-2601(01)80003-4

Dilworth, R. L. (2010). Explaining traditional action learning: concepts and beliefs. In *Action Learning* (pp. 3–28). Palgrave Macmillan. doi:10.1057/9780230250734_1

Ferguson, M. J., & Bargh, J. A. (2004). How social perception can automatically influence behavior. *Trends in Cognitive Sciences*, *8*(1), 33–39. doi:10.1016/j.tics.2003.11.004 PMID:14697401

Fernie, S., Green, S. D., Weller, S. J., & Newcombe, R. (2003). Knowledge sharing: Context, confusion and controversy. *International Journal of Project Management*, *21*(3), 177–187. doi:10.1016/S0263-7863(02)00092-3

Ford, D. P., & Chan, Y. E. (2003). Knowledge sharing in a multi-cultural setting: A case study. *Knowledge Management Research and Practice*, *1*(1), 11–27. doi:10.1057/palgrave.kmrp.8499999

Friesl, M., Sackmann, S. A., & Kremser, S. (2011). Knowledge sharing in new organizational entities: The impact of hierarchy, organizational context, micro-politics and suspicion. *Cross Cultural Management*, *18*(1), 71–86. doi:10.1108/13527601111104304

Fullwood, R., Rowley, J., & Delbridge, R. (2013). Knowledge sharing amongst academics in UK universities. *Journal of Knowledge Management*, *17*(1), 123–136. doi:10.1108/13673271311300831

Gopalakrishnan, S., & Santoro, M. D. (2004). Distinguishing between knowledge transfer and technology transfer activities: The role of key organizational factors. *IEEE Transactions on Engineering Management*, *51*(1), 57–69. doi:10.1109/TEM.2003.822461

Gourlay, S. (2001). Knowledge management and HRD. *Human Resource Development International*, *4*(1), 27–46. doi:10.1080/13678860121778

Greenberg, J. R., & Greenberg, P. J. (1991). *Oedipus and beyond: A clinical theory*. Harvard University Press.

Han, B. M., & Anantatmula, V. S. (2007). Knowledge sharing in large IT organizations: A case study. *Vine*, *37*(4), 421–439. doi:10.1108/03055720710838506

Hendriks, P. (1999). Why share knowledge? The influence of ICT on the motivation for knowledge sharing. *Knowledge and Process Management*, *6*(2), 91–100. doi:10.1002/(SICI)1099-1441(199906)6:2<91::AID-KPM54>3.0.CO;2-M

Hoegl, M., & Gemuenden, H. G. (2001). Teamwork quality and the success of innovative projects: A theoretical concept and empirical evidence. *Organization Science*, *12*(4), 435–449. doi:10.1287/orsc.12.4.435.10635

Holste, J. S., & Fields, D. (2010). Trust and tacit knowledge sharing and use. *Journal of Knowledge Management*, *14*(1), 128–140. doi:10.1108/13673271011015615

Hsu, M. H., & Chang, C. M. (2014). Examining interpersonal trust as a facilitator and uncertainty as an inhibitor of intra-organisational knowledge sharing. *Information Systems Journal*, *24*(2), 119–142. doi:10.1111/isj.12000

Huang, Q., Davison, R. M., & Gu, J. (2008). Impact of personal and cultural factors on knowledge sharing in China. *Asia Pacific Journal of Management*, *25*(3), 451–471. doi:10.100710490-008-9095-2

Huysman, M., & Wulf, V. (2006). IT to support knowledge sharing in communities, towards a social capital analysis. *Journal of Information Technology*, *21*(1), 40–51. doi:10.1057/palgrave.jit.2000053

Inkpen, A. C., & Tsang, E. W. (2005). Social capital, networks, and knowledge transfer. *Academy of Management Review*, *30*(1), 146–165. doi:10.5465/amr.2005.15281445

Jain, K. K., Sandhu, M. S., & Goh, S. K. (2015). Organizational climate, trust and knowledge sharing: Insights from Malaysia. *Journal of Asia Business Studies*, *9*(1), 54–77. doi:10.1108/JABS-07-2013-0040

Jeon, S., Kim, Y. G., & Koh, J. (2011). An integrative model for knowledge sharing in communities-of-practice. *Journal of Knowledge Management*, *15*(2), 251–269. doi:10.1108/13673271111119682

Joia, L. A., & Lemos, B. (2010). Relevant factors for tacit knowledge transfer within organisations. *Journal of Knowledge Management*, *14*(3), 410–427. doi:10.1108/13673271011050139

Jolaee, A., Nor, K. M., Khani, N., & Yusoff, R. M. (2014). Factors affecting knowledge sharing intention among academic staff. *International Journal of Educational Management*, *28*(4), 413–431. doi:10.1108/IJEM-03-2013-0041

Jones, M. C., Cline, M., & Ryan, S. (2006). Exploring knowledge sharing in ERP implementation: An organizational culture framework. *Decision Support Systems*, *41*(2), 411–434. doi:10.1016/j.dss.2004.06.017

Kankanhalli, A., Tan, B. C., & Wei, K. K. (2005). Contributing knowledge to electronic knowledge repositories: An empirical investigation. *Management Information Systems Quarterly*, *29*(1), 113. doi:10.2307/25148670

Killingsworth, B., Xue, Y., & Liu, Y. (2016). Factors influencing knowledge sharing among global virtual teams. *Team Performance Management*, *22*(5/6), 284–300. doi:10.1108/TPM-10-2015-0042

Kim, S., & Lee, H. (2006). The impact of organizational context and information technology on employee knowledge-sharing capabilities. *Public Administration Review*, *66*(3), 370–385. doi:10.1111/j.1540-6210.2006.00595.x

Lam, A., & Lambermont-Ford, J. P. (2010). Knowledge sharing in organisational contexts: A motivation-based perspective. *Journal of Knowledge Management*, *14*(1), 51–66. doi:10.1108/13673271011015561

Lee, H., Reid, E., & Kim, W. G. (2012). Understanding knowledge sharing in online travel communities: Antecedents and the moderating effects of interaction modes. *Journal of Hospitality & Tourism Research (Washington, D.C.)*, *38*(2), 222–242. doi:10.1177/1096348012451454

Lee, J. H., & Kim, Y. G. (2001). A stage model of organizational knowledge management: A latent content analysis. *Expert Systems with Applications*, *20*(4), 299–311. doi:10.1016/S0957-4174(01)00015-X

Lee, J. H., Kim, Y. G., & Kim, M. Y. (2006). Effects of managerial drivers and climate maturity on knowledge-management performance: Empirical validation. *Information Resources Management Journal*, *19*(3), 48–60. doi:10.4018/irmj.2006070104

Lee, S., Gon Kim, B., & Kim, H. (2012). An integrated view of knowledge management for performance. *Journal of Knowledge Management*, *16*(2), 183–203. doi:10.1108/13673271211218807

Levin, D. Z., & Cross, R. (2004). The strength of weak ties you can trust: The mediating role of trust in effective knowledge transfer. *Management Science*, *59*(11), 1477–1490. doi:10.1287/mnsc.1030.0136

Levin, D. Z., Cross, R., Abrams, L. C., & Lesser, E. L. (2002). Trust and knowledge sharing: A critical combination. *IBM Institute for Knowledge-Based Organizations*, *19*, 1–9.

Lin, H. F. (2007). Knowledge sharing and firm innovation capability: An empirical study. *International Journal of Manpower*, *28*(3/4), 315–332. doi:10.1108/01437720710755272

Lin, H. F., & Lee, G. G. (2004). Perceptions of senior managers toward knowledge-sharing behaviour. *Management Decision*, *42*(1), 108–125. doi:10.1108/00251740410510181

Lin, W. B. (2008). The effect of knowledge sharing model. *Expert Systems with Applications*, *34*(2), 1508–1521. doi:10.1016/j.eswa.2007.01.015

Maurer, I., Bartsch, V., & Ebers, M. (2011). The value of intra-organizational social capital: How it fosters knowledge transfer, innovation performance, and growth. *Organization Studies*, *32*(2), 157–185. doi:10.1177/0170840610394301

McAllister, D. J. (1995). Affect-and cognition-based trust as foundations for interpersonal cooperation in organizations. *Academy of Management Journal*, *38*(1), 24–59.

McDermott, R. (1999). Why information technology inspired but cannot deliver knowledge management. *California Management Review*, *41*(4), 103–117. doi:10.2307/41166012

McGivern, G., Dopson, S., Ferlie, E., Bennett, C., Fischer, M., Fitzgerald, L., & Ledger, J. (2016). "Epistemic fit" and the mobilisation of management knowledge in health care. *Mobilizing Knowledge in Health Care: Challenges for Management and Organization*, 23.

Mooradian, T., Renzl, B., & Matzler, K. (2006). Who trusts? Personality, trust and knowledge sharing. *Management Learning*, *37*(4), 523–540. doi:10.1177/1350507606073424

Mura, M., Lettieri, E., Radaelli, G., & Spiller, N. (2013). Promoting professionals' innovative behaviour through knowledge sharing: The moderating role of social capital. *Journal of Knowledge Management*, *17*(4), 527–544. doi:10.1108/JKM-03-2013-0105

Nahapiet, J., & Ghoshal, S. (1998). Social capital, intellectual capital, and the organizational advantage. *Academy of Management Review*, *23*(2), 242–266. doi:10.5465/amr.1998.533225

Newell, S. (2009). Managing knowledge work and innovation. (2nd ed.). Palgrave: Hampshire. doi:10.1007/978-0-230-36641-1

Nonaka, I. (1994). A dynamic theory of organizational knowledge creation. *Organization Science*, *5*(1), 14–37. doi:10.1287/orsc.5.1.14

O'Neill, B. S., & Adya, M. (2007). Knowledge sharing and the psychological contract: Managing knowledge workers across different stages of employment. *Journal of Managerial Psychology*, *22*(4), 411–436. doi:10.1108/02683940710745969

Oliver, S., & Kandadi, K. R. (2006). How to develop knowledge culture in organizations? A multiple case study of large distributed organizations. *Journal of Knowledge Management*, *10*(4), 6–24. doi:10.1108/13673270610679336

Orlikowski, W. J. (2000). Using technology and constituting structures: A practice lens for studying technology in organizations. *Organization Science*, *11*(4), 404–428. doi:10.1287/orsc.11.4.404.14600

Pan, S. L., & Leidner, D. E. (2003). Bridging communities of practice with information technology in pursuit of global knowledge sharing. *The Journal of Strategic Information Systems*, *12*(1), 71–88. doi:10.1016/S0963-8687(02)00023-9

Pan, S. L., & Scarbrough, H. (1998). A socio-technical view of knowledge sharing at Buckman Laboratories. *Journal of Knowledge Management*, *2*(1), 55–66. doi:10.1108/EUM0000000004607

Panahi, S., Watson, J., & Partridge, H. (2013). Towards tacit knowledge sharing over social web tools. *Journal of Knowledge Management*, *17*(3), 379–397. doi:10.1108/JKM-11-2012-0364

Pangil, F., & Moi Chan, J. (2014). The mediating effect of knowledge sharing on the relationship between trust and virtual team effectiveness. *Journal of Knowledge Management*, *18*(1), 92–106. doi:10.1108/JKM-09-2013-0341

Politis, J. D. (2003). The connection between trust and knowledge management: What are its implications for team performance. *Journal of Knowledge Management*, *7*(5), 55–66. doi:10.1108/13673270310505386

Porter, L. W., & McLaughlin, G. B. (2006). Leadership and the organizational context: Like the weather? *The Leadership Quarterly*, *17*(6), 559–576. doi:10.1016/j.leaqua.2006.10.002

Rapert, M. I., & Wren, B. M. (1998). Reconsidering organizational structure: A dual perspective of frameworks and processes. *Journal of Managerial Issues*, 287–302.

Renzl, B. (2008). Trust in management and knowledge sharing: The mediating effects of fear and knowledge documentation. *Omega*, *36*(2), 206–220. doi:10.1016/j.omega.2006.06.005

Rutten, W., Blaas-Franken, J., & Martin, H. (2016). The impact of (low) trust on knowledge sharing. *Journal of Knowledge Management*, *20*(2), 199–214. doi:10.1108/JKM-10-2015-0391

Ryu, S., Ho, S. H., & Han, I. (2003). Knowledge sharing behavior of physicians in hospitals. *Expert Systems with Applications*, *25*(1), 113–122. doi:10.1016/S0957-4174(03)00011-3

Salis, S., & Williams, A. M. (2010). Knowledge sharing through face-to-face communication and labour productivity: Evidence from British workplaces. *British Journal of Industrial Relations*, *48*(2), 436–459. doi:10.1111/j.1467-8543.2009.00762.x

Sankowska, A. (2013). Relationships between organizational trust, knowledge transfer, knowledge creation, and firm's innovativeness. *The Learning Organization*, *20*(1), 85–100. doi:10.1108/09696471311288546

Sharratt, M., & Usoro, A. (2003). Understanding knowledge-sharing in online communities of practice. *Electronic Journal of Knowledge Management*, *1*(2), 187–196.

Staples, D. S., & Webster, J. (2008). Exploring the effects of trust, task interdependence and virtualness on knowledge sharing in teams. *Information Systems Journal*, *18*(6), 617–640. doi:10.1111/j.1365-2575.2007.00244.x

Swan, J., Newell, S., & Nicolini, D. (Eds.). (2016). *Mobilizing knowledge in health care: challenges for management and organization*. Oxford University Press. doi:10.1093/acprof:oso/9780198738237.001.0001

Swift, P. E., & Hwang, A. (2013). The impact of affective and cognitive trust on knowledge sharing and organizational learning. *The Learning Organization*, *20*(1), 20–37. doi:10.1108/09696471311288500

Tamjidyamcholo, A., Baba, M. S. B., Tamjid, H., & Gholipour, R. (2013). Information security–Professional perceptions of knowledge-sharing intention under self-efficacy, trust, reciprocity, and shared-language. *Computers & Education*, *68*, 223–232. doi:10.1016/j.compedu.2013.05.010

Tohidinia, Z., & Mosakhani, M. (2010). Knowledge sharing behaviour and its predictors. *Industrial Management & Data Systems*, *110*(4), 611–631. doi:10.1108/02635571011039052

Tsai, M. T., & Cheng, N. C. (2010). Programmer perceptions of knowledge-sharing behavior under social cognitive theory. *Expert Systems with Applications*, *37*(12), 8479–8485. doi:10.1016/j.eswa.2010.05.029

Tsai, W. (2002). Social structure of "coopetition" within a multiunit organization: Coordination, competition, and intraorganizational knowledge sharing. *Organization Science*, *13*(2), 179–190. doi:10.1287/orsc.13.2.179.536

Van Den Hooff, B., & De Ridder, J. A. (2004). Knowledge sharing in context: The influence of organizational commitment, communication climate and CMC use on knowledge sharing. *Journal of Knowledge Management*, *8*(6), 117–130. doi:10.1108/13673270410567675

Van Wijk, R., Jansen, J. J., & Lyles, M. A. (2008). Inter-and intra-organizational knowledge transfer: A meta-analytic review and assessment of its antecedents and consequences. *Journal of Management Studies*, *45*(4), 830–853. doi:10.1111/j.1467-6486.2008.00771.x

Voelpel, S. C., & Han, Z. (2005). Managing knowledge sharing in China: The case of Siemens ShareNet. *Journal of Knowledge Management*, *9*(3), 51–63. doi:10.1108/13673270510602764

Wang, S., & Noe, R. A. (2010). Knowledge sharing: A review and directions for future research. *Human Resource Management Review*, *20*(2), 115–131. doi:10.1016/j.hrmr.2009.10.001

Wasko, M. M., & Faraj, S. (2000). "It is what one does": Why people participate and help others in electronic communities of practice. *The Journal of Strategic Information Systems*, *9*(2-3), 155–173. doi:10.1016/S0963-8687(00)00045-7

Wasko, M. M., & Faraj, S. (2005). Why should I share? Examining social capital and knowledge contribution in electronic networks of practice. *Management Information Systems Quarterly*, *29*(1), 35–57. doi:10.2307/25148667

Weick, K. E. (1995). *Sensemaking in organizations* (Vol. 3). Sage.

Widén-Wulff, G., & Ginman, M. (2004). Explaining knowledge sharing in organizations through the dimensions of social capital. *Journal of Information Science*, *30*(5), 448–458. doi:10.1177/0165551504046997

Willem, A., & Buelens, M. (2009). Knowledge sharing in inter-unit cooperative episodes: The impact of organizational structure dimensions. *International Journal of Information Management*, *29*(2), 151–160. doi:10.1016/j.ijinfomgt.2008.06.004

Wu, W. L., Lin, C. H., Hsu, B. F., & Yeh, R. S. (2009). Interpersonal trust and knowledge sharing: Moderating effects of individual altruism and a social interaction environment. *Social Behavior and Personality*, *37*(1), 83–93. doi:10.2224bp.2009.37.1.83

Wu, W. Y., & Sukoco, B. M. (2010). Why should I share? Examining consumers' motives and trust on knowledge sharing. *Journal of Computer Information Systems*, *50*(4), 11–19.

Wu, Y., & Zhu, W. (2012). An integrated theoretical model for determinants of knowledge sharing behaviours. *Kybernetes, 41*(10), 1462–1482. doi:10.1108/03684921211276675

Xue, Y., Bradley, J., & Liang, H. (2011). Team climate, empowering leadership, and knowledge sharing. *Journal of Knowledge Management, 15*(2), 299–312. doi:10.1108/13673271111119709

Yu, T. K., Lu, L. C., & Liu, T. F. (2010). Exploring factors that influence knowledge sharing behavior via weblogs. *Computers in Human Behavior, 26*(1), 32–41. doi:10.1016/j.chb.2009.08.002

Yuan, Y. C., Zhao, X., Liao, Q., & Chi, C. (2013). The use of different information and communication technologies to support knowledge sharing in organizations: From e-mail to micro-blogging. *Journal of the American Society for Information Science and Technology, 64*(8), 1659–1670. doi:10.1002/asi.22863

Zboralski, K. (2009). Antecedents of knowledge sharing in communities of practice. *Journal of Knowledge Management, 13*(3), 90–101. doi:10.1108/13673270910962897

Chapter 3
Knowledge Flows Through Unbounded Innovation

Ayse Asli Yilmaz
https://orcid.org/0000-0003-1784-7307
Atilim University, Turkey

Şule Tuzlukaya
Atilim University, Turkey

ABSTRACT

Beyond the boundaries of the organizations, they act fearlessly to adopt open innovation tactics and models in order to gain access to the necessary resources. In open innovation, "open" refers the sharing of organizational tacit knowledge. Knowledge management is essential in organizations because it promotes the development of a successful organizational business model and makes a difference in completing various organizational tasks and forms that may lead to the discovery of new knowledge. This journey starts from the flow of information and takes organizations toward innovation that has no boundaries. For this reason, the research question involves the kind of relationship that exists between knowledge flow and open innovation. This chapter aims to illustrate the importance of knowledge flow through unbounded innovation, particularly the correspondence between aspects of knowledge management and open innovation.

DOI: 10.4018/978-1-6684-4431-3.ch003

INTRODUCTION

From the beginning to the end of the 1960s, the authority of science and technology was shaken. Thomas Kuhn introduces the concept of "paradigm" in the development of science and technology as the mechanisms of science and technology change. This is the process by which science evolves through a series of crisis, scientific revolution, and normal science (Kuhn, 1962).

The organization has begun to develop innovative technologies that will provide it with an unrivalled competitive advantage. Understanding the origins and evolution of science and technology is a compelling works in both theoretical and practical aspects. The organization gains control of its own data, information and knowledge, which it can access whenever it wants without relying on any technology (Nonaka & Takeuchi,1995). The Fourth Industrial Revolution promotes knowledge management as an all-around oversight of the data stream, guaranteeing that the appropriate actor receives the relevant data and information at the right time. Knowledge management is defined as a discipline that effectively improves ability and substance in order to increase competency, agility, adequacy, and disruptive evolution in the organization (Al Mansoori et al., 2021).

Through the flawless of scientific continuum, innovation enables all balances to carry out the forms and make knowledge available to everyone at any time. Knowledge management has become more standardized, ubiquitous, successful, and less expensive in responding to organizational demands as a result of recent advances in innovation (Lee et al., 2017). Therefore, organizations are more likely to evolve their own application of open innovation, moving away from traditional bilateral arrangements like alliances and toward approaches like communities to consolidate their strength in an interactive relationship (Brunswicker & Chesbrough, 2018).

In the light of all, this chapter is designed that will be a roadmap for organizations and decision makers in the digital transformation journey. This journey starts from the flow of information and take organizations towards innovation that has no boundaries. For this reason, the question of what kind of relationship exists between knowledge flow and open innovation is the research question. Therefore, this chapter aims to illustrate the importance of knowledge flow through unbounded innovation, particularly the correspondence between aspects of knowledge management and open innovation. As a result, this chapter is designed in a logical sequence. First, the relationship between the digital transformation and learning organizations is discussed. The transition from close to open innovation is then presented. Finally, the conclusion is provided.

USING DIGITAL DISRUPTION TO GAIN A COMPETITIVE ADVANTAGE

Industry 4.0. and the digital transformation bring about radical changes in all sectors. These radical changes are predicted to continue radical or gradual realization for organizations. Particularly, the digital disruption, which has become the keyword of many studies, appears in every realm in business life. For example, organizations that adopt value-oriented strategies aim to think and act data-oriented, by evaluating technology as a tool rather than a goal in digital transformations. Or, the building the right strategy for the digitalization process might be the disputable for the organization. Because any organization's goals are survival first, followed by competitive advantage. Therefore, it is considered that innovation based on knowledge and environmental, social, and economic criteria enables the creation of a sustainable foundation for organizational competitiveness. Competitiveness emerges as a result of limited resources, as does the search for new strategies for organizational sustainability (Lopes et al.,2016) Being agile, establishing trust-based sustainable relationships, and moving forward knowing that employees are also a part of the transformation provide a significant competitive advantage at this point. Learning organizations are explained as the beginning of organizational transformation in the real sense by understanding the relationship between organizational transformation and business models, starting with digital transformation.

Digital Transformation and Learning Organizations

How will we develop the best strategy during the digitization process? This is a difficult question to answer. The world's borders have been redefined as a result of fast changing technologies. Organizations, institutions, small and medium-sized enterprises (SMEs), start-ups, and scaleups that follow the process must learn and adapt to the sine qua non of digital transformation in order to stay up with the dizzying pace of technology. Artificial intelligence, for example, is a must in today's organizations to be applied in common workflow in sectoral basis. Ultimately, regardless of structure, the majority of the organizations undergo that metamorphosis for the first time Furthermore, cooperation with technology requires the construction of satisfactory logics to address novel social issues such as productivity, job loss, quality of life, and social and ethical issues. (Boong et al., 2018).

Within this frame of reference, decision makers, particularly top management, play a critical role in the advancement of knowledge management systems by creating conditions that encourage people to use their knowledge, share it and reciprocally exchange it (Sousa & Rocha, 2019). Leaders have a critical role in this process of implementing creative transformation. One of the most important digital transformation strategies is to accept technology as a tool, not as a value creation goal. Value-oriented managers or decision-makers with short-, medium-, and long-term projections, as well as proactive leadership skills, are also seen as significant milestones on the way to digitalization. Improved knowledge is documented and archived on a regular basis, using reports, images, and even even metaphors, and made available to all members of the organization (Sousa & Rocha, 2019). Decision makers are supposed to act in a complimentary manner rather than as a single leader. Because members of organizations are prone to resisting change, they desire to act and collaborate with their leader during this transformation. Throughout this process, an organizational culture that can be data-driven, act data-driven, perceive, and absorb the digitalization process is required. The organizational objective is to have not just technology, but also a business framework that can invest as much as needed with the drive to acquire technology.

Organizational learning is the process that occurs via interaction in which information is produced by the organization either implicitly or explicitly and simultaneously transmitted to the organization's knowledge management applications. The external and internal environment of the company, its features and characteristics, organizational memory, and organizational culture all point to the need for organizational digitalization (Liao et al., 2017). As a result, organizational digital skills, the ability to enhance relationships with supporting parties, and learning capacity all have an impact on the digitalization strategy and transformation success. Organizations must be prepared in this situation, both organizationally and operationally.

Organizational Transformation and Business Model

An inquiry results in an understanding of the current situation and being aware of the situation. Then, action after the action, organizations are given the opportunity to mirror and interpret the inquiry and action in order to learn from the experience. As a result, the inquiry restarts for the second cycle in order to gain a better understanding of the current situation that has evolved as a result of the organizations' actions in the first cycle. Indeed, organizational partnerships required by the transformation are allowed in the query at the beginning of each new circle (Graham,2015). Partnership takes its real shape when the organizations' stakeholders combine their competencies.

Organizations are formed with the intention of organizing structures, relationships, cultures, and ideas. They are linked by a social interaction that pulls people together. Each component of the organization contributes to a strong synergy that is consistent with the company's mission. Each of these parts may be compared to the Lego pieces we used to play with as children. Because of the fast changes in technology in recent years, the term "transformation" has become highly common in businesses.

It is seen as a slow-motion process of transitioning from existing to adapting to new and developing situations. This method includes utilizing the organization's own resources and capacity, as well as adapting knowledge management to the organizational memory change. At this point, we come across the transformational leadership, which supports, plans and executes the transformation in every sense, and includes the features also expressed as 4C (creativity, communication; critical reflection, collaboration).In a managerial sense, the transformational leader is expected to take a futuristic role, encourage staff for open innovation, proactive and risk taking stance where all communication channels are open and personally participating in all collective works (Anderson& Jefferson, 2018)

Uncertainty is linked to the current state of things and trends. With emerging disruptive technologies, internal and external ideas are grouped together in open innovation processes inside different platforms, architectures in order to identify the needs for these architectures and systems (Bogers, et al., 2016). Therefore, organizational core competencies evolve in order to gain a competitive advantage.

It is necessary to express how organizations need open innovation in their transformation processes in an environment of fierce competition. Because open innovation enables the organization to reach new information and technology that cannot be reached. Open innovation allows the organization to expand into new markets. Open innovation helps the organization to be aware of technological standards and control this power. It prepares the environment for the organization to establish strategic partnerships on the path of digitalization (Leitão, 2019)

The business model is the theoretical foundation for open innovation as a strategy. It describes how the organization generates, distributes, and captures value. It helps in the identification of an organization's most obvious characteristics that set it apart from other competitors in the target market Although there are many definitions of business model in the literature, the most general definition is that it is a conceptual tool that consists of a set of elements and their relationships and allows explaining the business logic of a specific organization. The organizational value is, in fact, the most important factor here. The value of the organization presents many segments of customers and of the architecture of the organization. For generating profitable and sustainable revenue streams, organization's network of partners is developed in order to create, market, and deliver this value and relationship capital. Although this may seem like a business strategy at first glance, it is actually a business model. Strategy and model are separated from each other by various features. These are;

- **Creating value vs. capturing value**, in which the business model expresses the way an organization captures value, and the strategy clarifies how to create competitive advantage and create value,

- **Business value vs. Shareholder value**, in which the business model engages attention business value and business strategy on shareholder value,
- **Assumed knowledge levels**, in which the business model manages and study on a more limited environmental knowledge and the business strategy wants more certainty in the knowledge of the environment (Olofsson & Farr, 2006).

As can be seen from the point reached open innovation provides a secure platform with different relations with different actors. Because of collaborative partnership, all desired knowledge can be created and interpreted from the information obtained. Thanks to the business model prepared with the right moves, open innovative organization become global. Besides, fraud management and cyber security with artificial intelligence and machine learning is provided. Business model provides offline-online organization integration so that the organization develops agility, sustainability strategies. Thanks to open innovation, IT and technology works that unnecessarily occupies the organization are transferred to the other stakeholders so that the organization can focus on its main business. Therefore, reporting, situation analysis and agile strategies as well as real time data analysis with scalable software architecture are presented by business model.

In every moment of transformation, decision makers are expected to build an effective policy over open innovation that gives the value-added of openness to organization, but at the same time, also promote the investment and financial opportunities for transforming open initiatives into new technologies and new business models. Open innovation processes engage business models to specify the requirements for these architectures and systems (Bogers et al., 2018).

ENABLING THE ORGANIZATIONAL REVOLUTION TO BEGIN

Open Innovation vs. Closed Innovation

Chesbrough (2003) proposed a new innovation management model that contrasts the close innovation strategy on the requirements of companies to address internal and external technology advances. Whereas close innovation is based on "do it yourself" approach, open innovation is based on collaboration. Closed innovation, as the name implies, is based on a closed perfectionist framework. Therefore, the close innovation is in the middle of the controversy. It has limitations in following the dynamics of real science and technology.

Therefore, in other words, only smart and talented individuals work in organizations. The organization's own resources, self-discovery, developed values, and all it can control are deemed adequate for innovation, survival, core competencies, and adaptation to changing situations. The differentiating aspects of closed innovation are being the first in the field, being the best, having exciting ideas, and even being a trailblazer (Marques, 2014). In theory, success is unavoidable within well-defined boundaries. However, without external references and knowledge, it does not appear practicable. Ideas for solutions come from the right internal resources. Leaders and decision makers make critical judgments behind closed doors. Because it is considered that working with the greatest in their domains has distinct burdens than developing cross functional cooperation, coordination, and partnership. In other words, how does connectivity with the external environment in terms of knowledge transfer, knowledge sharing, and knowledge management affect organizational productivity the productivity or creativity, or how does organizational culture diversification affect connectivity performance (Boong et al., 2018)

In the paradigm of closed innovation, the competitive strategies are structured upon organizations' current business model so that it is expected to be motivated in internal R&D activities and is triggered to entry the new markets in this way. The close innovation paradigm is based on more static relationships with internal ideas, applications and solutions. However, new technological developments, digitalization in the organizations develop at an unprecedented pace due to the volatility, complexity, ambiguity and uncertainty of the environment. In an environment of uncertainty, organizations can operate with their own resources, internal dynamics and decision mechanisms, and relying only on their core competencies may lead them to mistakes. Because open innovation plays such an important role in effective strategic sustainable management, organizations have turned knowledge management into an asset that supports sustainable innovations that influence organizational sustainability (Lopes et al.,2016)

Organizations may find themselves in competence traps, learning myopia, and the compelling impacts of organizational and environmental variables as a result of digitalization and the catching up period. As a result of this situation, several organizational tactics evolve in order to survive and preserve a competitive advantage. To that end, an innovative paradigm based on more dynamic, collaborative, and open balances can be used.

In his 2003 book Open Innovation: The New Imperative for Creating and Profiting from Technology, Chesbrough presents the new paradigm "Open Innovation." The phenomena of the open innovation bases on that the organizations are to benefit from the external and internal ideas together in to different architectures, platforms and sectors. In order to improve their innovation success, there must be intentional reciprocal information sharing. The open innovation paradigm has become so popular in the constantly evolving and revolving cyber space that organizations such as start-ups, scaleups, SMEs, high- and low-tech industries, as well as not-for-profit organizations and public organizations, regardless of size, maturity, structure, and complexity...etc. from nearly all areas design their business model according to the disruptive innovative approach. High-tech industries, for example, act as net takers of free knowledge flows, thanks in part IP protection for outbound knowledge. As a result, according to Brunswicker and Chesbrough, outside-in open innovation is more commonly practiced than inside-out open innovation (Brunswicker & Chesbrough,2018). However, there is a lack of knowledge on how to integrate social and environmental perspective into the organizational essence of business, as well as how to overcome existing barriers and encourage organizations to fully implement sustainability in business processes (Lopes et al.,2016).

As digital technology allows the organizations to modify their business models so quickly, organizations that are constantly dependent on their existing business model feel resistance from internal and external factors leading to use of innovative technologies. Organizations are not required to operate a unique business model with their existing internal resources. Beyond the boundaries of the organizations, they act fearlessly to adopt open innovation tactics and models in order to gain access to the necessary resources. Open innovation is a dynamic and ever-changing journey involving diverse parties operating in the same business ecosystem (Priyono, et al.,2020). The most widely cited distinctions are between information technology and strategic knowledge that has been made explicit and knowledge that has remained tacit. There are two forms of knowledge created in organizations. The first is tacit (implicit) knowledge, whereas the second is explicit information. These categories of knowledge are sometimes expressed as coded (explicit) or uncoded (tacit) knowledge in the literature (Nonaka,1995).

All businesses that want to obtain a competitive advantage and actually prosper must meet certain requirements. These will include tactical demands that are expected to be met in the short term, as well as long-term requirements that will offer efficiency, sustainability, and adaptability in all aspects. Organizations with strict communication laws, conventional hierarchies, and predefined policies may face various hurdles in terms of innovation. In contrast to closed innovation, the open system approach benefits from both external and internal information flow. Because open innovation handles the transformation process while increasing absorptive and dynamic capabilities.

As a result, organizations that are able to expand their knowledge capacity are likely to get extra advantages from external stakeholders such as universities, industrial partners, private and public organizations, and so on. In that flat management approach, the more responsibility there is, the more productivity and creativity there is. The sine qua non of open innovation includes dynamic web relationships, agility, effective information sharing, and faster corporate learning and adaption (Leitão, 2019). Organizations frequently make intentional use of external inputs from stakeholders, or authorize them to access underutilized assets and knowledge, in order to improve their research and development productivity (Brunswicker & Chesbrough, 2018).

Knowledge Management and Open Innovation

In terms of knowledge management, Industry 4.0 offers new dimensions to both the inside of organizational learning (knowledge creation, codification, and transfer) and the outer of network actors. As the business and society transition to a digital state, organizational actors and stakeholders demand to get information at the appropriate moment. These attempts to keep up with the modern era are accompanied by a shift in the way information and knowledge are managed, connected, collaborated on, and learned across the business (North et al.,2018). In order to satisfy expectations, knowledge management uses a user-centred approach. The primary phenomena of the mechanism are knowledge, including know-how, which involves production, enrichment, verification for group performance, and sustainability (Saulais & Ermine, 2019).

The outside-in and inside-out aspects highlight the organization's knowledge flow. The literature persists on the significance of owing a well-structured intellectual property strategy from the beginning of the innovation partnership. In open innovation, "open" refers the sharing of organizational tacit knowledge. Innovation collaborations, in particular, foster socialization processes that are favourable to the sharing of tacit knowledge (Barbaroux et al.,2016). Organizations also engage in enterprise to expand their knowledge beyond their borders. They are to be welcomed to other management presumptions in addition to their own. Organizations generate outside-in innovation. Open innovation is encouraged by knowledge management. Successful businesses owe their success primarily to the competitive advantages that their innovative capabilities have created (Lopes et al.,2016).

Knowledge management is essential in organizations because it promotes the development of a successful organizational business model and makes a difference in completing various organizational tasks and forms that may lead to the discovery of new knowledge (Santoro, 2018). Organizations' increased dependence on knowledge management strategies has been observed in the formation of organizational practices. Furthermore, knowledge-intensive organizations, in particular, are required to have more advanced communication and computer equipment that facilitates the integration of interactive media for acquiring, processing, displaying, and storing data in innovative collaboration (Alshurideh et al., 2015).

The flow of internal and external information within organizations is referred to as open innovation (Wang et al., 2015). The link with reinforceable innovations appears when it is recognized that internal investments in specific resources are essential to boost the introduction of innovations through knowledge and competencies from stakeholders (Lopes et al.,2016).

By virtue of the high cost and uncertainty contained in research and development, designing in-house knowledge or utilizing available knowledge by a single organization is not always feasible. Organizations collaborate with external stakeholders to obtain resources that cannot be improved internally due to economic and/or technological constraints (Talab et al.,2018)

In the context of Industry 4.0, a diversity of sources provides the chance to gather knowledge that businesses may use to track and focus on innovation, plan activities, and build new interactions with other players in order to produce value (Bettiol et al., 2020). Knowledge, as one of the key dimensions of competitiveness and risk prevention, is an ever-changing strategic resource and factor for organizations. Whereas the digitalization provides new chances and possibilities, all actors in the organizations are to rearrange their structure, leadership, innovation, knowledge, and learning processes (North et al.,2018). Knowledge transfer among actors, such as people-to-people and people-to-document, is being transformed into various technological solutions in the cyber space, such as artificial intelligence, blockchain, the Internet of things. As organizations attempt to leverage Industry 4.0 technologies for knowledge management and competitive advantage, the knowledge management framework is in flux (Bettiol et al., 2020).

Organizations must be aware of their dynamic capabilities in open innovation. Digitalization has both advantages and disadvantages in terms of keeping up with the times and being innovative. Using disruptive technologies to transform raw data into knowledge and wisdom is seen as a fundamental competency in human-machine interaction. As a result, many companies will need to create a new framework for creating, storing, and protecting high-value knowledge (Pablos & Lytras, 2018). As a result, knowledge management systems and their business solutions enabled organizations to extend their access to their business partners and stakeholders' knowledge. (Sousa & Rocha, 2019).

Organisational technology can significantly promote enablers and process. These are two critical factors in knowledge management and open innovation. Both dimensions entail well designed coordination, collaboration and constant information exchange among partners and stakeholders. The knowledge was classified as fundamental facts and thoughts with the most basic degree of significance. While compared to data, information is stated as providing a greater degree of meaning, analysing current news, and creating an object to be employed when making a choice. It is a measure of the indispensable degree of usage of information technology in obtaining information and knowledge in the cyber era. The civilization has begun to develop novel technologies that will provide it with an absolute advantage over other societies, and it has now become a technology exporter. In terms of global interconnectedness, digital transformation plays an essential role in terms of value generation and open innovation from a social standpoint.

Provided that today's organizations' value creation is fundamentally knowledge-based, and if the fundamental rationale of inter-organizational cooperation is to co-create/co-use knowledge, knowledge classification must address organizational types. Furthermore, such a classification shapes the logic of organizational culture and intelligence. Understanding the knowledge roles of organizations allows for better alignment and orchestration of their reactions. The question "how the organizational types are associated with the knowledge classification" must be answered in order to understand inter-organizational knowledge interactions in domains of organizational intelligence and culture (Talab et al., 2018).

Following this, examples of current applications of the concepts of knowledge management and open innovation would be appropriate. Platforms such as APIs, for example, Amazon and Android, are more common and well-defined ways to encourage developers to add new service offerings (Burchardt, & Maisch, 2019). Crowdsourcing is another term for the process of obtaining anyone from the masses who can handle a problem that the organization does not have a solution for, rather than from its own employees or selected professional consultants or market experts. Because it is possible to do things much faster, in a much larger demographic, and, most importantly, at a much lower cost by harnessing the power of the innovative masses. Indeed, this talent pool has spread.

General market research (e.g. Telescope by Innosabi), software development resources (e.g. Topcoder) and variety of digital services (e.g. Mechanical Turk) are shown as examples of outsourcing of processes and jobs can be outsourced (Burchardt, & Maisch, 2019 Tom Goodwin (2015) exemplifies this collaboration by stating that "the world's largest taxi company (Uber) does not own a single taxi; the world's most popular media company (Facebook) does not produce a single piece of content; the world's most important retailer (Alibaba) has no stock; and the world's largest accommodation provider (Airbnb) does not own a single property(Forbes,2015).

Therefore, open innovation and knowledge management interactions involve not only knowledge and information sharing, but also but also project financing through the contributions of multiple parties. Furthermore, in addition to the crowdsourcing model, there are other tools for collaboration aimed at improving open innovation. These web-based software collaboration tools range from appointment scheduling (doodle) to real-time conversations (e.g., Skype) to document sharing and exchange (e.g., Dropbox) (Burchardt, & Maisch, 2019).

CONCLUSION

The term "innovation" refers to the process of redesigning scientific, technological, organizational, financial, political and managerial activities in order to generate and then commercialize unused knowledge. Andreessen Horowitz wrote an essay titled "Software is Eating the World" that was published in The Wall Street Journal in 2011. In order to sustain long term business, more hierarchical, structured, and traditional companies open their doors to the software industry. No matter its purpose or nature, regardless being technological, organizational or institutional, innovation is always presented and promoted by its creator with the purpose of satisfying the requirements (Barbaroux et al., 2016). Due to the nature of the thing, it is very difficult or even impossible for an organization to meet all its technological and innovative needs with its own resources within its borders. Because of closed innovative paradigm, the organization may deviate from its purpose and fall into the competency traps.

In the closed innovation, there is no bidirectional (inside-outside/outside-inside) or even multidirectional flow or leakage of information. Moreover, in this closed model, when there is an organizational problem, the organization depend exclusively on solutions and knowledge developed internally. Contrary to closed innovation, the open model has a relatively permeable structure. It actually means a partnership where innovation gains value with knowledge coming from and goes to inside and outside the organization. In here, the most important balance elements here are the measurement of partnership, the protection of the rights of all parties and the project-based sharing of information between the parties (Barbaroux et al., 2016)

Accepting innovation as merely the process of developing new technologies, or simply invention, would be a huge mistake. Organizations must innovate through their own (internal) efforts because the need for a new innovative design stems from the difficulty. According to the open innovation approach, knowledge is the crowning achievement of the entire process. External knowledge flows, whether tacit or explicit, are particularly magnificent (Lee et al., 2015). In recent years, it has been observed that the leading organizations that have taken steps with the open innovation paradigm have increased their production compared to other organizations, in terms of entering new markets, positioning and their economies have increased significantly (Bogers et al., 2018).

Organizations benefit from open innovation by receiving new business models and market opportunities. It draws attention at both the micro and macro levels. Because, in this system, the individual feels extremely valuable, works extremely hard, and freely expresses his ideas. Reduce stress, make fewer mistakes, and become more innovative makes full use of the spatial freedom provided by open innovation. Innovation goes on to evolve, and so policy regulations are to be arranged. At this point, in the VUCA environment of the digital age, leadership has a very important role (The acronym VUCA stands for Volatility, Uncertainty, Complexity, Ambiguity environment from US-American military jargon). A leader is expected to show a rough direction, contemplate the different scenarios, develop several options, become aware of weak signals, learn success and failure and be agile (North et al.,2018).

In the light of all these critical factors, an organization that goes fast on the path of digitalization will either undergo project-based short-term adaptation or accept a long-term metamorphosis. In fact, this is a decision that the organization, which is a living creature, will make with all its organs. Since it would be extremely unnecessary to take a step alone in this entire learning and transformation process, a business model should be established that includes a controlled, planned and coordinated partnership. It will be a kind of "core insight". For this reason, all employees in the organization, partners, potential stakeholders should believe that they are an integral part of this business model and are to be encouraged to participate in studies at all stages (Olofsson & Farr, 2006.). Thus, with open innovation, new forms of knowledge intensive digitally value creation is targeted in the organizations on the basis of knowledge management practices thanks to the partnerships, cooperation and collaboration.

REFERENCES

Alshurideh, M., & Alhadid, A. (2015). The effect of internal marketing on organizational citizenship behavior an applicable study on the University of Jordan employees. *Int. J. Mark. Stud.*, *7*(1), 138. doi:10.5539/ijms.v7n1p138

Anderson, M., & Jefferson, M. (2018). Transforming Organizations: Engaging the 4Cs for Powerful Organizational Learning and Change. Bloomsbury Publishing.

Barbaroux, P., Attour, A., & Schenk, E. (2016). *Knowledge management and innovation: Interaction, collaboration, openness* (Vol. 6). John Wiley & Sons. doi:10.1002/9781119330134

Bogers, M., Chesbrough, H., & Moedas, C. (2018). Open Innovation: Research, Practices, and Policies. *California Management Review*, *60*(2), 5–16. doi:10.1177/0008125617745086

Boong, K. C., Woon-Dong, Y., & Dong, K. W. (2018). The implication of ANT (Actor-Network-Theory) methodology for R&D policy in open innovation paradigm. *Knowledge Management Research and Practice*, *16*(3), 315–326. Advance online publication. doi:10.1080/14778238.2018.1471329

Brunswicker, S., & Chesbrough, H. (2018). The Adoption of Open Innovation in Large Firms: Practices, Measures, and Risks A survey of large firms examines how firms approach open innovation strategically and manage knowledge flows at the project level. *Research Technology Management*, *61*(1), 35–45. doi:10.1080/08956308.2018.1399022

Burchardt, C., & Maisch, B. (2019). Digitalization needs a cultural change – examples of applying Agility and Open Innovation to drive the digital transformation. *Procedia CIRP*, *84*, 112–117. doi:10.1016/j.procir.2019.05.009

Chesbrough, H., & Bogers, M. (2014). Explicating Open Innovation: Clarifying an Emerging Paradigm for Understanding Innovation. In *New Frontiers in Open Innovation*. Oxford University Press. https://www.forbes.com/sites/oracle/2015/04/20/digital-disruption-its-not-what-you-think/?sh=68f3a14a9e06

Graham, W. (2017). Developing organizations: A system of enquiry, action and learning. *Development and Learning in Organizations*, *31*(1), 12–14. doi:10.1108/DLO-03-2016-0023

Kuhn, T. S. (1962). *The structure of scientific revolutions*. University of Chicago Press.

Lee, K.-W., Lanting, M. C. L., & Rojdamrongratana, M. (2017). Managing customer life cycle through knowledge management capability: A contextual role of information technology. *Total Quality Management & Business Excellence*, *28*(13–14), 1559–1583. doi:10.1080/14783363.2016.1150779

Lee, M., Yun, J., Pyka, A., Won, D., Kodama, F., Schiuma, G., Park, H., Jeon, J., Park, K., Id, K., Jung, K., Yan, M., Lee, S., & Zhao, X. (2018). How to Respond to the Fourth Industrial Revolution, or the Second Information Technology Revolution? Dynamic New Combinations between Technology, Market, and Society through Open Innovation. *Journal of Open Innovation*, *4*(3), 21. Advance online publication. doi:10.3390/joitmc4030021

Leitão, J. (2019). *Open Innovation Business Modeling Gamification and Design Thinking Applications*. Academic Press.

Liao, S. S., Chen, C. C., Hu, D. C., Chung, Y. C., & Liu, C. L. (2017). Assessing the influence of leadership style, organizational learning and organizational innovation. *Leadership and Organization Development Journal*, *38*(5), 590–609. Advance online publication. doi:10.1108/LODJ-11-2015-0261

Lopes, C., Scavarda, A., Hofmeister, L., Thomé, A. M., & Vaccaro, G. (2016). An analysis of the interplay between organizational sustainability, knowledge management, and open innovation. *Journal of Cleaner Production*, *142*, 476–488. doi:10.1016/j.jclepro.2016.10.083

Marques, J. P. (2014). Closed versus Open Innovation: Evolution or Combination? *International Journal of Business and Management*, *9*(3). Advance online publication. doi:10.5539/ijbm.v9n3p196

North, K.,Maier, R. & Haas, O. (2018). *Knowledge Management in Digital Change New Findings and Practical Cases: New Findings and Practical Cases.* . doi:10.1007/978-3-319-73546-7

Olofsson, L.& Farr, R. (2006). *Business Model Tools and Definition - a Literature Review*. Academic Press.

Priyono, A., Moin, A., & Putri, V. N. A. O. (2020). Identifying Digital Transformation Paths in the Business Model of SMEs during the COVID-19 Pandemic. *Journal of Open Innovation*, *6*(4), 104. doi:10.3390/joitmc6040104

Randhawa, K., Wilden, R., & Hohberger, J. (2017). A Bibliometric Review of Open Innovation: Setting a Research Agenda. *Journal of Product Innovation Management*, *33*(6), 750–772.

Salloum, S. A., Al-Emran, M., & Shaalan, K. (2017). Mining text in news channels: A case study from facebook. *Int. J. Inf. Technol. Lang. Stud.*, *1*(1), 1–9.

Santoro, G., Vrontis, D., Thrassou, A., & Dezi, L. (2018). The Internet of Things: Building a knowledge management system for open innovation and knowledge management capacity. *Technological Forecasting and Social Change*, *136*, 347–354. doi:10.1016/j.techfore.2017.02.034

Sousa, M., & Rocha, Á. (2019). Strategic Knowledge Management in the Digital Age. *Journal of Business Research*, *91*, 223–226. doi:10.1016/j.jbusres.2018.10.016

Talab, A. H., Scholten, V., & van Beers, C. (2018). Knowledge Sharing and Open Innovation. In Open Innovation and Knowledge Management in Small and Medium Enterprises (pp. 117-140). doi:10.1142/9789813233591_0007

West, J., Salter, A., Vanhaverbeke, W., & Chesbrough, H. (2014). Open Innovation: The Next Decade. *Research Policy*, *43*(5), 805–811. doi:10.1016/j.respol.2014.03.001

West & Bogers. (n.d.). Open Innovation: Current Status and Research Opportunities. *Innovation. Organization & Management*, *19*(1), 43–50.

Yilmaz, A. A., & Tuzlukaya, S. E. (2022). Competency Trap in Organizational Learning: Turkish E-Government Gateway Application During the COVID-19 Pandemic. *International Journal of Electronic Government Research*, *18*(1), 1–13. doi:10.4018/IJEGR.288068

Section 2

Knowledge Sharing and Innovation: Knowledge Systems and the Empowerment of Collective Wisdom

Chapter 4
Work Tribes Present an Opportunity for Firms in Knowledge Management Systems

Amy Rosellini
https://orcid.org/0000-0001-6704-9333
New Western, USA

Jeff M. Allen
https://orcid.org/0000-0003-0551-0539
University of North Texas, USA

Malak Khader
University of North Texas, USA

Millicent Njeri
University of North Texas, USA

ABSTRACT

The phenomenon of work tribes is discussed widely in trade publications but is missing from scholarly research. A work tribe exists where people in the same job role demonstrate shared life experiences outside the work environment, loyalty to others in the work group regardless of social connection, and security or protection within the work group. The existence of work tribes is largely considered a positive force for companies to promote community at work. This chapter introduces a crossroads of social groups and work tribes that cause an opportunity for firms to identify and

DOI: 10.4018/978-1-6684-4431-3.ch004

understand how the work tribe plays a role in the knowledge management system. A case study of flight attendants with a U.S.-based international carrier provides a practical example of how firms can learn from work tribes. Understanding work tribes enables a company to identify the factors that impact knowledge management systems so companies can empower work tribes to propel knowledge forward.

INTRODUCTION

Academic research has failed to investigate and codify the concept of *work tribes*, which is discussed and studied within the practice of culture and knowledge management systems at companies and in trade publications. A work tribe is a collection of people associated through a job role where loyalty, security, and shared life experiences supersede job, company, and social connection. Work tribes are connected by occupational affiliation rather than through physical meeting, company affiliation, or geographic footprint. The work tribe goes beyond the connection and relationships of a typical work team because work tribes are not dependent upon social connections. The work tribe is identified as having a level of loyalty and membership that does not require physical social interaction, where members are connected through association to the tribe itself, rather than connection to each other.

This chapter investigates work tribes, the practical impact of work tribes on knowledge management systems, and the implication to further research work tribes. The study of work tribes within knowledge management systems benefits companies so they better understand how to align the values and goals of the knowledge management system with those of the work tribe to maximize outcomes.

Work tribes exist beyond the spectrum of work teams because of the increased identity, security, and support. Flight attendants are one example of a work tribe. Flight Attendants are present on aircraft with a primary job responsibility of safety and the comfort of passengers (BLS, 2021). The flight attendant population is regulated by the Federal Aviation Administration (FAA) and highly unionized, with the largest union the Association of Flight Attendants representing roughly 50,000 of the almost 250,000 flight attendants in the United States. The large level of oversight and demand for safety upon aircraft make the flight attendant a unique job role to study in knowledge management systems. The success of knowledge transfer to ensure both the safety of passengers and flight crew create a knowledge management system that, if it fails, can be a life-or-death situation.

The flight attendants are a classification of workers like EMS, police, floor nurses, etc., where their job demands force changes in lifestyle that are reflected outside of the workplace. Flight attendants work in a role with changing schedules, unpredictable destinations, and new/unknown coworkers daily.

BACKGROUND

Knowledge management systems exist within the broad context of human and social interaction. Knowledge is social in nature, and knowledge management systems are studied through the context of group dynamics, social groups, and Communities of Practice (COP). Research highlights the positive impact of social constructs within the company's knowledge management system without preparing companies for the downside of social relationships in knowledge management systems. According to the literature, strong knowledge management system adoption is strengthened in the presence of positive work culture, trust in leadership, social identity, group learning, strong inter-group identity, social category, and support from colleagues (Reagans & McEvily, 2003; Huang, 2009; Liu et al., 2020; Zarraga & Boanche, 2005).

Work tribes like other groups and social systems are a benefit to knowledge management systems, as they encourage workers to comply with the practices of the tribe itself. However, understanding how work tribes impact knowledge management systems requires a definition of work tribes and academic, peer-reviewed research to identify when and where work tribes happen and how they might influence knowledge management systems.

Identifying Work Tribes

Knowledge management processes are strengthened by culture and knowledge activities that incentivize workers (Iqbal, Latif, Marimon, Umnar, & Hussain, 2019). When a company understands the social models and work cultures that lead to the connections resulting in a work tribe, the company can enhance the flow of knowledge by engaging with the tribe itself. Identification of work tribes can also benefit companies helping them to identify the negative aspects of work tribes. The impact of not belonging in a culture where work tribes exist can be detrimental to employee engagement, worker performance, and ultimately knowledge management systems (Haldorai, Kim, Phetvaroon, & Jun, 2020). To do this, the company must first learn how to identify the social constructs that lead to work tribes and the nature of the job demands that provide a culture where work tribes will flourish.

Social Categorization and Social Groups

The study of groups and the social nature of individuals is critical to understanding work tribes. Tajfel's research in the 1970s and 1980s focused on social categorization. Tajfel defines social categorization as "the individual's knowledge that he belongs to certain social groups together with some emotional and value significance to him of the group membership" (1972, p. 292). Tajfel's research evolved in the 1980s to include social identification as a cognitive relationship to groups rather than a physical one. Turner and Tajfel find that group belonging is not dependent upon interaction; membership is based on knowledge of belonging to the same social category which drives behavior rather than social pressures or followership determining group behavior (1982).

While the research of social groups was prevalent for three decades, it was not until 2000 that Hogg and Terry linked social identification and social categorization finding phenomenon exists within social categories that drive behaviors in organizations. Their research provides a milestone for social research as it is investigated in relation to work behaviors and knowledge management in firms. Connections between social groups and knowledge management became inextricably linked upon the discovery that the social categorization and social identification impact work behaviors. Knowledge is social in that it is exchanged and transferred through people; understanding that knowledge behaviors can be driven by social groups adds more complexity to understanding the rich social nature of knowledge management systems.

Social Identification Model

While there is research that links social identity as a factor in knowledge management and knowledge transfer, it is not thoroughly studied. Social Identity can be defined as the feeling of belonging to a social group (Schutte & Barkhuizen, 2015, p.130-131). Kane, Argote, and Levine (2005, p. 57) state, "when individuals identify with or are categorized as members of a social aggregate, they are more likely to define themselves in terms of their membership in that group." They also state that when members of a group share a social identity, they feel more comfortable disseminating information with the members of their group.

Although social identity is defined by the common characteristics that a group of people share, the term "work tribes" takes the social identity theory to another level. Not only does it consider the social aspects of a group, but it also considers work dynamics, the effects of the work (whether that be physical, emotional, or mental) on the people, and common behaviors. Work is such a large component of people's lives that it tends to dominate the social aspects of their lives and can in turn, become a large part of their social life as well as their social identity. Because "work tribes" encompasses social identity and it can be expected to have an impact on knowledge management and sharing as well. In fact, organizational knowledge sharing is motivated by several factors including its use for validating information being spread throughout the organization. Kimmerle, Wodzicki, and Cress (2008) state that this is especially true if "they are uncertain that their information is correct, and they prefer to contribute information that can be validated by others. Consequently, they will not introduce information that is only uniquely available to them themselves (p.385)."

Communities of Practice

Originally, the term Communities of Practice (CoP) was used to refer to the coming together of individuals who had similar understanding about what they were doing and how this impacted them and their communities (Bolisani & Scarso, 2014). However, this notion has evolved over time and been adopted by researchers in the field of Knowledge Management. One of the recent formal definition of Communities of Practice (CoP) is "groups of people who share a concern, a set of problems, or a passion about a topic and who deepen their knowledge and expertise in this area by interacting on an ongoing basis" (Inger 2002, p. 4, as cited in Agarwal & Agarwal, 2016). It is based on the notion of collective learning and group expertise (Agarwal & Agarwal, 2016). The concept is used to demonstrate how knowledge is created and shared within an organization, and the basis of the social learning system (Bolisani & Scarso, 2014). Though the concept remains the same, the names used by different organizations vary. Some of the names used include learning clubs, tech forums, or thematic groups. Membership of the CoPs occurs personally and professionally as individuals exchange information and experiences. CoP can be an essential tool for problem solving and sustainable innovation in organizations (Agarwal & Agarwal, 2016).

Beyond the social nature of knowledge management, a knowledge management system is affected by factors outside of social relationships as well. When a job places additional stress or demands on workers that impact their personal life, companies may start to see the presence of social groups that develop deeper connection than that of a CoP. In-flight cabin crews are a work group that is connected beyond CoP, as their job demands outweigh those of many other occupations.

Job Demands

Chen and Chen (2014) defined job demands as "the physical, social, or organizational aspects of a job that require sustained physical or mental efforts and are therefore associated with certain physiological or psychological costs" (p. 46). Flight attendants are frontline employees hence their work can be viewed as emotional. They spend a great deal of time taking customers' requests and listening to their complaints and are expected to handle these complaints effectively (Karatepe & Vatankhah, 2015). In addition, their work includes long hours, confined workspaces, little autonomy, and demanding customers (Chen & Chen, 2014). The physical nature of the job and unusual environment of air travel promotes erratic sleep patterns, constant shifts in routine, as well as a job that is physically demanding. Researchers (e.g., Chen & Kao, 2012) have found that high job demands lead to increased stress, burnout, low productivity, and organizational commitment, and hinders cooperation among employees. This in turn can lead to increased employee turnover which would cost the airlines a lot of money.

Job Demands Impact Life Experiences

The flight attendant work group experiences physical and emotional demands that go beyond job role work groups. While belonging and social identification are present for many work groups like engineers, accountants, or other office jobs, flight attendants have measurable physiological similarities that stay with them even when they leave work.

A flight attendant's job has much to do with the customers and customer service. Part of their skills include surface acting (SA) and deep acting (DA) that affects their emotional labor. SA requires the flight attendant to exhibit an emotion that they do not necessarily have to feel. In other words, they use a facade to let the customer know that they are being heard. DA, on the other hand, requires the flight attendant to attempt to feel the emotion they are displaying. Both levels of acting have an impact on emotional well-being of FAs (Jeon, 2016, p. 348).

Additionally, a study conducted by McNeely et al. (2014, p.3) shows that 15% of flight attendants report having acute or chronic emotional illness such as sleep disturbances, depression, and/or anxiety. When faced with these emotional demands, Chen and Chen (2014, p.50) state that flight attendants "may not only hesitate to carry out proactive safety behaviors, such as taking the initiative in promoting safety programs or communicating any they have safety concerns to managers but may also neglect basic safety routine duties."

The work environment for a flight attendant has difficult emotional demands beyond those of most occupations (Bakker, Demerouti, & Verbeke, 2004; Williams, 2003). When considering that the safety of passengers is dependent upon the ability of the flight attendant to perform essential job functions (Kao, Stewart, & Lee, 2009), it is critical for businesses to understand how emotional and physical demands of a work group impact MS.

Flight attendants are subject to radiation, poor air quality, elevated ozone levels, pesticides, high occupational noise levels, and hypoxia (Ballard et al., 2006; Griffiths & Powell, 2012; Grajewski, et al., 2016; Rayman, 2002). Flight attendants also experience intense physical job demands (McNeely et al., 2018).

The physical job demands of the flight attendant work group leads to health problems (Chen & Chen, 2012). In McNeely et al.'s (2014) study after adjusting for age of the general population, flight attendants have a three-time greater risk of chronic bronchitis with lower smoking levels than the general population and a greater than three-time risk of cardiac disease though they have less cases of hypertension and obesity than the general population. Flight attendants also have a higher rate of reproductive cancers, sleep disorders, and fatigue. As flight attendants increase tenure, they also increase their risk of sleep disorders, alcohol abuse, cancer, foot surgery, and infertility.

Emotional job demands present similar physiological similarities in flight attendants. Stress and disengagement occur when job demands outweigh the resources provided to manage the job demands (Bakker & Demerouti, 2007; Demerouti et al., 2001). Flight attendants endure a great deal of emotional labor, especially female flight attendants. Female flight attendants are perceived to be more subordinate than male flight attendants, so as a result they endure behavior from passengers that could affect them emotionally; these behaviors towards flight attendants include complaints about their airline services and passengers speaking to them rudely (Williams, 2003, p.516).

When Social Groups Become Work Tribes

Shared Life Experience

The nature of the flight attendant work tribe reaches beyond the definition of a social group because health and lifestyle factors connect flight attendants beyond social group and CoP. Flight attendants are in a job category that suffers from chronic health issues due to their work environment, sleep deprivation, irregular schedules – issues that stay with them even as they leave work and enter their home environment.

The presence of a work tribe occurs when the workers have a connection beyond their job. In the case of flight attendants, fluctuating schedules, physiological demands, and the emotional toll of SA and DA connect the tribe even after the flight attendant is clocked out. Where social identity promotes association and actions as determined by the group, the phenomenon of the flight attendant study suggests that the association to the tribe dictates not only actions within the work environment but outside of it as well.

Security

In addition to shared life experience outside of work, flight attendants depend upon one another for safety. An aircraft may provide as few as two or as many as six flight attendants on an aircraft where their job is to maintain the safety of the passengers and cabin crew. The flight attendants' dependence upon one another for security in the air transfers to the knowledge management system where they realize proper training and improved knowledge transfer will impact their personal safety and that of the other passengers and workers on future flights. The security provided by flight attendants can save their lives, and it has become a critical factor in the identification of a work tribe.

Loyalty

Perhaps as a result of the shared life connections and protection provided to one another in the work tribe, the third factor found in work tribes is loyalty. Loyalty is discussed at length in academic articles in terms of customer loyalty. Attention is also paid to the concept of employee loyalty to the company. In work tribes, the concept of loyalty is regarding loyalty to one another – worker loyalty to other workers. In the presence of a work tribe, loyalty is demonstrated through workers acting on behalf of the tribe, even when those actions conflict with personal or company goals. The worker sees the tribe as an extension of themselves and views loyalty to the tribe as loyalty to self.

UNDERSTANDING THE PRESENCE OF A WORK TRIBE

For the remainder of this chapter, the concept of a social group with high job demands and similarities in both physiological and emotional health issues is referred to as a work tribe. The concept of the work tribe in the flight attendant case study, the prevalence of work tribes in industry publications, and the problem researchers face in not addressing work tribes will be discussed.

Work tribes exist in companies and identifying their presence can serve as a benefit to leaders and to the organization (DeRouw, 2019; Godin, 2008; Logan & Fischer, 2008; Murphy, 2019). Work tribes serve as a catalyst in knowledge management systems as they are a social group that naturally puts CoP into place to promote the security of the tribe. Flight attendants specifically demonstrated this phenomenon in the Operating Experience of first-time flight attendants.

In a two-year study of knowledge management systems with flight attendants at an international United States-based airline, the flight attendants revealed the existence a *work tribe*. The flight attendant case study followed and measured flight attendants and supervisors throughout the Operating Experience (OE). The OE is the FAA-mandated final evaluation of first-time flight attendants. During the OE, first-time flight attendants are expected to demonstrate competency in required job safety tasks with little or no coaching from an onboard supervisor.

According to academic research, a strong company culture with trust in leadership, social identity, group learning, and communities of practice (COP) leads to a strong knowledge management system. The flight attendant work tribe demonstrated many of these same attributes throughout the study and therefore their impact on the knowledge management system went unmeasured and unchecked.

Identifying where work tribes exist, how they positively impact company results, and how they can negatively impact results will improve the company's understanding of what is occurring within the knowledge management system itself.

Failure to Identify the Work Tribes

Flight attendants learn their roles through close interaction during group training, mentorship, and colleague support. Since the managers are on the ground during flights, flight attendants build a social network that is not reliant on management, but on their fellow team members. The nature of the flight attendant's role requires their presence on aircraft for the safety of passengers. Due to the high safety knowledge required to do their job, flight attendants rely on each other (not just the company) for the knowledge and skill transfer required to be successful in their job. A CoP is critical in the success of the flight attendant job. Successful knowledge management systems take the social nature of the work group into account when developing internal learning systems to navigate how workers will learn their job role. This result is the development of an elevated level of trust between workers, frictionless knowledge management systems, and the ability to accurately measure knowledge transfer.

A Case Study

At a U.S.-based international airline, a work tribe was identified as a group within the corporate culture that behaves in similar manners in various parts of the country regardless of the individuals not having met each other. Over the course of observing 29 flights and 6 focus groups in various parts of the United States, the research led to the presence of underlying similarities in answers, suggestions, and discussions from flight attendants. To maintain confidentiality, the airline took precautions to ensure that flight attendants did not attend the focus group with acquaintances or friends within the airline. The precautions included emails, surveys, and conversations with supervisors reminding the flight attendants that participation in the study is confidential.

Without prior connections to each other, both the flight observations and the focus groups allowed researchers to see how quickly connections were made among participants and how the tribe, rather than existing personal relationships, dictated the behavior of the group.

The purpose of the flight observations and focus groups was to examine knowledge transfer measurement tools. However, through the two-year study of the flight attendants at one airline, researchers discovered the presence of social connections that superseded social group or the social identification model discussed at the beginning of this chapter. Though it was not the purpose of the focus group study, researchers quickly learned that unexpected behaviors existed within the knowledge management system leading to frictionless knowledge transfer regardless of setting. The settings where flight attendants were observed included the training environment, an in-air flight, and a focus group discussion in a conference room. The flight attendant behaviors were consistent in each setting and with each new set of flight attendants.

The researchers named the presence of these deep social connections a work tribe and reviewed transcripts to determine what factors revealed the presence of the work tribe and how the work tribe appeared to present deeper connections between individuals than that of social categorization or social groups. The factors that presented repeatedly in the different settings were (1) shared life experience outside of work, (2) loyalty to one another – even those workers they had not met previously, and (3) a need to protect or feel security within the work tribe. Once researchers identified work tribes, they were able to review the data collected to find evidence of the work tribe.

Through the 29 observed flights, the willingness of workers to share and transfer knowledge in the OE of first-time flight attendants was the most important finding of this study. Including both explicit knowledge transfer (that which can be shared) and tacit knowledge transfer (that which cannot be easily documented or verbalized), flight attendant supervisors executed formal and informal instruction to first-time flight attendants on 29 flights in this case study. As first-time flight attendants began their OE, supervisors were seen and heard showing empathy, care, support, and affirmation to the first-time flight attendants. The flight attendant supervisors were heard sharing information above and beyond what is provided in the multi-week training program.

The impact on the knowledge management system when flight attendants willingly transfer knowledge above and beyond what is expected of them is that first-time flight attendants receive additional tacit knowledge that they may have had to learn on their own over time. Instead, first-time flight attendants receive knowledge and skills more quickly allowing them to master their role with the support of the tribe.

Unlike some knowledge management systems that show an unwillingness for workers to transfer knowledge as they fear that sharing knowledge can make themselves less valuable to the organization. With the existence of the work tribe, the tribe is more concerned with the needs of the tribe rather than the needs of the individual, allowing for less friction in the knowledge management system, less egos with individuals who transfer knowledge, and a knowledge management system that aligns with the work tribe: to get as much useful information into the hands of the new flight attendant as possible.

Through focus groups, the researcher understood through tacit knowledge transfer that flight attendants were offering the same suggestions and speaking about unrelated requests in the focus group, altogether avoiding the questions that the focus group was aimed to answer. Rather than addressing researchers' questions directly, the flight attendants suggested mentor programs and additional job resources that were unrelated to the focus group questions. When examined through the lens of current research and knowing the high job demands of the flight attendants' role, the focus groups produced a work tribe requesting increased job resources to counterbalance the high job demands.

The focus group inquired as to flight attendants' use of a training evaluation tool and instead were informed about the values and needs of the work tribe. Utilizing NVivo Software, the five focus group transcriptions were coded and placed into categories based on theme. Out of 38 total themes identified, five themes were outside the parameters of what the study was measuring and also included references in 80% of the focus groups and at least 20 independent references to that theme (Table 1).

Table 1. References to themes outside of case study scope that flight attendants referenced in focus groups

Theme	Number of Focus Group References to Theme	Number of Independent References to Theme
Federal Aviation Administration (FAA)	5	22
Mentor/Mentor Program	4	50
New Flight Attendants are nervous/anxious	5	29
New Flight Attendant is relatable	5	28
New Flight attendant's personality (positive or negative reference)	5	56

The flight attendants revealed through the transcript that they collectively identified the same themes though they did not attend focus groups in the same geographic locations or meet to discuss the focus group prior to their arrival in the room. The solutions brought to the focus groups provided the airline with critical information that allows the company to address potential gaps in the knowledge management system.

Success of the Work Tribe

The company benefited from taking a qualitative approach to understanding the measurement tools with the knowledge management system. The qualitative approach allowed for inductive analysis revealing that the CoP in work tribes goes beyond in-person collaboration and towards a group think where individuals of the tribe reach the same conclusions because of their similar circumstances. The company benefitted from the work tribe when the focus group openly shared solutions to improve the knowledge management system while also revealing how the workers proactively work through obstacles presented within the knowledge management system. The obstacles were not brought up to the company previously because the work tribe solved the problem themselves without intervention from the company.

Numerous successes were revealed through the work tribe including several informal mentorship programs that individuals adopted when no formal mentorship programs were in process. The work tribe found methods to balance nerves and anxiety with new flight attendants while measuring job performance in the new flight attendants' first trip. The work tribe found ways to relate to the experiences of new flight attendants and use those to coach and assist them in learning how to perform job duties.

In addition to informal mentorship, flight attendant supervisors stepped into roles as coaches and teachers of first-time flight attendants. Though first-time flight attendants had just completed weeks of training when they entered the first flight OE, the supervisors found ways to transfer tacit knowledge that only comes from years of experience with the aircraft and company.

The benefits of the work tribe in the knowledge management system were evident throughout the case study and allowed the company to uncover gaps in the current system to ensure the company meets the needs of both supervisors, new flight attendants, and ultimately work tribe.

The Three Factors of the Work Tribe

Work Tribes Identify Solutions Based on Shared Experience

As the literature review outlined, in-flight cabin crew work in a culture with physical and physiological job demands that exceed most occupations. The focus group revealed connections among never-before-introduced flight attendants where there was immediate comradery and connection. Dialogue between focus group participants recounted travel schedules, stressful situations, and the exchange of tacit knowledge ranging from how to handle work situations to managing travel conflict.

The flight attendants were unfamiliar with the literature suggesting that the best recourse for high job demand is to provide workers with additional resources. Regardless of city or state, the focus groups continued to offer solutions that pointed towards more resources rather than solutions to improve the evaluation of knowledge transfer measurement tools. The presence of the work tribe, the quick connection and trust built among co-workers allowed the company insight into problems the work tribe diagnosed. Even better, the work tribe had ready-made solutions for the company to put into place.

Protection and Loyalty of the Work Tribe

In contrast to the many benefits of work tribes noted here, it is possible for work tribes to create an obstacle for companies looking to measure knowledge transfer. Flight attendants are part of a unique work tribe that relies on a certain level of comradery and sisterhood (or brotherhood) that is not taken into consideration with the rigorous demand of the one-on-one job observation mandated by the FAA. While the FAA requires that a supervisor objectively evaluate the work of a trainee, that is not the world the flight attendants inhabit. On an anonymous survey, flight attendants were able to answer performance measurement scenarios with approximately 50% accuracy. In multiple face-to-face focus groups, not one flight attendant stated that they would evaluate performance measurement accurately if it meant giving a negative score. Not one. As researchers dug deeper, they uncovered flight attendants' willingness to score others based on how they predicted the flight attendant would perform in the future. These statements of loyalty to the tribe itself trumped loyalty to the company.

The decision to provide evaluations based on feelings rather than evidence was also seen when flight attendants responded that they often evaluate a trainee not on how they perform, but on how they feel the trainee will perform when they are not nervous. The evaluation score was based on connection to the tribe and association with the individual's position. In the focus groups, flight attendants are often equated scoring the evaluation form based on how the evaluator felt when they were a trainee, rather than associating the score with the feeling or job behaviors of the trainee. The disassociation of the score reflecting the performance of the trainee further establishes that the score reflects the association with a tribe rather than the individual score of the flight attendant. In each focus group, the supervisors made statements based on scenarios and trainees they had never met. The practice of scoring higher than earned, based on personal experience or association with the tribe was about protecting the tribe.

After completing months and years of research in the airline industry, the dangers of the flight attendant job are evident. In addition to health and emotional problems described earlier in this chapter, feelings of isolation associated with the travel and the job demands are also present as flight attendants address solutions that would not impact knowledge transfer measurement (as knowledge transfer measurement was the purpose of the focus groups).

Security and the Quick Induction into the Tribe

When flight attendants arrive at work, they have a few moments to build a relationship with a co-worker that they will then spend hours with within a dangerous job. Flight attendants rely on each other for emotional, sometimes physical support. They have demanding customers, health issues because of their profession, and other personal issues that come from the inconsistency of their sleep schedule. In most cases, the relationship they build with a coworker is fleeting and one-time-only. Yet their relationship to the tribe strengthens the loyalty and connection with the tribe with every new relationship.

The elevated level of stress and work demands require a kinship to be developed quickly for the flight attendants to rely on each other as an additional resource to do their job. As flight attendants are hired and trained to provide a safe passage to travelers in the air, they spend much of their time interacting with passengers, de-escalating demanding passenger situations, and pouring one hundred drinks in under an hour. Given the strenuous job demands, it is understandable why flight attendants need the resources of a tribe.

Fast relationships were formed with flight attendants attending the focus group sessions. At the onset of this study, the research questions did not include an investigation of work tribes. If work tribes were a construct of this study, the qualitative design might have included a measurement of body language and facial expressions to understand more of the unspoken language of the work tribe. What was discovered in the study is each focus group repeatedly encountered flight attendants who shared names with each other and built relationships quickly. The study design intentionally kept the flight attendants out of the conference room before focus group sessions to remove the opportunity to build rapport and learn names, which could accidentally be used in the transcription.

No matter what steps were taken, the flight attendants met like old friends. They spoke the same language. They had the same experiences. They knew each other without knowing each other. Their relationship was not purely social, they were tribal. They had (figuratively) been to war together even though they had never met.

Informal and Formal Leadership of the Tribe

Within the focus group, work tribe leaders were often identified through their engagement with the case study discussion, willingness to share personal information, and tenure with the company. Flight attendants that received affirmation and agreement from the rest of the group appeared as informal leaders, and they shared the characteristics of expressing ideas, sharing personal insight, and working for the company longer than other flight attendants in the room.

The purpose of the case study was not to uncover the leaders existing within the work tribe, but the presence of informal leadership will be discussed further at the end of this chapter.

SOLUTIONS AND RECOMMENDATIONS

A solution to firms understanding a work tribe is identifying when a work tribe is present, what resources the tribe needs to counterbalance high job demands, and how the values of the organization are (or can be) aligned with the values of the tribe.

Identify the Work Tribe

The Work Tribe builds on the Social Identification Model, which does not require human interaction or cohesion to exist to have a social identity to a group. A work tribe consists of some of the same characteristics of a social group where there is a value to the individual member and emotional connection. However, the Work Tribe goes beyond social identity in the work environment and touches all aspects of workers' lives. Like a tribe of people with customs, language, belonging, and identity that is unique to them and translates to all parts of life: home, family, and work, the work tribe eclipses the expectations of the company and prioritizes the tribe needs and expectations. This can be of invaluable benefit to the company when the work tribe goals and values align with those of the company. The work tribe can serve as an obstacle when the goals and values of the tribe and company are not aligned.

The Work Tribe also builds on the work relating Communities of Practice (COP) to knowledge management systems. When informal communities of practice exist and without manager oversight, as is the case with flight attendants, a company has little ability to intercede on the knowledge transferred between workers. The benefit to companies with positive work culture and trust in leadership is that often the work tribe values align with the values of the company. When both sets of values are aligned, the CoP works for the benefit of the company and can serve as a catalyst in knowledge management systems.

The Work Tribe, Defined

A Work Tribe exists at the intersection of the social group with three additional work factors. First, the job demands outweigh the resources needed to complete the job, leading to high stress on the job. The limit of resources is stretched due to changes in air travel with COVID19. Second, the work environment encroaches on home, personal, family, and other non-work-related life. Flight attendants have increased health risks compared to the public and lifestyle issues like sleep deprivation and irregular schedules that further alienate the group from the population. The third factor is emotional problems that connect the social group. The combination of the three factors with a community of practice where social groups already exist leads to a company that lacks the ability to control aspects within the knowledge management system.

Figure 1 provides a visualization of the factors that, when all are present, produce an environment where a work tribe is likely. As the case study noted, workers have a sense of comradery and loyalty to each other due to what they endure on the job. Work tribes emerge when there is a sense of security when the group is dependent upon one another for safety in the workplace. The work tribe is also a result of lifestyle experiences that impact the worker beyond the workday/night. Examples of shared lifestyle experiences outside work for flight attendants include fluctuating schedules, high altitude work environment, and a high physical/emotional toll. With these three shared and unique needs among a group of workers, it is hard to dismiss the fact that the natural sense of a tribe is formed or can be formed.

The workers acted in accordance with the needs of the work tribe itself, rather than aligning with the expectations or priorities set forth by the company. At times, this group think benefited the company in terms of knowledge transfer. The outcome of the tribe acting outside of the knowledge management system design is that the measurement tool loses its effectiveness.

Figure 1. Work Tribe model demonstrates the three factors that lead to the presence of Work Tribes: shared life experience beyond the demands of the job, loyalty to tribe members over company or job, and protective behaviors ensuring the security of the tribe

Theme	Number of Focus Group References to Theme	Number of Independent References to Theme
Federal Aviation Administration (FAA)	5	22
Mentor/Mentor Program	4	50
New Flight Attendants are nervous/anxious	5	29
New Flight Attendant is relatable	5	28
New Flight attendant's personality (positive or negative reference)	5	56

Identify the Culture Where Work Tribes Exist

The understanding of work tribes helps companies to impact knowledge management systems. As companies understand how a work tribe both positively and negatively impacts the operations of both formal and informal knowledge management systems, they can implement strategies to employ or counter-act the impact of work tribes.

The first steps to identifying a work tribe is to determine if the three factors - shared life experience, loyalty, and security – are present. If so, the company investigates the presence of a work tribe and how that presence impacts the success, and potential obstacles, of the knowledge management systems.

Examining Work Tribe Factors

The results of the two-year study of flight attendants overwhelmingly pointed to the company's success in providing an environment where the work tribe improves the effectiveness of a knowledge management system while at the same time experiences a loss of control in the measurement of knowledge transfer. While this case study revealed that work tribes have a mostly positive impact on knowledge management systems, it is unlikely that is the case in all companies with work tribes. The first step to understanding how a company can work alongside the work tribe to improve the knowledge management system is to properly identify where work tribes exist, who are the informal leaders, and what are the values of the work tribe.

Since work tribes can have both positive and negative impacts on knowledge management systems, the awareness that workers identify feelings and value by their association with their job role is helpful to companies. Companies should work to understand the values and feelings of the work tribe to see how the company aligns with the group's values. Where there is alignment, there is less room for friction. Where the company and work tribe are not aligned, the company may need to alter messaging or core values to better align with its workers – especially if those workers represent a sizable portion of the population.

Consider how Figure 2 provides an example to firms where their knowledge management system can be positively and negatively impacted by the presence of work tribes. Knowledge management systems grow stronger when values are aligned. In addition, trust in leadership and a positive company culture where workers feel supported aids in the effectiveness of knowledge management systems. Companies must also consider how the natural behaviors of the work tribe work within the knowledge management system. For example, flight attendants are hired for their ability to protect passengers through following safety procedures while also providing elevated levels of customer service. Flight attendants tend to exhibit empathy, care, and friendliness both on and off the job. Companies who understand the behaviors of the flight attendant work tribe can design a knowledge management system allowing for flight attendants to communicate and socially engage in other ways so that the knowledge management systems complement the flight attendants' behaviors.

Conversely, a company's failure to recognize a work tribe can negatively impact the knowledge management system. Identifying the existence of the work tribe allows companies to understand how a work tribe impacts the knowledge management system – even when the impact is positive. When a company fails to identify the knowledge management system, it is possible that the company will continue to dedicate time and resources into strategies that the company believes propels the system forward while the tribe is transferring tacit knowledge and ensuring knowledge sharing. When the company is unaware of the knowledge behaviors and informal knowledge systems the tribe puts into place, the company may be crediting the wrong intercession with producing a positive impact on the knowledge management system.

In the flight attendant case study, workers were observed and readily communicated their willingness to evaluate first-time flight attendants based on aspects of the work tribe – loyalty, shared life experiences, and security – rather than evaluating based on job performance. While this may have a negative impact, it is counterbalanced by the positive impacts workers had on the knowledge management system. The supervisors act as coaches, trainers, and mentors for as long a period as needed regardless of whether the company offers a formal mentorship program.

Figure 2. Work Tribes' impact on knowledge management systems

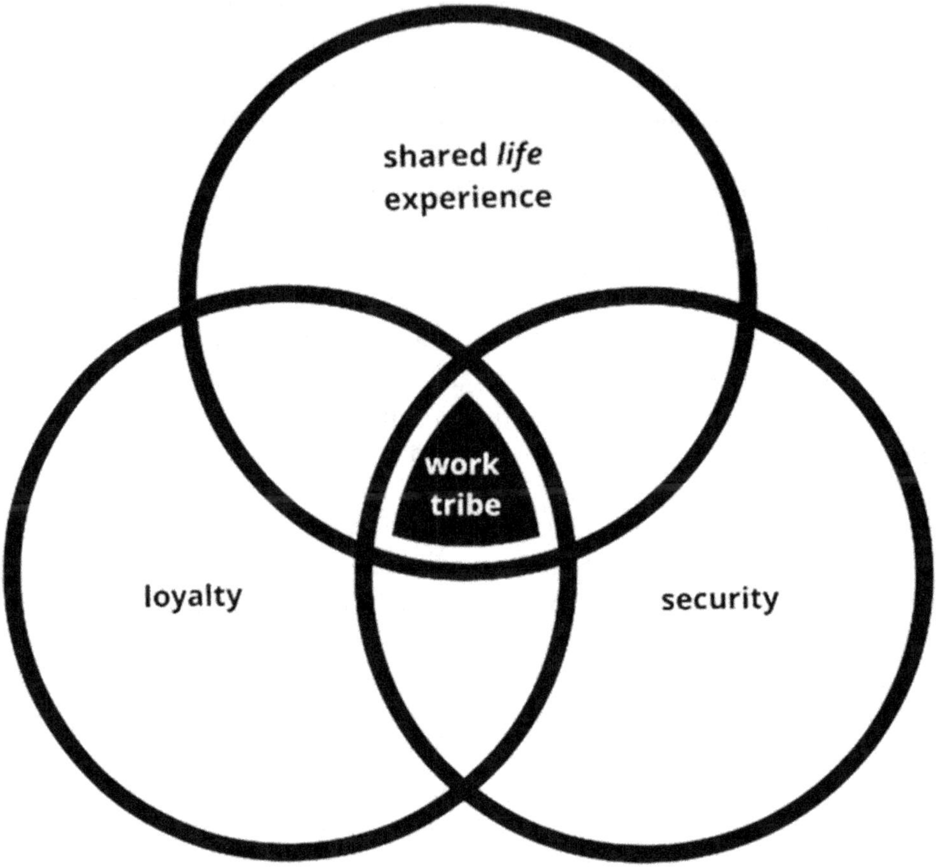

Identifying work tribes is increasingly important in companies with poor work culture or low trust in leadership. The success or failure of the knowledge management system can be improved upon, but companies should start by understanding their population, including where social groups exist, how CoP are active in the company, and where work tribes have formed.

To mitigate job demands, companies need to provide the workers with job resources. Xanthopoulou et al. (2008) define job resources as "those physical, psychological, social or organizational aspects of the job that: (1) are functional in achieving work goals; (2) reduce job demands and the associated costs; and/or (3) stimulate personal growth, learning and development (p. 345). Job resources can be classified into two types of motivators: intrinsic and extrinsic motivators. Job resources that are intrinsic motivators promote employees' individual growth and satisfy their basic needs. For example, when the FA are provided support by their colleagues and supervisors, their need for belonging is met. Extrinsic motivators, on the other hand, promote employees' job productivity (Xanthopoulou et al., 2008). When job demands outweigh job resources, the firm has an opportunity to survey workers and understand what resources will make the biggest impact. When firms provide resources to counterbalance high job demands, workers feel more motivated and less stressed, resulting in a greater capacity to perform their job.

Providing resources and designing knowledge management systems that anticipate job demands help workers to work through the challenge of the job and perform their job roles. Job resources allow workers to counterbalance the heavy job demands. The ability of workers in dangerous roles like flight attendants perform safety duties directly associated with the number of resources they are given in their roles. Resources include the training provided to them by the company, job autonomy in their role, social connections that they build at work (Chen & Chen, 2014), and feedback (Chen & Kao, 2012).

Lastly, workers in dangerous or emotionally-taxing jobs do not expect a company to remove all risk. However, aligning the company values with the tribe values ensures that the tribe continues to be a benefit to the knowledge management system. When physiological and emotional problems are an outcome of the work environment, companies can measure and understand the degree that physiological and emotional problems impact workers and provide health and safety resources to improve the lives of workers. Multiple options such as on-site clinics, discounted mental health services, increased vacation pay, and other solutions may provide some relief to workers to lessen potential negative impacts.

CONCLUSION

The presence of work tribes presents an opportunity for companies when measuring the success of knowledge management systems. A work tribe is connected to the tribe over the company and causes members of the tribe to behave in a way that expresses loyalty and protection to act in favor of the tribe. The behavior of a work tribe impacts knowledge management systems and has shown a positive impact on the function of knowledge management systems.

Human beings are social beings and have a need for belonging which motivates them to find and maintain group membership (Haldorai et al., 2020). Work tribes are the kinships that exist at work and provide the workers with a sense of belonging. The sense of belonging stimulates the belief that one is respected, supported, and in general, the other workers are interested in one's well-being and success. Individuals who experience a sense of belonging tend to portray positive emotions and as a result perform beyond what is expected of them (Haldorai et al., 2020). Tribes at work are especially important as they provide employees with a collective goal and are viewed as a way that increases their odds of success in the workplace. In some cases, these tribal ties are so strong that even after employees leave their places of work, they continue to stay connected with their former colleagues. Organizations should identify where work tribes exist and celebrate how they positively impact knowledge management systems. Companies should also ensure the values of the company continue to align with the values of the work tribe. When a work tribe is seen to have a negative impact on the measurement of a knowledge management system, companies can work with informal leaders to understand the gaps in the system and make the necessary changes.

Work tribe leadership, even if informal, provides a crucial resource for companies to stay aligned with the needs and values of the tribe. The company should work to recognize if and where informal leadership exists to ensure that there are shared goals between the organization and the tribe.

As professional and industry journals explore the presence of work tribes and their impact on business, researchers within knowledge management must explore how work tribes engage and interact with knowledge management systems. The success of knowledge management systems is dependent upon firms recognizing how external factors impact the success of knowledge transfer and behavior change in the work environment.

The lack of research today defining work tribes, assessing the value of work tribes, and understanding the impact of work tribes on knowledge management systems provides a large research gap. The priority for future research is to test additional groups that meet the factors indicating a work tribe is present and determine if they have an impact on knowledge management systems. Additional studies need to be completed to understand if it is true that work tribes have a mostly positive impact on knowledge management systems, while having an adverse effect on the measurement of these systems.

The work tribe is not unique to the aviation industry and in-flight crews. It is likely that air pilots may also operate within work tribes. In addition, hospital staff, first responders, FEMA, rough necks, social workers, military, and other work groups have similar work roles that encroach on family life and home environments. The combination of security, loyalty, and shared life experiences is evident in more communities of workers where a social group at a company becomes a work tribe. Studying additional populations will identify and strengthen the criteria that make-up work tribes.

FUTURE RESEARCH

Future research opportunities exist within additional industries like healthcare, emergency response, oil and gas, and active military to understand if the same phenomenon of work tribes impact knowledge management systems. A study to determine how best to identify the factors: shared life experience, security, and loyalty would build upon the evidence of contributing work tribe factors from this study.

More research and evidence are needed to evaluate when work tribes serve as a catalyst and when they serve as an obstacle in knowledge management systems. The focus group in the study revealed less friction when workers are transferring knowledge resulting in greater tacit knowledge transfer; an opportunity for future study is to measure the impact work tribes have on tacit knowledge transfer.

An additional opportunity for future research is to assess how a company can interrupt or break the cycle where a work tribe is having a negative impact on one aspect of a knowledge management system. An example of interfering with the knowledge management system is a study where the company increases job resources to balance job demands. The opportunity to further research how additional job resources impact not only job demands, but also the strength of work tribes is a potential future study for this topic. As job resources are increased, knowledge management systems may see a positive impact on knowledge behaviors that produce a better functioning knowledge management system.

The emotional tax of work tribes may also provide insight into how stronger emotional ties both enhance and disrupt the knowledge management system. Loyalty and security can serve as both a resource and a weapon; future examination may lead to a greater understanding of pitfalls within the factors present in work tribes.

This research received no specific grant from any funding agency in the public, commercial, or not-for-profit sectors.

REFERENCES

Agarwal, N., & Agarwal, R. (2016). Why communities of practice (CoP) are 'still' relevant for the organizations? *Studies in Asian Social Science*, *3*(2), 17–25. doi:10.5430ass.v3n2p17

Association of Flight Attendants-CWA. (n.d.). *About AFA*. https://www.afacwa.org/about_afa

Ballard, T., Romito, P., Lauria, L., Vigiliano, V., Caldora, M., & Mazzanti, C. (2006). Self-perceived health and mental health among women flight attendants. *Occupational and Environmental Medicine*, *63*(1), 33–38. doi:10.1136/oem.2004.018812 PMID:16361403

Bolisani, E., & Scarso, E. (2014). The place of communities of practice in knowledge management studies: A critical review. *Journal of Knowledge Management*, *18*(2), 366–381. doi:10.1108/JKM-07-2013-0277

Chen, C., & Chen, C. (2012). Burnout and work engagement among cabin crew: Antecedents and consequences. *The International Journal of Aviation Psychology*, *22*(1), 41–58. doi:10.1080/10508414.2012.635125

Chen, C., & Chen, C. (2014). Investigating the effects of job demands and job resources on cabin crew safety behaviors. *Tourism Management*, *41*(4), 45–52. doi:10.1016/j.tourman.2013.08.009

Chen, C. F., & Kao, Y. L. (2012). Investigating the antecedents and consequences of burnout and isolation among flight attendants. *Tourism Management*, *33*(4), 868–874. doi:10.1016/j.tourman.2011.09.008

De Rouw, S. (2019). *The importance of a work tribe and how to find yours.* Medium. https://medium.com/joingoodcompany/the-importance-of-a-work-tribe-and-how-to-find-yours-544d3ba1614c

Godin, S. (2008). *Tribes: We Need You to Lead Us*. Portfolio/Penguin.

Grajewski, B., Whelan, E., Nguyen, M., Kwan, L., & Cole, R. (2016). Sleep disturbance in female flight attendants and teachers. *Aerospace Medicine and Human Performance*, *87*(7), 638–645. doi:10.3357/AMHP.4512.2016 PMID:27503044

Griffiths, R., & Powell, D. (2012). The occupational health and safety of flight attendants. *Aviation, Space, and Environmental Medicine*, *83*(5), 514–521. doi:10.3357/ASEM.3186.2012 PMID:22606869

Haldorai, K., Kim, W. G., Phetvaroon, K., & Li, J. J. (2020). Left out of the office "tribe": The influence of workplace ostracism on employee work engagement. *International Journal of Contemporary Hospitality Management*, *32*(8), 2717–2735. doi:10.1108/IJCHM-04-2020-0285

Haldorai, K., Kim, W. G., Phetvaroon, K., & Li, J. J. (2020). Left out of the office "tribe": The influence of workplace ostracism on employee work engagement. *International Journal of Contemporary Hospitality Management*, *32*(8), 2717–2735. doi:10.1108/IJCHM-04-2020-0285

Hogg, M., & Terry, D. (2000). Social identity and self-categorization processes in organizational contexts. *Academy of Management Review*, *25*(1), 121–140. doi:10.5465/amr.2000.2791606

Huang, C. (2009). Knowledge sharing and group cohesiveness on performance: An empirical study of technology R&D teams in Taiwan. *Technovation*, *29*(11), 786–797. doi:10.1016/j.technovation.2009.04.003

Iqbal, A., Latif, F., Marimon, F., Umar, F. S., & Hussain, S. (2019). From knowledge management to organizational performance: Modelling the mediating role of innovation and intellectual capital in higher education. *Journal of Enterprise Information Management*, *32*(1), 36–59. doi:10.1108/JEIM-04-2018-0083

Jeon, A. (2016). The effect of pre-flight attendants' emotional intelligence, emotional labor, and emotional exhaustion on commitment to customer service. *Service Business*, *10*(2), 345–367. doi:10.100711628-015-0273-2

Kane, A., Argote, L., & Levine, J. (2005). Knowledge transfer between groups via personnel rotation: Effects of social identity and knowledge quality. *Organizational Behavior and Human Decision Processes*, *96*(1), 56–71. doi:10.1016/j.obhdp.2004.09.002

Karatepe, O. M., & Vatankhah, S. (2015). High-performance work practices, career satisfaction, and service recovery performance: A study of flight attendants. *Tourism Review*, *70*(1), 56–71. doi:10.1108/TR-01-2014-0004

Kimmerle, J., Wodzicki, K., & Cress, U. (2008). The social psychology of knowledge management. *Team Performance Management*, *14*(7), 381–401. doi:10.1108/13527590810912340

Liu, F., Wu, J., Huang, X., & Fong, P. S. W. (2020). Impact of intra-group coopetitive incentives on the performance outcomes of knowledge sharing: Evidence from a randomized experiment. *Journal of Knowledge Management*, *24*(2), 346–368. doi:10.1108/JKM-05-2019-0256

Logan, D., & Fischer-Wright, H. (2008). *The five stages of work "tribes."* Gallup. https://news.gallup.com/businessjournal/106903/five-stages-workplace-tribes.aspx

McNeely, E., Gale, S., Tager, I., Kincl, L., Bradley, J., Coull, B., & Hecker, S. (2014). The self-reported health of U.S. flight attendants compared to the general population. *Environmental Health*, *13*(1), 1–11. doi:10.1186/1476-069X-13-13 PMID:24612632

McNeely, E., Mordukhovich, I., Tideman, S., Gale, S., & Coull, B. (2018). Estimating the health consequences of flight attendant work: Comparing flight attendant health to the general population in a cross-sectional study. *BMC Public Health, 18*(1), 346–358. doi:10.118612889-018-5221-3 PMID:29566648

Murphy, S. (2019). *Work Tribes: The Surprising Secret to Breakthrough Performance, Astonishing Results, and Keeping Teams Together*. Harper Collins Leadership.

Rayman, R. (2002). Cabin air quality: An overview. *Aviation, Space, and Environmental Medicine, 73*(3), 211–215. PMID:11908887

Reagans, R., & McEvily, B. (2003). Network structure and knowledge transfer: The effects of cohesion and range. *Administrative Science Quarterly, 48*(2), 240–267. https://doiorg.libproxy.library.unt.edu/10.2307/3556658. doi:10.2307/3556658

Schutte, N., & Barkhuizen, N. (2015). Knowledge management and sharing in local government: A social identity theory perspective: EJKM. *Electronic Journal of Knowledge Management, 13*(2), 130–141.

Tajfel, H., Billig, M. G., Bundy, R. P., & Flament, C. (1971). Social categorization and intergroup behaviour. *European Journal of Social Psychology, 1*(2), 149–178. doi:10.1002/ejsp.2420010202

Turner, J. C. (1982). Towards a cognitive redefinition of the social group. In H. Tajfel (Ed.), *Social identity and intergroup relations* (pp. 15–40). Cambridge University Press.

U.S. Bureau of Labor and Statistics. (2021, September 8). *Flight attendants*. https://www.bls.gov/ooh/transportation-and-material-moving/flight-attendants.htm

Williams, C. (2003). Sky service: The demands of emotional labour in the airline industry. *Gender, Work and Organization, 10*(5), 513–550. doi:10.1111/1468-0432.00210

Xanthopoulou, D., Bakker, A., Demerouti, E., & Scjaufeli, W. (2007). The role of personal resources in the job demands-resources model. *International Journal of Stress Management, 14*(2), 121–141. doi:10.1037/1072-5245.14.2.121

Zarraga, C., & Bonache, J. (2005). The impact of team atmosphere on knowledge outcomes in self-managed teams. *Organization Studies 26*(5), 661-681. https://doi-org.libproxy.library.unt.edu/10.1177/0170840605051820

Chapter 5
Enhanced Knowledge Sharing Adoption Model in the Halal Food Industry

Siti Zakiah Melatu Samsi
Multimedia University, Malaysia

ABSTRACT

Knowledge sharing (KS) is one method for businesses to build knowledge within their walls and create a learning environment. It enables the achievement of common goals, which improves organisational performance and competitiveness. The willingness to contribute and participate in knowledge-sharing activities are the most important issues that must be addressed and for which a management solution is required. This chapter will investigate the factors that influence Halal food organisation staff to participate in and contribute to the organization's knowledge sharing activities. A phenomenology approach was used to investigate employees' attitudes or levels of adoption toward knowledge sharing in a case study of one Halal food organisation in Malaysia. The enhanced adoption model for Halal organisations is established using the TOE framework as the theoretical lens and the concept of knowledge sharing from an Islamic perspective.

INTRODUCTION

According to the Janus (2016), knowledge, specifically how a community produces, processes, and integrates knowledge into their lives, is a critical factor in organizational development. Understanding how to effectively encourage knowledge sharing among staff is a critical challenge for today's organizations in increasing their intellectual

DOI: 10.4018/978-1-6684-4431-3.ch005

capital. The importance of knowledge sharing has been elucidated in other research in different contexts, such as in preserving knowledge in institutes of higher learning (Muda et al., 2017), promoting organisational sustainability in supply chains (León-Bravo et al., 2017), enhancing teams' communications, performing in project management (Cui, 2017), as well as helping organisations achieve competitive advantages (Degbey and Pelto, 2021). Knowledge sharing should be a culture in all organizations, including Halal food organizations, because it promotes social interaction and the exchange of knowledge, experience, and expertise, as well as the recreation of knowledge, all of which contribute to innovation and organizational performance (Maizza et al., 2019).

Despite the fact that Halal food is the leading segment within the overall global Halal industry, it is still plagued by a lack of standardised rules and regulations due to the different doctrines that exist in Islam (Abdallah, 2021), which makes it difficult for multinational food companies to enter the industry (State of the Global Islamic Economy Report 2016/17, 2016; Al-Mubarak, 2015). One example is the debate among religious organizations and authorities over the use of stunning procedures in Halal animal slaughtering (Riaz et al., 2021). Many countries still allow animals to be slaughtered without being stunned, although western countries make it mandatory for animal welfare reasons. Halal regulators had a challenge in maintaining conformity among industry participants from different countries as a result of this issue therefore need further explanations by religious experts and scholars known as *"ulama"* and "*mufti*". With the help of religious experts, complete instructions can be supplied to Halal organizations and stakeholders, allowing for the development of standard practices for reference. Thus, at the organizational level, Halal knowledge is the most important knowledge to be shared among the staff and stakeholders so that everyone in the organization understand the whole concept of Halal. Knowledge sharing as part of management solutions may provide one of the best approaches in improving Halal organizations' performance.

Thus, this research aims to explore how knowledge sharing can be adopted in the Halal food industry by answering the following research questions (i) what is the knowledge sharing practices in the selected Halal food organization and (ii) what are the factors that influence the adoption of knowledge sharing in Halal food organization.

This chapter begins with the introduction section that elaborate the motivation of the study followed by the review of the literature. The research methodology then explained and justified followed by the theoretical background and the conceptual framework. The findings and discussion section elaborates the findings from the interviews followed by the presentation of the adoption model and conclusion of the research outcomes.

LITERATURE REVIEW

Halal Food Industry

Halal is a comprehensive concept for the protection of Muslims. It covers not only religious requirements like avoiding alcohol and pork, but also the safety, health, and cleanliness aspects of products. This concept is known as "*Halalan Thoyyiban*", which denotes the all-inclusive nature of Halal. The Islamic law has clearly stated the criteria of Halal food that do not solely depend on the ingredients used. To ensure that a product is Halal, all stages of production, from the determination of raw materials, preparation, handling, storage, and packaging to the final process before the product reaches the final consumers must comply with Halal rules and regulations. The Halal concepts are stated in the holy Qur'an and Hadith (the Prophet Muhammad Sayings). One of the Qurânic verse about Halal - "*O mankind! Eat of that which is lawful and good on the earth*" (Al-Baqarah, 168). This verse refers to the guideline given in Islam that clearly mentions "lawful" and "good". Lawful is interpreted as the Halal guidelines provided by Islamic law while "good" interpreted as the purity, safety and the cleanliness of all aspects of the food source.

Halal food products can be categorized based on their sources such as animals, plants, natural minerals, and chemicals or types such as food additives, nutritional food and supplements, as well as fully-processed food. The Halal status does not only apply to food; it covers other industries like tourism, finance, cosmetics, pharmaceuticals, and healthcare ("Market Information," 2013).

Though Halal does not necessarily refers to Halal food, the industry of Halal food is still the most predominant, with its global market value of approximately 1.4 trillion U.S. dollars in 2017 and are expected to reach 2.6 trillion U.S. dollars in 2023 (M. Shahbandeh, 2018).

Knowledge Sharing

Knowledge sharing is one of the most important processes in knowledge management (Asrar-ul-Haq and Anwar, 2016). Specifically, the exchange of information, data, and expertise to solve problems, develop new insights, or implement rules or measures is referred to as knowledge sharing (Kader Jilani et al., 2020). According to the World Bank, knowledge sharing is defined as a subset of knowledge management activities which involve the exchange of knowledge within and across organizations (Janus, 2016). Rohman *et al.*, (2020) have described knowledge sharing as a process of social interaction that involves knowledge exchange, expertise and skills between people within an organization that contribute to the improvement of an organization.

Knowledge sharing is a mutual interaction between a sender, who delivers knowledge, and receivers, who are seeking knowledge, in which information learned from experiences is exchanged to support an individual working toward a common objective (Alotaibi et al., 2017). Knowledge sharing includes the creation and transfer of knowledge via media like documents, and communications between individuals, groups, as well as organisations (Hussain Alsayed et al., 2012). This carries a lot of benefits, including the reduction of barriers within organizations, improvement of performance, better decision-making skills, and development. Knowledge sharing can happen in different directions either vertically or horizontally within an organization (Muhammed and Zaim, 2020). Vertical knowledge sharing is based on contacts with supervisors or subordinates, which can occur either upward or downward in the organizational hierarchy. Horizontal knowledge sharing, on the other hand, comprises sharing knowledge with peers, co-workers, and other persons within the organization who may or may not be on the same level of the organizational hierarchy.

A willingness to participate in knowledge sharing can be attributed to various factors, including the existence of collaborative technologies (Hussain Alsayed et al.,2012); leadership and reward systems (Cyril Eze et al., 2013); alignment with organizational strategies (Jafari et al., 2007); organizational learning cultures (Yen and Yen, 2016); openness to experience, conscientiousness, extraversion, agreeableness, and neuroticism (Cui, 2017); trust and team effectiveness (Alsharo et al., 2017); and enjoyment in helping others along with monetary rewards, management support, change of knowledge-sharing behaviour, and recognition (Razmerita et al., 2016) .

Knowledge-Sharing from an Islamic Perspective

The acquisition of knowledge is promoted in Islam as it is part of the obligation as a Muslim. Knowledge in Islam is a revelation from Allah and is transferred to human beings through multiple channels (Yaakub, 2011). Many verses in the holy Qur'an have stated that mankind is the vicegerent of the Earth, and are hence responsible for carrying out the duty to pursue and distribute knowledge (Yaakub, 2011; Azizan, Alahoul, Alwi, & Mohd Zarif, 2016; Hussain et al., 2014). The first verse in the Qur'an – *Surah al-'Alaq* – has emphasized on knowledge-seeking, and discovery-making in this world (Ghafar, Don, & Awang, 2009; Ghafar et al., 2009). Yaakub (2011) concluded that knowledge co-exists with mankind and therefore, it is incumbent of the latter to seek and apply knowledge for their needs. Hussain et al. (2014) elaborated on faith and virtue, which are part of the dimensions of knowledge management in Islam. Faith is defined as the inner beliefs, thoughts, and behaviors towards Islam which must be possessed by every Muslim in order understand the basis for the creation of mankind in this world. On the other hand, virtue is an implication of faith, whereby a Muslim has attained the goals of their life in this world. In Islam, seeking for knowledge or learning is considered act of worship (Robinson, 1992). The rewards and importance of knowledge is also written in the Hadith by the Prophet Muhammad (peace be upon him):

Do you know who is most generous? ... God is the Most Generous, then I am most generous to humankind, and the most generous people after me will be those who will acquire knowledge and then disseminate it. (They) will come on the Day of Resurrection singly, like a ruler. (Tirmidhi, 93)

According to Ghafar et al. (2009), Islam has built a basis for knowledge sharing from the prophet's time, where knowledge has been distributed in a systematic manner through the construction of educational infrastructures and the role of leaders. The Prophet Muhammad's speech on knowledge sharing was recorded by Abu Bakr As-Siddiq, the first Caliph of Islam who succeeded the Prophet's leadership following his death. The Prophet said:

No doubt your blood, property, the sub-narrator Muhammad thought that Abu Bakr had also mentioned and your honor (chastity), are sacred to one another as is the sanctity of this day of yours in this month of yours. It is incumbent on those who are present to inform those who are absent." (Muhammad the Sub-narrator used to say, "Allah's Messenger told the truth.") The Prophet repeated twice: "No doubt! Haven't I conveyed Allah's message to you (Abu Bakr, 47)

The foundation of knowledge sharing promoted by the Prophet is applicable in the current Islamic economic environment. The increasing number of Islamic-related industrial organizations in Malaysia, for instance, has created a necessity to explore the aspects of knowledge sharing from an Islamic perspective (Ahmad et al., 2010). However, the motivation to adopt knowledge sharing in Islamic related organizations such as Halal food organizations are influenced by two principles under Islamic perspective namely (i) religiosity and (ii) Islamic work ethics.

Religiosity

Islam encourages its true believers to engage in business by providing a comprehensive set of guidelines, including what is permitted and prohibited in the Holy Qurán (Abeng, 1997) and demonstrated by the Prophet Muhammad, who was also a businessman prior to being appointed as Islam's messenger (Salahudin et al., 2016). Beekun and Badawi, (2005) are also highlighted that the two primary sources of business principles in Islamic religion are the Holy *Qurán*, and the *Hadith* i.e., the words, actions and the approval of the Prophet Muhammad. It is an obligation as a Muslim to strictly follow the Islamic teachings in all aspects of life including in business management. Individuals who are deeply religious and committed to their beliefs are more likely to follow their religion's laws and customs (Mallasi & Ainin, 2015). The commitment of believers to the religion's laws and customs is known as religiosity. A religious Muslim believes that performing his duties and playing his roles and responsibilities in an organization is an act of worship as a servant of Allah (God) therefore they uphold the principles like trust, justice, promoting goodness, and preventing evil not only for the personal or material benefits but also for Allah's pleasures (Sulaiman et al., 2013). Religiosity is reflected in Islamic management principles and practices in an Islamic organization and defined as the discipline that approaches organizational management from the perspective of revealed and other Islamic sources of wisdom, resulting in applications that are compatible with Islamic beliefs and practices (Ahmad et al., 2010). It is also can be explained as the process of planning, organizing, leading, and controlling the efforts of organizational stakeholders and other resources while relying on Allah's (SWT) and His Prophet's guidance with accountability, honesty, and integrity mentality in order to achieve predefined goals (Sulaiman et al., 2013).

In terms of knowledge sharing, true Muslim understands that it is one of the obligations that must be fulfilled, and it is a good deed that will be rewarded by Allah. By completing this obligation in an organizational context, one has contributed to the dissemination of knowledge as directed in the Qurán and Hadith.

Islamic Work Ethics

Islamic work ethics is an ethical notion founded on Islamic teachings and principles that are based on faith (Salahudin et al., 2016). It is also defined as a set of moral standards that control and steer employees' behaviors and attitudes at work, based on the teachings of the Qur'an and the words of Prophet Muhammad (Udin et al., 2022). The Islamic work ethics emphasizes that in any organization, a Muslim employee is actually carrying his duty towards the god, the creator of the earth for the sake of the Islamic community (Muslim Ummah) (Chanzanagh & Akbarnejad, 2011).

Islamic work ethic dimensions are being established based on the Islamic ethics principles that promote unity, justice, trusteeship and balance (Rice, 1999). Tawheed, or unity, is a term that refers to a person's relationship with God and other people. It is a concept that whatever is done in this world has a strong relationship to what will be gained in the hereafter, thus by adhering to this unity principle, a Muslim will constantly be encouraged to give their best in their profession. On top of that, a Muslim must treat other people as a brother or sister therefore cooperation and equality of efforts are promoted. Islam promotes its followers to remove any signs of injustice, exploitation, and oppression from society through the justice or 'Adalah concept. In promoting justice, Islamic work ethics emphasis on the well-being and welfare of others and avoid of being individualistic (Udin et al., 2022). Trusteeship on the other hand refers to the concept where being a Muslim one is a vicegerent of the earth (Rice, 1999). As a trustee all economic activities are considered as a responsibility rather than wealth creation and therefore will be treated as the character of worship. Balance is also one of the Islamic work ethics where as a Muslim one is suppose to be moderate in all affairs to ensure social well-being and fair development of all human being covering all aspects of human potentials (Rice, 1999).

Upholding Islamic work ethics therefore will be a driving factor for knowledge sharing in Islamic-related organizations. For example, the unity concept encouraged a true Muslim to consider other people's development as part of the mutual advantages from knowledge sharing activities, while also nurturing the relationship with Allah by completing a good deed. Justice, trusteeship as well as balance principles in Islamic work ethics are also supporting the knowledge sharing behavior among Muslim employees in Islamic related organizations in this research context, Halal food organizations. A Muslim, according to Hussain et al., (2014), need strong willpower in order to conduct and act sincerely in Allah's favor. Understanding of religiosity and Islamic work ethics concepts have an impact on strong willpower.

Both religiosity and Islamic work ethics are the items under Islamic perspective dimension in the proposed knowledge sharing adoption model for this research.

THEORETICAL BACKGROUND

Technology – Organization - Environment (TOE) Framework

The Technology – Organization - Environment (TOE) framework describes that the adoption and implementation of a technology in an organization are influenced by three different perspectives, namely (i) technology, (ii) organization, and (iii) external environment (Oliveira et al., 2011). This framework, which was introduced by Tornatzky and Fleischer (1990), has been applied in diverse research, especially those on the adoption of information systems in various fields. Alqahtani (2016) argues that the advantage of this framework is that it provides adequate details to enable its adaptation in an organizational context. Its flexibility has become a source of motivation for researchers to adapt the model to various studies on the potential impact of an innovation towards an organization (Alqahtani, 2016). Therefore, the TOE framework is the adoption theory of choice for this research, and has been improved upon by the addition of new perspectives, specifically the individual perspective and moderated by Islamic perspective. Figure 1 below depicts the original TOE framework:

Figure 1.

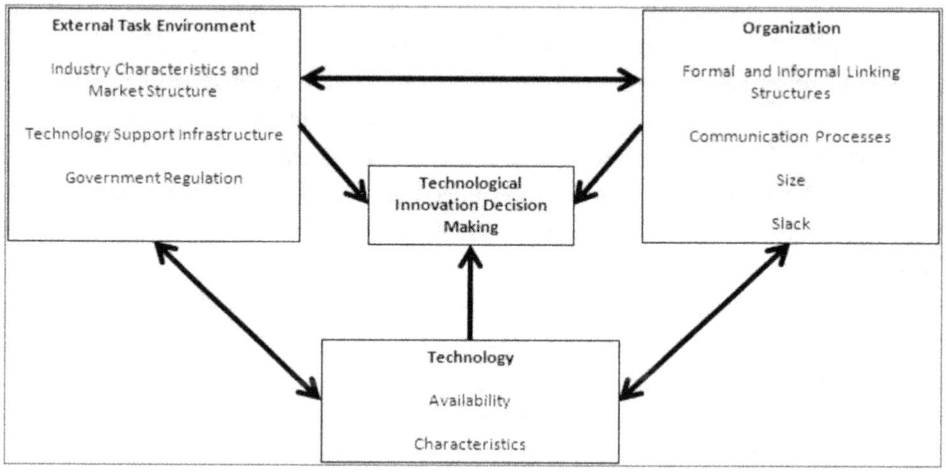

Technology is the main factor for the success in adopting an innovation (Alqahtani, 2016). The technological aspect of a firm refers to the technology, internal or otherwise, which is relevant to the firm (Roger, 1990; Hoti, 2015). Meanwhile, the organizational aspect denotes the structure, size, resources, and employees of a firm, as well as the linkages between the employees. Likewise, the environment aspect refers to the general structure of an industry, competitors, governmental regulations, as well as the constituents of the market. According to Alqahtani (2016), organizational culture has a great influence towards the acceptance of change. The organizational aspect also includes the managerial support for and the employees' knowledge of technology adoption (Chiu et al., 2017). Additionally, the environment aspect encompasses the external aspects that influence adoption, which include industrial and government pressures as well as consumer factors (Hoti, 2015).

TOE framework has been demonstrated to be an effective theory in adoption research but is not intended to be a fix theory (Balaid et al., 2014). Many researchers have proposed that the TOE framework be used as an introductory theory for adoption research, but that it be integrated with other theories in order to make it relevant to the specific research context. Alqahtani (2016) also highlighted that the said framework has the capacity to be expanded via the addition of more factors. Since Halal food organizations are being established based on the Islamic principles such as the Islamic law of Halal food preparation and handling with the ultimate aim to gain Allah's pleasure by upholding the religiosity and Islamic work ethics principles, this research therefore, is modifying the original TOE framework by adding the Islamic perspective dimension. The modified TOE framework resulting in enhanced knowledge sharing adoption model for Halal food industry.

CONCEPTUAL MODEL

The TOE framework provided the basis for the factors that could have influenced the existence of knowledge sharing practices in an organization. From the Islamic perspective, knowledge sharing is a responsibility of a Muslim (and hence, Halal organizations), and it creates more meaningful associations with knowledge sharing practices in Halal food organizations. Understanding one's responsibility as a Muslim as Allah's vicegerent under the religiosity principle and Islamic work ethics makes the implementation of information sharing easier for Halal food firms.

Hussain Alsayed et al. (2012) believed that knowledge sharing would not be successful without technological elements, especially if it involved wide geographical areas. This context referred to the current and future states of technology. According to a research by Sandhu, Jain, & Ahmad (2011), a lack of information technology (IT) systems is a major barrier to the success of knowledge sharing. The inability to provide a good IT platform will reduce the efficiency of knowledge sharing initiatives in an organization. Alsharo *et al.*, (2017) also highlighted that the technology used may have an impact on the development of trust and the knowledge shared by team members. However, according to Hussain et al. (2014), technology acts as the platform, media or tool to facilitate knowledge sharing activities by providing easy access to data, converting them to information and wisdom. In technology perspective, prior studies ranked relative advantage or perceived benefits, compatibility and complexity as the top three adoption factors followed by security and privacy.

The organizational perspective lists numerous factors based on the nature of the business and organization where knowledge sharing adoption is being strategized. An organization's readiness refers to the resources owned by the organization to adopt technology, including resources such as financial, people, infrastructure and facilities that support the adoption. The size of the organization where the bigger the organization, the adoption level towards an innovation will be higher due to availability of resources that can facilitate adoption successfully.

The last perspective is environment, which focuses on the influence of external factors such as competition, government support, external partners as well as industry pressure (Gangwar et al., 2015).

METHODOLOGY

This research has used qualitative phenomenology approach in light of its aim to evaluate the comprehension and perceptions of the respondents regarding knowledge sharing in their organization. Phenomenology approach was introduced by Husserl (1970) which focuses on the several individuals who shared same experience of the phenomenon being investigated – in this research, knowledge sharing phenomenon. In order to come up with a more focused and in-depth inquiry, only one organization was selected for this study which is Ayamas Food Cooperation Sdn. Bhd, a well-established Halal food organization in Malaysia. The initial meeting with the company Deputy General Manager has confirmed that knowledge sharing is being practiced in the organization.

Table 1. List of respondents and justification of selection

Level, position & department	Code	Interview method	Justification for selection as respondent
Top level Management Deputy General Manager	R1	Face to face	Among the top leaders, he has the authority to give instructions and initiate activities. Upon joining the company in early 2017, he introduced knowledge sharing activities in the Human Resources Department.
Manager Quality Assurance Department	R2	Face to face	In leading her department, she interacts with a lot of people, especially vendors and suppliers where knowledge sharing is essential to her job.
Executive Human Resources Department Executive	R3	Face-to-face	This respondent is one of the active participants in knowledge sharing activities in the organization.
Executive Industrial Relations Executive, Human Resource Department	R4	Face to face	This respondent is one of the active participants in knowledge sharing activities in the organization.
Executive Shari'ah Compliance Unit Executive	R5	Phone interview	This respondent is responsible for Halal compliance matters in the organization including Halal awareness, training, certification, and auditing.
Temporary worker Industrial Attachment Staff, R&D Department	R6	Phone interview	Even though this respondent is only a temporary worker, his observation and experience of the knowledge sharing practices in the organization is also required. He involved in a special project at the organization and it requires him to interact with different people at different levels and departments.

Semi-structured interviews were conducted where staff from different departments and levels of management, in addition to their roles, were identified and interviewed. Interview protocol was developed as a guideline for the interview process. This exercise examined their current knowledge sharing activities and experiences, the results of which would be used to develop the final enhanced knowledge sharing model for the Halal food industry. Six staff were selected to be the respondents and their roles and justification of selection are summarized in Table 1 below:

Following the interviews, data were transcribed and analysed using qualitative data analysis software, Atlas.ti, with thematic analysis used to identify codes and themes before being interpreted in the research findings' section. Atlas.ti has generated the quotations and document numbers automatically during the coding process and that will be the reference in the finding section. The quotations will be presented in this format; (Respondent Code-Document number: quotation number). For example, "R1-1:20" refers to respondent 1, document 1 and quotation 20.

FINDINGS AND DISCUSSION

Knowledge Sharing Practices in the Halal Food Industry

The first research question that had to be addressed in this research was "what are the current knowledge sharing practices in the Halal food organization?". Five themes have been identified with regards to this research question during the analysis stage of the study, namely knowledge sharing as a new initiative, leader's role, knowledge sharing embedded in policies, formal and informal sessions, and technology as a connector. The following are the summary of the themes for this research question:

1. Knowledge sharing as a new initiative - Knowledge sharing sessions have been introduced informally in the HR department. Every morning, all staff gathered for morning talk and knowledge sharing, prayers, and sharing of individual activities. Staff were encouraged to share anything with team members, even if it had nothing to do with their jobs. There were also inductions, trainings, and informal face-to-face sessions that encouraged knowledge sharing, according to the respondents. They were able to not only learn from each other, but also understand each other's tasks, routines, jobs, and responsibilities. The following quotations were found in the interview transcripts to support this finding: "Knowledge sharing in this office has started in March this year when the new Deputy General Manager joined this department. He proposed a short stand-up session every morning so that everybody can share anything related to work as well as any knowledge that benefits the staff" (R3-4:20).

This statement is supported by the Deputy General Manager himself who is also one of the respondents for this research (R1) as per following quotations: "So, we initiate the morning prayer and morning talk in HR. We start internally in HR. Once it becomes the culture in HR, then we introduce it to other departments" (R1-2:15). "This is not instructed by anyone; this is my own initiative. I knew that this is a good thing so why not we proceed with that. I called up a meeting and I told them I want to proceed" (R1-2:43). "We will call the head of departments for meetings and brief them. The head of departments will share the knowledge with their staff. However, in terms of making the staff understands, it is under the responsibility of their superiors" (R5-14:14).

2. Leaders' role - Leaders were critical in establishing the knowledge sharing culture, procedures, and initiating events that enabled knowledge sharing in the organization. The top management and parent company of this organization have established some procedures for knowledge distribution and knowledge sharing among all employees. The leaders initiated the internal SOPs to ensure that all employees had all of the necessary knowledge to understand the company's directions, new initiatives, and strategies. These would make it easier for staff from various departments and units to understand why they were assigned certain tasks, initiatives, and activities. The importance of the leaders' roles in the knowledge sharing practices in the organization has shown in the following quotations:

At the high level of management, knowledge sharing happens very fast under the supervision of the top management. The management brings a new culture that is very clear where we can see the way that knowledge is distributed to the next level. For example, right after a meeting with the top management, another meeting will be initiated for the head of departments, subsector leaders, and restaurant managers to share the outcomes from the top management. It is expecting that the leaders will share and deliver the same outcomes until it reaches the lower-level staff. (R6-1:56)

It is also a leader's responsibility to establish guidelines for how Halal knowledge is distributed throughout the organization. The organization's Shariáh Compliance Unit for example is required to ensure that all new employees at all subsidiaries, including restaurant chains, are exposed to Halal-related knowledge. Head of each department is also responsible to ensure that all departmental staff understand the meaning of Halal and Halal processes in the company as quoted from the interview transcripts: "From management at the head of department (HOD) level, training will be conducted at least once to understand the Halal certification process. So, at the end of the day, the HODs will brief to their staff" (R5-14:13). "There are a few units under human resource and each unit has its own HOD. So HOD will play their role to inform and update the latest development as well as the current issues" (R3-3:4).

3. Knowledge sharing embedded policies and procedures – knowledge sharing has been formalized through organization's policies and procedures such as induction sessions for new hired, trainings, talk, briefings, audits, and visits that involved other multiple people including external stakeholders. These can be found in few interview transcripts with the respondents. "Normally, we will share the Halal knowledge through an induction program organized for the new staff. We will explain all the existing processes, we will show our corporate video and all other videos that we have" (R1-2:4). "For knowledge sharing related to Halal, we have training. It is related to Halal practices and Good Manufacturing Practices (GMP). All staff are compulsory to attend that training at least once" (R5-14:1). "When our new customers would like to purchase from us, they are visiting our plant to audit our processes. From that audit exercise, we will share our practices, policies, and standards. We will bring them for tour in our sites to show our real practices" (R6-14:22). "Sometimes, we export our products to Brunei and Singapore. Brunei for example, is very strict in terms of Halal. So, they call these people from Brunei to check and visit the site. Every time we would like to send our products to Brunei, they will come and check our production. It means that, every time they come, knowledge sharing will happen" (R6-1:62).
4. Formal and informal knowledge sharing sessions - The knowledge in this organization is shared with others, either in formal or informal sessions. Some of the informal sessions are the individual face-to-face sessions where discussions might be related to the individual and confidential issues. Some of the quotes depicted in the interviews: "Most of the discipline problems in my department for example will be discussed with other members in the department so that we can exchange opinions and ideas especially from previous experiences and knowledge on action that should be taken" (R3-3:26). "In my case, I love to share. I will inform others what I am doing, what had happened yesterday, and what is going on today. We share so that our officemates know what is going on. It is not necessarily office matters, there are other things that can be shared in 10–15 minutes sessions" (R4-4:19). "We can have informal sessions like gathering, communal work, and organize a potluck where knowledge and experience exchange can happen informally in the engaging situations" (R4-4:12).

5. Technology as connector - The staff were utilizing current technologies, such as emails and Whatsapp, for knowledge exchange and distribution. However, for the staff who have no access to the technology during working hours, for example, the staff at the production lines and slaughtering plants, knowledge was cascaded down to that level through meetings, face-to-face interactions, or interactions with superiors as well as formal trainings and briefing sessions. For example, "We will use email and whatsapp to distribute and share information about any progress, event and activities with other staff" (R3-3:3).

The importance of communication channel as medium of delivery had been highlighted seriously by one of the respondents as quoted below:

Channel is a tool or something that can link people in order to materialize the knowledge sharing. For example, we use email to share messages between different departments. However, we are not sure whether the channel is effective or not. How about action? Is email the best channel that can share message and at the same time encourage prompt action? Therefore, we need to identify the most effective channel that enable understanding and direct to the right person. (R6-1:50)

TOE Analysis of Knowledge Sharing in Halal Food Industry

The second research question of this study is answered based on the TOE framework. The research question is "What are the factors that influence the implementation of knowledge-sharing in the Halal food industry?". The interview transcripts were coded and themed based on the TOE framework namely technology, organization, and environment. However, the dynamics of TOE framework allowed additional theme found in the transcripts added in the final model which is Islamic perspective that will be added in the final adoption model.

Technology

Knowledge sharing would be adopted if the technology platforms exist to enable the communication and interaction between the staff and stakeholders as stated by (R3-3:3) and (R6-1:50) during the interviews. Technology can be a delivery medium to improve the impact of the knowledge shared. Therefore, to pursue with knowledge sharing adoption strategy, the organization must identify the technology gap between the staff and stakeholders so that knowledge sharing could successfully be implemented. Technology that is being used for knowledge sharing should be compatible with the individual staff characteristics. Different staff in the Halal food industry have different access to technology and different education levels based on their job area. As example, the staff at the production line have no access to the technology while performing their jobs in the manufacturing plant. Thus, the organization should do something to overcome this problem. In this context, the organization should be able to identify other compatible the technology platforms for knowledge sharing activities so that no one will be left behind in the organization. This issue is highlighted in the interview by R6 as quoted below.

Yes, knowledge sharing practice is there. However, the knowledge does not reach people at the bottom level. Sometimes we are also not sure whether the knowledge already distributed to the low levels or not. I give you one example. Let's say the knowledge are distributed and shared using the email as a channel. Maybe we thought that email is the best channel for knowledge sharing. But the question is, is email being used by everybody in the company? How about people at the production line? Do they know how to use email? In fact, they don't use email to perform their daily routines. So, how? (R6-1:121)

Organization

Leadership, the roles of the stakeholders, organizational policies and non-technology channels are the items found under the organization perspective of this research. Knowledge sharing can be successfully adopted in the organization with supportive leaders. Leaders should initiate, plan, and strategize on how knowledge sharing could be embedded in daily routines of all staff at all levels. Some of the quotations that mentioned leaders' role for knowledge sharing initiative are; "Yes, initiated by the leader. The leader knows which channel is the most suitable for the knowledge sharing" (R6-1:43), "HOD will play their roles where they will interact with other staff to update and discuss the current developments and issues" (R3-3:4). "I don't think all staff support at the beginning. However, they have to participate because it is the instruction from the head of department. Once the head started, they have to do it. Even though at the beginning they don't like it, but after some time, they become willing to participate" (R4-4:8).

The organization has many internal and external stakeholders. Organizations should be able to identify their stakeholders and their roles (general or specific) so that knowledge sharing initiative includes the stakeholders as the enabler. The quotes that highlighted the roles of stakeholders in knowledge sharing adoption are; "The benefit is we can share, for example, we understand IR department tasks, what is he doing today, what are the activities that will happen today. If there is anything that they will do, he shares with us so that we know. So, I can see it is good to share knowledge" (R3-4:2). "From the staff perspective the training will be able to make them exposed to what other departments are doing. For example, the staff might be working in the cutting department only. So, they don't know what is going on in slaughtering, how the chickens are slaughtered etc. Therefore, we explain how it is being practiced in the plant" (R6-14:9).

Knowledge sharing adoption is only successful if this initiative is embedded in the organization's policy, procedures, and business practices. In Ayamas for example, knowledge sharing elements are embedded in the training, induction, purchasing, quality control as well as the new product development strategies as quoted in the interview transcripts (R1-2:4), (R5-14:1), (R6-14:22) and (R6-1:62) highlighted in the previous section.

Knowledge sharing adoption in Halal food industry needs to consider staff that have limited access to technology. It is therefore the organization must have proper channel either proper procedures or methods to enable knowledge exchange between stakeholders. This finding discovers that innovation adoption does not necessarily solved by technology existence. Evaluation towards the nature of the organization especially its people should be done to ensure adoption strategy is successful.

Environment

External stakeholders support is one of the key factors that influences the knowledge sharing adoption in the industry. An organization cannot stand alone in producing, delivering, and providing its services to the end consumers. It is able to ensure both the knowledge sharing initiative and the strategy are successful. Some of the quotes that highlighted the stakeholders supports are: "It can be on certain topics, certain area, certain department, there are topics that covered by certain departments which will be organized by them. If it is inter-departmental topics, the related departments will organize together. But if we call outsiders, for example, lab-related people, new technology, skills from outside of the company, we will call them and organize the session" (R2-10:21). "We have to organize more collaboration events where at the same time, we will be able to share our information, company direction in a more informal situation." (R3-4:10).

Additional Findings for Knowledge Sharing Adoption Factors

Other than three perspectives of TOE framework discussed in the previous section, there are additional perspectives found such as Individual and Islamic perspectives.

Individual

The individual perspective highlighted that individual attitude, job relevancy, awareness and perceived importance as factors that contribute to the knowledge sharing adoption in the Halal food organization. The staff attitude includes their willingness to share, grab, and distribute the knowledge as well as positive attitude toward the knowledge sharing initiative in the organization. The staff are only willing to participate and support the knowledge sharing initiatives when they think that the activities and processes are related to their job. For example, the product development staff know that it is important for them to collaborate and share the knowledge with staff at the production plant so that new product are able to be introduced to the market as expected. Stakeholders' awareness on the importance and impacts of knowledge sharing is an important factor for knowledge sharing adoption. The importance of individual factor for knowledge sharing adoption are highlighted in the following quotes: "We have to make our staff understand that knowledge sharing is important because we have to make them realize that they are working in a very sensitive industry" (R1-2:30). "The staff are positive because they know it is part of the requirement for them to gain the knowledge in order to perform their job. Otherwise, they cannot do their work" (R2-10:8). "I will be willingly sharing my knowledge if it is instructed and as part of my KPI" (R4-1:45). "For me people will only listen if the knowledge is related to their job. Otherwise, we also do not know do we have to participate in this" (R6-1:52).

Knowledge sharing can be successfully adopted if the organization with positive attitudes of individual staff towards the initiative.

Islamic Perspective

The teaching of Islam is the whole foundation of Halal. The industry, business, stakeholders, and the whole environment in the Halal food industry should be based on the Islamic worldview and the way of life. As a Muslim majority company, the respondents believe that knowledge sharing is part of obligation in Islam. Seeking knowledge as well as sharing the knowledge with others are the responsibility as a vicegerent in the Earth. This perspective is the most dominant aspect in the knowledge sharing adoption of the Halal food organization which is understood as religiosity. The respondents admitted that they are willing to participate in knowledge sharing because of their understanding on Islamic teachings. Islam encourages the knowledge sharing, learning, and promotes learning environment. The evidences are found in the following quotes:

As a staff in Halal food organization, the understanding toward the *amanah* or trust concept as a worker in the Halal company is essential. This can be found in the following quotes in the transcripts: "In the context as a Muslim, we have to look beyond that. What we are doing in this world will be brought to hereafter" (R1-2:37). "Staff has to understand that Halal is not only for the production of Halal products. But we have to make sure that people eat Halal food. Ensuring this is also considered as an act of worship. In my opinion, when we guarantee that Muslims and the public eat Halal, that is our obedient to the god" (R3-3:11). "For me, our staff must be internally and externally okay. They know their responsibilities as a staff toward the company as well as the responsibilities as a Muslim" (R4-2:34). "I am already 50, maybe today or tomorrow I will be no longer in this world. So every day, I must do something good. That is the *Amanah* that given to me" (R1-2:38). "It is our responsibility as a Muslim. Every process must be Halal and compliance to Islamic law. When they understand that, share with them all the time, and they understand that their contributions to the people are actually very big" (R1-2:31). "About the knowledge related to Halal, because we are a Muslim, it is our obligation to know about it" (R4-4:15). The Islamic work ethic elements shown by the staff are the evidence that it has contributed a lot in motivating the staff to adopt knowledge sharing in the organization.

The Islamic perspective is the most influential contribution in this study that shows the uniqueness of this study as compared to other adoption study findings in other industries. The whole perspective of knowledge sharing adoption should be based on the Islamic perspective.

Knowledge Sharing Adoption Model in Halal Food Industry

From the elaboration, there are a lot of themes that can be retrieved and contributed to the knowledge sharing adoption model development in the Halal food industry. Figure 2 below is the illustration of the model which is an enhancement of the original TOE that consists of five main perspectives namely, (i) technology, (ii) individual, (iii) organization, (iv) environment and (v) Islamic perspective.

The technology perspective includes the existence of the technology as the communication channel and compatibility of the technology with the internal working environment. The individual perspective includes the attitude, relevancy to the job, awareness and perceived importance of the individual staff towards knowledge sharing importance in the organization. The organization perspective on the other hand includes leadership, stakeholder identification, organization's policy and non-technology channel. The environment perspective includes external stakeholders' support and customers' expectations. The external stakeholders' supports related to the willingness of the external stakeholders to be part of knowledge sharing initiative in the organization. Based on the experiences of the respondents, the external stakeholders such as potential customers, vendors, suppliers and relevant government agencies always being part of the organization's knowledge sharing activities whenever required. The customers' expectations have become one of the push factors for the company to practice knowledge sharing.

Figure 2.

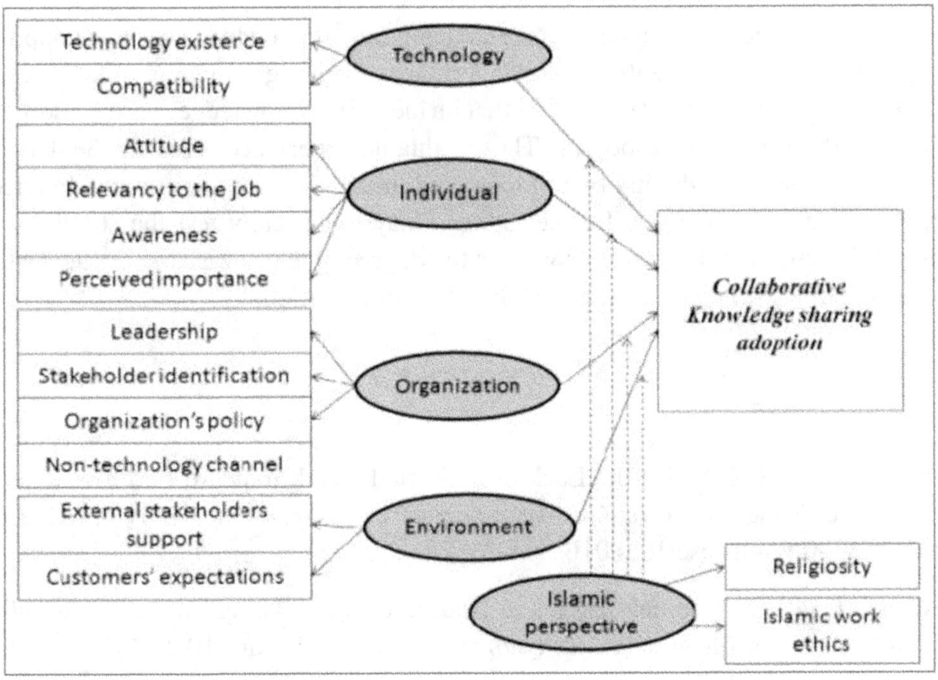

The Islamic perspective is the factor that moderates the individual, organization and environment factors towards knowledge sharing adoption in Halal food industry. Islamic perspective refers to the overall understanding of the Islamic belief and values that crafted the Halal industry itself. Religiosity influences the individual, organization, and environment context of the framework. How the individual reacts and behaves toward something depends on how the religion principles influence them as argued by Ibrahim (2015). At the same time, the organization that establishes based on the religion principles i.e. Halal also shapes its policies, procedures, and the leadership qualities based on the Islamic principles. Islamic work ethics is the way an individual or stakeholder perform their job based on Islamic teachings, beliefs and faith. The Islamic work ethics that constituted within Islamic perspective is the foundation for all decisions, actions and behaviors of the stakeholders towards something including knowledge sharing adoption.

CONCLUSION

This study provides the fundamental understanding of knowledge sharing adoption in the halal food organization. The experiences of the respondents in knowledge sharing were explored and the factors that influence the knowledge sharing adoption are identified from the responses. These valuable experiences provide the data on how can knowledge sharing be implemented in the similar organizations in terms of planning and strategies. Further studies may empirically test the strengths of every dimension and variable as well as the degree of every variable influence the adoption of knowledge sharing in Halal food organizations.

REFERENCES

Abdallah, A. (2021). Has the Lack of a Unified Halal Standard Led to a Rise in Organised Crime in the Halal Certification Sector? *Forensic Science*, *1*(3), 181–193. doi:10.3390/forensicsci1030016

Abeng, T. (1997). Business Ethics in Islamic Context: Perspectives of a Muslim Business Leader. *Business Ethics Quarterly*, *7*(3), 47–54. doi:10.2307/3857312

Ahmad, A., Burgoyne, J., & Weir, D. (2010). The Learning Organization from an Islamic Perspective: A Case Study in Islamic Organization. *8th International Academy of Management and Business (IAMB 2010)*, 1–9.

Alqahtani, F. N. K. (2016). *Identifying the Critical Factors that Impact on The Development of Electronic Government using TOE Framework in Saudi E-Government Context : A Thematic Analysis*. Academic Press.

Alsharo, M., Gregg, D., & Ramirez, R. (2017). Virtual Team Effectiveness: The Role of Knowledge Sharing and Trust. *Information & Management*, *54*(4), 479–490. doi:10.1016/j.im.2016.10.005

Asrar-ul-Haq, M., & Anwar, S. (2016). A Systematic Review of Knowledge Management and Knowledge Sharing: Trends, Issues, and Challenges. *Cogent Business & Management*, *3*(1), 1127744. Advance online publication. doi:10.1080/23311975.2015.1127744

Azizan, N., Alahoul, M. R., Alwi, N. H., & Mohd Zarif, M. M. (2016). Islamic Knowledge: Factors Effective Islamic Knowledge Transfer for Visually Impaired Users via Malaysia e-Learning Websites. *Seminar Perpustakaan Islam Serantau*, 1–19.

Balaid, A., Rozan, M. Z. A., & Abdullah, S. N. (2014). Conceptual Model for Examining Knowledge Maps Adoption in Software Development Organizations. *Asian Social Science*, *10*(15), 118–132. doi:10.5539/ass.v10n15p118

Beekun, R. I., & Badawi, J. A. (2005). Balancing ethical responsibility among multiple organizational stakeholders: The Islamic perspective. *Journal of Business Ethics*, *60*(2), 131–145. doi:10.100710551-004-8204-5

Chanzanagh, H. E., & Akbarnejad, M. (2011). The Meaning and Dimensions of Islamic Work Ethic: Initial Validation of a Multidimensional IWE in Iranian Society. *Procedia: Social and Behavioral Sciences*, *30*, 916–924. doi:10.1016/j.sbspro.2011.10.178

Gangwar, H., Date, H., & Ramaswamy, R. (2015). Understanding Determinants of Cloud Computing Adoption Using an Integrated TAM-TOE Model. *Journal of Enterprise Information Management*, *28*(1), 107–130. doi:10.1108/JEIM-08-2013-0065

Ghafar, A., Don, H. J., & Awang, J. (2009). Knowledge Management and its Impact on Islamic Da ' wah : A Historical Perspective. *Journal of Islamic and Arabic Education*, *1*(2), 61–68.

Hussain, S., Al-Hudawi, V., Musah, M. B., & Hamdan, A. R. (2014). Islamic Worldview on Knowledge Management: Implication for Muslim Education System. *World Journal of Islamic History and Civilization*, *4*(2), 66–74. doi:10.5829/idosi.wjihc.2014.4.2.185

Hussain Alsayed, M., Mohamed Dahlan, H., & Che Hussin, A. R. (2012). Knowledge Sharing in Collaborative Research Activities. *Journal of Information Systems Research and Innovation*, *2*, 1–8.

Husserl, E. (1970). *The Crisis of European Sciences and Transcendental Phenomenology: An Introduction to Phenomenological Philosophy*. Northwestern University Press. doi:10.100713398-014-0173-7.2

Ibrahim, A. (2015). *The Fast Food Consumption Experiences and Identity Construction of British Muslims : A Phenomenological Study*. Issue March.

Janus, S. S. (2016). *Becoming a Knowledge Sharing Organization: A Handbook for Scaling Up Solutions through Knowledge Capturing and Sharing*. World Bank Group. doi:10.1596/978-1-4648-0943-9

Kader Jilani, M. M. A., Fan, L., Islam, M. T., & Uddin, M. A. (2020). The influence of knowledge sharing on sustainable performance: A moderated mediation study. *Sustainability (Switzerland), 12*(3), 1–18. doi:10.3390u12030908

Maizza, A., Fait, M., Scorrano, P., & Iazzi, A. (2019). How Knowledge Sharing Culture Can Become a Facilitator of the Sustainable Development in the Agrifood Sector. *Sustainability (Switzerland), 11*(4), 952. Advance online publication. doi:10.3390u11040952

Mallasi, H., & Ainin, S. (2015). Investigating Knowledge Sharing Behaviour in Academic Environment. *Journal of Organizational Knowledge Management*, 1–19. 10.5171/2015.643253

Market Information. (2013). *Halal Knowledge Centre*. http://www.hdcglobal.com/publisher/hkc_market_information#overview

Rice, G. (1999). Islamic Ethics and the Implications for Business. *Journal of Business Ethics, 18*(4), 345–358. doi:10.1023/A:1005711414306

Robinson, F. (1992). Knowledge, its Transmission and The Making of Muslim Societies. In *The Cambridge Illustrated History of the Islamic World*. Cambridge University Press. https://pure.royalholloway.ac.uk/portal/en/publications/knowledge-its-transmission-and-the-making-of-muslim-societies(13bfabeb-c589-47ec-ad86-21757eb52983).html

Rohman, A., Eliyana, A., Purwana, D., & Hamidah, H. (2020). Individual and Organizational Factors' Effect on Knowledge Sharing Behavior. *Entrepreneurship and Sustainability Issues, 8*(1), 38–48. doi:10.9770/jesi.2020.8.1(3)

Salahudin, S. N., Baharuddin, S. S., Abdullah, M. S., & Osman, A. (2016). The Effect of Islamic Work Ethics on Organizational Commitment. *Procedia Economics and Finance, 35*, 582–590. doi:10.1016/S2212-5671(16)00071-X

Sandhu, M. S., Jain, K. K., & Ahmad, I. U. K. B. (2011). Knowledge Sharing Among Public Sector Employees: Evidence from Malaysia. *International Journal of Public Sector Management, 24*(3), 206–226. doi:10.1108/09513551111121347

Shahbandeh, M. (2018). *Market Value of Halal Foods Worldwide from 2017 to 2023*. https://www.statista.com/statistics/562857/market-value-of-halal-products-worldwide/

Sulaiman, M., Sabian, N. A. A., & Othman, A. K. (2013). The Understanding of Islamic Management Practices among Muslim Managers in Malaysia. *Asian Social Science, 10*(1), 189–199. doi:10.5539/ass.v10n1p189

Udin, U., Dananjoyo, R., Shaikh, M., & Vio Linarta, D. (2022). Islamic Work Ethics, Affective Commitment, and Employee's Performance in Family Business: Testing Their Relationships. *SAGE Open*, *12*(1), 1–12. doi:10.1177/21582440221085263

Yaakub. (2011). Islamic Conceptualisation of Knowledge Management. *American Journal of Economics and Business Administration, 3*(2), 363–369. doi:10.3844/ajebasp.2011.363.369

Chapter 6
Leveraging Collective Wisdom to Impact Workplace Culture

Jeff M. Allen
https://orcid.org/0000-0003-0551-0539
University of North Texas, USA

Amy Rosellini
https://orcid.org/0000-0001-6704-9333
New Western, USA

Malak Khader
University of North Texas, USA

Millicent Njeri
University of North Texas, USA

ABSTRACT

Wisdom, both personal and collective, is largely missing in both information science and knowledge management literature. Workplace culture and shared vision impact every level of organizations in a positive or negative direction. A healthy culture and optimistic shared vision can provide a climate for knowledge sharing and provide opportunity for rich transfer of collective wisdom in our workplace communities. Wisdom is evolved from knowledge and can be cultivated by knowledge and learning specialists. This chapter places wisdom as the desired result of successful knowledge management and provides an opportunity for scholars, students, and practitioners to leverage this rich resource in organizations and extends the models, processes, and theories.

DOI: 10.4018/978-1-6684-4431-3.ch006

INTRODUCTION

"Wisdom is the pinnacle of human cognitive performance" (Allen, 2022, p. 114). Organizations seek competitive advantages to leverage effectiveness and productivity. Knowledge managers are responsible for the tacit and explicit knowledge sharing tools, functions, and processes needed to ensure that individuals can access and utilize institutional knowledge and resources needed to effectively complete their job duties. Current theories, models and information science, knowledge management and Human Resource Development (HRD) offer little significant insight into this area of scholarship. The broad topic of wisdom has gained some traction in business and management journals, training magazines as well as within HRD/training function of organizations seeking avenues to better understand and enhance knowledge discovery, acquisition, sharing, and implementation. Wisdom is not a philosophical exercise but a viable avenue to a competitive edge in our global knowledge economy.

This chapter presents an extension of scholarship presented in "Fostering Wisdom at Work" (Allen, 2022) and is catered for knowledge management scholars and practitioners. The purpose of the chapter is to open the field of wisdom to knowledge management scholars so that, as a field, we can further our understanding of individual and collective wisdom to impact organization culture. It should serve as a reference for students learning about wisdom and a roadmap for KM to help leaders and learners in different segments.

The chapter begins by describing the relationship of wisdom to information science and provides an overview of wisdom from a knowledge management and learning perspective. An understanding of classical individual wisdom provides a solid theoretical foundation to explore the cultivation of collective wisdom in organizations. Finally, the researchers explore collective wisdom as it applies to workplace communities and organizations. Wisdom is highly prized yet remains a largely untapped resource in knowledge organizations.

DIKW

To understand wisdom, within the current context of our field, we need to review how wisdom is most often presented. In the field of information science, the DIKW hierarchy is used to characterize information organization and is often expressed as a hierarchical pyramid with data at the base and wisdom at the apex. The DIKW model, attributed by Ackoff (1989), prescribes a direct, and building relationship between data, information, knowledge, and wisdom.

"Data are a collection or set of facts (numbers, measurements, observations, or descriptions) that can be quantitative or qualitative in nature" (Allen, 2022, p. 119). Data is seldom useful for decision making, but it is raw material for decision making that needs to be processed and organized in a meaningful way to become information. As knowledge managers we must capture accurate data and transform data to information.

Data can *transform* to information when it is contextualized. "Information is structured data with attached meaning, connection, and significance" (Allen, 2022, p. 118). Information is learned from data and is sufficient to make decision making. As knowledge managers we ensure that the information is each to find, use, share and learn from to facilitate organizational knowledge.

Knowledge can be *created* from information when it is internalized by a person so that it can be put into practice (Davenport, 1998). As knowledge managers we are concerned with knowledge acquisition, knowledge curation and knowledge sharing of tacit, explicit, and embedded knowledge.

Wisdom can *evolve* from knowledge when an individual uses their knowledge, experience and understanding to identify patterns, make connections, and underlying principles to make sound judgements and wise decisions. As knowledge managers, we are challenged to move beyond knowledge acquisition and knowledge transfer to foster individual and collective wisdom that not only include the knowledge and experience but an understanding self and understanding others. This cultivates a benevolent implementation of knowledge solutions that produce a beneficial course of action for the individuals, workplace community, larger organization, and society.

The hierarchical aspect of DIKW implies a "building block" relationship. First data, then information, then knowledge and finally wisdom. The hierarchy is easy to understand yet implies that we start from raw data and can build to knowledge. This knowledge is then applied to create wisdom. If this hierarchy is transferred on a continuum or possess, we might see that Data is raw and unorganized. Information is *learned* from data as it is organized to become structured and useful. Knowledge is *created* from information as it is contextualized and synthesized. However, knowledge may *evolve* to wisdom.

The hierarchical nature of the DIKW model has been called into question by researchers (e.g., Frické, 2009; Rowley, 2007) due to the conservative definitions of the four concepts. For example, the distinction between data and information is not so clear as some view information as a type of data. The relationship between wisdom and knowledge is complicated and is not simply an accumulation of data, information, and knowledge, but rather than simply connecting principles and applying knowledge to practice. The complex relationship between wisdom and knowledge *is much more than* connecting principles and applying knowledge to practice, but an integration of a complete array of human traits that work in partnership with knowledge application and experience. The next sections explore this complex relationship and discuss how collective wisdom can be cultivated in the workplace community.

WISDOM

Wilson (1999) stated "The world henceforth will be run by synthesizers, people able to put together the right information at the right time, think critically about it, and make important choices wisely. (p. 294)". Development of wisdom not only benefits the individual but benefits the organization as a whole. As wisdom is fostered in the individual, and collective wisdom is cultivated in the workplace community our organizational knowledge will flourish over time. This parallels the system that the grandparents impart their wisdom to the younger generation to enhance the survival of the species. In the same way, within our organization, we must develop strategies to not only grow wisdom but develop mechanisms for discovery, acquisition, and transfer of both knowledge and wisdom.

Wisdom can be classified as tactic, explicit, or embedded in nature in parallel to knowledge categories. Wisdom can be discovered, wisdom can be curated, wisdom can be shared. Allen states that "Collective wisdom is a shared understanding of wise behaviors that are collected and curated by an interconnected group to create a beneficial course of action for the group, communities, and society." (2022, p. 119).

As a society, we have created many advanced measures of knowledge and intelligence and use these instruments to assess progress and create development plans to enhance knowledge acquisition and transfer. Yet, there is an enormous lack for research, modeling, and instrumentation for wisdom in business. "Growing research suggests that wisdom is a personally and socially useful construct; it has been linked to better overall physical and mental health, well-being, happiness, life satisfaction, and resilience" (Jeste & Ellen, 2019, p. 129).

The field of knowledge management, and information science in general has little published research or scholarly work around wisdom that provides theories, models, theories, processes to guide professionals in the area of wisdom or collectively wisdom. Wisdom has been investigated by the fields of management, business, or leadership. Within the last 10 years, business and management have turned to the subject of wisdom to better develop business and leadership ethics. Wisdom is a "uniquely human virtue combining compassion, intuition, knowledge, experience, and sound judgment to create a beneficial course of action for individuals, communities, and society." (2022, p. 18). For knowledge managers, religious, philosophical, and sociological perspectives can provide some insight into the theoretical construct of individual wisdom. Learning specialists and knowledge managers must have tools to better understand, model and leverage the acquisition and sharing of wisdom in organizations.

Allen (2022) advances that individual wisdom contains three separate constructs that include: knowledge and experience, understanding self, and understanding others. These three aspects, or dimensions, of wisdom provide a comprehensive perspective of wisdom that can assist knowledge managers to better understand all aspects of this complicated human virtue. Unlike data, information, and knowledge, wisdom is set apart by its virtuous characteristics. Contextualized through experience, capable of viewing from the self- and others-lens, wisdom surpasses knowledge in its intrinsic ability to see the whole of knowledge complete with feeling, perspective, and depth.

Figure 1. Wisdom construct model (Allen, 2022)

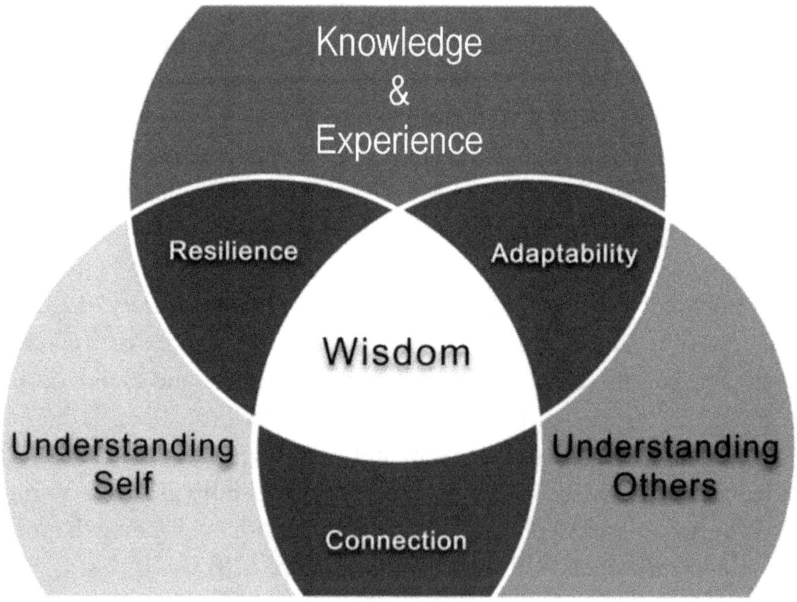

Knowledge and Experience

"Experience is the practice or the application of knowledge over a period of time. Knowledge is the depth and breadth of information and skills acquired through interaction, participation, observation integrated with an individual's comprehension of connected experiences" (Allen, 2022, p. 119). There is a strong relationship between our depth and breadth of experience and the depth and breadth of knowledge. Depth of knowledge grows considerably when we spend time learning a narrow field (subject-matter expertise). The downside of specialization is a reduced breadth of knowledge and experience. Our breadth of knowledge and experience grows when we study and can connect multiple disciplines or related areas of knowledge.

The modern figure of speech, *"A Jack of all trades, master of none."* aptly describes the subject matter expert. However, the original phrase more aptly describes the generalist when stated as the full quote, *"Jack of all trades, master of none, but oftentimes better than master of one."* Rather than a narrow path that focuses on a narrowly defined expertise and experience, we may be better served by balancing a depth and breadth of knowledge. This balance provided individuals to not only gain knowledge in one area but gain new knowledge of multiple disciplines. It requires both learning and unlearning, abstract reasoning, and systematic thinking to apply knowledge across experiences. Both depth and breadth of knowledge and experience are critical to fostering wisdom in individuals and cultivating collective wisdom.

Personal characteristics of knowledge and experience may be observed as: abstract reasoning, competence, explicit knowledge, implicit knowledge, insight, intuition, learning, unlearning, systematic thinking, objectiveness, perception, sound judgment, systematic thinking, and unlearning.

Understanding Self

The second construct of wisdom is understanding self. Strength of character and resilience are enhanced by overcoming adversity. Resilience is a key to understanding self. Understanding self is concerned with an ability to better understand how we respond to adversity in our lives. Adversity is an underutilized leverage to build resilience. Both individuals and organizations cycle through periods of comfort and time of adversity. However, adverse situations provide opportunities for self-growth. "Resilience speaks to our ability to bounce back and grow despite adversity. Resilience is a key between self-reliance and sound judgment." (Allen, 2022, p. 118).

From a personal perspective, individual resilience is strengthened from encountering and overcoming adversity (Luthar, Crossman, and Small, 2015). This is true for individuals or organizations (Herbane, 2019). Research in the areas of multiple and emotional intelligence (Garner, 1983; Goleman 1995) provides tremendous insight into both understanding self and understanding others. Understanding self is independent of other people. A person living alone or in isolation or working independently in an organization can grow their knowledge and experience and understanding self independently.

Shaolin monks are a prime example of individuals with high levels of self-understanding dedicating a portion of their life to understand how to overcome adversity in both physical martial arts and meditation. Understanding self is not building comfort, perfection, or even mastery. It is built with a personal drive for growth requiring creativity that matches the adversity facing the individual. We build understanding and resiliency through persistence, growth, learning and unlearning during challenging or adverse situations that stretch our ability to adapt to change.

As knowledge managers, adversity provides unique opportunities for understanding organizational response to the adversity and building resilience to future adversity. Personal characteristics of understanding self may be observed as: agency, belief systems, courage, drive, flexible, mindfulness, optimism, patient, perseverant, self-direction, self-growth, self-reliance

Understanding Others

The third construct of wisdom is understanding others. Our workplace communities depend on understanding others. Adaptability is a key to understanding others. Goleman (1995) introduction of emotional intelligence to provide insight in our ability to assess our understanding of self (self-awareness, and self-management) and our interaction with those around us (social awareness and relationship management). The intelligence domains demonstrate that not only do we need skills to manage our ourselves, but we also need skills and competencies to connect and interact with others. We must not only create and capture knowledge, but we need to share and apply knowledge and wisdom in a knowledge global economy. As stated in emotional intelligence frameworks, empathy, influence, and inspiration (Goleman, 1995) are important characteristics for relationship management and awareness. Wisdom is a generational activity that moves knowledge from one generation to the next (Smith, 1991). Knowledge and wisdom are both unique resources that are shared yet not given away. In other words, when we share knowledge or wisdom, we do not lose it, but we spread it to others. While explicit knowledge is the easiest to document and share, tacit knowledge and much of wisdom is implicit and intuitive wisdom therefore more difficult to evolve from knowledge to wisdom. When cultivating the collective wisdom we are not only looking for leaders/coaches/mentors, but caring individuals that demonstrate a benevolence in sharing knowledge and a compassionate generosity toward their workplace community. Consider the impact on our workplace communities if knowledge managers are able to build work cultures of benevolence and compassion for wisdom to flourish.

Personal characteristics of understanding others may be observed as: accountable, Benevolence, compassionate, empathy, ethical, generosity, influential, inspiring, listener, responsible, sacrificing, sharing

ORGANIZATIONAL CULTURE AND CHANGE

Knowledge managers are key figures in organizational hierarchy, but seldom lead cultural change. There is an inherent disadvantage to leading organizational change except from the top. Organizational culture is complex and difficult to change. Zheng, Yang and McLean (2008) have shown that knowledge management plays a role in the relationship between organizational culture, structure, strategy and organizational effectiveness. They explain further that "culture has the strongest positive influence on knowledge management. This implies that knowledge management practices need to center on incorporating culture-building activities to foster an environment that is knowledge-friendly." This is area research that connect perception of organizational learning and knowledge management is well founded on a large body of research that emphasizes the critical importance of learning and knowledge management in organization culture (e.g., Chun, 2013; Gold, 2001; Davenport and Prusak, 1998; Watkins and Marsick, 1996 and 2003). Zheng, et al. (2008) states "Organizations that are adaptive, consistent in their values, engaging to employees, and embracing common missions in their cultures have a higher tendency to probe into issues, to seek methods to reduce costs, to look into the future, and to act proactively in their strategies" (p. 770).

Knowledge managers have a significant role in developing a learning organization and further connect activities to organizational culture and leverage knowledge and wisdom to better impact organizational effectiveness. Our learning cultures are important and are impacted by factors such as connection, continuous learning, inquiry and dialog, collective learning, embedded systems, employee empowerment (Egan, Yang, & Bartlett, 2004; Shuck, 2011), and leadership.

Organizational culture is a set of shared values, beliefs and assumptions that employees share about the organization. This culture governs the way that employees behave and interact in the workplace. This culture established norms and should bring all employees together to help understand and solve problems encountered by the organization. Weak cultures feature poor decision making, lack of transparency, high attrition rates, siloed work structures, low focus on effectiveness. On the other hand, strong cultures emphasize belongingness, widely accepted values and purpose, stability, innovation, team and outcome orientation, and support. Lack of advancement, lack of challenge, unethical behavior, ineffective leadership, and lack of development are drivers of employee turnover. Our global knowledge economy will need to emphasize courageous leadership, employee belongingness, appreciation, shared purpose, opportunity, growth, innovation, and success.

Knowledge managers and learning can best impact organizational outcome by improving the learning culture of their organization. Senge (1990) popularized the term learning organization with the goal of continuous and system learning. As a systems scientist he and others prescribed that organizations build innovation and through systems thinking. This included team learning, shared vision and personal mastery. Allen (2022) argues that "learning organizations are a foundation from which we can build wise organizations. A wise organization is a step forward, as adding 'fostering wisdom' is a natural next step in progression of organizational learning and growth" (p. 108). Knowledge management requires a major shift in organizational culture and a commitment from the firm to make it work (Chang & Tung-Ching, 2015).

Shared Models

The knowledge management process is described by many authors across multiple fields. Managing the knowledge management process is difficult. Knowledge is not easily stored (Gopal & Ganon, 1995). Allee (1997) describes properties of knowledge: messy, self-organizing, seeks community, travels via language, slippery, likes looseness, changes and experiments, perishable; self-organizing, evolves organically, multimodal, and multi-dimensional.

Given the instability of knowledge properties, knowledge workers are challenged to develop a model to help them process wisdom in their organization. Knowledge managers can utilize many existing knowledge management tools with minimal modification. For example, the knowledge management process can be modified or reimagined to accommodate wisdom:

Just as knowledge is created from information, wisdom *evolves* from knowledge. When an individual uses their knowledge, experience and understanding to identify patterns, make connections, and recognize underlying principles, they make sound judgements and wise decisions. Learning Science has few avenues to teach individual wisdom. Rather, wisdom is fostered in individuals and collective wisdom is cultivated through shared growth.

Our models, tools and processes of knowledge management can be utilized to accommodate wisdom with few modifications, however wisdom is much rarer than knowledge. Allen (2022) offers "behavioral characteristics and traits that are woven in virtually every discussion on the topic of identifying the wise:

While not every wise person has all these virtues and characteristics, they are often used to describe both the locally and globally wise" (p. 8). Individual wisdom is a topic that has been discussed for centuries, yet, we have little understanding of how to individually become "wise." For the purpose of the discussion, individual wisdom is largely used to provide an understanding of collective wisdom in the context of an organization.

Figure 2. Knowledge management process

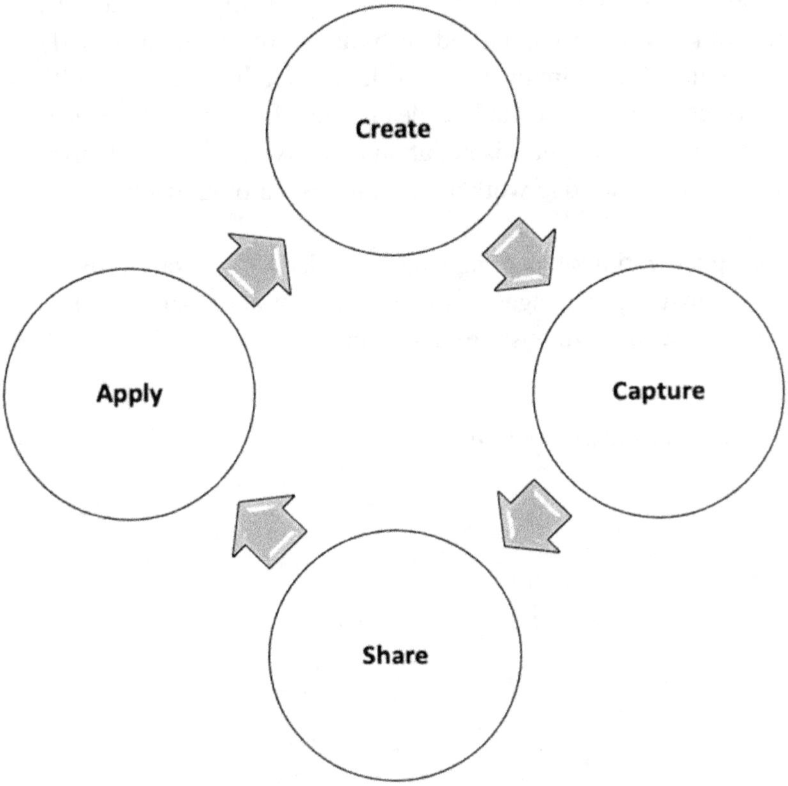

Table 1.

Knowledge & Experience	*Understanding Self*	*Understanding Others*
Abstract reasoning	Agency	Accountable
Competent	Belief system	Benevolent
Explicit knowledge	Courageous	Compassionate
Implicit knowledge	Driven	Empathetic
Insightful	Flexible	Ethical
Intuitive	Mindful	Generous
Learner	Optimistic	Influential
Objective	Patient	Inspiring
Perceptive	Perseverant	Listener
Sound judgment	Self-directed	Responsible
Systematic thinking	Self-growth	Sacrificing
Unlearning	Self-reliant	Sharing

Imagine an organization of wise individuals versus an organization of knowledgeable individuals. Both types of organizations sound ideal, but an organization of knowledgeable individuals is attainable given the tested knowledge models and applicability of innovative knowledge tools and techniques. The learning organization that produces knowledgeable individuals is well within reach today. An organization of wise individuals is not attainable given the lack of current research and models to aid knowledge workers in building an organization with collective wisdom.

The conceptualization of an organization guided by collective wisdom does not exist today. Knowledge managers will require new approaches to understanding how to evolve knowledge to wisdom in organizations.

Figure 3. Wisdom cultivation process

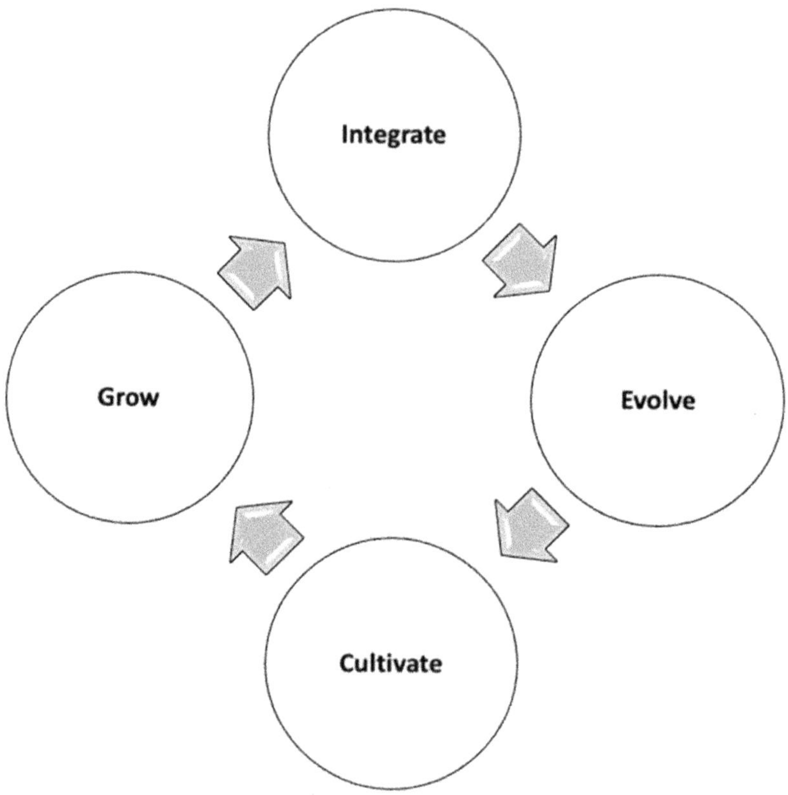

This wisdom management model provides a conceptual re-framing of the knowledge management process to better address the process of developing collective wisdom in our organizations.

Integrate: We integrate new knowledge into existing knowledge and experience. This integration involves assessment of current environment and conceptualization of future use. The assessment and conceptualization require human interaction as different perspectives are integrated into new wisdom. This may involve learning new and unlearning old perspectives, integrating new ideas and processes, or conceptualizing and innovating. Integration requires a great deal of change and adaptation, an integral piece for wisdom.

Evolve: Wisdom evolves from integrated knowledge. Evolution involves dramatically changing the original into something new with inherent characteristics from which it was born. While evolution can take time and happen over generations, knowledge managers who understand how wisdom is born can duplicate this process in knowledge systems by understanding how wisdom evolves. Wisdom is uniquely human and involves characteristics such as insight, intuition, judgement, connection, learning and unlearning. Wisdom requires an evolution from information by integrating knowledge and experience, understanding self, and understanding others to create a deeper level of cognizance.

Cultivate: Integrated knowledge can evolve into individual wisdom, but cultivation allows for individual wisdom to become collective wisdom. Unlike knowledge, wisdom may be best understood as fostering individual wisdom to cultivate collective wisdom. Collective wisdom is cultivated in a trusting community of individuals that offer mutual support and inspiration. Cultivation is dependent on empathizing with the individual – listening to and sharing with – in way that builds *Understanding Others* to promote collective wisdom.

Grow: Growth is a key outcome of wisdom. As collective wisdom is cultivated in an organization, the wisdom-cultivating community grows; as the wisdom-cultivating community grows, wisdom grows. We trust our mentors who generously offer wise input. Wise decisions lead to a beneficial and shared course of action. Growth can be attributed to the size and wisdom flourishing in the community as individuals learn to flex and adapt with the gained perspective of collective experiences. As with any cyclical model, growth and increasing numbers of individuals into the community leads to further integration and the cycle continues.

As the pinnacle of human performance, wisdom is often considered unattainable and meant only for a chosen few. However, wisdom is both obtainable for both individuals and groups. It's unfair to an individual's wisdom as against the remarkably wise (e.g., Martin Luther King, Jr., Mahatma Gandhi, Nelson Mandla). Wisdom should be assessed within the context of an individual's community. In the same way the collective wisdom can be assessed within the context of community need.

Wisdom moves us beyond knowledge and experience to understanding ourselves and others. It moves us into the implicit and away from the tacit. Wisdom is more difficult to understand and cultivate but consider how an organization might change by focusing on evolving toward wisdom rather than knowledge acquisition, sharing and application.

WORKPLACE COMMUNITY

Organization culture and people intersect in the workplace community. Simply, it's where the rubber meets the road. Not unlike a living organism, collective wisdom or a community does not flourish without a healthy culture. A strong and healthy organizational culture should emphasize belongingness, widely accepted optimistic values and purpose, stability, innovation, outcome orientation, and support. These positive cultural characteristics provide the foundation for building a strong and healthy workplace community.

A workplace community consists of a group of engaged colleagues that offer mutual support and that influence and inspire work within the larger organization. Each day we, as individuals, enter our organization as a member of a team, department, division or organization. Depending on the size of the organization, individuals typically define their workplace community as a segment of colleagues rather than a larger organization. For most individuals, their workplace community is the boundary of their overall organization interaction. The workplace is where we develop relationships, gain mentors, identify our belonging and perform critical activities that support organizational success. We value the community where we belong and receive both support and security as a member of the community.

Staudinger (2010) pointing out that "a complex pattern of personal characteristics and experiential features have to coalesce in order for wisdom to emerge" (p. 641). Allen, Bracey, Gavrilova and Zimmerman (2020) further this point stating that wisdom characteristics "can be observed in individuals from every race, creed, color, and society and have no requirements, of age, educational background, or job/social title. When linked and enhanced, these characteristics can foster not only a knowledgeable workforce, but a workforce that leverages wisdom to provide deep understanding of data, information, and knowledge, ultimately providing wise advice within organizations. While a "wise" person is a unique golden nugget found in an organization, aspects and characteristics of wisdom can be bolstered to enhance a corporate workforce in this dynamic and changing knowledge economy" (p. 159).

Knowledge managers need to decide of where they can best impact growth and development. While knowledge managers seldom define and implement organization vision, culture, and strategic direction, they are often involved with supporting implementation at all levels of the organization. Knowledge manager establishes and maintains a healthy learning environment in the organization that facilitates growth and organizational success.

The development of individual wisdom and collective wisdom are happening in parallel for both the individual and the workplace community. The healthy workplace community provides an opportunity for fulfilled individuals to evolve and grow adaptability, to build resilience, and connect with others in their community. As social learners we interact and grow with others by cooperatively investigating and solving complex problems that test knowledge, skills and abilities.

Cooperative mentoring is a natural outgrowth of social learning and growth. Individual's value cooperative relationships, leverage knowledge and experience of others in the mission of building capacity. Cooperative social growth provides collective success of the workplace community. Within a community of practice demonstrate wise decision making, while sharing knowledge and growing collective wisdom to create a better future for the community for ourselves and our colleagues.

WORKPLACE CULTURE

There's not a commonly accepted term for wisdom that is akin to management of knowledge. Terms such as cultivating and fostering move us away from an authoritative structure of "management" to the idea of a caretaker of wisdom. In the same way, bankers manage their money as farmers care for their crop. Living organisms, whether plants, animals, or humans thrive in fertile climates that provide the necessities for growth. Some environments provide a safety and comfort (kind environments) others require a hardiness (wicked environments) that requires greater resiliency.

Theodore Roosevelt is misattributed as stating "*Do what you can, with what you have, from where you are.*" The statement rings true for the question, "How do we make an impact?" Knowledge managers work in many different parts of the organization and interact with employees and systems throughout the organization. Healthy workplace culture is the basis for advanced cognitive development, employee satisfaction and retention (Brunges & Foley-Brinza, 2014). As knowledge manager, our focus on employee training, education and development has a direct impact on the learning culture of the organization and therefore overall workplace culture.

Lack of advancement opportunities, lack of career growth and advancement, lack of challenge, lack of engagement (Shuck, 2011), mismanagement and poor leadership, lack of transparency, lack of voice, stress and negativity each deteriorate individual wellbeing and overall organizational climate and culture (REF). Knowledge manager can indirectly impact many of these factors through knowledge sharing, collaboration, systems management, and both individual and collective development of employees that build belonging, challenge, and growth.

Allen 2022 describes twelve qualities of culture that serve to optimize our wise organizations and workplace communities:

Ethics are vital to an organization. A trusting culture based on sound ethics is the first step to building shared purpose, engaging employees, and providing a professional climate that invites ideas, and connected reliance.

Shared Purpose is a promise/agreement with our collaborative partners. It provides the "why?" of our work. As social creatures it provides us a catalysis for engagement, beyond self, to support and be supported by the community to achieve a common purpose.

Leadership (formal and informal). The best of our leaders influence, inspire and support their followers. Our leaders are the champions. Leaders are not only champions of organizational purpose, but equally champions and advocate the ideas and concerns of their followers.

Support is needed for individuals to take risks and provide honest feedback. If trust, ethics, and psychological safety are in question at any level of the organization, individuals cannot feel safe to fully engage and contribute toward a shared purpose. Leadership must take the lead in creating a safe environment where everyone feels comfortable contributing, learning and developing.

Connection is a key to building relationships between ourselves and others. Individuals must connect both to their colleagues and organizational purpose. We cannot access empathy, compassion, empathy, and generosity without a connection to our community and larger organization.

Belongingness is a human need to give and receive support and security as an engaged member of a group. With belonging comes mentoring, development, sacrifice, learning, growth. I cannot hope to engage individuals that don't feel that they belong - even if they are included.

Positive Disruption is good for the organization. Positive disruptors see opportunities for improvement and move away from group think. Collective wisdom is derived from the collective wise behaviors that we have in our organizations. Our positive disruptors look for new ways of doing ordinary things in a more efficient and effective way. We need adaptability, open-mindedness, innovativeness, and ways to leverage our capabilities and capacities. Wisdom comes from our growth, adaptability, connection, and resilience, not from stagnation and contentment.

Incubator of Innovation is a culture that supports innovative programs at the risk of failure. This innovation can lead to new resources, technologies, markets and customers. We take risks and get honest feedback from the failures. Innovation at risk to failure can only exist in a safe and engaged culture.

Resilience is our capacity to adapt and recover from difficult situations, adversity or challenge. If we take risks we will eventually fail and must learn to bounce back and grow despite adversity. Good judgement comes from overcoming bad experiences and judgements. Resistance to change and failure provide the opportunity for agile change and rapid innovation.

Learning and Unlearning are windows to new knowledge and wisdom. Our models of the world are temporary and we must become adaptive to change. While we are taught that learning is positive, unlearning is weighing, judging, comparing, discerning and deciding if a new model or paradigm should replace outdated ones in order to adapt to new circumstances. As we grow in complex social environments, we learn from rich diverse experiences that challenge our assumptions and we must be willing to disengage from old models, evolve and grow.

Systematic thinking allows us to see the processes and diverse communities that span across the hierarchy of the organization to overcome natural barriers to mentorship, learning, efficiency and effectiveness. It's very easy to see our independent system in the organization and miss how it is interconnected to other systems in the same organization toward the shared purpose.

Optimism is an attitude that positivity will result from an attitude or an action. Optimism provides more agency because you are responsible for the positive attitude even in face of challenge and adversity. (p. 111 - 113)

PERSONAL WISDOM

The purpose of the chapter is not to discuss how to foster individual wisdom, but to shed light on the concept and tools of cultivating collective wisdom in the workplace. Personal and collective wisdom are related, but personal wisdom is independent of others, independent of the workplace, independent of family, independent of location. It's a personal quest that few seek, but is attainable by anyone with the drive to delve deep and develop a wide range of characteristics that are uniquely human in composite. As knowledge management professionals, we can serve as compassionate mentors that listen and engage.

We know from many centuries of studying wisdom that wise individuals are relatively rare. For every 100 or 200 people that we consider knowledgeable we will only count one to three of those individuals as wise. We, as a society, value the wise beyond all others.

Wisdom is contextual and is not dependent on background, religion, socioeconomics, race or age. Wisdom people exist everywhere on earth, and they are considered wise within the context of their group, community or society. Everyone has an opportunity to become wise regardless of other circumstances of life. Wisdom and wise people exist in the jungle villages of the Amazon, rural rice farms China, the Suburb of the United States, and in the high-rise of Dubai. Yet, the idea of becoming individually wise remains mysterious and largely unstudied from a learning perspective. We develop a healthy culture that fosters individual wisdom while evolving, integrating, cultivating and growing collective wisdom in our workplace communities and organization. For knowledge management professionals, it should be noted that growing wisdom is more akin to development than either education or training education.

In order to generate wisdom, we must also create an environment of growth (learning and unlearning) that provides challenges. This challenge includes not only an expanding of the breadth and depth of cognitive knowledge, but by expanding individual understanding of self and others. While the individual is responsible for growth, knowledge managers can cultivate a culture of learning and development that enhance career and personal development.

Figure 4. Five values of collective wisdom

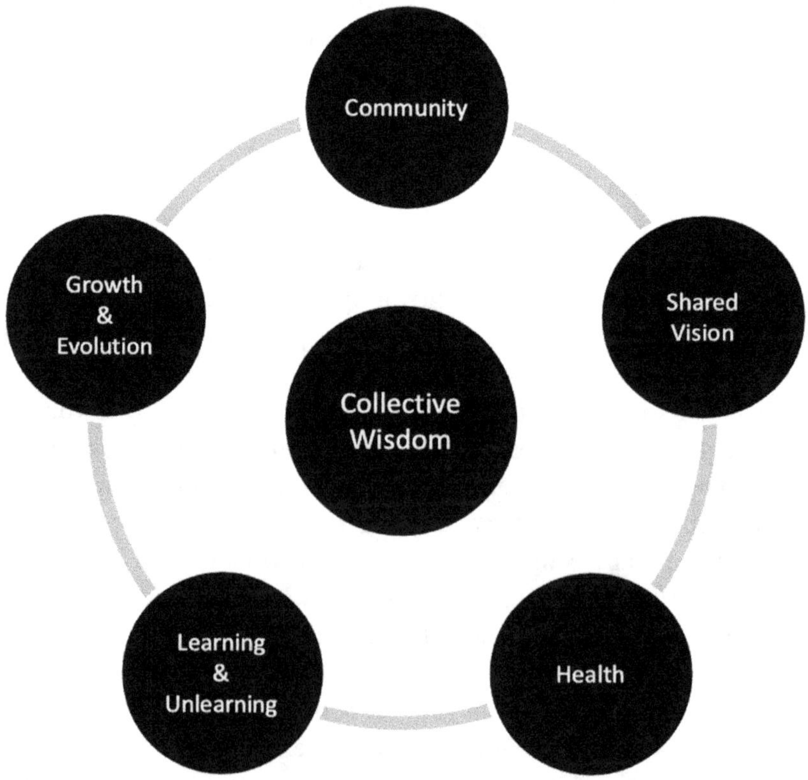

CULTIVATING COLLECTIVE WISDOM

Wisdom evolves through complicated interaction of many different characteristics and virtues that can be clustered in three constructs of knowledge & experience, understanding self, and understanding others. Wisdom can evolve from knowledge when an individual, or group of individuals, use their knowledge, experience and understanding to identify patterns, connections, and underlying principles to make sound judgements and wise decisions. Collective wisdom is developed and refined with an integrated collection of wise behaviors that are cultivated and grown by an interconnected group for the purpose of identifying a beneficial course of action for the group, communities, and society. Collective wisdom is a community activity.

Community

A community is a connected group of individuals with shared interest, values, and purpose. There is not a limit on the size of a community. A small group, team, family, tribe, department, division or a small organization can operate as a community. "Community" can wildly vary depending on organizational structure, but for the purpose of wisdom they are best when they are diverse and contain a rich depth and breadth of knowledge, experience, and backgrounds.

Three decades of research in Communities of Practice (CoP) provides a rich resource for understanding of how individuals work together with shared purpose. Cox (2010) provides a very good review of the four seminal works to define CoP as "a relatively informal, intra-organizational group specifically facilitated by management to increase learning or creativity" (p. 538). CoP literature is a good beginning for Knowledge Managers working to leverage learning in their organization.

Workplace communities must provide connection, support, and belonging. As social learners, we grow by interacting with others and working cooperatively to investigate and solve problems. Connection is a first step in building community. This connection can be a shared purpose, but more importantly to come to a shared understanding of others in the community to begin a deeper social connection. A workplace community supports others in the community beyond simply a connection between co-worker guided by productivity goals. To leverage collective wisdom, trust and support work together to begin to move from representation in the community to inclusion in the community where an individual's ideas and perspective are shared and valued by the community.

Belongingness must be a community goal when moving toward collective wisdom. Humans have an inherent need to be included as a member of a community but belong to the community. Belonging implies that the individual is fully accepted into the community where their ideas, knowledge, experience, understandings, beliefs, and values are integrated into the collective values of the community. Belonging is a critical goal if we are to build a community of mentors that are dedicated to cultivating collective wisdom for the betterment of the community

Shared Vision

An optimistic shared vision is critical to a healthy culture. Shared vision builds a collective goal by providing a strategic picture of the future. This shared commitment to a community vision guides principles and practices. Where group think creates an environment that blocks knowledge and wisdom growth, shared vision is related to a value system. Shared vision is more closely related to collective outcome that a community shares and often requires individuals with many different talents, backgrounds, and experiences contributing to the benefit of the whole; whereas group think does not allow for differences to be celebrated or demonstrated.

Both the organization and community vision must be shared, discussed, and modified as the organization grows and changes over time. To build collective wisdom, members of the workplace community should have a shared vision or purpose to which everyone contributes. Shared purpose establishes collective goals for everyone in the community or organization. Even with diverse activities a shared vision provides a common sense of purpose and that can be supported by every member of the community.

Health

A healthy organization or organizational culture is transparent, adaptable, resilient and innovative. In a global knowledge economy, the health of the individuals and the organization are interconnected so that the health of the organization is critical to moral, communication, relationship and retention.

Organizational transparency does not mean that everyone in the organization has access to all information in the organization, but that everyone in the organization perceives that they belong in the organization to the extent that their voice is heard, questions can be answered. "Transparency is the perceived quality of intentionally shared information from a sender" (Schnackenberg & Tomlinson, 2014, p. 1788). Without this transparency, organizational vision suffers because it is no longer shared intentionally. Since there is not a sense of ownership or connection to the vision and purpose in the community, the organization will not experience collective wisdom.

Adaptability to obstacles and facing adversity provide teaching moments in which knowledge can foster wisdom. Organizations and communities must be able to rapidly adapt to change and become resilient to adversity. "Healthy and fulfilled individuals adapt, grow resilience, and thrive in adverse and challenging environments." (Allen et al., 2020). As our workplace communities become resilient to adversity they learn self-reliance, resilience, and how to best communicate to build relationships. These tenets foster the integration of new knowledge and experience to evolve our collective wisdom for future conditions of adversity. An agile and healthy organization should be resilient, innovative and adaptable to fast-changing chaotic global markets.

Learning and Unlearning

Senge (1990) presents that a learning organization is one that continually learns and improves. Humans are social learners that seek knowledge and crave learning. Learning is essential for our existence. In the same way that food nourishes the body, information, knowledge, and connection nourish our mind through the active process of learning. Learning is critical in aiding us to acquire critical skills and interacting with others. Learning is a lifelong process that requires curiosity, observation, reflection, integration, and application to develop knowledge, skills, attitudes, and abilities for future success. Learning must be a part of every individual's personal and professional activities to flourish in a rapidly changing global economy. Workers must employ learning skills to be effective in today's landscape; learning skills include creativity and innovation, critical thinking and problem solving, communication, and collaboration (Battelle for Kids, 2019).

The Greek philosopher Antisthenes states, in 400 BC, that the most useful piece of learning for the uses of life is to unlearn what is not true. A diverse and global workforce requires adapting existing models or constructing new ones to explain phenomena. It is essential to unlearn previously held beliefs and devise solutions and rapidly adapt to change.

The amount of learning, and therefore unlearning, is exponentially larger in our modern and global knowledge economy and it's expected to continue to grow.

Growth and Evolution

The greatest threat to personal and collective wisdom is comfort and stagnation. Wisdom, creativity, compassion, intuition, perception, drive, courage, insight, and optimism are all attributes of humans that are difficult to replicate in artificial intelligence. Humans have a desire to learn and grow socially with other humans so that they can evolve ideas, knowledge, and experience to improve their environment.

Growth happens in many ways and growth is not always linear, continuous, or steady. Collective wisdom changes as the knowledge, experience, people, and the environment change. In adverse situations, productivity may slow but growth will continue due to an increase in the depth and breadth of knowledge and experience. Growth may not remain positive. Healthy, active, engaging, and challenging environments cultivate positive growth. Knowledge managers must tend not only to discovery, acquisition, sharing and application of knowledge. They must also develop strategies that activate challenge, engagement, and connection with others to grow the collective strength of workplace communities.

Evolution is a gradual change over time for a better chance of surviving environmental threats. From a biological viewpoint the character changes happen incrementally over many generations in the evolution of a species. While this may be a relatively fast process in single cell organisms, these incremental changes happen very slowly for more advanced primates. The process of transforming knowledge into wisdom is both incremental and complicated. Collective wisdom provides the opportunity to formalize sharing of knowledge, perspective, insight, and sound judgement through mentorship and community collaboration.

FINAL THOUGHTS

The collective wisdom of our knowledge workforce is tremendous. Knowledge managers are positioned to act as agents of change in their organization. The ability of knowledge workers to adapt to the global learning economy depends upon the recognition that the next phase of growth lies in collective wisdom. To produce organizational wisdom, knowledge managers must recognize their role in promoting transparent, healthy cultures within organizations, and promoting models within knowledge management systems that foster the growth of wisdom in individuals.

We have the tools, processes, and theories to manage knowledge organization, however there is a wealth of untapped wisdom that has yet to be leveraged to improve our organizations' culture and productivity. As a field, we should begin to revise, adapt, reimagine, or even unlearn what we understand about managing knowledge to better cultivate wisdom in our organizations. The inability to cultivate wisdom from knowledge managers will not only hinder their organization's growth and development but will stunt it. Understanding the importance of integrating this change is not only necessary for the health of the organization, but it is integral for the success of the workers and the organization as a whole.

Wisdom is a growth and next step in the evolution of the knowledge economy. In order to establish organizational wisdom, both knowledge workers and organizations as a whole must choose to grow and evolve.

REFERENCES

Ackoff, R. (1989). From Data to Wisdom. *Journal of Applied Systems Analysis, 16*, 3–9.

Allee, V. (1997). 12 principles of knowledge management. *Training and Development Journal, 51*(11), 71–74.

Allen, J. (2022). *Fostering Wisdom at Work*. Rutledge Taylor & Francis Group. doi:10.4324/9781003018759

Allen, J., Bracey, P., Aguilar, M., & Zimmerman, T. (2020). Supporting Workforce Wisdom in a Global Economy. In C. Hughes (Ed.), *Strategies for Attracting, Maintaining and Balancing a Mature Workforce*. IGI Global. doi:10.4018/978-1-7998-2277-6.ch007

Ardelt, M., Pridgen, S., & Nutter-Pridgen, K. (2018). The relationship between age and three-dimensional wisdom: Variations by wisdom dimensions and education. *The Journals of Gerontology. Series B, Psychological Sciences and Social Sciences, 73*(8), 1339–1349. doi:10.1093/geronb/gbx182 PMID:29401232

Batelle for Kids. (2019). *21st century framework for learning*. Retrieved from http://www.battelleforkids.org

Bergsma, A., & Ardelt, M. (2012). Self-reported wisdom and happiness: An empirical investigation. *Journal of Happiness Studies, 13*(3), 481–499. doi:10.100710902-011-9275-5

Brunges, M., & Foley-Brinza, C. (2014). Projects for increasing job satisfaction and creating a healthy work environment. *AORN Journal, 100*(6), 670–681. doi:10.1016/j.aorn.2014.01.029 PMID:25453685

Chang, C., & Tung-Ching, L. (2015). The role of organizational culture in the knowledge management process. *Journal of Knowledge Management, 19*(3), 433–455. doi:10.1108/JKM-08-2014-0353

Chun, W. (2013). Information culture and organizational effectiveness. *International Journal of Information Management, 33*(4), 775–779. doi:10.1016/j.ijinfomgt.2013.05.009

Cox, A. (2005). What are communities of practice? A comparative review of four seminal works. *Journal of Information Science, 31*(6), 527–540. doi:10.1177/0165551505057016

Davenport, T., De Long, D., & Beers, M. (1998). Successful Knowledge Management Projects. *Sloan Management Review*, *39*(2), 43–57.

Egan, T. M., Yang, B., & Bartlett, K. R. (2004). The Effects of Organizational Learning Culture and Job Satisfaction on Motivation to Transfer Learning and Turnover Intention. *Human Resource Development Quarterly*, *15*(3), 279–301. doi:10.1002/hrdq.1104

Frické, M. (2009). The knowledge pyramid: A critique of the DIKW hierarchy. *Journal of Information Science*, *35*(2), 131–142. doi:10.1177/0165551508094050

Gardner, H. (1983). *Frames of mind: The theory of multiple intelligences*. Basic Books.

Gold, A., Malhotra, A., & Segars, A. (2001). Knowledge management: An organizational capabilities perspective. *Journal of Management Information Systems*, *18*(1), 185–214. doi:10.1080/07421222.2001.11045669

Goleman, D. (1995). *Emotional intelligence*. Bantam Books.

Herbane, B. (2019). Rethinking organizational resilience and strategic renewal in SMEs. *Entrepreneurship and Regional Development*, *31*(5-6), 476–495. doi:10.1080/08985626.2018.1541594

Jeste, D., & Lee, E. (2019). The Emerging Empirical Science of Wisdom: Definition, Measurement, Neurobiology, Longevity, and Interventions. *Harvard Review of Psychiatry*, *27*(3), 127–140. doi:10.1097/HRP.0000000000000205 PMID:31082991

Luthar, S., Crossman, E., & Small, P. (2015). *Resilience and Adversity. Handbook of Child Psychology and Developmental Science* (7th ed.). Wiley. doi:10.1002/9781118963418.childpsy307

Rowley, J. (2007). The wisdom hierarchy: Representations of the DIKW hierarchy. *Journal of Information Science*, *33*(2), 163–180. doi:10.1177/0165551506070706

Schnackenber, A., & Tomlinson, E. (2014). Organizational transparency: A new perspective on Managing trust in organization-stakeholder relationships. *Journal of Management*, *42*(7), 1784–1810. doi:10.1177/0149206314525202

Senge, P. (1990). *The Fifth Discipline: The Art and Practice of the Learning Organization*. Doubleday/Currency.

Shuck, B. (2011). Integrative Literature Review: Four Emerging Perspectives of Employee Engagement: An Integrative Literature Review. *Human Resource Development Review*, *10*(3), 304–328. doi:10.1177/1534484311410840

Smith, R. (1991). Where is the wisdom...? *BMJ (Clinical Research Ed.)*, *303*(6806), 798–799. doi:10.1136/bmj.303.6806.798 PMID:1932964

Staudinger, U. (2010). Older and wiser? Integrated results on the relationship between age and wisdom-related performance. *International Journal of Behavioral Development*, *23*(3), 641–664. doi:10.1080/016502599383739

Watkins, K. E., & Marsick, V. J. (1996). *In action: creating the learning organization*. American Society for Training and Development.

Watkins, K. E., & Marsick, V. J. (Eds.). (2003). Make learning count! Diagnosing the learning culture in organizations. *Advances in Developing Human Resources*, *5*(2), 132–151. doi:10.1177/1523422303251341

Wilson, E. (1998). *Consilience: The Unity of Knowledge*. Vintage Books.

Zheng, W., Yang, G., & McLean, G. (2010). Linking organizational culture, structure, strategy, and organizational effectiveness: Mediating role of knowledge management. *Journal of Business Research*, *63*(7), 763–771. doi:10.1016/j.jbusres.2009.06.005

KEY TERMS AND DEFINITIONS

Belongingness: A human need to give and receive support and security as an engaged member of a group.

Collective: Wisdom: A shared understanding of wise behaviors that are collected and curated by an interconnected group to create a beneficial course of action for the group, communities, and society.

Community: A connected group of individuals with shared interest, values, and purpose.

Connection: A key to building relationships between ourselves and others. Individuals must connect both to their colleagues and organizational purpose.

Data: A collection or set of facts (numbers, measurements, observations, or descriptions) that can be quantitative or qualitative in nature

Experience: The practice or the application of knowledge over a period of time.

Information: Structured data with attached meaning, connection, and significance

Knowledge: The depth and breadth of information and skills acquired through interaction, participation, observation integrated with an individual's comprehension of connected experiences.

Optimism: An attitude that positivity will result from an attitude or an action.

Organizational: Culture: A set of shared values, beliefs, and assumptions that employees share about the organization.

Resilience: Our capacity to adapt and recover from difficult situations, adversity, or challenge.

Section 3

Data Analytics, Visualization, Cybersecurity, and Knowledge Management Systems in KM Governance

Chapter 7
How Agile Are the Organizations Against Cyber Threats?

Ayse Asli Yilmaz
https://orcid.org/0000-0003-1784-7307
Atilim University, Turkey

Mustafa Hafizoglu
https://orcid.org/0000-0003-4935-7791
Atilim University, Turkey

Sule Tuzlukaya
Atilim University, Turkey

ABSTRACT

Some of the tasks of organizations in the digital age include information formation, coding and increasing value, data mining, and encoding information to make it accessible to others. As disruptive technology permeates all aspects of social life, new threats and vulnerabilities emerge. Cyber threats and cyber-security incidents may affect organizations, whether public or private, individuals, and all social network actors. The idea of a system that must defend against all possible attacks has given rise to the cyber resilience phenomenon. In public organizations, cyber resilience is obtained in various ways such as storing private classified data assets and records on independent backup platforms. Regardless of whether one platform is in danger, the other can provide a copy of missing or maliciously encrypted data immediately. Given the preceding discussion, this chapter focuses on agility, which is now regarded as a core competency in organizations in terms of cyber management, cyber resilience, knowledge management, and artificial intelligence in the cyber cosmos.

DOI: 10.4018/978-1-6684-4431-3.ch007

INTRODUCTION

Disruptive technologies have had a significant impact on our lives. The incorporation of knowledge and disruptive technologies has altered the social fabric. In the "digitalized knowledge-based society," digital transformation paves the way for new and distinct goals.

On the one hand, traditional knowledge management practice focuses on knowledge compilation and welcomes social networks, including technology. On the other hand, there is a business-centric viewpoint that focuses on total transformation, particularly on organizational aspects such as artificial intelligence, the internet of things, cloud computing, big data, learning analytics, adaptive engines, and so on (Klaus et al., 2018). Interconnected digital technology has created unprecedented opportunities for both individuals and organizations, and such change not only benefits public organizations but also strengthens and ensures social welfare. The assets and technologies available to public organizations as well as the tools and skills required to maintain them, are changing and gradually improving. As processes are integrated into software and the role of data, analysis, and artificial intelligence systems in operations and administrative decisions expands, the concept of organization itself evolves.

Organizational core competencies evolve to gain a competitive advantage, and public organizations are no exception. Some of the tasks of public organizations in the digital age include information formation, coding and increasing value, data mining, and encoding information to make it accessible to others.

As disruptive technology permeates all aspects of social life, new threats and vulnerabilities emerge. Cyber threats and cyber security incidents may affect organizations, whether public or private, individuals, and all social network actors. In general, public organizations have regular, static, inflexible, and bureaucratic structures, which reflect on the operating system (Denning, 2018). Cyberspace's interconnectedness enables large organizations to become more agile, flexible, and adaptive.

In light of all of this, this chapter is designed to illustrate how cyber space offerings have accelerated the adoption of agility, which was previously regarded to be slow in the public sector. Big data, artificial intelligence, the internet of things, robots, quantum technologies, and distributed registry systems all play a role in knowledge management with digital products based on end-to-end and additive technologies. Therefore, virtual and augmented reality technologies are becoming increasingly important in organizations, particularly in the public sector (Chesalin et al., 2020). Organizations that want to catch innovation may be vulnerable to cyber threats while using a variety of technology tools for knowledge management. In the face of cyber threats, the learning and adaptation process of public organizations with more central and even more hierarchical structures, which are likely to resist change, will be explained. In terms of cyber management, cyber resilience, and knowledge management in the cyber space, this chapter focuses on digital transformation and agility, which is currently considered as a core competency in public organizations,

CYBER THREATS AND CYBER SECURITY

The cyberspace as phenomenon, which we used to only see in science fiction movies and try to understand from books on beyond our dreams, has quickly entered our personal and social lives. The cyberspace and its physical, logical, and social components enable humans to communicate, collaborate, and control in previously unimaginable ways. As the physical and virtual worlds have become inseparable, humans have shifted many aspects of their lives to the online worlds. Humans are given excellent opportunities in cyberspace to realize their full potential. The free flow of information is reliant on disruptive technologies that freely connects human opinions and knowledge. This freedom necessitates trust. Humans want to be in a safe virtual ecosystem. Organizations are seen as living organisms as well. To keep up with future technological, social, and logical network changes, management system must also evolve. The ability to understand the internal and external balances of the organization in all of its dimensions and to follow the digital era is related to management in the cyberspace. Management is defined as the global coordination of human actions in domestic, social, political, and other contexts, as well as in organizations (Kaehler & Grundei, 2018). As settled, orderly structured public organizations try to adapt to the cyberspace, things become more complicated on the verge of chaos.

Organizations leverage existing knowledge and create new ones in today's complex and unleashed global system (Obitade, 2019). Cyber threats and attacks are increasing in number and complexity on a daily basis as well as becoming more sophisticated. Therefore, organizations undergoing digital transformation require protection against threats and vulnerabilities (Abomhara & Køien, 2015). Simply said, providing knowledge is a dangerous activity information sharing is a risky activity that must be justified through interaction with both external and internal stakeholders. Classified knowledge includes external factors such as financial situation, market evaluations, regulations and sources, as well as internal issues such as r reorganization, business strategy, and risk appetite. (Refsdal et al., 2015). So, it entails the availability of technological infrastructure, superstructure, software, and hardware in cyberspace.

Cyber-systems are increasingly being surrounded by public organizations, social networks, welfare, and public services such as health, banking, trade, energy, and transportation. (Refsdal et al., 2015). Cybersecurity is explained as a procedure and process for protecting data, information and/or systems/services against damage, unauthorized access, theft, or loss by maintaining high levels of intimacy and privacy whenever required. This entails the maximum authenticity value added for both tangible assets like devices and intangible assets such as services, information and data (Abomhara & Køien, 2015).

At this point, artificial intelligence solutions provide great convenience in identifying and solving organizational weaknesses created by developing technology. Artificial intelligence techniques build complex predictive models, identify patterns, structure data, and detect anomalies (Chesalin et al., 2020). The more the impact and sophistication of cyberattacks increase, the more the ability to detect and respond to threats develop. Organizations are restructured in order to survive by changing strategies.

In public organizations, cyber resilience is obtained in various of ways such as, storing private, classified data assets and records on independent backup platforms. Regardless of whether one platform is in danger, the other can provide a copy of missing or maliciously encrypted data immediately. As a result, in order to comprehend what it may imply for different systems, the agility of the system's architectural design must be heterogenic (Pogrebna et al., 2019). Cyber agility is the organizational capability to respond quickly and rapidly to cyber threats and attacks. That is the reason cyber agility is important for organizations' continuation (Obitade,2019). The idea of a system that must defend against all possible attacks has given rise to the cyber resilience phenomenon. Cyber resilience adds a dimension to the holistic strategic approach by giving the organization a new capacity to deal with cyber incidents through a variety of actions ranging from minor, such as small adaptation, to major, requiring complete transformation (Ferdinand, 2015).

Within organizational contexts, the interrelationship between all of these domains is based on a series of managerial decisions based on effective systematic thinking and leadership in the cyber cosmos. Decision makers play a proactive role in shaping organizational culture. Every organization has its own culture, which is comprised of a set of assumptions that direct the course of actions toward adaptability. Looking back is a natural for organizational memory because lessons are learned from the past. However, looking ahead is unavoidable in the organizational real world of the cyber cosmos. In the Rhizome (golden triangle) framework, which consists of human, technology, and adaptiveness, cyber security is critical to establishing trust. Some metaphors of cognitive space are the digital library, database management, archival information services, electronic mail, electronic market, digital commerce, digital money, and digital property, geographical and social settings and network navigations, and groupware (Fourkas, 2004). A security culture is defined as a set of norms, values, and codes of conduct that are developed and shaped by individuals within an organization in relation to various aspects of security (Ertan et al., 2020).

In general, cyber security generally refers to the ability to control access to networked systems and the data contained within them. Where cyber security controls are viable, cyberspace is regarded as a trustworthy, adaptable, and dependable computerized framework (Bayuk et al.,2012). Trojans, viruses, malware, phishing and social engineering; targeted attack; crypto and ransomware as well as lack of precaution and untrained employees against cyber threats are considered most expensive and well recognized attacks for organizations (Diogenes& Ozkaya, 2018). As a result, some cyber security policy and regulations are reorganized and formally implemented by a governing authority in public organizations. Because all citizens, public-related institutions (political, military, economic, critical infrastructures, social, and so on), and even foreign stakeholders are covered by cyber security policy. At that point, the goals of cyber security in public organizations differ from those of private companies (Bayuk et al., 2012). They take a proactive approach to cyber threats, developing customized protection measures not only for complex network systems, but also for damaging cyber-attacks.

Cyber security systems belonging to public organizations, in particular, fight cyber-attacks, data breaches, and identity theft. Because the public sector must have a strong understanding of network security and contingency preparations in the event of a cyber-attack (Seemma et al., 2018). As a result, risk management has become a core competency of public organizations. Because risk management is the process of assessing and controlling threats stemming from technological uncertainty on, legal liabilities, or natural disasters, and other factors. Thus, in terms of knowledge security in public organizations, risk management is considerably more critical. Whereas fundamental freedoms, privacy and free flow of information have gained prominence; citizens private lives and personal data, among other things, are regarded as equally important in public organizations' cyber security solutions. Being a decision maker in a series of digital, changeable universes that can even be communicated with virtual reality glasses entails being an innovator in every way.

As a result, in order to understand vulnerabilities in the cyber space, decision-makers in public organizations must be situationally aware. Creative decision makers capable of taking the initiative and making the public organization agile enough envision a shared and clear vision of the desired future state (Srinivas et al., 2007). To achieve interoperability with secure networks, the method best suited to the application of each public organization must be customized (Isaksen & Tidd, 2007).

RELATIONSHIP BETWEEN AGILITY AND KNOWLEDGE MANAGEMENT

As organizations attempt to leverage Industry 4.0 technologies for knowledge management and competitive advantage, the knowledge management framework is in flux (Bettiol et al., 2020). Knowledge, as one of the key dimensions of competitiveness and risk prevention, is an ever-changing strategic resource and factor for organizations. Organizational actors and stakeholders expect to receive information at the appropriate time. Knowledge management takes a user-oriented approaching order to meet expectations. Knowledge, including know-how, is the central phenomenon of the mechanism, which includes creation, enrichment, verification for collective performance and sustainability (Saulais & Ermine, 2019).

From the perspective of knowledge management, Industry 4.0 introduces new dimensions to both the interior of organizational learning (knowledge creation, codification, and transfer) and the exterior of network stakeholders in terms of managing knowledge. Because they focused on maintaining business value through strategies such as staff reductions, technological adaptation, and an explosion of content, information, and knowledge (Murray, 2007). In the context of Industry 4.0. a great number of sources offer the opportunity to obtain knowledge that organizations follow and focus on innovation, organize activities, and develop new relationships with other actors in order to create value (Bettiol et al, 2020). So, new operational skills in addition to being innovative, flexible, and effective, for example, in areas such as marketing, logistics, and human resources are developed, in organizations.

The role information systems and communication technologies evolve on a daily basis. Knowledge transfer among actors, such as people-to-people and people-to-document, is being transformed into various technological solutions in the cyberspace, such as artificial intelligence, blockchain, the Internet of things. As a result, in the virtual ecosystem, knowledge creation, analysis, and evaluation occur alongside social dynamics. Therefore, organizational learning, organizational memory, and knowledge management are all considered interconnected concepts that contribute to organizational effectiveness, resilience, and agility of an organization. In particular, the relationship between organizational learning and knowledge management, resembles a cause-and-effect relationship. Because in organizational learning, the organization continues to learn itself in order to better carry out the activities that are considered to be the founding purpose. As a result, organizational learning occurs when actors use knowledge in a comprehensive information network. Organizational memory and knowledge management have a similar relationship. Organizational memory is what information technology support organizations do, such as superstructure and knowledge artifact infrastructure (Jennex, 2007).

When a stand-alone concept, organizational agility refers to an organization's ability to efficiently redeploy/redirect its resources in order to value-create and protect higher-yield activities as internal and external conditions warrant (Teece et al., 2016). It is critical for organizations to be agile in terms of organizational learning and adaptation at this point. As a result, organizations are expected to be more alert, adaptive, flexible, and quick to respond to the increasingly dynamic cyberspace. There is a subtle distinction between flexibility and agility. While flexibility refers to the ability to quickly change task-oriented conditions, agility provides the organization with the ability to respond quickly to unexpected organizational ecosystem changes (Jennex, 2007). In the human and machine interaction, transforming raw data into knowledge and wisdom by disruptive technologies is considered core competencies. Because this enables innovative services and smart decision making for new business models (Pablos & Lytras, 2018)

At this point, agile methods that support decision-making processes can be used as an example. Because organizations want to improve their ability to manage changing priorities, increase productivity, and enhance software quality. The adoption of changes, which is perpetual with traditional methods, is a critical point of agile methods. Methods for managing knowledge works include Scrum and Karban, for example. Scrum is an agile system that includes ideas and practices that help organizations present new products in continuous progress and with rapid adaptation to changes, whereas Kanban is a continuous management technique established by Toyota based on the experience of other agile processes. The elimination of waste and delays is the primary goal of Kanban. Because it contributes to the optimization of the workstream. The Kanban system is based on the Just-In-Time technique, which is based on job scheduling and necessitates correct task description and execution (Brezonik, et al., 2016).

During citizen and public organization relations, a massive amount of information is accumulated, collected, mined, and exploited in the cyberspace, just as it is in other organizational external and internal interactions. These relationships are established to benefit all stakeholders, including citizens, the government, public administrative offices, and businesses. Nations' e-government projects are excellent examples of virtual public organizations. E-government systems enable the coordination and complexity of institutional activities. As a result, nations are improving the quality of e-government services on a daily basis in order to increase effectiveness, awareness, engagement, and collaboration among all actors. (Yilmaz&Tuzlukaya, 2022).

However, even as we benefit from new technologies, there are always risks and challenges in the cyber cosmos. When cyberattacks are directed at nations, public organizations, and citizens, public organizations are expected to be agile in order to protect national security or individual privacy, as well as to develop the ability to adopt new technologies in the aftermath of cyberattacks (Valle-Cruz et al.,2019).

RHIZOME MODEL: DIGITAL TRANSFORMATION AND KNOWLEDGE MANAGEMENT

Digitalization and digital transformation have been defined in various ways. Reis et al. (2020) reviewed 16 different definitions of digitalization from 16 articles and proposed the following definition: "Digitalization is the phenomenon of transforming analog data into digital language (i.e. digitization), which, in turn, can improve business relationships between customer and companies, bringing added value to the whole economy and society". This definition explains why and how digitalization works, as well as what it is. In terms of its emphasis on change, digital transformation differs from digitization. The term "digital transformation" refers to the changes to a company's business model, products, processes, and organizational structure that will be implemented (Hess, 2016). As a result, when executives participate in digital transformation projects, one of the top three concerns is change management (Sailer et al., 2019).

The economic value of any technology that leads to digitalization remains unrealized until it is commercialized. (Chesbrough, 2010). Instead of focusing solely on operational goals such as increasing efficiency, the goal of digital transformation is to transform the business model and support a better knowledge management infrastructure. Eggers and Bellman (2015) conducted a survey of over 1,200 government officials from over 70 countries on digital transformation and discovered that digital strategies at early-stage public organizations are more operational in nature.

Digital transformation necessitates a mindset shift as well as the incorporation of agile structure (Eggers & Bellman, 2015). According to the Oxford Dictionary, being agile means being able to move quickly and easily, as well as thinking quickly and intelligently. Agile also implies being adaptable at all times and gaining flexibility in order to meet current needs while maintaining the vision (Sailer et al., 2019). In order to be prepared for their digital transformation, competitive competencies such as innovation necessitate agility and a learning culture with a mature knowledge management infrastructure (Stronen, et al., 2019).For public organizations, agility is the key to gaining flexibility in the face of increasing uncertainty and complexity. Figure 1 shows how to achieve digital transformation with an agility mindset which is driven by an effective knowledge management using the Rhizome Model® (Rhizome is the underground part of the plant that runs horizontally and has the ability to produce root).

The rhizome is first used as a metaphor for chaotic root structures by Deleuze and Guattari (1987) in order to draw attention to complex movement, activity and change in which connectivity and heterogeneity are defining characteristics (Pick, 2017).

Figure 1. Rhizome model®

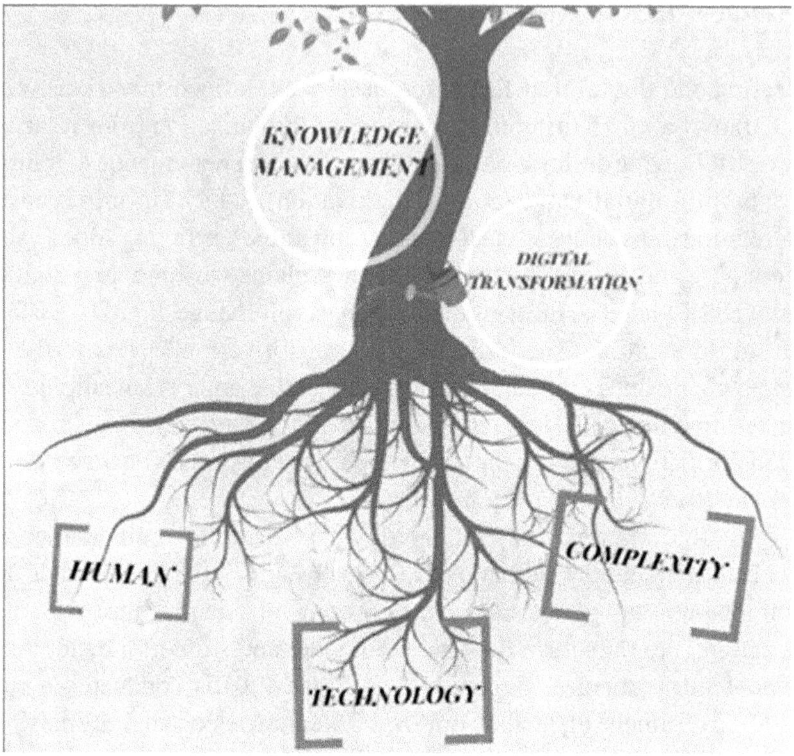

Rhizome Model® is constructed on three core concepts from a perspective of everything is connected to everything else:

1. *Human,*
2. *Technology,*
3. *Complexity.*

These, like the roots of a tree, must be carefully handled in order for an organization's growth to be achieved through digital transformation, which will also enable improved knowledge management. Creating a digital world culture reflects the human side. Many governments have appointed new transformation directors, as well as chief digital officers in departments and agencies, to encourage culture change by allowing influential people to agitate and challenge the status quo (Eggers & Bellman, 2015).

Digital transformation is all about the human (Sailer et al., 2019). Sailer et al. (2019) researched the reasons for high failure rates of digital transformations and the number one reason was found to be the culture: *"There is a lack of openness to digitalization, sometimes even pushback from traditional entities. It takes time for both leadership and employees to adopt the necessary information-sharing mentality and cope with continuously changing conditions"*.

Employees should learn not only to work with digital tools but also work with new business models. Moreover, they should gain new skills and capture the right talents. "*People build up business, not machines*" (Sailer et al., 2019). People should develop an agile mindset, establish flexible working models, and learn how to work in the digital world to implement a better knowledge management in business settings.

Technology enables agility, flexibility, adaptability, and growth. Adoption of technological solutions for the development of new business models, products, and best practices increases organizations' innovation capacity and allows them to meet the needs of a constantly changing environment (Gomez et al., 2020). These technological solutions which may provide opportunities for knowledge management to get improved are classified into four categories: (1) Big Data, (2) Artificial Intelligence (AI), (3) Internet of Things (IoT), and (4) Blockchain.

Big Data is not only a smart and insightful way of analyzing data. It also uses of real-time data from sensors and radio frequency identification devices to better understand the business environment in order to develop new business models, products, and services (Davenport et al.,2012). Public organizations, for example, may collect real-time health information from citizens and pave the way for treatments and cures for life-threatening diseases. Di Viao and his colleagues (2021) investigated the role of digital transformation in knowledge management systems, with the findings revealing that Big Data and IoT provide access to large flows of data and information, allowing for the application of useful knowledge across various company departments. Alveranga and his colleagues (2020), on the other hand, confirm that knowledge management is also a crucial aspect in the success of digital transformation.AI systems can make decisions and reach different conclusions on their own, without the need for human intervention, by learning and identifying patterns (Sousa et al., 2019). Souse and his colleagues identified AI solutions for the public sector such as knowledge management and data processing automation, fraud detection, work effectiveness analysis, irrigation optimization, pollution detection, traffic analysis, and disease prediction. On the other hand, the application of AI in the public sector is still very slow due to concerns about code and data fraud, the high cost of error in these systems such as the scalability of making automatically-biased decisions that can affect large sectors of the population, and the need for people to be replaced in various daily activities as a result of automation (Cruz et al., 2019).

The Internet of Things (IoT) is a growing open and comprehensive network of intelligent objects that communicate with one another and with other internet-enabled devices over the Internet and have the ability to react and act in response to situations and changes in the environment (Brous et al., 2020; Wirtz et al., 2019). The Internet of Things (IoT) is one of the key trends that governments are looking into in order to become a "smart government," which is the highest level of modernization for public organizations (Wirtz et al., 2019). Connecting to the Internet, on the other hand, means communicating with potential cyber threats, and the expansion of IoT increases these risks (Tawalbeh et al., 2019). Using IoT for access control to enter public transformation, for example, may improve efficiency, whereas eliminating the human element of conductors may introduce new risks (Brous & et al., 2020). To mitigate these risks, a new agile structure should be implemented.

Blockchain is a specialized technology for peer-to-peer transaction platforms that records all transaction data using decentralized storage, shifting away from centralized structures (banks, exchanges, trading platforms, energy companies) and toward a decentralized system (end customers, energy consumers) (PWC, 2016). The analysis of a group of pioneering public service developments shows that blockchain technology can reduce bureaucracy, improve administrative process efficiency, and boost trust in public record keeping (Allessie et al., 2019), making the entire system more flexible, as many previously manual work tasks are now carried out automatically (PWC, 2016).

Organizations become more information-intensive as uncertainty and complexity increase. Despite the increase in uncertainty and complexity, many organizations currently lack such adaptability (Janssen & Voort, 2016). To gain adaptability and cope with the complexity, established governance mechanisms and decision-making patterns should be transformed into an agile structure. Employees benefit from adaptability because it allows them to tailor their tasks to local information (Dessein & Santos, 2006). Dessein and Santos (2006) discovered that the better the coordination between employees, the more flexibility they receive and, as a result, the higher the returns to further improving coordination, which increases adaptability in the complex environment. Most government organizations lack a digital transformation strategy (Eggers & Bellman, 2015).

The right strategy should be based on the Rhizome Model, namely, human, technology, and complexity, and the new governance structure should be guided by an agile mindset. If public organizations can start their digital transformation with this strategy, they will be able to capitalize on new opportunities in the cyber universe, deal with threats, implement a better knowledge management system and become more resilient in the cyber space.

CYBER RESILIENCE AND DYNAMIC CAPABILITIES

Cyber resilience is one of the most important characteristics of today's organizations. The Rhizome Model depicts cyber resiliency as a structural axis from the root to the branches, similar to the trunk of a tree. The ability to recover and move forward in the face of adversity while maintaining critical organizational core competencies is referred to as cyber resilience If the unthinkable occurs the organization must be ready with a crisis response and strategy plan. Improving cyber resilience strategy benefits organizations in a variety of ways. Despite the fact that the majority of organizations have little experience with cyber threats, the strategic plan focuses on streamlining efforts to prepare for tomorrow's cyber security threats (Siegel and Sweeney, 2020). As a result, decision-making authorities must have a thorough understanding of cyber threat vulnerabilities, penetration, protection, security assessment, and so on, as well as an understanding of all steps in crisis response planning with dynamic capabilities (Cordes, 2013).

Individuals and organizations must actively participate and interact socially in order to manage in the cyber universe. To break free from organizational myopia and competency traps, new innovative ideas are required. Organizational structure and adaptability are related to dynamic capabilities. Being reactive and proactive on the reactive and proactive sides of dynamic capabilities provides organizations with agility and cyber resilience in the cyber cosmos (Ferdinand, 2015).

Dynamic capabilities learn about their internal and external environments and then change their resource configurations based on this knowledge to assist organizations, whether centralized or decentralized, in achieving their goals. When it comes to centralized, inflexible, and hierarchical public organizations, the situation is different in cyberspace. While cyberspace enables public organizations to demonstrate their dynamic capabilities in terms agility, flexibility and adaptability, the organizational structure and central decision-making mechanism may inhibit innovative improvements.

As a result of such disruptive factors, public institutions are unable to develop dynamic capacities, causing them to fall behind the times. Public sector organizations may become more vulnerable to cyber threats. In the context of cyber security, appropriate collaboration among public and other stakeholders is required; internally, from bottom to top, from macro to micro, all actors must be trained on the cyber strategic plan's course of action. Furthermore, public organizations' cyber agility, cyber resilience, and dynamic capabilities enlightened humans on their rights and responsibilities in cyber security, cyber threats, and cyber law by utilizing convenient technological solutions such as Big Data, Artificial Intelligence, Internet of Things, and Blockchain to improve their individual and organizational adaptability in the cyber cosmos.

CONCLUSION

Digital technologies not only provide a high degree of information storage, but they also provide dynamic and timely knowledge utilization and provide new prospects for knowledge management. The Rhizome Model explains the most important ideas to focus on in order to accomplish a successful digital transformation that leads to good knowledge management, namely technology, human, and complexity. Digitalization, on the other hand, places public information and knowledge in cyberspace. As a result of digitization and the sophistication of disruptive technologies, enterprises are becoming increasingly exposed to cyberattacks.

As a result, a new structure for producing, storing, and securing high-value knowledge is required by many businesses. Traditional knowledge management capabilities, on the other hand, are rendered outdated due to the complexity and dynamic nature of cyber threats and attacks. Cyber security is a dynamic knowledge environment in several aspects. Because cyberspace is increasingly becoming the new battleground for national security, decision-makers must reevaluate and refocus on the strategies, technology, and procedures utilized to identify cybersecurity threats (Obitade, 2019; Malviya & Malmgren, 2019).

Over the last few years, the increase in digitalization, cultural change, and effectiveness in managing knowledge have created an environment in which public organizations can seize the opportunity to be agile. COVID-19 has evolved into a kind of catalyst for (1) the adoption and increasing use of digitalization in the workplace (Amankwah-Amaoh et al., 2021; Hassani et al., 2021; Raimo et al., 2021) and more use of technology, (2) cultural shifts in organizations such as remote working (Amankwah-Amaoh et al., 2021), and (3) knowledge management, which is also a vital component of the digital transformation (Mahdi & Nassar, 2021).

The coronavirus pandemic has accelerated society's digital transformation (Kloos et al., 2021) and digitilization of public organizations by developing new and quick applications e-portals such as a coronavirus testing program, travel allowance, and a dashboard showing statistics on coronavirus cases and deaths. (Yilmaz & Tuzlukaya, 2022). According to Amakwah et al. (2021), there are three main drivers for the Covid -19 effect: Covid-19 (1) compelled many organizations to work remotely, (2) hastened the transition from paper-based to electronic-based processes and procedures, and (3) imposed travel and social distancing constraints, forcing firms to operate online. The value created by the pandemic was also captured by public organizations that were structurally and technologically ready or quickly adapted. The challenges were faced by public organizations that lacked technological infrastructure and had institutional constraints such as an underdeveloped education system, a lack of access to a stable internet connection, or a lack of government investment in infrastructure (Amakwah-Amaoh et al., 2021).

The pandemic also pushed these organizations to work harder to find solutions to these problems in a shorter period of time. Agility necessitates a cultural shift. The Covid-19 pandemic has also accelerated this change. For example, professors who were hesitant or unwilling to take advantage of the opportunities provided by digital technologies were suddenly forced to teach with them (Kloos et al., 2021). Similarly, organizations discovered how to hold virtual meetings, and working from home, which was once considered unusual, became the norm (Tome & Gromova, 2021). These cultural changes had already begun prior to the pandemic, but they were hampered by significant obstacles.

The pandemic accelerated cultural change. The COVID-19 outbreak has changed organisational learning processes and their impact on operational performance (Tortorella et al., 2021). This crisis necessitates novel approaches to knowledge strategies as well as novel models to foster dynamic capabilities (Mahdi & Nassar, 2021) (Mahdi & Nassar, 2021). Although Tortorella et al. (2021) refer to the Covid-19 crisis as a crisis of knowledge capabilities, Tome and Gromova (2021) demonstrated that the home office work environment positively mediates the impact of organizational learning on operational performance during the pandemic. The pandemic has had a significant impact on organizations, causing them to abruptly restructure their processes in order for businesses to continue operating (Tortorella et al., 2021), which has also contributed to agility.

The increase in virtual network relations and transactions as a result of the pandemic has led attackers all over the world to see the covid-19 situation as a golden opportunity to carry out various malicious activities and attacks (Yadav, 2021; Lallie et al., 2021; Baz et al., 2021). Public organizations continuously improve their cybersecurity efforts to protect their digital networks by achieving a balance between agility and digitalization. According to Baz et al. (2021), security leaders must embrace these initiatives that are driven by leveraging emerging technologies and service models that have been transformed to do more with less.

With the shifting dynamics and opportunities afforded by digital transformation and agility, public organizations are paying more attention to knowledge management. However, by investing in cyber security, these firms should be careful to secure the knowledge that is stored in cyberspace.

REFERENCES

Abomhara, M., & Køien, G. (2015). Cyber Security and the Internet of Things: Vulnerabilities, Threats, Intruders and Attacks. *Journal of Cyber Security.*, *4*, 65–88. doi:10.13052/jcsm2245-1439.414

Allessie, D., Sobolewski, M., & Vaccari, L. (2019). Blockchain for digital government. EUR 29677 EN, Publications Office of the European Union.

Alvarenga, A., Matos, F., Godina, R., Joao, C., & Matias, M. (2020). Digital Transformation and Knowledge Managementin the Public Sector. *Sustainability, 12*, 5824. doi:10.3390u12145824

Amankwah-Amoah, J., Khan, Z., Wood, G., & Knight, G. (2021). COVID-19 and digitalization: The great acceleration. *Journal of Business Research, 136*, 602–611. doi:10.1016/j.jbusres.2021.08.011 PMID:34538980

Bayuk, J., Healey, J., Rohmeyer, P., Sachs, M., Schmidt, J., & Weiss, J. (2012). *Cyber Security Policy Guidebook*. Cyber Security Policy Guidebook., doi:10.1002/9781118241530

Baz, M., Alhakami, H., Agrawal, A., Baz, A., & Khan, R. A. (2021). Impact of covid-19 pandemic: a cybersecurity perspective. Intelligent Automation & Soft Computing, 27(3).

Bettiol, M., Di Maria, E., & Micelli, S. (2020). *Industry 4.0 and Knowledge Management: An Introduction*. Building Digital Government Strategies Principles and Practices. doi:10.1007/978-3-030-43589-9

Brezočnik, L., & Majer, Č. (2016). *Comparison of agile methods: Scrum*. Kanban, and Scrumban.

Brous, P., Janssen, M., & Herder, P. (2020). The dual effects of the Internet of Things (IoT): A systematic review of the benefits and risks of IoT adoption by organizations. *International Journal of Information Management, 51*, 51. doi:10.1016/j.ijinfomgt.2019.05.008

Chesalin, A., Grodzenskiy, S., Nilov, M., & Pham, V. (2020). Intelligent quality management tools for digital production and knowledge management system for their application. *IOP Conference Series. Materials Science and Engineering, 862*(4), 042032. doi:10.1088/1757-899X/862/4/042032

Chesbrough, H. (2010). Business Model Innovation: Opportunities and Barriers. *Long Range Planning, 43*(2-3), 354–363. doi:10.1016/j.lrp.2009.07.010

Davenport, T. H., Barth, P., & Bean, R. (2012, Fall). How Big Data is Different? *Sloan Management Review, 54*.

Denning, S. (2018). *The Age of Agile: How Smart Companies Are Transforming the Way Work Gets Done*. AMACOM.

Dessein, W., & Santos, T. (2006). Adaptive Organizations. *Journal of Political Economy, 114*(5), 956–995. doi:10.1086/508031

Di Vaio, A., Palladino, R., Pzzi, A., & Kalisz, D. E. (2021). The Role of Digital Innovation In Knowledge Management Systems: A Systematic Literature Review. *Journal of Business Research, 123*, 220–231. doi:10.1016/j.jbusres.2020.09.042

Diogenes, Y., & Ozkaya, E. (2018). *Cybersecurity Attack and Defense Strategies.* Packt Publishing.

Eggers, W. D., & Bellman, J. (2015). *The journey to government's digital transformation.* Deloitte University Press. https://www2.deloitte.com/content/dam/insights/us/articles/digital-transformation-in-government/DUP_1081_Journey-to-govt-digital-future_MASTER.pdf

Ertan, A., Crossland, G., Heath,C., Denny, D.& Jensen, R. (2020). *Cyber Security Behaviors in Organizations.* Academic Press.

Faraj, S., Renno, W., & Bhardwaj, A. (2021). Unto the breach: What the COVID-19 pandemic exposes about digitalization. *Information and Organization, 31*(1), 100337. doi:10.1016/j.infoandorg.2021.100337

Ferdinand J. (2015) Building organizational cyber resilience: A strategic knowledge-based view of cyber security management. *J Bus Contin Emer Plan, 9*(2), 185-95.

Fourkas, V. (2004). What is 'cyberspace'? *Media Development.*

Hassani, H., Huand, X., & Silva, E. (2021). The Human Digitalisation Journey: Technology First at the Expense of Humans? *Information (Basel), 2021*(12), 267. doi:10.3390/info12070267

Hess, T., Matt, C., Benlian, A., & Wiesbock, F. (2016). Options for Formulating a Digital "Transformation Strategy. *MIS Quarterly Executive, 15*(2), 123–139.

Iansiti, M., & Lakhani, K. (2021). *Competing in the Age of AI: Strategy and Leadership When Algorithms and Networks Run the World. Harvard Business Review Press.*

Isaksen, S. G., & Tidd, J. (2007). *Meeting the Innovation Challenge: Leadership for Transformation and Growth.* Wiley.

Janssen, M., & Voort, H. (2016). Adaptive governance: Towards a stable, accountable and responsive government. *Government Information Quarterly, 33*(1), 1–5. doi:10.1016/j.giq.2016.02.003

Jennex, M. (2007). *What is Knowledge Management?* doi:10.4018/9781599042619.ch001

Kaehler, B. & Grundei, J. (2018). *HR Governance: A Theoretical Introduction*. doi:10.1007/978-3-319-94526-2

Klaus, N., Maier, R., & Haas, O. (2018). Knowledge Management in Digital Change. In *Progress in IS*. Springer.

Kloos, C. D. (2021). Towards a Cloud-Based University Accelerated by the Pandemic. *IEEE Global Engineering Education Conference (EDUCON)*, 1642-1649. 10.1109/EDUCON46332.2021.9453967

Lalli, H. S., S., L. A., Nurse, J. R. C., Erola, A., Epiphaniou, G., Maple, C., & Bellekens, X. (2021). CyberSecurity in the Age of COVID-19: A Timeline and Analysis of Cyber-Crime and Cyber-Attacks during the Pandemic. Computers & Security, 105.

Mahdi, O. R., & Nassar, I. A. (2021). The Business Model of Sustainable Competitive Advantage through Strategic Leadership Capabilities and Knowledge Management Processes to Overcome COVID-19 Pandemic. *Sustainability*, *13*(17), 9891. doi:10.3390u13179891

Malviya, A., & Malmgren, M. (2019). *Big Data for Managers: Creating Value*. Academic Press.

Nuottila, J., Aaltonen, K., & Kujala, J. (2016). Challenges of adopting agile methods in a public organization. *International Journal of Information Systems and Project Management*.

Obitade, P. (2019). Big data analytics: A link between knowledge management capabilities and superior cyber protection. *Journal of Big Data*, *6*(1), 71. Advance online publication. doi:10.1186/s40537-019-0229-9

Pablos, P. O., & Lytras, M. (2018). Knowledge Management, Innovation and Big Data: Implications for Sustainability, Policy Making and Competitiveness. *Sustainability*, *10*(6), 2073. doi:10.3390u10062073

PWC. (2016). *Blockchain – an opportunity for energy producers and consumers?* https://www.pwc.com/gx/en/industries/assets/pwc-blockchain-opportunity-for-energy-producers-and-consumers.pdf

Raimo, N., De Turi, I., Ricciardelli, A., & Vitolla, F. (2021). Digitalization in the cultural industry: Evidence from Italian museums. *International Journal of Entrepreneurial Behaviour & Research*, 1355–2554. doi:10.1108/IJEBR-01-2021-0082

Refsdal, A., Solhaug, B., & Stølen, K. (2015). Cyber- *Risk Management*. Advance online publication. doi:10.1007/978-3-319-23570-7

Reis, J., Amorim, M., Melao, N., Cohen, Y., & Rodriguez, M. (2020). Digitalization: A Literature Review and Research Agenda. *Proceedings on 25th International Joint Conference on Industrial Engineering and Operations Management*, 443-456. 10.1007/978-3-030-43616-2_47

Sailer, P., Stutzman, B., & Kobold, L. (2019). *Successful Digital Transformation*. Siemens Advanta. https://www.siemensadvanta.com/system/files/202011/Successful%20digital%20transformation_whitepaper%20by%20SIEMENS%20Advanta.pdf

Saulais, P., & Ermine, J.L. (2019). *Understanding and Deploying a KM Plan within a Learning Organization*. Academic Press.

Seemma, P. S., Sundaresan, N., & Sowmiya, M. (2018). Overview of Cyber Security. *IJARCCE*, *7*, 125–128. doi:10.17148/IJARCCE.2018.71127

Siegel, C. A., & Sweeney, M. (2020). Cyber Strategy: Risk-Driven Security and Resiliency. Auerbach Publications.

Sousa, W. G., Melo, E. R. P., Bermejo, P. H. D., Farias, R. A. S., & Gomes, A. O. (2019). How and where is artificial intelligence in the public sector going? A literature review and research agenda. *Government Information Quarterly*, *36*(4), 36. doi:10.1016/j.giq.2019.07.004

Srinivas, J., Kumar, D. A., & Neeraj, K. (2018). Government regulations in cyber security: Framework, standards and recommendations. *Future Generation Computer Systems*, *92*, 178–188. Advance online publication. doi:10.1016/j.future.2018.09.063

Stronen, F., Ronning, V. H., & Breunig, K. J. (2019). Innovation Capabilities in Banking: The Case of Norwegian Mobile Payment. *Proceedings of the 20th European Conference On Knowledge Management (ECKM 2019)*, 998-1005.

Tawalbeh, L., Muheidat, F., Tawalbeh, M., & Quwaider, M. (2020). IoT Privacy and Security: Challenges and Solutions. *Applied Sciences (Basel, Switzerland)*, *10*(12), 4102. doi:10.3390/app10124102

Teece, D., Peteraf, M., & Leih, S. (2016). Dynamic capabilities and organizational agility: Risk, uncertainty, and strategy in the innovation economy. *California Management Review*, *58*(4), 13–35. doi:10.1525/cmr.2016.58.4.13

Tomé, E., & Gromova, E. (2021). Development of emergent knowledge strategies and new dynamic capabilities for business education in a time of crisis. *Sustainability*, *13*(8), 4518. doi:10.3390u13084518

Tortorella, G., Narayanamurthy, G., & Staines, J. (2021). COVID-19 Implications on the Relationship between Organizational Learning and Performance. *Knowledge Management Research and Practice, 19*(4), 551–564. Advance online publication. doi:10.1080/14778238.2021.1909430

Valle-Cruz, D., Ruvalcaba-Gomez, E. A., Sandoval-Almazan, R., & Criado, J. I. (2019). A Review of Artificial Intelligence in Government and its Potential from a Public Policy Perspective. *20th Annual International Conference on Digital Government Research.*

Wirtz, B. W., Weyerer, J. C., & Schichtel, F. T. (2019). An integrative public IoT framework for smart government. *Government Information Quarterly, 36*(2), 333–345. doi:10.1016/j.giq.2018.07.001

Yadav, R. (2021). Cyber Security Threats During Covid-19 Pandemic. *International Transaction Journal of Engineering Management & Applied Sciences & Technologies, 12*(3).

Chapter 8
Tools and Technologies for the Governance of Knowledge Management

Bindi Varghese
Christ University, India

Yakkala B. V. L. Pratyusha
Infelearn, India

ABSTRACT

Knowledge management is a consolidation of various endeavours and disciplines. This chapter assesses the space of knowledge management and examines the significance of running a successful business with an efficient management system. To have a smooth management in a company, all the employees in the company need to access all the required information, which may be comprised of documents, collaboration of teams, policies in various departments, etc. All of these require an efficient knowledge management system. A framework for characterising the various tools and techniques available to knowledge management practitioners are well explored in the chapter.

INTRODUCTION

To run a Successful Businesses, an efficient management system is mandatory. And to have smooth management in a company, all the employees in the company need to access all the required information, which may comprise documents, Collaboration of teams, policies in various departments, etc.; (Harrinson, 2021) All of these require

DOI: 10.4018/978-1-6684-4431-3.ch008

an efficient knowledge management system. The Process of Accessing, managing, and sharing the information within an organization is knowledge management (Eisenhauer, 2021). In other words, we can call it a tool for running a successful organization. It helps in managing documentation, guidelines, lists, Databases, memos, and files. This also helps in managing team members, which will be resulted in enhancing the organisation. Knowledge is power, and when properly harnessed, it fuels a successful company. (Chetty, 2017) ICT has a tremendous impact on knowledge management. Currently few knowledge management techniques are followed in the market, but these are not up to the mark to match the requirements of the present organization needs (Wang, 2018). Here we are going to discuss a few current trends which change the face of knowledge management where it will be evolved as a response for meeting our demands and challenges.

RESEARCH SETTING

Businesses in general, work towards improvising the effectiveness of information systems in database management (Alberto Ferraris, 2019) and explore navigational techniques and custom-made applications. Perhaps, organizations in a post- pandemic scenario introduced extensive and massive restructuring process to banish redundant jobs and thereby (Daniele Giampaoli, 2021), the manpower. This process has moved the business process in a leaner organizational structure. In a globally competitive business environment; knowledge management has been finding its way in a sophisticated manner to meet the requisites of a consumer. To stay competitive, organizations are narrowing and streamlining their work-flow processes (DaSilva, 2021). Knowledge Management (KM) not only leads to a managerial efficiency but also a cost-efficient technique in handling security issues (Derrick McIver, 2017), decision making process and overall problem solving to execute an competitive edge. This chapter, we discuss the basic tools of KM followed by idealistic practices (Trees, 2019), and challenges. We conclude with remarks on the future of KM with implications.

STATEMENT OF PROBLEM

With the growth of ICT (Ball, 2020)and innovations in telecommunications technology, KM methods are supported by the need for an efficient time/space boundaries. It is significant for the expansion of firms (Arne Isaksen, 2021), ICT innovations pave way for sharing information as an imperative measure for the firm's continued survival. Newer organizational theories substantiates the competitiveness of organizations by devising measures to apply KM innovatively (Kent, 2021). Two major trends in KM are: developing measurement indexes for the intellectual capital of an organization and Mapping the knowledge with information technology. KM from a discipline details the intervention of artificial intelligence (Metaxiotis, Ergazakis, Samouilidis, & Psarras, 2003), from a system centric perspectives and expert systems, relating to knowledge engineering and knowledge dispersion. The crux of this approach outlines core development of a knowledge with a smart engine that consolidates information to disparate locations with differing databases (Eisenhauer, 2021)into knowledge. This can be used anywhere in the organization at any point of time.

AIM

Security Issues and Privacy also are key determinants (Randeree, 2006) in Knowledge Management Systems (KMS). There are many security threats and risks that are applicable to information systems in general which rather apply to Knowledge Management Systems (Petros Belsis, 2005). Organizations develop KMS to help their project teams and departments to disseminate and reuse knowledge about procedures, technical issues and functional processes. Knowledge Management Systems are significantly developed to ensure organizational information on the project are available for various functional subject areas (Avrahami, 2021). This chapter details on the KM technologies and various innovative tools for devising a good KMS for organizational knowledge dissemination and reuse of data for firm's competitiveness.

KNOWLEDGE MANAGEMENT TECHNOLOGIES: TOOLS AND TECHNIQUES

Content Automation

In 2021, an upcoming newer trend is content automation in the domain of knowledge management systems. The knowledge repository is generally content-driven, and Knowledge Management (KM) is a field that spans several disciplines. Psychology, epistemology, and cognitive science are all included in KM (Birzniece, 2011). Knowledge management aims to make it easier for people and organisations to collaborate, exchange, produce, consume, and reuse information. From an individual and organisational standpoint, understanding KM enhances performance and increase creativity (Eisenhauer, 2021). Organizations can assign manpower usage with relevant work by combining the power of automation with content aggregation. Many businesses utilize high-performance Artificial Intelligence systems (Education, 2021), such as chatbots, to communicate important information when it's needed. To construct powerful information centres, AI-focused technologies and chatbots can process data from ueries and search histories (Metaxiotis, Ergazakis, Samouilidis, & Psarras, 2003). All of this contributes to the establishment of a comprehensive knowledge foundation for future information needs. Automated version control is one way that businesses can benefit from content automation. Some businesses go about their business as usual, and their knowledge management systems help them accelerate or maintain their growth. (Metaxiotis, Ergazakis, Samouilidis, & Psarras, 2003) The foundation for a comprehensive knowledge management system is laid by cloud technologies, the hybrid workspace, graph databases, artificial intelligence, and language processing tools. Because of the pandemic, these technologies are being adopted at a faster rate. Many organizations, on the other hand, had already begun to plan for their digital transition before COVID. These efforts' contributions provide solutions to complicated work situation. (Snell, 2019). AI enables machines to collect, process, and apply information to execute tasks, as well as unlock knowledge that can be communicated to humans to help them make better decisions (Chetty, 2017).Knowledge management allows for the understanding of knowledge, while artificial intelligence (AI) allows us to grow, utilise, and create knowledge in ways we haven't yet envisioned (Daniele Giampaoli, 2021). The link between knowledge management and artificial intelligence has paved the way for cognitive computing.

Cloud Technology

In the Current scenario work-from-home is the best possible option where we can carryon with daily routines in a normal way, in short, we can call it as new normal. This new normal can be possible because of Cloud technology. According to the National Institute of Standards and Technology (NIST) definition (Mell and Grance, 2011), "Cloud technology is a model for enabling ubiquitous, convenient, on demand network access to a shared pool of configurable computing resources (e.g., networks, servers, storage, applications, and services) that can be rapidly provisioned and released with minimal management effort or service provider interaction". In other words, we can say Employees can access all the information and all also able to connect with their Colleagues with the help of Cloud based technologies like Paas, Saas, Iaas. Platform-as-a-Service (PaaS) is a cloud component that allows application development and deployment, whereas Software-as-a-Service (SaaS) is a cloud component that offers online applications. Infrastructure-as-a-Service (IaaS), on the other hand, provides cloud storage, servers, and networking. This model has various benefits like Cost reduction, Convenience and elasticity in barring workloads

Demands which can manage all the resources in the workplace like (e.g., CPU, Storage, Memory and Bandwidth) are pooled, which has great scope in satisfying the customers' demands. These advantages are primary reason for Growing traction for this technology in various fields.

Table 1. Elements of knowledge management system

Themes	Elements of KM and KMS	Authors
Knowledge Creation	ICT enabled Knowledge Creation process	(Avrahami, 2021)
Knowledge Sharing	Factors creating knowledge sharing Tools and Techniques knowledge sharing	(Birzniece, 2011) (Hartmann, 2008)
Implications of Knowledge Management System	Effects of KMS on Organizational performance Opportunities for KMS and Governance Knowledge Management Technologies	(DaSilva, 2021) (Trees, 2019)
Knowledge Conversion	Framework to align the Knowledge creation Process and encourage Knowledge sharing to establish sustainable competitive advantage	(Hanson; Birzniece, 2011) (Harrinson, 2021)
Knowledge Management System	Importance of Kms to increase the ability of organisation to perform well	(Lawes, 2021)
Knowledge management solutions	Usage of latest technologies in knowledge management for sustaining their position in the market.	(John Lannon, 2020) (Arne Isaksen, 2021)
Knowledge Management Trends	Customising knowledge management software using ICT according to organisation needs.	(Eisenhauer, 2021)
Knowledge Graph	Visual representation of data is effective and new way of working.	(Education, 2021)
Implementation Knowledge Management	Case study of a Retail bank which effectively use KM to decreases its operational risks.	(Daniele Giampaoli, 2021) (MOGOLE, 2014)
Enterprise Knowledge Management	Use technologies like NLP, Data analytics unstructured data is organised	(Alberto Ferraris, 2019)
Hybrid KMS	Technologies like content automation, cloud sharing integrated with KM to collaborate with several disciplines.	(Ball, 2020) (Meenu Dave, 2013)
Secure Knowledge Management	The role information security system in building effective Knowledge management System	(Randeree, 2006)

The Researches in the field of knowledge management by cloud technology came up with concepts like Enterprise knowledge Delic and Riley (2009) (EKM). Cloud based system where all the information about the organisation/ Enterprise can termed as EKM. This EKM may further divided into 4 Components which are Infrastructure, Applications, Content and Users. The infrastructure may comprise of data centres that act as Storage centres, network allocators and also helps in computing which depends on cloud-based system chosen by the organisation. Respectively Applications will help in dealing with software's, operating systems as well as Programming Environment. The aspects like Capture, represent, process and deliver the needs of enterprise will be can take care by Content components whereas User Component helps in setting of various goals of skills in order to process gather and deliver the knowledge of business which are in line with the Contemporary Users by using Cloud Components. These Applications of Cloud technology is Self-Adaptable (Maurer et al 2010). Cloud Computing also facilitates default logic, situation calculus and case-based reasoning (CBR) and interpretation of data (Cruz et al 2011). This CBR helps in measuring data from datacentres and trigger the appropriate actions according to the assigned goal which also prevents in violating any service level Agreements. Cloud computing also disruptive technology which helps in creating new products, Strategies and business model for the Enterprises which can survive in this dynamic and competitive markets (Sultan 2013).

Graph Database

The network of real-world qualities and entities such as events, concepts, and circumstances are known as a knowledge graph. Knowledge graphs can show how various elements are related internally. These knowledge assets are used by organisations to describe their organisational structure, procedures, and other resources. (Chetty, 2017) . Enterprises will utilise knowledge graphs to refine searches, the content assembly systems, and recommendation engines in 2021 (Ball, 2020). Individuals can get immediate answers to their search questions by using knowledge graphs, which include boxes of targeted search results. They have the ability to connect various sorts of datasets in a meaningful and relevant way. Artificial intelligence and machine learning technologies are used by businesses to uncover in-depth data trends. The future of information management technology is the knowledge graph (Education, 2021), which is combined with AI/ML-based predictive capabilities. This is a huge step forward from current knowledge management initiatives. Graph technology connects disparate pieces of data with the appropriate context, allowing for exceptionally quick and versatile querying (DaSilva, 2021).

When graphs are combined with AI/ML-based recommendations or predictive capabilities, searches not only provide particular results, but also a rich range of highly relevant alternate suggestions and answers to complex problems in real time (Ball, 2020). To streamline their processes and acquire company data, modern firms employ a variety of apps. Google Drive, Slack, Salesforce, and Zendesk, to mention a few, are undoubtedly among them (Hanson).

We all know how beneficial they are for increasing our daily productivity, but you may not have regarded the data as a gold trove for the company. Document metadata pulled from Google Drive and ingested into Neo4j (Ball, 2020)(a software that aids in the creation of knowledge graphs) can, for example, tell you what document topics are currently popular, which projects are receiving a lot of attention, and who are organization's Google Drive super users (i.e. people who review/edit a lot of documents) (Ball, 2020) are. The possibilities are unlimited, and the analysis' ability is only limited by the amount and quality of data you have. Similarity of papers, identification of reusable content, employee skills inventory, client projects, technologies used, talents necessary, and much more are among the additional business insights (MOGOLE, 2014).

NLP and Text Analytics

Another trend redefining the knowledge Management System is Natural Language Processing (NLP) and Text Analytics. Artificial intelligence (AI) is used with NLP and text analytics for interpreting language. For years, KM experts have struggled with existing technologies (Wang, 2018). These technologies all serve the same basic objective in terms of knowledge management (Wang, 2018). To be successful in current dynamic world and sustain a position in the market, data and its quality become essential for every organisation. The issue now is one of size. We are generating data at an incredible rate. According to some estimates, by 2025 (Alberto Ferraris, 2019). KM professionals confront data to interpret (Trees, 2019). Intelligent machines and intelligent interfaces are required to detect signals in the noisy world of big data. (Birzniece, 2011)Text analytics and natural language processing (NLP) can help with this. If the company is considering implementing these tools, here are some best practises to get you started. Text analytics is the technology that allows you to search and analyse enormous amounts of data intelligently. It is used by scientists and pharmaceutical businesses to examine COVID-19 and its variations data (Arne Isaksen, 2021). Text analytics is used to synthesise findings, connect publications to clinical breakthroughs, and uncover patterns (Daniele Giampaoli, 2021).

Text analytics can also be used to forecast consumer behaviour, monitor customer mood, track compliance, and discover fraud by analysing text, emails, and social media (Snell, 2019). Text analytics and speech-to-text services are available through Azure Cognitive Services, allowing businesses to take advantage of these capabilities. Natural language processing (NLP) uses computers to interpret the meaning of written or spoken language and respond appropriately. Researchers predicted a market slowdown as a result of decreased customer interactions and supply chain concerns in the manufacturing (Snell, 2019), consumer products, and transportation and logistics industries. Dynamic growth is predicted by interactive virtual assistants and chatbots, which provide benefits such as cost savings. By 2023, Juniper Research forecasts savings of $11 billion in banking, retail, and healthcare. According to Mordor Intelligence, the global market for text analytics will be $5.5 billion in 2020, growing at a rate of 17% per year over next 5 years. NLP, on the other hand, is expected to expand at a rate of 20% each year from 2020 to 2026, according to Mordor Intelligence. Markets and Markets, on the other hand, share the same forecast. Before moving forward, we have to first examine and improve the quality of our data. According to some estimates, up to 96 percent of businesses have experienced data quality issues as a result of adopting AI into their operations. This isn't merely a technical issue. According to some estimates, poor data costs the United States around $3 trillion every year (Harrinson, 2021).Data quality is predominant with text analytics and NLP. It must also be a top priority for the company. The most successful businesses allocate an interdisciplinary team to this task (Muhammad Rafiq, 2016).Of course, we're dealing with unstructured data in both text analytics and NLP.

Unfortunately, many businesses assume that because they are working with unstructured data, quality is unimportant. Working with unstructured data, the technologies utilized should be carefully integrated (Wang, 2018). As international data quality assessment standards support many businesses ; accuracy of most natural language recognition algorithms is reliable. When opposed to putting meaning and intent together, recognising words is a fundamental function. And there's a lot of disagreement on how to approach NLP (Snell, 2019).The two basic approaches are statistical and metaphorical. The former is precisely what it sounds like: you train the system on a large corpus of data, it recognises patterns, creates a model, and then uses probability to predict the meaning of a piece of English. However, determining NLP engine based on the needs and data is a straightforward best practise (Muhammad Rafiq, 2016).After all, it's all about the numbers. These technologies are built on data, run on data, and generate massive volumes of data. As a result, it's critical for the evaluation-which is data-driven. In the end, data will be the resource that propels business and economic progress in the twenty-first century (Trees, 2019).

THE HYBRID WORKPLACE

The Hybrid workplace is the work model using by the organisations to regroup and redefine the work place by bringing the balance between remote place and office work. (Avrahami, 2021) This model helps the employees to be flexible and also not to miss any of the office elements. Organisations are embracing this new work culture which gives way for the remote teams and tools for being engaged, productive and happy. Enterprise Knowledge management (Avrahami, 2021) is the software used by the organisations for blending in and implementing this approach to the successful management of work. (Avrahami, 2021). EKM helps in Seamless Project work, Easier Collaboration and Improved Productivity can enabled with this Software. (Avrahami, 2021). These systems are according to the organisations and employee needs. Even if the pandemic subsides, technology-supported Collaboration will certainly rise dramatically, and the hybrid work environment will become the norm. Collaboration platforms are becoming more popular, and COVID is helping to accelerate their adoption. For example, Microsoft reported a fivefold growth in daily active Teams users from November 2019 to October 2020. The use of collaboration platforms increased by at least 50% between April and October 2020 (Eisenhauer, 2021). Adroit Market Research, on the other hand, forecasts a $45 billion market by 2025 (Ball, 2020).As a solution to the aforementioned issues, we must first understand how elements in the organisation interact, according to Feldman. "Understanding how elements in the organisation interact is key to designing a solution that is easier than asking a co-worker" Begin by compiling a list of knowledge requirements from around the organisation so you can understand what people are looking for and how they're finding it.

(Harrinson, 2021)Unified search returns results from multiple data stores at the same time, allowing employees to get more information with less effort. Employees who are responsible for the maintenance and tweaking of federated search will have less work to do. "You'll need a unified search if you want to make sure individuals can discover the right information," Chase added. (Daniele Giampaoli, 2021). The results are linked to the company's values, (NEVO, 2003)Starting small is one of the best approaches in developing a knowledge management plan since it allows you to gain a solid understanding of one subject at a time (Hartmann, 2008). The knowledge management effort will acquire traction as individuals learn about triumphs in one area. Taking advantage of that opportunity is critical to the project's success. As the discovery process progresses, you can realign the knowledge management strategy by starting small and gaining greater staff buy-in. Feldman (2012) explained that this is critical since the change management process never ends.

Seamless Collaboration Tool

Many intranet packages will have flexible and diverse collaboration options in 2021. You'll notice a shift away from Gantt charts in favour of features that allow for simple scheduling, transparency, and tracking (Eisenhauer, 2021). Some of the various collaboration options to look for include task management, spaces, wiki pages, cases, and forums. The number of US employees who worked from home "at least half the year" increased by 115 percent between 2005 and 2017... This figure is expected to climb in the future (DaSilva, 2021). As a result, solutions that enable seamless Collaboration, editing, and communication – regardless of user location – (Birzniece, 2011)will be a key knowledge management trend.

Visuals are Replacing Lists

Users had to search through long lists, intricate file names, and large amounts of text to find documents in early versions of knowledge management software. Those days are long gone. A key knowledge management trend for 2021 (Birzniece, 2011)will be an image-focused and minimalist design. It's all about user-friendly navigation—finding the information you need quickly and simply. Visual tools are the big assets in achieving them (Eisenhauer, 2021). Visual tools assist us in more effectively communicating our message. The widespread usage of visual tools in is and km attests to their practical importance in both fields. Frameworks, models, procedures, and evaluative techniques all use visual tools in KM (Ball, 2020). The Core Capabilities and Activities framework is an example of where visual tools are used. Visual aids for simplifying or summarising complicated events may improve communicability, but they may also contribute to misinterpretation.

Flexible and Fine-Grained Permissions

Many businesses value roles and permissions because they want to stimulate the creation and exchange of information without turning their intranet into the Wild West (Trees, 2019). As a result, the focus of knowledge management is shifting from control to cultivation, allowing the team to share information naturally while maintaining content governance (Eisenhauer, 2021). Permission settings that are flexible will be a knowledge management trend to watch. Employees will be able to add to the knowledge base while quality will be monitored with as much or as little oversight as needed.

Organised Content through Tags

Content classification that is more refined is a continuing knowledge management trend. Users will be able to filter content in a variety of ways in 2021, making it more searchable and selective. Tags will be used to provide blogs, articles, and wikis a unique and easily searchable home (Eisenhauer, 2021). Information can also be found by format, author, or department. This reduces ambiguity and makes knowledge management a more participatory experience (DaSilva, 2021).

Easy to use Segmented Space

Let's get one thing straight: you should be segmenting the departments or groups if you aren't already (Hartmann, 2008). Knowledge management system is a social community where people share, refine, and organise information assets. Businesses, on the other hand, frequently experience information overload, especially during moments of rapid expansion and success (Eisenhauer, 2021). The workers are most valuable asset, and they require their own digital workspace to organise information and establish a sense of belonging within the company (Chetty, 2017). Although digital workspaces or divided groups are not new, increased user-friendliness will be a major knowledge management trend in 2021 (Lawes, 2021). Create private or public groups, and give members access to as many tools as you want that space, and send immediate notifications to users.

Consistent and Immediate Notifications

Knowledge management trends have evolved in recent years away from email, which has been the major mode of communication for decades, and toward more rapid and direct forms of Collaboration (Eisenhauer, 2021). Can you count on more than one hand how many needless emails you've received in the last week? You'll probably need a couple of hands (DaSilva, 2021). In 2021, notifications will be the answer. Members of a space or workflow can avoid having their inboxes clogged with announcements and relevant messages from team members (Chetty, 2017).

Easy Customisation and Scalability

Easy-to-use customization options are required for a knowledge management platform to genuinely be a one-size-fits-all solution. When we mention customization, we are referring to the look and feel of the knowledge management system, as well as the tools you wish to enable, their names, and their locations (DaSilva, 2021). We will be able to do it without an IT crew by 2021. Customization is critical to a successful software installation, especially during the rollout of intranet (Eisenhauer, 2021). Keep sites well-equipped with the necessary tools so that people are eager to get to work.

Focus on Employee 360 Angle View

Organizations can generate a consolidated perspective of a topic by combining knowledge from many sources, according to the "360-degree" notion. (Eisenhauer, 2021) Employee 360-degree solutions are increasingly being used by businesses to generate a holistic view of their people, their actions, their capabilities, and any other relevant data. An employee 360-degree solution, when implemented appropriately (Ball, 2020), may assist businesses in tracking employees from the time they are hired until the time they leave. Organizations may efficiently increase employees' skill sets and evaluate their growth during employment using a 360-degree solution (Harrinson, 2021).The employee life cycle encompasses an employee's complete connection with their employer. Attraction, recruiting, onboarding, development, retention, and separation are the steps that make up this process. Because all components of the employee's hiring process and retention are mapped and visible, having 360-degree perspectives on this life cycle ensures that all of the employee's needs are addressed (DaSilva, 2021). HR managers and existing team members can use the 360-degree knowledge graph to manage the entire employee life cycle in one place.

An IT firm looking to add a new product programmer to the development team; require input from the development team, budget information from finance and own HR skills to draught the function description and publish it to the optimal channels (Lawes, 2021). Organizations link essential information together by using knowledge graph enabled by Employee 360 (Lawes, 2021): To map out the required skills and to evaluate if the prospects are a good match for the requirements (Ball, 2020). The goal of this exercise is to create a knowledge graph that can be used by both employers and employees to manage the life cycle and promote ongoing enrichment during their time at the organisation (Education, 2021). Search indexing is becoming more accessible and is an powerful search engine is essential for any knowledge management platform, especially as content continues to develop. Consider the following scenario: you work for a huge company with a large knowledge base (Education, 2021).

Figure 1. Tools - knowledge management (Source: Developed by the Authors, 2022)

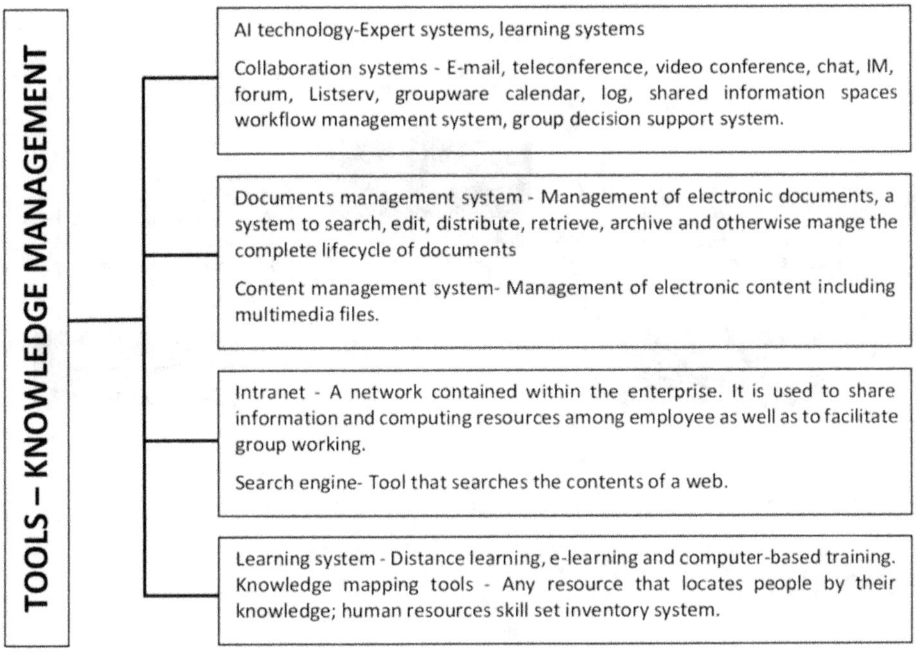

IMPLICATIONS

Knowledge management challenges are mounting issues for organizations which are extensively working towards KM and allied knowledge intensive areas (Avrahami, 2021). Collaborators and consulting organizations are directly engaged in selling knowledge. Perhaps, certain indicators are imperative for the organization's to disseminate and apply knowledge (Chetty, 2017). However the creation, dissemination and use of knowledge within the organization can generate a strategic impression with the effective use of an efficient KM system. The role of ICT and information technology in the KM program can be critically be an significant aspect in knowledge creation (Daniele Giampaoli, 2021).

Figure 2. Knowledge management process for organizational efficiency (Source: Developed by the Authors, 2021)]

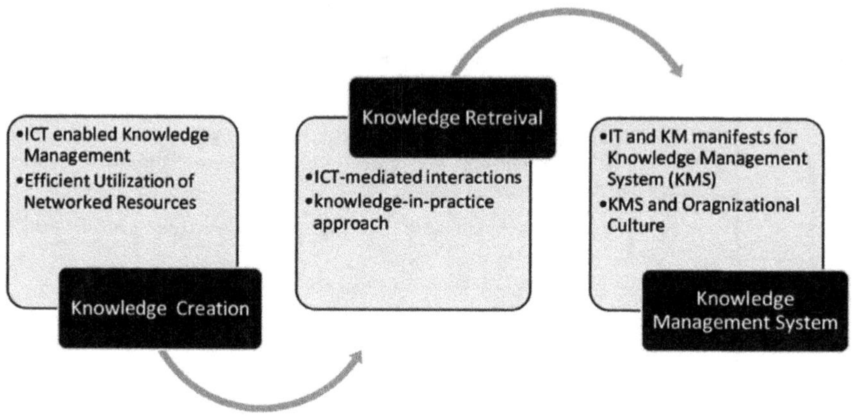

CONCLUSION

Efficient Management of Knowledge become a valuable resource for all Organisations. For creating sustainable competitive advantage any organisation efficient knowledge management system is required. (Daniele Giampaoli, 2021).This chapter focuses on determining varied perspectives towards knowledge management and architypes of governance and examining the role of Content automation is at its best. This chapter accentuates perspectives on cloud technology, graph database, NLP and text analytics, Seamless collaboration tool, Flexible and fine-grained permissions and Organised content through tags. By capturing implicit information within an organization's database, search indexing combined with knowledge management software can provide immediate value. Knowledge management tools search indexing features have progressed beyond simple searching to assist enterprises with information dissemination.

The future of knowledge management determines and demand a changed perspective through a shift in the culture of an organization culture (Umar Farooq Sahibzada C. J., 2020). Analysing the commitment at varied levels of the organization enhance the learning and improves communication (Eisenhauer, 2021). The technological infrastructure, determines the need of an organization, and facilitates required tools with a new dimension to connect and configure information and accelerates necessary action for better KM efforts (Ball, 2020). Firms are required to harness the knowledge to remain competitive, with an innovative pedagogy to build an "intelligent organizations".

REFERENCES

Alberto Ferraris, A. M. (2019). Big data analytics capabilities and knowledge management: Impact on firm performance. *Management Decision*, *57*(8), 1923–1936. doi:10.1108/MD-07-2018-0825

Amjad Iqbal, F. L. (2019). From knowledge management to organizational performance: Modelling the mediating role of innovation and intellectual capital in higher education. *Journal of Enterprise Information Management*.

Arne Isaksen, M. T. (2021). Digital transformation of regional industries through asset modification. *Competitiveness Review*, *31*(1), 130–144. doi:10.1108/CR-12-2019-0140

AvrahamiH. (2021). Retrieved from https://www.kmslh.com/blog/how-to-support-hybrid-work-with-enterprise-knowledge-management/

Ball, H. (2020). Retrieved from neo4j.com: https://neo4j.com/blog/building-enterprise-knowledge-graph/

Birzniece, I. (2011). *Artificial Intelligence in Knowledge Management:Overview and Trends. Scientific Journal of Riga Technical University Computer Science.*

Chetty, L. (2017). *Enhancing the effectiveness of a knowledge management toolkit in a professional services firm*. Academic Press.

Daniele Giampaoli, F. S. (2021). Integrating knowledge management with intellectual capital to drive strategy: A focus on Italian SMEs. *VINE Journal of Information and Knowledge Management Systems*.

DaSilvaA. (2021). Retrieved from https://www.poolparty.biz/what-is-customer-360-in-enterprise-360/

Derrick McIver, D. A. (2017). Effects of knowledge management on unit performance: Examining the moderating role of tacitness and learnability. *Journal of Knowledge Management*.

EducationI. C. (2021). Retrieved from https://www.ibm.com/cloud/learn/knowledge-graph#:~:text=A%20knowledge%20graph%2C%20also%20known,the%20term%20knowledge%20%E2%80%9Cgraph.%E2%80%9D

Eisenhauer, T. (2021). Retrieved from axerosolutions.com: https://axerosolutions.com/blog/17-hot-knowledge-management-trends-for-2021

Hanson, K. (n.d.). *Integrating Knowledge Management and E-Learningto Enhance Knowledge Creation and Conversion for Competitive Advantage*. Academic Press.

Harald Vacik, C. T. (2013). *The role of knowledge management tools in supporting sustainable forest management*. Academic Press.

HarrinsonE. (2021). Retrieved from https://www.kminstitute.org/blog/learn-top-5-knowledge-management-trends-2021

Hartmann, R. S.-d. (2008). The use of tacit knowledge within innovative companies: Knowledge management in innovative enterprises. *Journal of Knowledge Management*, 14.

John Lannon, J. N. (2020). Paradoxes and partnerships: A study of knowledge exploration and exploitation in international development programmes. *Journal of Knowledge Management*, 8–31.

KentE. (2021). Retrieved from https://blog.coveo.com/4-steps-to-knowledge-management-in-hybrid-offices/

LawesT. (2021). Retrieved from https://www.symphonysummit.com/itil/automating-your-knowledge-management/

Meenu Dave, Y. S. (2013). Cloud Computing and Knowledge Management as a Service: A Collaborative Approach to Harness and Manage the Plethora of Knowledge. BVICAM's International Journal of Information Technology Bharati Vidyapeeth's Institute of Computer Applications and Management, 619-622.

Metaxiotis, K., Ergazakis, K., Samouilidis, E., & Psarras, J. (2003). Decision support through knowledge management: The role of the artificial intelligence. *Information Management & Computer Security*.

Mogole, E. (2014). *A South African Retail Bank's Readiness for Knowledge Management Implementation*. Academic Press.

Muhammad Rafiq, A. B. (2016). Innovative Trends in Knowledge Management: A Cloud Computing Perspective. ME14 DUBAI Conference.

Mujeye, D. (2016). *Investigating The Effectiveness Of Concept Maps In Facilitating Tacit Knowledge Conversion During Requirements Elicitation: A Quantitative Evaluative Study*. Academic Press.

Nevo, D. (2003). *Developing Effective Knowledge Management Systems*. Academic Press.

Peter Sharp, A. E. (2003). *Visual Tools within Make- A Knowledge Management Method*. Academic Press.

Petros Belsis, S. K. (2005). Information systems security from a knowledge management perspective. *Information Management & Computer Security*, *13*(3), 189–202. doi:10.1108/09685220510602013

Randeree, E. (2006). Knowledge management: Securing the future. *Journal of Knowledge Management*, *10*(4), 145–156. doi:10.1108/13673270610679435

Sahar Hayaeian, R. H. (2021). The impact of knowledge management strategies on the relationship between intellectual capital and innovation: Evidence from SMEs. *Journal of Intellectual Capital.*

Snell, J. (2019). *Text Analytics and Natural Language Processing: Knowledge Management's Next Frontier*. Academic Press.

TreesL. (2019). Retrieved from https://www.apqc.org/blog/5-reasons-why-knowledge-management-moving-cloud

Umar Farooq Sahibzada, C. J. (2020). Fueling knowledge management processes in Chinese higher education institutes (HEIs): The neglected mediating role of knowledge worker satisfaction. *Journal of Enterprise Information Management*, *33*(6), 1395–1417. doi:10.1108/JEIM-07-2019-0197

Umar Farooq Sahibzada, J. C. (2020). Knowledge management processes, knowledge worker satisfaction, and organizational performance: Symmetric and asymmetrical analysis. *Aslib Journal of Information Management*, 112–129.

Wang, C. (2018). *Integrating Data Analytics & Knowledge Management: A Conceptual Model.* Academic Press.

Chapter 9
Information Overload and the Use of Data Analytics and Visualization Tools in Organizations

Tereza Raquel Merlo
https://orcid.org/0000-0002-2042-5415
University of North Texas, USA

Suliman Hawamdeh
https://orcid.org/0000-0001-7018-6945
University of North Texas, USA

ABSTRACT

This chapter examines information overload and its impact on organizational performance and productivity, the level of use of data analytics tools by organizations to address the information overload problem, and reports on the results from some of the data collected from an online survey about the use of visual analytics tools in organizations. The survey was aimed at gathering users' experiences in dealing with information overload and their level of exposure to data analytics tools. The results from the survey show that email is still the most time-consuming application, with a reported increase in remote access via handheld devices. A relevant percentage of respondents (65%) confirmed having knowledge and experience using some sort of data analytics tools, while 69.23% stated that the exposure to large amounts of information at work causes stress and anxiety.

DOI: 10.4018/978-1-6684-4431-3.ch009

INTRODUCTION

The remarkable amount of digital information created worldwide and exchanged on a daily basis in organizations of all types, and society in general, has been redefining the idea of information usefulness, knowledge value, and perception (McKeown and Philip, 2003). Numerous sources of data in a digital information era often prompt confusion when considering the fast spread of ideas and knowledge that are not necessarily trustworthy or reliable. The 21st century has been marked by the phenomenon of excessive information and disinformation parallelly, characterized by a notable misuse of information for political, economic, and personal gains that in many cases are catastrophic. The notion that information is becoming so fragile now that it is "free" for all in a web-based format could not have been conceived by the first guardians of information behind church and library walls. From the Guttenberg Bible (c. 1450) to the worldwide web, the invention of Tim Berners-Lee (1989), the relationship between humans and knowledge has been transformative in many significant and troubling ways.

Through a process of turning data into information and knowledge, society has been reshaping its organizational system, and knowledge is an asset that must be used to increase productivity and the well-being of knowledge workers (Mohanta, Kannan and Thooyamani, 2006). The approach to information consumption as a powerful organizational strategy is strictly related to the organizations' commitment to allow decision makers to act on the most up-to-date information about business processes, procedures, and products. Proper data processing and data analysis must be succinctly presented with effective data visualization methods and techniques, so that information is easily processed and consumed, translating in quick operations and decision making by individuals in all levels of the organization. This is especially true of most modern boardrooms, where organizations are encouraged to have independent directors that may not have the same industry or organizational expertise as non-independent directors (Roy, et. al., 2017). Problems such as the aforementioned *information overload* (too much information with excessive data that overburdens and prohibits the ability to assimilate because of cognitive limitations & time constraints) and *information asymmetry* (difference between information available to management and what is presented to the board (especially with independent directors) hamper the decision-making process and subject the organization to legal liability and operational viability (Roy, et. al., 2017), ultimately affecting profitability and competitiveness.

The use of visual data analytics tools can reduce the problem of information overload and the amount of information that employees need to process on daily basis (Dillon, Vossen and Rastrick, 2013). Areas that have been investigated in the literature and the study discussed here have covered information overload and the use of information systems in organizations. The studies also highlighted the human aspect of data management and production that decisively impacts profitability, creativity, and competitiveness in organizations. The main questions that have been addressed in these studies focused on two general ideas. The first one is the impact of information overload on productivity in the work environment, and the second is the extent that organizations use data analytics tools to deal with information overload (IO). The principal benefits of addressing these questions are the ability for organizations to recognize that information overload is a serious problem and help devise certain mechanisms that will contribute to business processes improvement and business performance and pipeline success management.

INFORMATION OVERLOAD

As information technology evolves there is an increasing volume of data being generated in various formats and from a variety of sources, prompting information and organizational anxiety that inevitably affects the workplace dynamic, productivity, and time management. Roetzel (2018) defends that information overload occurs due to four different factors: databases, social networks, information source design, and source preferences. The author asserts that: "While the core issue of providing a too high amount of information or too complex information when using management information systems, databases, etc., may confuse its users, it may also affect their ability to prioritize or complicate the retrieval of information" (p. 506).

One of the benefits of this ongoing battle is the advanced technology being made nearly constantly to combat IO, among other internet-related obstacles. However, hackers are never too far behind in the exploitation realm, and are even ahead of the security of some organizations in recent events. One of the benefits of this ongoing battle is the advanced technology being made nearly constantly to combat IO, among other internet-related obstacles. However, hackers, in some sense, are never too far behind in the exploitation realm, and are even ahead of the security of some organizations in recent events. Information overload in organizations is continually growing in this digital age, and so are the issues related to it. However, with the correct tool and right organizational culture, managers can overcome the feeling of being overwhelmed with information and employees across the board will have a better understanding and be able to efficiently use the information systems available. An example in the hospitality industry is analyzed by Saxena and Lanest (2018) who investigated the reviews of websites like Hotels.com, Expedia, TripAdvisor, Facebook, and Twitter to see all the comments related to the organizations and their employees' performance. Both positive and negative reviews were read, but there is never enough time to go through all the submitted feedback, prompting participants to say that: "This has made it a lot more difficult because you could get lost. It is information overload, that you could get into these reports and be gone for a week." Most managers appear to perceive information as overwhelming at times and that data cannot be tamed. They had to adapt quickly or risk having a mental breakdown (p. 29).

Lavenda (2017) advocates that when there is so much information that it is no longer possible to effectively be used, we are dealing with information overload. The data visualization process is a way to take the large amount of data that is being generated and present it in a cohesive way that can be used to gain value. Organizations generate huge amounts of data, and from data, visualization designers can create systems that can take a single point of data and correlate it to other points of data to give the information meaning, which can then be used by decision makers to maximize gains within an organization. Larose (2014) argues that: "Information provides meaning to the decision maker by correlating data within a context, and knowledge is a grouping of information that has value or provides benefit to the decision-maker, such as solving a problem" (as cited in Moore, 2017, p. 129).

DATA ANALYTICS AND VISUALIZATION

Data visualization can challenge a variety of these issues, especially in cases of suboptimal information source presentation mode, content recommendation, and extraneous information in datasets (noise). Data visualization technology uses models to predict human interpretation of information and allows the user to make complex connections in otherwise unstructured datasets to tackle the issue of information overload. "The prior research regarding system or user adaption is characterized by a strong orientation toward "hard" technical characteristics such as algorithm efficiency, availability, compatibility, system feature design, and visualization". (Roetzel, 2018, p. 507). Qin, Zhao, Mou, and Zhang (2018) propose an algorithm for creating a "personal knowledge map" that can be used when sharing knowledge in a peer-to-peer environment without causing information overload. Through this approach, information is organized in a way that the receiver or knowledge seeker can then apply what they already know from their past experiences to this new knowledge in order to learn it more efficiently (Qin et al., 2018, p. 399). The drawback to this is the possibility that the knowledge seeker does not have the right kind of previous knowledge to absorb the new knowledge. Qin et al. (2018) term this "the cold start problem" (p. 409). This can cause difficulty in retaining the new knowledge without the assistance of association or familiarity.

There are many benefits of implementing a data visualization tool as part of a KM technology approach in order to mitigate information overload. The popular software Tableau, for example, helps organizations analyze data and transform it into useful visualizations that are easy to share and communicate. The ability to connect almost any type of data to Tableau in the form of spreadsheets, databases, cloud, etc., is an undeniable benefit that supports the idea that most organizations will have compatible data sets (Tableau Software, 2019). It should also be mentioned that these data connections between the organization and Tableau can happen in real-time because Tableau supports both live and scheduled updates (Tableau Software, 2019). Another benefit to the incorporation of Tableau is the intuitive insight that it offers in the form of guidance and automated visualizations.

Data visualization assists with sense-making by extrapolating meaning from complex datasets and uses the human visual system to create insight regarding conceptual information. Several researchers defend that humans are, by nature, visual learners, and that acquiring knowledge visually allows a more effective understanding and exchange of ideas, knowledge production, and knowledge sharing; therefore, enabling a deeper human connection and interaction and a better understanding of concepts. Dasgupta, Poco, and Wei (2015) defend that data visualization is a methodically developed graphic which represents data in a manner that allows one to obtain insights, develop understanding, identify patterns, trends, or anomalies faster, promoting engaging discussions.

The many possible interfaces are filled with helpful ways to generate useful knowledge that is yet to be discovered. For example, Visual Analytics can be aided by Tableau's ability to leverage best practices using fields the user may be interested in as it suggests "Automatic Marks" and the "Show Me view" are helpful features to facilitate access and the display of data. The foremost use of Tableau is the ability to share and communicate the data findings through the "Dashboards" and "Stories," which offer a variety of actions such as interactive Images and Web Pages, URL Actions, and Dashboard Extensions (Tableau Software, 2019). Overall, the leading advantage that Tableau and similar data visualization tools provide to the organization in the reduction of information overload is the ability to bridge the gap between information that is available and information that is useful.

The manipulation of large data sets by data visualization software can be accomplished by other tools such as Google Analytics or Microsoft Power BI, both considered relevant tools by participants in this study. An organization can mitigate information overload by choosing to implement a data visualization tool within their KM processes that meets the organization's needs (Koltay, 2017). Roetzel (2017) defends that: "Information overload is seen as a decisive issue across all disciplines within business administration and economics" (p. 15). According to the author: "information overload is a decisive factor driving negative work environments [that] are killing productivity, dampening creativity, and making us unhappy" (Roetzel, 2019, p. 480) and in that sense, data visualization tools have been proven efficient in simplifying and organizing data representation, making data easily comprehended and visually appealing to audiences of both knowledgeable and inexperienced professionals in a way that is manageable.

Tableau and Microsoft Power BI

For the types of data analytics tools used by organizations, there are several leading solutions available in the current market, many highlighted by Gartner, the global research advisory firm that provides information and advice focusing on IT, among other services in business and management. Gartner (2022) claims that data virtualization technology "is based on the execution of distributed data management processing, primarily for queries against multiple heterogeneous data sources, and federation of query results into virtual news" (Gartner…, 2022, para. 4). In terms of the product features and ratings in data visualization software, the most critical features include data deployment, content management, a customizable dashboard, relational display, reporting/analytics, search filters, visual discovery, and price. The graphic below contains a list of the top data visualization software utilized by companies participating in this study, with Power BI and Tableau dominating the market, as shown in the infographic word cloud below:

Known as the "grand master of data visualization software" (B. Marr, 2018) Tableau earned its spot due to interface and visual aesthetics, but also due in large part to how well the technology can handle big data. When handling such large amounts of data through a given interface, user navigation and information needs to change periodically, creating the need for organizations to have the same in site structure and navigation, further enhancing users' browsing efficiency. (M. Chen, 2018). Tableau supports the creation of Visuals/Graphics. This feature introduces various analytical tools, including forecasting, clustering, trend lines, average lines, etc., making it simple to color code, create categories, and even use geolocation fields and a custom dashboard that is interactive. Another feature is storytelling, used to describe the visuals for story points on demand and helping to create stories from images. The study developed by Hoelscher and Mortimer (2018) emphasizes the importance of data analysis through the usage of data visualization software and demonstrates how Tableau helped facilitate the "understanding of data and how it can be transformed into information to enhance the decision-making process" (p. 49). The investigation describes a case study in a small start-up manufacturer investigated for six months, tracking sales transactions and the importance of data analytics for decision-making and profitability.

Figure 1. Infographic: Most identified data analytics and visualization tools utilized by survey respondents.

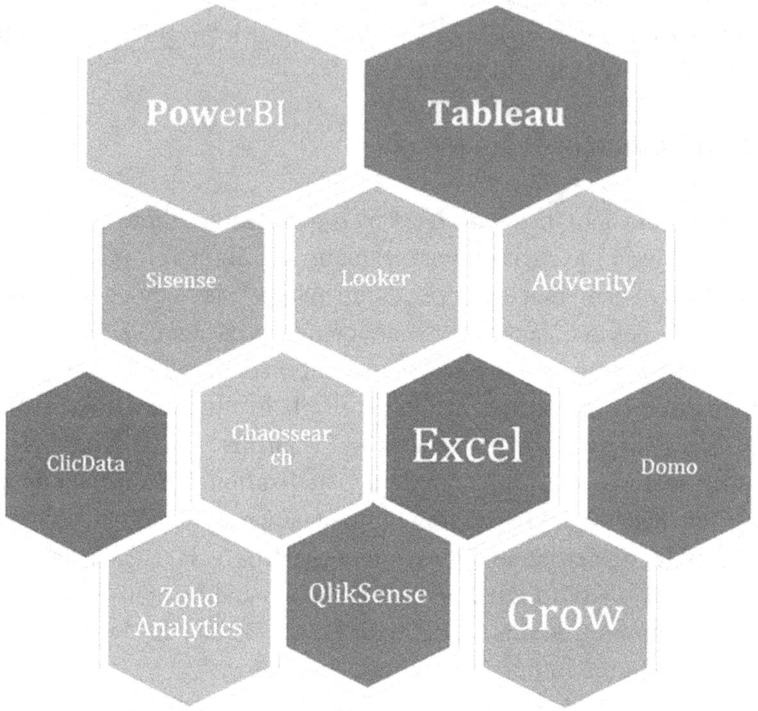

Three types of services for business are offered: Online, Public, and Desktop, allowing users to create dynamic, interactive data visualization presentations shared in a way that everyone in the organization, from employees to CEOs, can see the data that counts most for their role in the organization (Batt; Grealis; Harmon and Tomolonis, 2020), and "by using visual elements like charts, graphs, and maps, data visualization tools provide an accessible way to see and understand trends, outliers, and patterns in data" (Tableau. 2019b, para. 1).

Microsoft Power BI "has a set combination of services, such as applications, connectors, and services to transform the raw data gathered into understandable, consistent, and visually interactive information." (Sousa, et al., 2021, p. 12). It allows users to transform raw data into meaningful, consistent, and understandable information that, like Tableau, contains interactive features and is compatible with multiple sources of information connecting vast data sources and formats, from Excel to SQL.

Similar to Tableau, Power BI will allow the creation of reports, dashboards, and visual interactive features that makes data analysis and visualization flexible, easy, and customizable. It allows also connection with multiple devices and applications, creating business insights. Sarveswar (2021), discusses the theories of Kopáčková and Škrobáčková (2006) regarding Business Intelligence (BI), corroborating that it helps companies improve decision-making using contextual, historical, and current data. BI helps with a better analysis of strategic investments and better positioning in the market. The author defends that BI is a valuable tool for identifying market trends, increasing sales and revenue, and supporting businesses in the following ways:

- Helping to identify ways to increase profit
- Helping to analyze customer behavior
- Helping to compare data with competitors
- Helping to track their own performance
- And finally, helping to predict success (Sarveswar, 2021, p. 87)

Effective use of data visualization helps to mitigate these decision-making problems by allowing decision makers to visualize and assess the value of the decisions they are about to make before defining the Key Performance Indicators (KPIs) and setting clear business strategies and operations goals. A data visualization presentation given to a board of directors "must provide simplicity, clarity, intuitiveness, insightfulness, gap, pattern and trending capability in a collaboration enabling manner, supporting the requirements and decision objectives" (Moore, 2017) of the organization. Furthermore, attributes like confidence, consumption, and speed must be represented in data visualization presentations through a respected peer to peer open decision-making approach (consumption), contrasting design elements like color, charts, and graphs to highlight anomalies and areas of interest (speed), and the confidence the presenter exhibits and projects onto the decision makers by knowing the technology and affirming the accuracy and integrity of the data being presented (Moore, 2017).

Phusava (2013) stated that productivity indicates the "ability of all related activity to produce. Instead of independently and separately focusing on the input and output sides, productivity represented a major philosophical shift in how a work system (including a workstation, an assembly line, a process, and a plant) would be analyzed for continuous improvement" (p. 25). The author defends that "the higher productivity level implies the lower operating cost", indicating that "being productive is equivalent to being competitive" (p. 25). The author stresses that, historically, productivity has always been associated with industrial engineers, with its key founding members inventing the term back in the late 1800s. Moving from an individual perspective to a systematic level, engineers are traditionally expected to analyze processes and present solutions in order to increase efficiency and efficacy, reducing "the use of resources while increasing the outputs that one generates." (p. 25). In terms of workforce, the motion and efforts that are individual must be transformed to a system level effort, allowing better use of resources, an easy flow of information, and higher productivity, thereby avoiding a waste of human and technological resources. Phusava (2013) affirms that "productivity measurement and analysis have gained more recognition from researchers and higher acceptance from practitioners over the past three decades. It has evolved from merely linking individual and accounting-related to more comprehensive information that contains both financial and non-financial information." (p.23), while Deming (1986) defends that: "You cannot manage what you cannot measure," Both authors present theories based on the belief that "productivity (as well as other performance aspects) measures is one of the greatest single determiners of an organization's effectiveness as a system." (p.24), inferring that the improvement of productivity measurement is as critical in service industries as it is in manufacturing.

That approach to productivity in an era of digital information only reaffirms the singularity of a society driven by access and consumption of information and the generation of systems that will enable valuable information to be transformed into knowledge, innovative products and services, higher profitability, and competitiveness for organizations of all segments, and data visualization and management tools will allow individuals and organizations to achieve that level of desired productivity/ competitiveness.

IMPACT OF INFORMATION ON PRODUCTIVITY

The impact of information overload on productivity is widely recognized and well documented in the available literature (Roetzel, 2019). The studies of Karr-Wisiniewski and Lu (2010) concluded that more information technology usage in the workplace can potentially lead to an increase in unproductivity, finding that information and information technology overload negatively impacts knowledge workers' performance, noting that researchers must find strategies to mitigate the effects of overload to maximize the use of information technologies and knowledge workers' productivity.

Drawing from different theories, the consensus that the modern economy is based on information, information technologies, and knowledge sharing defines a new model that helps understand the new approach to productivity as based on the employment of information to drive decisions and business solutions. Bulkley and Alstyne (2004), in their examination of the influence of information in productivity, discuss the historical overview connecting information and productivity defending that the systematic, computational, and statistically applied use of information in problem solving raise productivity. The authors claim that the relationship between information productivity is complex, and that information technologies and human interactions are critical for productivity.

With respect to the study presented here, participants were recruited via the authors' LinkedIn network using an online survey created on SurveyMonkey targeting knowledge professionals in the field of business and information technology, although knowledge professionals in related fields that deal with data management and information systems management of sorts, particularly with heavy data sets, business intelligence, and business analysis, data managers, knowledge managers, librarians, professors, and researchers were also included. The results from the survey show that 70% of participants agreed that they are exposed to too much information in the workplace, 14% stated that there is too much irrelevant information, while 42% of the respondents agreed that they are exposed to "too much disorganized/ unstructured information coming through.". See **Figure 2** below:

Figure 2. Participants understanding of information overload problem.

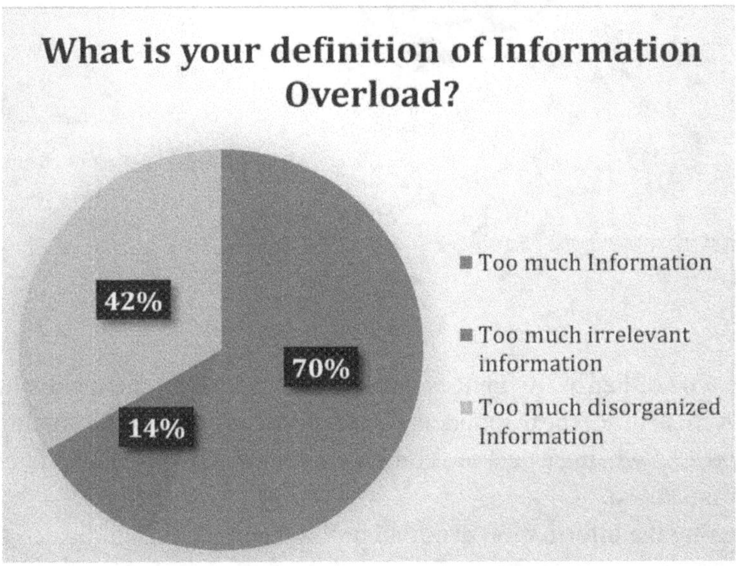

When asked about how often they were exposed to information systems at work, respondents declared spending between 35-40% of their time accessing multiple information systems, 20% of the respondents indicated only accessing the system a few times a day, and 17.5% reported having the need to access the information systems a few times per week. That data shows that participants are connected and exposed to new sets of data and information numerous times per hour and feel overwhelmed and unable to keep up with the volume, mostly due to its random and unstructured nature. In addition, most information is judged to be irrelevant to the respondents' job responsibilities, as illustrated in **Figure 3,** below:

Figure 3. The frequency in which employees access organizational Information Systems.

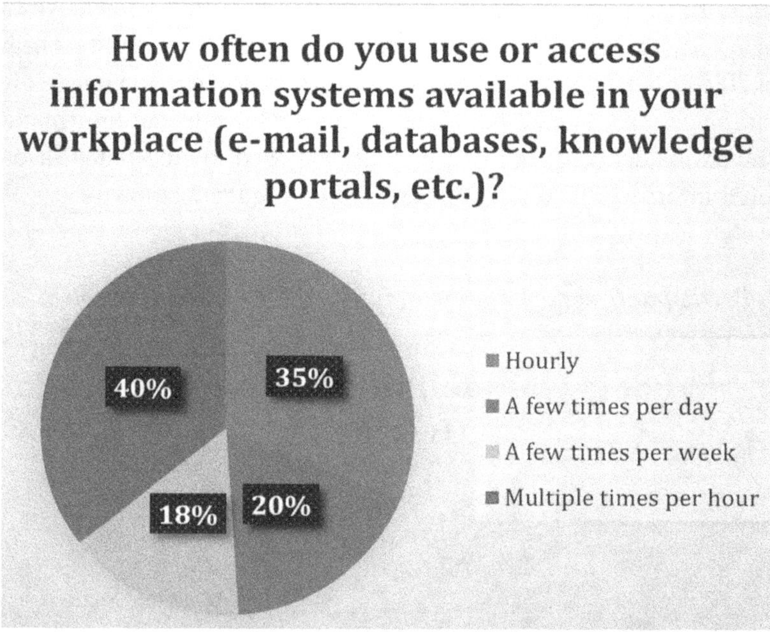

For the type of hardware devices used at the workplace, the results **in Figure 4** below show that 70% of the respondents use laptops, followed by 55% using handheld devices, and 22.5% using a desktop computer. 32.5% of respondents stated that they use "all of the above."

In assessing the information overload problem, employees indicated that e-mail (total 67.5%) is the most demanding application in terms of the time spent answering and responding (see **Figure 5** below). E-mail is the most widely used computer-mediated communication tool and the increase in the use of e-mail as a method of communication defines what many researchers call e-mail overload or e-mail related stress (Whittaker, Belloti and Gwizdka, 2006), which Lutchyn (2016) concluded to negatively correlate with productivity. This is followed by the Internet and Intranet at 52.5% and office applications tools like word processing and spreadsheets at

35%. While 30% of respondents assessed databases and other information systems applications as being time consuming, e-mail is the most time-consuming application, and is often accessed via multiples devices and applications, with an increase in the use of handheld devices and laptops.

Figure 4. The type of hardware used by respondents.

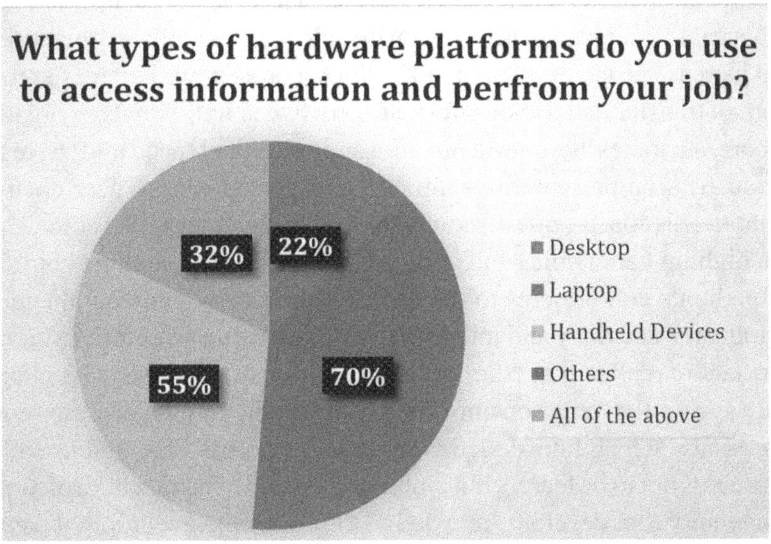

Figure 5. Application that is perceived as the most time consuming at the workplace.

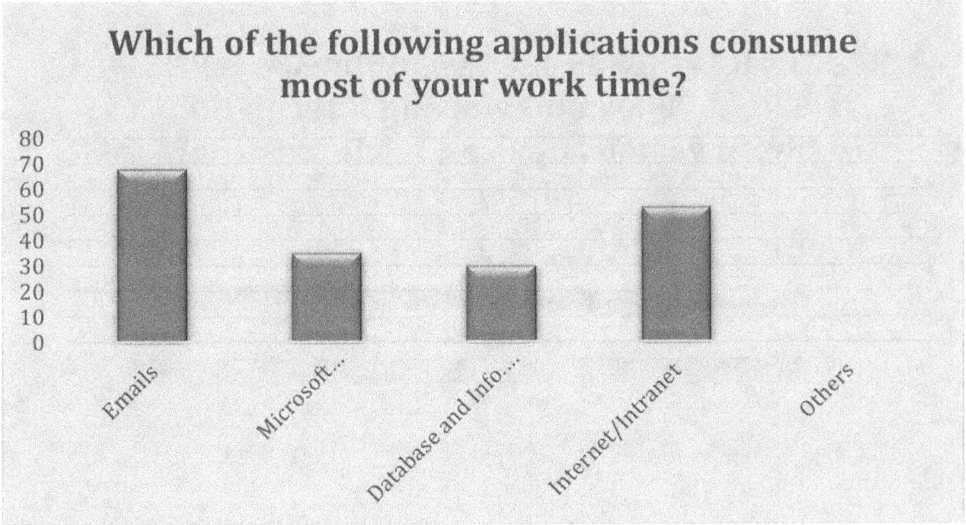

The assessment of the time employees spend viewing information on various devices including their smartphones during the worktime indicated that 45% of participants spend between 30-60% of their time accessing work related information via smart phones and various devices, while 42.5% acknowledged spending over 60% of their time doing so, which raises the question of accessibility from remote work and the impact of the COVID-19 pandemic, illustration in **Figure 6** below:

According to Torabi and El-Den (2017), "Organizational management's main objective is to ensure effective and efficient use of its diverse resources such as labor, capital, materials, energy and information in their quest to achieve competitiveness as well as to increase productivity." (p. 300). Such a process will increase profitability and a smooth transfer and use of information between individuals in organizations. Furthermore, attributes like confidence, consumption, and speed must be represented in data visualization presentations through a respected peer to peer open decision making approach (consumption), contrasting design elements like color, charts, and graphs to highlight anomalies and areas of interest (speed), and the confidence the presenter exhibits and projects to the decision makers by knowing the technology and affirming the accuracy and integrity of the data being presented (Moore, 2017). It is important to realize that "the 'original position of knowledge' is one in which we are always on the verge of information overload, simply as a consequence of the processes by which knowledge is reproduced across time and space" (Fuller, 2017), a process not to be feared, but embraced, considering that information utilizes human ingenuity that develops knowledge to further the evolution of intelligence, and in business, ensure business intelligence.

Figure 6. Percentage of time spent viewing online information on Various devices.

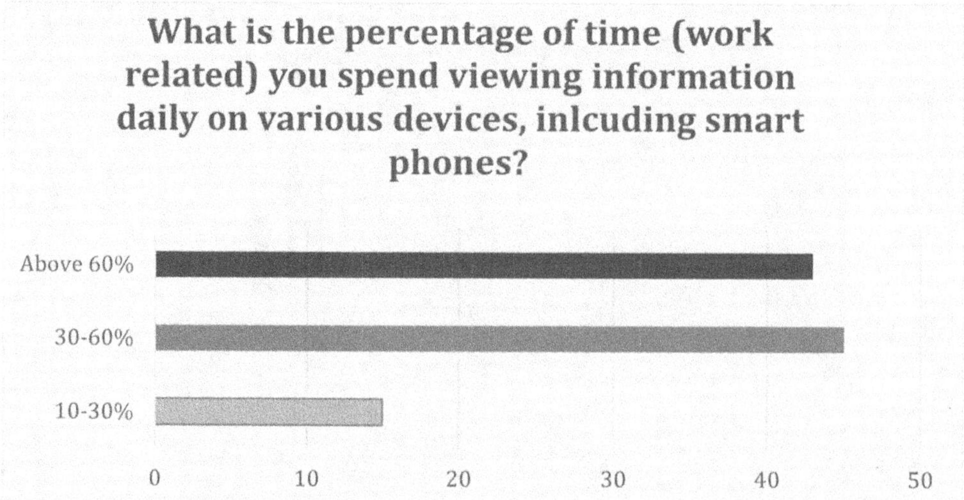

ORGANIZATION USE OF DATA ANALYTICS TOOLS

Studies related to the use of data analytics tools to address information overload are few. There is still a gap in the literature concerning the level of adoption and use of data analytics tools in organizations to help employees reduce the influx of information by filtering unwanted information. Recent studies by Li et.al. (2022) and Shamim et. al., (2019) show that big data analytics have a positive impact on decision making quality. What differentiates one organization from another is the ability of the organization to make timely decisions using information based on data that gives an organization a competitive advantage. However, the data generated using automated processes can be a big, complex, and require advanced data analytics tools to turn it into useful knowledge (Gupta and George, 2016). Advanced analytics utilize software, hardware, algorithms, and data processing method and strategies used to perform data and text mining functions. These capabilities are increasingly becoming an essential part of organizations' daily functions due to the amount of data that they generate (Wolfert, et. Al., 2017; Pham and Stack, 2018).

The adoption of data analytics and visualization tools by organizations is not only important in mitigating and lessening the impact of information overload, but also helps to make more informed decisions based on the data and improving the decision-making process. For the survey study in question, with regard to the respondents' level of experience and exposure to data analytics and data visualization tools and techniques, 65% of the participants indicated that they have knowledge and experience using data visualization tools and 37.5% stating not having experience at all. According to data from the Gartner report dated 2021, some of the top data visualization software utilized by companies that were also indicated by participants in this study include: Power BI and Tableau, dominating the market and leading the results, followed by Adverity, Looker, Sisense, Chaossearch, ClickData, Domo, Zoho Analytics, QlikSense, Grow, and Excel application was mentioned several times.

In some of the most meaningful responses to the open-ended portion of the survey, participants were able to better address the question about the data management and visualization information system available for use in their companies in their own words. Participants mentioned the use of *"infographics created through Canvas or similar websites, charts, graphics, from Excel."* While other participants have stated: *"...since COVID they have reduced email and have websites for less important items."*. Some participants testified that: *"I use infographics created through canvas or similar websites, charts, graphics, from excel."; "...limited views specific to task."; "...we've been asked to curb meetings to 30 minutes max."; "They have planned training for employees in how to cope with it and be productive to some degree"; "They have regular employee feedback to get suggestions on how to improve this area."; "Unified Communications (UC) is the system of choice."*

Two participants from the survey we conducted shared that their organizations are taking actions to address the improvement of data access and quality by managing productivity and worktime though the adoption of new practices. Analyzing the impact of information overload on employees' well-being, data results show that 69.23% of participants believe that the information overload process in their organizations causes stress and anxiety, while 61.54% agree that information overload both affects the ability to learn, remember, and absorb, and affects productivity at work. Interestingly, 15.38% of the respondents believe that information overload affects close relationships, and 12.82% said they were affected by it very little or not at all. Respondents, for the most part, indicated that there is a non-existent feeling of informational overload in their personal lives, with a 42.5% agreeing that they "easily navigate personal information, which includes e-mails, e-commerce, and related." 32.5% stated that they don't feel overloaded with the amount of personal information. However, 25% of respondents agreed that the amount of personal information they manage outside of their work-related information responsibilities makes them feel extremely overloaded, see **Figure 7 and 8** below:

Figure 7. Respondent well-being and perceived exposure.

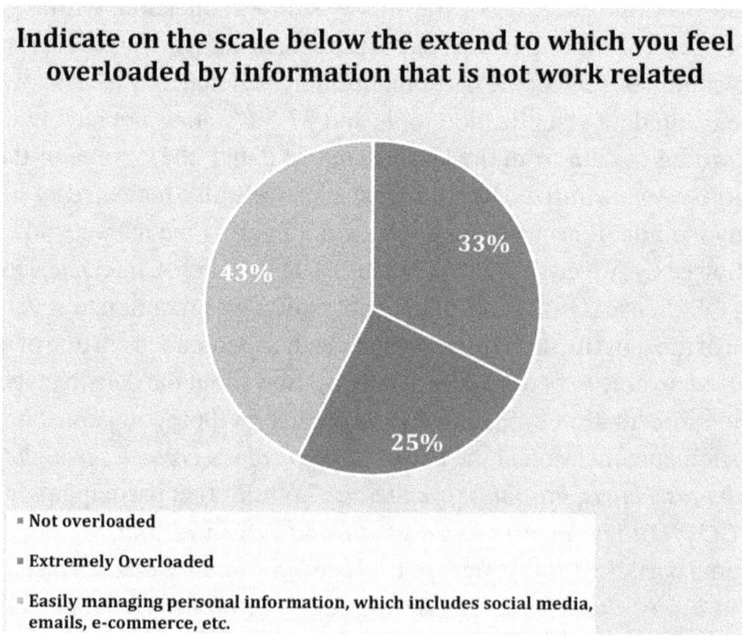

Figure 8. Types of issues experienced as a results of information overload.

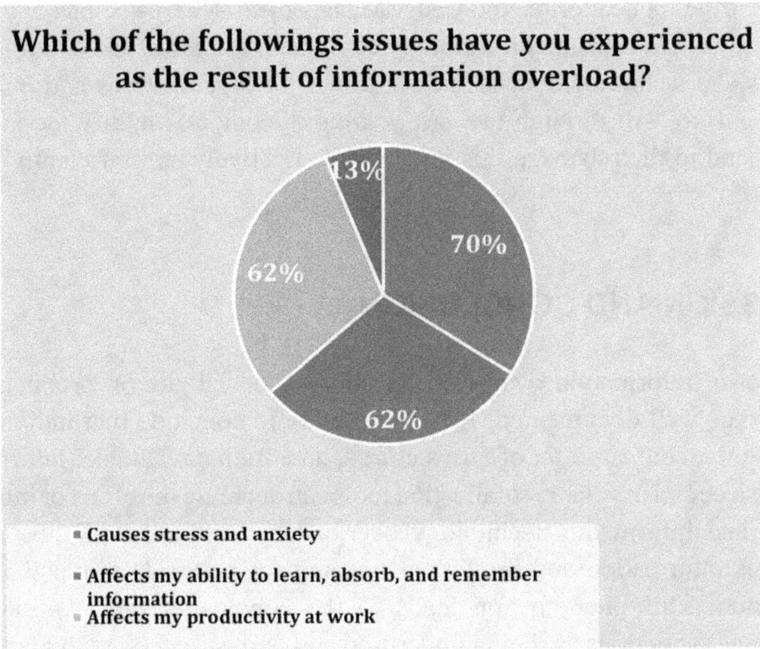

Although it is an effect of several emerging factors, information overload can best be described as the consequence of "the ever-widening gap between information that is available to us and that which is usable" (Koltay, 2017). Results of this survey found that the high level of anxiety and stress reported as the result of work-related information overload implies that future investigations assessing the extent to which information and information technologies overload are impacting individuals' productivity in organizations are warranted. Studies have shown that approximately 28% of individuals' daily work is "consumed by interruptions propagated by technology which cost the US economy approximately $588 billion a year." (Spira and Goldes, 2007; Kar-Wisiniewski and Lu, 2010, p. 1061). Kar-Wisiniewski and Lu (2010) found that in measuring information and information technology overload, three dimensions affect the loss of productivity: information overload: communication overload, systems feature overload.

While most technology organizations continue to invest in computer-based advances, knowledge workers are pursuing user-friendly business intelligence systems that will improve productivity. The organization's inability to manage, filter, and use information causes information overload that will likely obstruct a user's ability to complete a transaction or task in a manner and time that is desirable and conducive to productivity. Companies should address the need to manage their knowledge and knowledge workers more effectively in order to avoid information overload and overlap, and the application of Knowledge Management (KM) principles and practices in the form of KM tools and technology could help as part of the solution. Useful KM tools and technologies will make it easier for organizations and information professionals to "sift through the vast volume of content, identify the knowledge of value, and to then manage this knowledge effectively and efficiently" (Dalkir, 2017, p. 45).

DISCUSSION AND CONCLUSION

The effect of information overload and information fatigue on productivity and employees is well documented. It is appropriate to conclude that individuals are struggling with the large set of unstructured, and often unvaluable, information in the workplace and that data visualization tools can decrease the effect of information overload and information technology overload by mitigating the absorption of extraneous information and providing meaning for better data organization and presentation. This phenomenon leads to the conclusion that: 1) Information Technologies adoptions are being underused and or misused, 2) Individuals are not being as productive as they could or should be, and 3) managers are not understanding and prioritizing solutions that lessen the negative impact of information overload on productivity. It is clear from the literature and the present online survey that knowledge professionals in organizations are aware and have knowledge and experience with data analytics and data visualization tools of some sort and feel comfortable using them. It is also clear that effective use of information systems apparatuses integrating methods of communication and knowledge sharing allows users to prioritize data in meaningful ways and align it with the business processes, purpose, and goals, and most importantly the strategies.

Employees reported familiarity with business analytics and data visualization tools, while a staggering number of almost 38% stated not having familiarity with data analytics tools. Assuming that most companies are heavily digitalized and allowing remote work, particularly during a period when the world was facing a pandemic (COVID-19), it is rational to assume that those individuals are utilizing some sort of data analytics unbeknownst to them. Some have admitted using Excel to process and represent data, while others use more complex software such as Tableau and Power BI, and Canvas for educational purposes. Another relevant aspect of the findings from the literature and the survey is the percentage of time employees reported spending online during worktime, with a total of 45% of participants stating that they spend between 30-60% of their time accessing work-related information, and prompting a question about productivity and time management, as well as content access and creation during worktime. It was also concluded that information and productivity are directly correlated and that the excessive use of information technologies are negatively impacting information consumption, sharing, the decision-making process, knowledge workers, and the overall organizational performance, which ultimately impacts profitability.

REFERENCES

Bawden, D., & Robinson, L. (2009). The dark side of information: Overload, anxiety and other paradoxes and pathologies. *Journal of Information Science*, *35*(2), 180–191. doi:10.1177/0165551508095781

Bowman, B., Grupe, F. H., Lund, D., & Moore, W. (1993). An examination of sources of support preferred by end-user computing personnel. *Journal of End User Computing*, *5*(4), 4–11. doi:10.4018/joeuc.1993100101

Buchanan, J., & Kock, N. (2001). Information overload: A decision making perspective. In *Multiple criteria decision making in the new millennium* (pp. 49–58). Springer. doi:10.1007/978-3-642-56680-6_4

Bulkley, N., & Alstyne, M. (2004). *Why information should influence productivity*. Center for eBusiness @ MIT. Retrieved from: http://citeseerx.ist.psu.edu/viewdoc/download?doi=10.1.1.295.7563&rep=rep1&type=pdf

Bumblauskas, D., Nold, H., Bumblauskas, P., & Igou, A. (2017). Big data analytics: Transforming data to action. *Business Process Management Journal*, *23*(3), 703–720. doi:10.1108/BPMJ-03-2016-0056

Chen, M. (2018). Improving website structure through reducing information overload. *Decision Support Systems*, *110*, 84–94. doi:10.1016/j.dss.2018.03.009

Dalkir, K. (2017). *Knowledge management in theory and practice*. The MIT Press.

Dasgupta, A., Poco, J., Wei, Y., Cook, R., Bertini, E., & Silva, C. T. (2015). Bridging theory with practice: An exploratory study of visualization use and design for climate model comparison. *IEEE Transactions on Visualization and Computer Graphics*, *21*(9), 996–1014. doi:10.1109/TVCG.2015.2413774 PMID:26357283

Dillon, S., Stahl, F., Vossen, G., & Rastrick, K. (2013). A Contemporary Approach to Coping with Modern Information Overload. *Communications of the ICISA*, *14*(1), 1–24.

Edmunds, A., & Morris, A. (2000). The problem of information overload in business organisations: A review of the literature. *International Journal of Information Management, 20*(1), 17–28. doi:10.1016/S0268-4012(99)00051-1

Fuller, S. (2017). Prolegomena to a Deep History of "Information Overload.". *Journal of Information Ethics, 26*(1), 81–92. http://search.ebscohost.com/login.aspx?direct=true&db=lls&AN=123908416&scope=site

Gartner. (2021). Data Virtualization. *Gartner Peer Insights.*

Gupta, M., & George, J. F. (2016). Toward the development of a big data analytics capability. *Information & Management, 53*(8), 1049–1064. doi:10.1016/j.im.2016.07.004

Hiltz, S. R., & Turoff, M. (1985). Structuring computer-mediated communication systems to avoid information overload. *Communications of the ACM, 28*(7), 680–689. doi:10.1145/3894.3895

Jackson, T. W., & Farzaneh, P. (2012). Theory-based model of factors affecting information overload. *International Journal of Information Management, 32*(6), 523–532. doi:10.1016/j.ijinfomgt.2012.04.006

Jacoby, J. (1984). Perspectives on information overload. *The Journal of Consumer Research, 10*(4), 432–435. doi:10.1086/208981

Jin, Z., Zhangwen, W., & Naichen, N. (2019). Helping consumers to overcome information overload with a diversified online review subset. *Frontiers of Business Research in China, 13*(1), 1–25. doi:10.118611782-019-0062-1

Karr-Wisniewski, P., & Lu, Y. (2010). When more is too much: Operationalizing technology overload and exploring its impact on knowledge worker productivity. *Computers in Human Behavior, 26*(5), 1061-1072. doi:10.1016/j.chb.2010.03.008

Koltay, T. (2017). The bright side of information: Ways of mitigating information overload. *The Journal of Documentation, 73*(4), 767–775. doi:10.1108/JD-09-2016-0107

Kwon, B. C., Kim, S. H., Duket, T., Catalán, A., & Yi, J. S. (2015). Do people really experience information overload while reading online reviews? *International Journal of Human-Computer Interaction, 31*(12), 959–973. doi:10.1080/10447318.2015.1072785

Larose, D. T. (2014). *Discovering knowledge in data: An introduction to data mining*. John Wiley & Sons.

Li, L., Lin, J., Ouyang, Y., & Luo, X. R. (2022). Evaluating the impact of big data analytics usage on the decision-making quality of organizations. *Technological Forecasting and Social Change*, *175*, 121355. doi:10.1016/j.techfore.2021.121355

Lutchyn, Y. (2016). Email Duration, Batching and Self-interruption: Patterns of Email Use on Productivity and Stress. *CHI '16: Proceedings of the 2016. CHI Conference on Human Factors in Computing Systems*, 1717–1728. 10.1145/2858036.2858262

Maes, P. (1995). Agents that reduce work and information overload. In *Readings in human–computer interaction* (pp. 811–821). Morgan Kaufmann. doi:10.1016/B978-0-08-051574-8.50084-4

Marr, B. (2018, July 6). *The 7 Best Data Visualization Tools Available Today*. Retrieved from https://www.forbes.com/sites/bernardmarr/2017/07/20/the-7-best-data-visualization-tools-in-2017

McAfee, A., Brynjolfsson, E., Davenport, T. H., Patil, D. J., & Barton, D. (2012). Big data. The management revolution. *Harvard Business Review*, *90*(10), 61–67. PMID:23074865

Mohanta, G. C., Kannan, V., & Thooyamani, K. P. (2006). Strategies for improving productivity of knowledge workers-An overview. *Strength Based Strategies*, 77-84.

Moore, J. (2017). Data Visualization in Support of Executive Decision Making. *Interdisciplinary Journal of Information, Knowledge & Management, 12*, 125–138. doi:10.28945/3687

Moore, J. (2017). Data Visualization in support of executive decision making. *Interdisciplinary Journal of Information, Knowledge, and Management, 12*, 126–134. doi:10.28945/3687

Murayama, K., Blake, A. B., Kerr, T., & Castel, A. D. (2016). When enough is not enough: Information overload and metacognitive decisions to stop studying information. *Journal of Experimental Psychology. Learning, Memory, and Cognition*, *42*(6), 914–924. doi:10.1037/xlm0000213 PMID:26595067

Pham, X., & Stack, M. (2018). How data analytics is transforming agriculture. *Business Horizons*, *61*(1), 125–133. doi:10.1016/j.bushor.2017.09.011

Phusavat, K. (2013). *Productivity Management in an organization: measurement and analysis*. Bangkok: ToKnoPress.

Qin, C., Zhao, P., Mou, J., & Zhang, J. (2018). Construction of personal knowledge maps for a peer-to-peer information-sharing environment. *The Electronic Library*, *36*(3), 394–413. doi:10.1108/EL-03-2017-0071

Roetzel, P. G. (2018). *Information overload in the information age: A review of the literature from business administration, business psychology, and related disciplines with a bibliometric approach and framework development.* Business Research. doi:10.100740685-018-0069-z

Roetzel, P. G. (2019). Information overload in the information age: a review of the literature from business administration, business psychology, and related disciplines with a bibliometric approach and framework development. *Business Research, 12*(2), 479-522.

Roy, M. C., Roy, M. J., & Bouchard, L. (2017). Improving Board Knowledge with Information and Communication Technologies. *Electronic Journal of Knowledge Management, 15*(4), 215–224. http://search.ebscohost.com/login.aspx?direct=true&db=lls&AN=126281196&scope=site

Saxena, D., & Lamest, M. (2018). Information overload and coping strategies in the big data context: Evidence from the hospitality sector. *Journal of Information Science, 44*(3), 287–297. doi:10.1177/0165551517693712

Shamim, S., Zeng, J., Khan, Z., & Zia, N. U. (2020). Big data analytics capability and decision making performance in emerging market firms: The role of contractual and relational governance mechanisms. *Technological Forecasting and Social Change, 161*, 120315. doi:10.1016/j.techfore.2020.120315

Sousa, R., Miranda, R., Moreira, A., Alves, C., Lori, N., & Machado, J. (2021). Software Tools for Conducting Real-Time Information Processing and Visualization in Industry: An Up-to-Date Review. *Applied Sciences (Basel, Switzerland), 2021*(11), 4800. doi:10.3390/app11114800

Torabi, F., & El-Den, J. (2017). The impact of Knowledge Management on Organizational Productivity: case study on Koosar Bank of Iran. *Procedia Computer Science, International Conference, ISICO*, 300-310. 10.1016/j.procs.2017.12.159

Whittaker, S., Bellotti, V., & Gwizdka, J. (2006). Email in personal information management. *Communications of the ACM, 49*(1), 68–73. doi:10.1145/1107458.1107494

Wolfert, S., Ge, L., Verdouw, C., & Bogaardt, M.-J. (2017). Big data in smart farming – A review. *Agricultural Systems, 153*, 69–80. doi:10.1016/j.agsy.2017.01.023

Zeggelink, E. (1994). Dynamics of structure: An individual oriented approach. *Social Networks, 16*(4), 295–333. doi:10.1016/0378-8733(94)90014-0

Section 4

Metrics in Knowledge Management

Chapter 10
Designing Records Management Programmes:
Key Performance Indicators in South African Universities

Nkholedzeni Sidney Netshakhuma
https://orcid.org/0000-0003-0673-7137
University of Mpumalanga, South Africa

ABSTRACT

This chapter assessed the design of records and archives key performance indicators of universities to achieve a strategic objective. The records and archives key performance indicators are informed by overall university key performance indicators. Establishment of university records and archives management indicators is necessary to ensure compliance with regulatory frameworks such as the Constitution of the Republic of South Africa, 1996; National Archives and Records Service Act of 1996; The Public Finance Management Act; Protection of Personal Information Act; and International Organisation Standards.

INTRODUCTION

This chapter assesses the records management practices, policies, legislation rules, and procedures for managing records. Effective records management is a key element of good governance. This study established that the National Archives and Records Service Act 43 of 1996 is the legal framework for the management of university records in South Africa. The challenges facing South African universities

DOI: 10.4018/978-1-6684-4431-3.ch010

are ineffective records management system, implementation of policies, rules, procedures for managing records and the availability of records management standards. After introducing the research problem and the approach, thereof, this chapter reviewed the literature to allow the researcher to understand the records and archives management programme of universities in South Africa. The researcher then reviewed studies and evaluations that have attempted to examine the effectiveness of records management systems.

PROBLEM STATEMENT

The lack of records management policies, rules and procedures is a challenge for most South African universities. Hence, there is a need for universities to comply with the National Archives and Records Service Act 43 of 1996 on the preservation of public records. The review of the literature shows that records management practices, policies, rules, procedures and standards are not monitored regularly. Hence, monitoring records management programme is necessary to improve teaching, learning and research. In the past, there has been a limited university evaluation system linked to the records management programme. This chapter answer the following research questions:

- What are the current practices of managing the records?
- What are the mechanisms, policies, rules, procedures and legislation in place for managing records?
- Which records management standards are in place for managing records?

Developing records and archive management key performance indicators that integrate business processes might seem idealistic and unattainable to the university, especially as the mandate of the university is teaching, learning and research (Shacketon, 2006). Despite deliberate efforts in ensuring records management programmes, records management was not recognised as part of a university strategy.

Hence, a strategic plan is informed by policy direction, implementation strategies, actions and benchmarks for implementation, monitoring and evaluation and expenditure framework to allow adjustments in areas for development during implementation (Van Wyk and Moeng 2014, p. 138). The university's strategic plan should align with its strategic goal. The review of the literature shows that research was conducted on records and archives management programmes, especially in the corporate world. Less explored, however, is the integration of records management programmes into the organisation's strategy. Furthermore, the records management division frequently contends with intangible value, which is a challenge to define and measure records management function. As a result, records managers emphasize tangible outputs that do not reflect the value presented by this discipline. South African universities were concerned about the performance of the records management system in South Africa.

Challenges related to organisations' records management are as follows:

- Failure to assume a broad decision-making role
- Lack of a comprehensive records management programme
- Fail to address strategic issues
- Lack of management, business and planning skills
- Lack of research, or measure outputs rather than outcomes
- Lack of integration of the function into its larger organisation domain
- Are reactive, awaiting decisions by the Vice-chancellor rather than being proactive

These challenges led most of the university divisions to view records and archives management as only administrative functions serving no strategic purposes within an organisation.

RECORDS MANAGEMENT

Records management is the discipline that involves the management of records from their creation until their disposal. The records management programme is established to achieve transparency and accountability. The guiding principle of records and archives management is to ensure information available when is requested (Matangira 2016, p 67) As a management function, it is the responsibility of an institution to ensure that records are managed strategically to support a university's strategic objectives. Records Management programme involves the creation of records, records retention, disposal of records and records archival. The effects of achieved results and represent the indicators are assessed. The programme impact of the programme should be assessed. The archives and records management program must be assessed regularly.

Records are strategic resources to support organizational decision-making, ensuring operational business continuity and demonstrating effective, transparent and responsible governance, impartial administrative action and enabling access to information. Records management programmes are necessary to protect the legal rights and entitlements of both internal and external clients.

The records management programme is established to preserve institutional memory

The effective decision making of any organisation is based on records management
To control the creation, retention and disposal of records
To reduce the costs of operation.

Records support businesses to become efficient and effective, underpin e-government and service delivery, assist in accountability, transparency and corporate governance and are a source of information (McLeod and Childs and Heaford 2007 P. 216). To improve efficiency and productivity, records management contributes to accountability, transparency and good governance (Mojapelo and Ngoepe 2019). Records management has the potential to improve the flow of information and knowledge sharing. Proper management enhances access to information.

The value of information lies in information created by organisations to achieve their goals. Universities develop records management systems to ensure that records are accessible, accurate, completely relevant, reliable, timely, secure, simple, economical and verifiable. Information has value to assist the university to achieve its objectives.

DEMARCATION OF THE STUDY

This research is limited to South African public universities. The reason is that South African universities have been reputed for underestimating the value of intangible facets, especially in the area of records management. However, the results of this research may be generalised to other universities around Africa.

The study focus on the current practises of managing the records, policies, rules, procedures and legislation in place for managing records, records management standards which are in place for managing records examining the development of records management key performance indicators for records management within the university sector to capture intangible and tangible value to contribute to records management programmes in general.

The records and archives management program's purpose evaluation activities are to provide quality service to the university community (Grimard, 2004). Universities set a standard on records and archives management services to achieve institutional objectives. A records service standard must be based on a records and archives management programme strategy. The literature on information science provides information on measurement methods. External measures, internal measures are important to answer questions related to the performance and pertinence of programs. Measures should be based on the strategic objectives of the university.

HISTORY OF RECORDS AND ARCHIVES MANAGEMENT PROGRAMME IN SOUTH AFRICAN UNIVERSITIES

Political and public management redefine performance management in South Africa. Political transformation in South Africa from the apartheid system to democracy led to the recognition of the records and archives management programme as a strategic area. South African public services introduced a performance measurement system to improve service delivery (Mosimege and Masiya 2021). In the case of universities, performance management systems were necessary to comply with legislation such as the National Archives and Records Service Act 43 of 1996 and Protection of Personal Information Act No 4 of 2013. Universities in South Africa are required by archival legislation such as the National Archives and Records Service Act (Act No. 43 of 1996) to establish a records management programme (Ngoepe and Ngulube 2014, 142). The performance management system was developed because of demands by the university to comply with the National Archives and Records Service Act 43 of 1996 and the Promotion of Access to Information Act No. 2 of 2002. Therefore, the outcomes approach demonstrates an innovative orientation to build and establish a result-oriented approach in universities.

Over the past 27 years of democracy in South Africa, universities were slow to recognize the practices of managing the records, the mechanisms, policies, rules, procedures and legislation in place for managing records, and records management standards are in place for managing records to aid to achieve their mandate of teaching, learning and research. This is so because limited South African universities establish records and archives management programmes (Netshakhuma 2019). After 1994, the enactment of the Constitution of the Republic of South Africa in 1996 is a basis for the establishment of a records and archives management programme. Section 195 of the Constitution of South Africa requires information to be accessible, transparent and accountable. South African universities introduced records and archives management programmes to manage records and archives as part of universities' resources.

Performance measurement generated interest in the private sector during the transition from apartheid to a democratic system in South Africa's public management (Mosimege and Masiya 2021). South African universities adopted a performance management system to modernise and re-engineer a records and archives management programme.

South African universities are required to establish records and archives management programmes. This also requires universities to reaffirm the role of the university archives as an administrative function rather than an academic function. By the end of 1996, only a small portion of universities placed their university archives administratively within the library (Netshakhuma, 2019). So, most records managers report to university librarians. The fact that records and archives management function was placed under library division, department and implied that records management function was not recognised by universities as strategic

It seems that the records and archives management programme was viewed as the functions to improve teaching, learning and research. The performance management system is introduced in a university to achieve financial and operational measures. These are the drivers of organisational performance. Measures are taken to improve internal university business processes. There is a need to measure the performance of the university.

RESEARCH METHOD

The author reviews the literature on performance evaluation related to records and archives management programmes. The review of the literature shows that university develops and follow their methodology to develop and implement their programme. Records Management function measurements are intangible. The literature review focus on the role of key performance in the Records and Archives Management programme. It seems that universities followed different models to manage records. The literature review suggests that the performance management framework of the university was most similar to most universities. Key document related to university strategic plan and annual performance plans.

COMPLIANCE WITH LEGISLATION

Universities are required to comply with legislation and policies on records management. This statement is alluded to by Pereira (2018) who stated that archival legislation is a tool for the public sector to ensure the management, preservation and access to national documentary heritage. Performance management practices adopted in the public sector are fostered by mandated central government policies and initiatives (Siti – Nabiha and Jurnali 2020). Several policies shaped monitoring and evaluation. Universities are accountable to the public. Divisional managers are to be familiar with the National Archives and Records Service Act 43 of 1996. The only way an organisation can be sure reasonably that is in full compliance with laws and regulations is by ensuring an effective and efficient records and archives management programme (Ambira and Kemoni 2011, p. 02). Therefore, records managers are to possess legal skills. These skills will enable them to comply with the legislative framework.

Since the advent of democracy in 1994, legislators passed several pieces of legislation that provide a framework for records management. South African government enacted policies and legal frameworks to address records management issues. Section 141 and 195 (1) (f) of the Constitution of South Africa (1996) state that government should be accountable and transparent. Section 195 of the constitution provides among others, for the effective, economical and efficient use of resources, provision of timely, accessible and accurate information and requires the public to be accountable. The Constitution of the Republic of South Africa requires the state to deliver services and uphold the rights enshrined in the Bill of Rights of Section 195. it states that the efficient, economic, and effective use of resources must be promoted. The Constitution promotes the accessibility of information and promotes transparency.

The enactment of the National Archives and Records Service Act 43 of 1996 formed the basis of the establishment of records and archives management programmes at South African universities (Ngoepe and Ngulube 2014). The National Archives of South Africa play a role in ensuring that universities adopt records management programmes programme of public organisations.

Promotion of Access to Information Act (Act No. 2 of 2000) provides the framework and procedures for the university community to exercise their constitutional rights to access information. The Act aims to foster a culture of transparency and accountability in the public and private bodies by giving effect to the right of access to information and promoting a society in which the people of South Africa have effective access to information to enable them to exercise and protect their rights more fully. Section 11 (1) of this Act provides for records requester to be provided access to a record of a public body if that requester complies with all procedural requirements in this act. For information to be accessed, it has to be organised in such a way that it can be retrieved within a limited period. Section 25 (1) provides for the Information Officer to grant (or deny access within 30 days after the request is received. In an environment, that has ineffective records management systems, an office will find it difficult to provide the requester with the relevant record within the stipulated period, in which case it will have seem a refusal in terms of Section 27 of the Act. A good records management system depends on effective records management systems. Access to information is impossible without effective records management programme. Universities should adhere to good records management principles to expedite university community rights of access to information.

Minimum Information Security Standard (MISS) provides minimum access to information. MISS was developed as an official government policy document on document security. Information created by universities is to be maintained. The underlying assumption is that all universities possess at their disposal, records that are to some extent sensitive in nature and requires security measures. The degree of sensitivity determines the level of protection, which implies that records must be classified according to a different level. In terms of this policy document, records are classified according to restricted, confidential, Secret or Top Secret levels. MISS as a policy document has implications on how records are managed in universities. Universities are obliged to give particular attention to the elements of records management. These elements include the creation of registries, development, implementation and maintenance of records classification system and document security.

The Promotion of Administrative Justice Act (Act No. 3 of 2000) provides effect to the right to administrative action that is lawful, reasonable and procedurally fair and to the right to written reasons for administrative action as contemplated in Section 33 of the Constitution of South Africa, 1996. This Act has as its objective, the creation of a culture of accountability, openness and transparency in universities. In terms of Section 3(1) of this Act "administrative action which materially and adversely affects the rights or legitimate expectations of any person must be procedurally fair. In terms of Section 5 (1) any person whose rights have been materially and adversely affected by administrative action and who has not been given reasons for the action may, within 90 days after the date on which that person became aware of the action or might reasonably have been expected to become aware of the action or might reasonably have been expected to become aware of the action, request the administrator concerned to furnish written reasons for the action. If an administrator fails to furnish adequate reasons for administrative action, it must, "Subject to Subsection (4) and in the absence of proof to the contrary, be presumed in any proceedings for judicial review that the administrative action was taken with good reason. Although there is no reference to records in this Act, indeed, the most effective way by which an administrator proves an administrative action to be procedurally fair is through recorded information. Administrators in universities are by implication required to create and keep recordings of proceedings in which administrative action is taken. Records of such proceedings must be managed according to records management practices. University administrators are increasingly responsible for the management of information.

Higher Education Act of 1997 provides a guideline on the management of university records. 41. (1) The council of a public higher education institution must keep records of all its proceedings, and (b) keep complete accounting records of all assets. This is an indication that the Higher Education Act of 1997 promotes effective and efficient management of university records.

Electronic Communication and Transactions Act (Act No 25 of 2002) provides for the facilitation and regulation of electronic communications and transactions. However, it is the role of a Records and Archives Management division, departments or units to ensure that information reported to stakeholders is of high quality.

E-governance offers the potential to bring citizens closer to their government (Hsu, Chen and Wanga 2009). Departments are required to customise records according to the needs of clients. Measure performance needs to be defined. Section 15 (1) makes provision for the rules of evidence in legal proceedings not to be applied to deny the admissibility of a data message in evidence. Electronic records management systems should therefore be developed and designed in such a way that, elements such as security, integrity and authenticity are managed effectively.

The Protection of Personal Information Act of 2013 was enacted to protect personal information processed by public and private bodies and introduced conditions to establish minimum requirements for the processing of personal information. To provide for the establishment of an Information Regulator to exercise powers and to perform duties of the Act and the Promotion of Access to Information Act, 2000, to provide for the issuing of codes of conduct, to provide for the rights of persons regarding unsolicited electronic communications and automated decision making, to regulate the flow of personal information across the borders for the Republic and to provide for matters connected therewith. Then the processing of personal information of a university is guided by an effective records management programme. Information Regulator set standards for all South African universities to comply with. The Information Regulator provide the structure for the measurement of the set of programme to be followed.

The Public Finance Management Act regulate public finance records. The act was enacted to control the public financial system. This act also plays a role to reduce corruption. Section 40 (3) (a) of the Public Finance Management Act, 1999 (Act 1 of 1999) (PFMA) mandates accounting officers to submit annual reports, which include an assessment of pre-determined objectives (Mosimege and Masiya 2021). Therefore, universities are to comply with the prescription of the Act on financial management. However, the increase in university autonomy has involved an overall public university funding system. The South African government allocated universities based on their research outputs and the size of the university. The Department of Higher Education and Training assessed how universities fund their projects. Allocation of funds to universities has shown a better performance of universities. The application of predetermined objectives provides the basis for public sector entities to assess how well they are progressing towards achieving predetermined outcomes and to decide on future initiatives to initiate performance improvements. Determine the predetermined performance required review of information management systems.

The Auditor-General South Africa plays a role in audit South African university's projects. The audit was conducted following universities' internally developed instruments and the National Archives' guidelines for the planning, execution, reporting and follow-up of records audits. The audit tool was adopted and designed to reflect and address issues specific to South African universities. The development of a performance management system was based on university strategic objectives. Universities provide performance levels in terms of the Department of Higher Education. Universities are required to report on their strategic objectives. The performance indicators of universities are to be aligned with the allocated budgets. The annual report of South African universities needs to include inter alia, an audited financial statement and a statement of programme performance. Section 20 (1c) of the Public Audit Act (25 of 2004) requires Auditor-General to express an opinion on reported information of the auditee against pre-determined university objectives. The auditor- General feed into the overall monitoring process and serves as a key indicator of university institutional performance. Furthermore, the Auditor-General of South Africa plays a role in discretionary performance audits which are related to evaluation. The benefits of conducting external auditing are to ad credibility to the information provided and assist in the strengthening of oversight, accountability and governance in the public sector (Mojapelo and Ngoepe 2021, p. 37). The records management standards are to be in place for an organisation to conduct an effective audit. This also assists in the transformation of financial management in the public sector and provides insight into the management of the public sector

RECORDS MANAGEMENT STANDARDS

There are various mechanisms or standards used by universities to assess the effectiveness of records and archives management programmes. One of the methods used to assess the university is the survey of users' experiences. Standardised user satisfaction survey methods were applied in universities. To measure their value and user satisfaction. Consumers' surveys assess the experience of records management delivery as viewed by users. This process involves surveying various divisions, departments and units of a university. This is done to verify the level of satisfaction with the records management programme. The customer provides considerable information on the condition, status attitudes and behaviour of staff after they receive records management services. Officers are required to use correct techniques to collect information from various actors within an organisation.

The university may use a third party to evaluate its records and archives management programme. Comprehensive driving performance evaluation relates to not only drivers themselves but also external factors (Zhou, Li Wang 2021). Identifying customers and their needs and formation of campus-wide planning is a responsible committee responsible for developing the university strategy, key performance indicators and short term and long term goal (Grant, Mergen & Wildrick 2007). This shows the significance of continuous assessment of the university programme. This form of assessment is voluntary and combines internal self-assessment with external audits. This includes assessing universities' programmes against the International Organisation to Standardisation (ISO) certification, peer review and accreditation.

Researchers conducted research on benchmarking and the evaluation of project performance in the records management discipline. Records management programmes need to be benchmarked against international standards organisations (ISO 15489). Reviewing records and archives management programmes requires the involvement of other organisations.

However, it seems most universities around the world are not valuing records as a strategic area. The rationale behind a strategic plan is not likely to be progress unless monitoring and evaluation introduced (Van Wyk & Moeng 2014, P. 139). Monitoring is the system used by organisations to assess the implementation of a records management programme. Monitoring records management programme assists to track progress against pre-set objectives and desired outcomes and for this reason, is important. Monitoring is conducted to strengthen the contributions of divisions or departments to meet university strategic goals. It provides learning opportunities for university community members The Monitoring process involves actions directed at the consolidation of information at specific central points. The process involves quarterly monitoring against division Annual performance plans., Management performance monitoring, monitoring records and archives management programme against the national plan, monitoring of individual performance. This implies staff members sign a performance contract, Quarterly outcomes monitoring.

RECORDS MANAGEMENT PRACTICE AT UNIVERSITIES

The implementation of a records and archives management programme is dependent on division, department or unit interaction. Stakeholders ensure public accountability and transparency. Records and Archives Management sections have developed records archive management programmes in their development programme. Developing inter-departmental requires vision and determination from various stakeholders. University divisions, departments or units rely on partners to provide records management programmes. Practitioners and executive management believe that records and archives management activities' functions may not be measured because it is viewed as intangible assets. The records management function is a shared responsibility. Therefore, the implementation of records management requires an executive management support administrator responsible for the implementation of all records management programmes. Therefore universities are to develop controls to ensure that responsibilities are successfully executed. Universities apply performance systems to measure programme outcomes and inputs. Performance enables to improve the organisation. Effective and efficient records management improves the performance of the institutions in Nigerian universities (Umar 2019, p. 06). Demonstrating quality and accountability by measuring and evaluating the quality of records is an integral part of higher education institutions (Leonard and Niskala 2021, 302). Performance indicators represented division or department's Key Performance indicators.

Performance indicators are the factor to achieve an organisation's objectives (Koike 2013, p. 350). However, organisations are to determine key performance indicators in line with the organisation's strategic objectives. All divisional heads directors and managers are to enter into performance contractors with their employees. It seems that there is a lack of links between the annual performance plan, operational plans and performance agreements. Key performance can be created for the records management department and practitioners, as well as records and archives management in general. This is necessary to embrace aspects of the records and archives management programme of universities. Key performance areas are to be measured and be allocated time frame.

The university leadership such as the council is responsible for the university management. The University Council is the highest body of the institution responsible to establish a performance management system. This implies that the Management is responsible to develop a performance management system committed to providing leadership in quality and promoting organisational change. The committee is responsible to allocate resources and establishing strategic goals. Promoting quality improvement teams, reviewing key indicators of quality, estimating the cost of quality and ensuring adequate training of employees. Management is also responsible to rewards the best performing staff. The committee to establish a customer satisfaction survey. The university management committee should be a member of the committee to drive the performance programme of universities. The performance of the university should be driven by a vision/ mission statement. This should drive the university to prepare, develop and implement an action plan for the university.

The review of the literature shows that the lack of culture in records and archives management remains a challenge experienced by universities. Universities need to develop a culture of creation, maintenance, use and disposal of records. Barriers to restructuring information flow and integration of information include position bias, sub-unit goal optimisation and focus on goals that are related to the manager's position (Burger, 2015, p 30). The proper records and archiving culture ensured the management of records within an organisation.

An effective records and archives management programme require the allocation of resources. Therefore, It is necessary to allocate a budget to implement a records and archives management system. Universities are assessed based on programme efficiencies. Efficiencies are dependent on resources allocated to universities programme. organisations are to assign resources to ensure that the objectives of organisations are achieved. This statement is alluded to (by Hsu, Chen and Wang (2009, p 462) who stated that the measurement of ERMS performance can bring a direction for resource allocation in e-government.

The implementation of the records and archives management programme is dependent on the measured archives and records management indicators. Most organisations did not achieve key performance indicators because of their staff's lack of staff competency. The lack of staff with performance management skills affected to development of a key performance management system. For example, In Uganda, the issue of professional qualifications and training effect records management performance (Tumuhairwe e ad Ahimbisibwe 2015). The research recommended that future research on the level of professional capacity of officers involved in records management responsibilities and duties. Such a study should assess how officers have trained and the type of succession plans.

Archives services influence the skills and competencies, attitudes, and behaviours of archives users (Dunns 2021, P. 326). The benefits that universities experience from using archives services can be reviewed in terms of knowledge gained, improved records and archives management programmes. Even if universities measure the performance, staff are responsible for ensuring an effective and efficient records management system. Proactive measures are taken by all universities to ensure that vacant posts are filled with skilled and qualified staff. The establishment of a records management programme in line with the university structure is recommended.

Records Management should be seen as a specialized area. As such the common practice of shifting personnel without records management expertise to records management units should be eliminated. Appointing officials against records management posts but lacing them in other sections undermines all initiatives to capacitate the function. Records management staff establishment of all universities should be aligned to that of South African universities as far as the records functions are concerned. The staff structures of records management programmes.

University Records Management divisions should develop and implement a systematic training programme. Such training should be extended to other units within a university. Records management awareness workshops should be conducted within the division to sensitize all officials about the value of the records management system.

Information Communication Technology is a key dimension that universities require to leverage competitive advantage. The impact of Information Communication Technology lies in the fact that it is, in most cases, the medium through which development has taken place. There are a few studies that assess information communication technology models in the higher education sector. Conducting such a study may be an achievement to improve the records and archives management programme in South African universities. The efficient implementation of a strategic planning process is based on a well-functioning and integrated information and communication system (Van Wyk and Moeng 2014, p. 142). Information Communication technologies are an enabler to achieving university strategy. Lack of enforcement of records management systems and practices exposes an organisation to risks accruing from ineffective records keeping regimes, ultimately undermining the records management system (Ambira and Kemoni 2011, p. 03). Universities need to implement information management systems that enable increased performance on records and archives management systems (Mukred, Yusof, Alotaibi, Mokhtar and Fauzi 2019). Some institutions use e-resources as strategic resources. . This is so because e-resources play a role in the university's competency, enhancing the evaluation of performance. Universities' performance indicators are based on the utilisation of records and archives management systems. University cannot function effectively without an effective Electronic Records Management System. The performance management system depends on the utilisation of records and archives management system, sustainability and good quality performance record management system.

University strategy is informed by the Higher Education Act of 1997. Universities are guided by strategy to set objectives. Universities departments will set performance measures. This implied that the university develop a risk management register to determine the risk encountered by a university in the execution of its activities. A performance measurement system should contain comparisons so that university officials can better assess whether their university archives and records management programme performance is good or bad.

Organisational measurement models developed by the records management professions determine the state of records and archives management performance indicators. This study assesses the tools to manage types of records within an organisational records and archives management programme. The performance is significant to the university to understand the area which needs improvement. Assessing performance can be done through a survey. The system performance may be used to assess evaluation. The survey will provide experience on the system users

Archives and Records Management key performance indicators need to be customised and developed based on the strategic objectives and the critical success factors of the university. The development of Key performance indicators should be in such a way, that it measures the communication efforts of the entire university, and not just the efforts of the records and archives management division. The researcher has discovered that records management outcomes could have improved tremendously if records management exercises were implemented before the university implementation of a records management programme. This study hence gives an insight as to why the university should take records management seriously in their project execution to improve the performance of their institutions.

Implementation of the records management programme requires the university to develop annual objectives., devise policies, motivate employees and allocate resources. This will lead to the implementation of the university strategy. For a records management programme to contribute to organizational performance, records managers must embark on awareness campaigns in a form of seminars and workshops on the influence of records on the promotion of governance in the institutions (Umar 2019, p. 07). There was an increase in awareness of records and archives management. From the records and archive managers' perspective, it is evident that all records and archives managers practitioners should be aware of what the organisation expects of the Records and Archives Management Programme. The development of records and archives management programmes should be attached to the value of an organisation. It is necessary to determine whether a performance measurement model exists in the organisation or not. There are various models used by universities to assess their performance of universities. The most performance measurement system was the Balanced Scorecard. The Balanced scorecards provided an overview of the entire university's functions or university. The performance scorecard is linked to the operation of the university. Universities need to establish a model to ensure that records and archives functions are aligned with university strategy.

RECOMMENDATIONS

Measuring records and archives management performance improves reporting and performance of institutions. It is essential accountability to an organisation. Universities are to establish performance indicators to evaluate records and archives management programmes. The programme Performance Information Framework provides for the collection of performance. The framework needs to be utilised in compliance with the records and archives management programme within a university.

It is also necessary to build confidence in a records management system.

We should be able to measure contribution to organisation development based on key performance areas.

Universities need to develop a five-year strategic plan covering records and archives management programmes. From a developed strategic plan, universities develop annual performance plans. The strategic plan is informed by a university vision and mission. University must translate the strategy to operational terms. The development of strategy is necessary to evaluate organizational performance. Universities are to select appropriate performance indicators to assess the level of performance. Performance measures selected by division are monitored on annual basis.

The organisation should align and integrate its strategy with the daily job, increasing buy-in at all levels, the ability to make strategy continual process, ability mobilise change through executive leadership, the ability improve participative and consultative management style and the ability to move the organisational culture toward an achievement culture. The records and archives management key performance indicators should link to the university organisation plan. The records management strategy is informed by the overall university strategy. A performance management plan was introduced to assess the university programme. Records Management is an integral part of the business function of universities.

Performance measurement should be introduced to the university to be accountable to the public and to improve services to the university community by motivating employees to improve the quality and outcomes of the services. This builds trust in the community in their university. Feedback received from stakeholders determines a strategy of an organisation. The absence of organisation performance excluding records and archives management is the dearth of a records management programme.

Institutional performance depends on quality information and can be achieved by a systematic process to ensure data collection. Therefore the definition of quality should be clear (Tammaro, 2008). However, universities are to have clear objectives to be measured and monitored. The performance needs to be SMART to be assessed.

The South African government ensures that control is in place to measure records management processes (Duma 2020).

CONCLUSION

Evaluating a records and archives management programme is not a new phenomenon. The university depends on best practices to implement an effective records management programme. The review of the literature shows that most South African universities lack effective mechanisms, policies, rules, and procedures to manage records. The records management programme in South African universities must be guided by the National Archives and Records Service Act 43 of 1996. The international and national standards on records and archives management programmes should be followed by different university standards.

Most South African universities did not incorporate records and archives management processes into the performance measurement model. Hence, the Records Management programme is successful when university employees are made aware. Although extremely difficult to achieve, Staff are required to include a key performance area on records and archives management.

The role of the records and archives management programme in measuring university performance was limited. Most South African universities lack systems to measure records and archives management performance. It seems that universities lack systems to outline roles and responsibilities in the management of records and archives management systems. Hence universities have a mandate in terms of legislation to manage all forms of records within a university. The review of the literature shows that records and archives are not utilised to manage records management systems. It seems that some universities have the infrastructure to manage all forms of records within an organisation. While other universities lack systems to manage records within a system of universities. The study established that there was a lack of adequate support from management to support the records and archives management programme.

IMPLICATIONS FOR RESEARCH AND PRACTICES

The current National Archives and Records Service Act 43 of 1996 should be amended to give an adequate and specific guideline for the management and preservation of university records.

AREAS OF FURTHER STUDIES

Several countries develop key performance indicators to measure the performance of their records management programme. Use some time aspects of time measurement in their suite of Key Performance Indicators. However, before using the Key performance indicators, it may be beneficial to analyse the records management profile attending records management to ensure that records are managed effectively.

REFERENCES

Ambira, C., & Kemoni, H. (2011). Records management and risk management at Kenya Commercial Bank Limited, Nairobi. *South Africa Journal of Information Management, 13*(1).

Burger, N. P. (2015). *The role of Management Information Systems in Measuring Organisational Performance in the Kwazulu- Natal Department of Arts & Culture*. Stellenbosch University.

Duma, G. M. N. (2020). Assessment of records management practices among the senior managers in a South African Municipality. Master in Business Administration. North-West University. Potchefstroom, South Africa.

Dunn, A. (2021). *Monitoring and Evaluation of Public Libraries: A Case of Public Libraries in Namibia*. Wiley Library.

Grant, D., Mergen, E., & Wildrick, S. (2007). A Comparative Analysis of Quality Management in US and International Universities. *Total Quality Management & Business Excellence*, *15*(4), 423–438.

Grimard, J. (2004). Program Evaluation and Archives: "Appraising" Archival Work and Achievements, Counterpoint. *Archivaria*, *57*, 69–87.

Hsu, F-M., & Chen, T-Y., & Wang. (2009). Efficiency and Satisfaction of electronic records management systems in e-government in Taiwan. *The Electronic Library*, *27*(3), 461–473.

Koike, O. (2013). Institutionalizing performance management in Asia: Looking East or West? *International Journal of Public Sector Management*, *25*(5), 347–360.

Leonard, S., & Niskala, R. (2021). *Do Quality Assessment Matter in an Academic Library? A case study of the University of Namibia Library*. Academic Press.

Matangira, V. (2016). Recordkeeping in Zimbabwe in Colonial and Post – Independence Contexts. *ESARBICA Journal*, *35*, 67–88.

McLeod, J., Childs, S., & Heaford, S. (2007). Records management capacity and compliance toolkits: A critical assessment. *Records Management Journal*, *17*(3), 216–232.

Mojapelo, M., & Ngoepe, M. (2021). Contribution of Auditor-General South Africa to Records Management in the Public Sector in South Africa. *New Review of Information Networking*, *26*, 1–2.

Mosimege, B.S & Masiya, T (2021). Assessing audit outcomes of pre-determined objectives in a public institution (South Africa). *International Journal of Productivity and Performance Management*. https://doi.org/ doi:10.1108/uppm-02-2021-0091

Mukred, M., Yusof, M. Z., Alotaibi, M. F., Mokhtar, A. U., & Fauzi, F. (2019). The Key Factors in Adopting an Electronic Records Management System (ERMS) in Educational Sector: A UTAUT-Based Framework. IEEE, 7, 35963-35980.

Netshakhuma, N. S. (2019). The Blurry Line between archives and records management at the universities in South Africa. *Journal of the South African Society of Archivists*, *52*, 62–78.

Ngoepe, M., & Ngulube, P. (2014). The need for Records Management in the Auditing Process in the Public Sector in South Africa. *African Journal of Library Archives and Information Science*, *24*(2), 136–150.

Pereira, R. (2018). Assessing the implementation of the National Archives and Records Services Act at Eduardo Mondlane University in Mozambique. *ESARBICA Journal*, *37*, 221–239.

Shackleton, C. (2006). *Developing Key Performance Indicators For Corporate Communication in the Information Technology Industry. MCOM in Communication Management*. The University of Pretoria.

Siti-Nabiha, A. K., & Scapens, R. W. (2005). Institutional work and the implementation of performance measurement and management system in a developing country. *Journal of Accounting and Organisational Change. Accounting, Auditing & Accountability Journal*, *18*(1), 44–73.

Tammaro, A. M. (2008). *Performance indicators in Library and Information Science (LIS) education: towards cross-border quality assurance in Europe*. Conference paper presented at the Universita Di Parma.

Tumuhairwe, R., & Ahimbisibwe, A. (2016). Procurement records compliance, effective risk management and records management performance. Evidence from Ugandan public procuring and disposing entities. *Records Management Journal*, *26*(1), 83–101.

Umar, H. (2019). Records Management and Accountable Governance in two tertiary institutions of learning in Taraba State. *Bakundi Journal of Technology, Agriculture and Entrepreneurship*, *1*(1), 1–8.

Van Wyk, C., & Moeng, B. G. (2014). The Design and Implementation of a Strategic Plan in Primary School. *International Business & Economics Research Journal*, *13*(1), 137–143.

Wickman, D. (2009). Measuring performance or performing measurements? Measuring the impact and sustainability of the PARBICA Recordkeeping For Good Governance Toolkit. *Archives and Manuscript*, *37*(2), 114–126.

Zhou, J., Li, X., Zhao, X., & Wang, L. (2021). Driving performance grading and analytics; learning internal indicators and external factors from multi-source data. Driving performance grading. *Industrial Management & Data System*. https://www.emerald.com/insight/0263-5577.htm

ADDITIONAL READING

AlRababah, A. A. (2017). A new model of information systems efficiency based on key performance indicators (KPI). *Management*, *4*(8).

Cohen, K., & Bruijns, S. (2018). Describing Key Performance Indicators for waiting times in emergency centres in the Western Cape Province, South Africa, between 2013 and 2014. *South African Medical Journal*, *108*(7).

Hawash, B., Mokhtar, U. A., Yusof, Z. M., & Mukred, M. (2020). The Adoption of electronic records management system (ERMS in the Yemeni oil and gas sector: Influencing factors. *Records Management Journal*, *30*(1), 1–22. doi:10.1108/RMJ-03-2019-0010

Kim, E., & Han, S. (2022). A study on the Development of Operational Evaluation Indicators for Special Subject Archives. *Journal of Korean Society of Archives and Records Management*, *22*(10), 133–157.

Massegare, P., & Ngoepe, M. (2018). A framework for incorporating implementation indicators of corporate governance for municipalities in South Africa. *Corporate Governance: The International. Journal of Business and Society*, *18*(4), 581–593. doi:10.1108/CG-11-2016- 0216

Mintah, C., Gabir, M., Aloo, F., & Ofori, E. K. (2022). Does business records management affect business growth? *PLoS One*, *17*(3), e0264135.

KEY TERMS AND DEFINITIONS

Archives Management: It is the area of management concerned with the maintenance and use of archives materials.

Benchmarking: It is a process of measuring the performance of university services or processes against those of another business considered valuable to be the best in the records management industry.

Key Performance Indicators: It is a measurement value that shows how effectively a university is achieving key business objectives.

Records Management: It is the process of the creation, receipt, maintenance, use and disposition of records.

Strategic Plan: It is the organisation's process to identify its goals, the strategies necessary to accomplish those goals and the internal performance of an organisation.

Chapter 11
Strategic Implications of Key Performance Indicators for Knowledge Management Success in Organizations:
The Balanced Scorecard Framework

Tereza Raquel Merlo
https://orcid.org/0000-0002-2042-5415
University of North Texas, USA

ABSTRACT

The exponential growth of digital data generation and consumption in the past decade has ignited new discussions about the relevance and impact of knowledge management (KM) on individuals and businesses. This chapter presents a literature review examining knowledge management and systems of learning as well as some of the critical factors to be considered in the design, implementation, and evaluation of metrics for KM implementation success. It highlights the role of leadership and the importance of valuing knowledge workers for effective KM and KMS practices, and the design of knowledge metrics focused on learning and growth within the scope of the balanced scorecard framework and the possibilities of a Web 4.0 data processing environment in a competitive globalized market.

DOI: 10.4018/978-1-6684-4431-3.ch011

INTRODUCTION

In an era driven by data and the ability to use information to produce and share knowledge, businesses are significantly impacted by massive data production, the demand for data processing and use, and professionals with the skills to competitively manage data in organizations. Unquestionably, society has shifted from a form of production based on material goods and services, which is based on a concept that involves the logistical distribution and delivery of goods and services to create intellectual capital, defined by many researchers as the knowledge economy (Housel and Bell, 2001). This approach to capitalism attributed economic power to the core existence and understanding of society, the exploitation of labor, and the historically contingent strategic nature of class conflict in production and exchange (Skillman, 1996).

Skillman (1996) argues that “capitalist exploitation is instead best understood in terms of Marx’s historical-materialist theory of profit, which depicts capitalist production relations as a historically contingent strategic response to evolving conditions of class conflict over the creation and distribution of surplus product.” (p. 1). Carchedi (2005) contends that modern capitalism is based on the development of a Marxist theory of production of knowledge, where the theoretical structure accommodates mental production. The idea of production technologies and the future of work often parallel advances in technology, the creation of new machines, and the rise of artificial intelligence (Rifkin, 1995; Karakilic, 2020) which prompts recurring questions about whether machines will ever replace humans in the workplace.

In conjunction with the change in production processes progressively moving from physical labor to the use of intellect, the value of knowledge becomes a key factor in organizations, and the measurement of it becomes critical for performance evaluation and profitability. The notion of intellectual capital and collective intelligence is not new; however, the intensified advance in the production, adoption, and use of smart machines (artificial intelligence, machine learning, IoT, and algorithms, for example) imposes the urge to rethink knowledge production. Pettersen (2018) defends that “knowledge work can be assisted and enhanced, but not replaced, by computers” (p. 8).

Currently, the discussion around data access is marked by the evolution of the internet and how it brought a new paradigm to the communication process on an unimaginable global scale. It is imperative to understand the principles and impact of the evolution of the web as we strive to understand both data management and knowledge management and the impact they have on social and business activities. This insight allows effective creation of practices, policies, and an organizational culture that is designed to allow the rapid flow of information and knowledge in organizations, which impacts efficiency and innovation.

In that context, Aghaei, Nematbakhsh, and Farsani (2012) discuss the evolution of the internet, which the authors define as the "techno-social system that enhances human cognition, communication, and co-operation" (p.1). The authors highlight the evolution from Web 1.0, a readable platform where users had access to content but not the ability to change it, to Web 2.0 where the format was mostly read-write with a community centered approach, and the ability to share content. Then came Web 3.0, which introduced platforms for live-streams, smart applications, and more significant user engagement. Web 4.0, known as the symbiotic web, is an evolving current concept that considers self-learning systems and relates to the interaction between man and machine. (Almeida, 2017).

This chapter will discuss some critical factors for successful knowledge management implementation and metrics, from conceptualizing knowledge management and knowledge management systems to how an organizational culture focused on effective learning innovation will enable the use of performance metrics to track and measure the value of knowledge to organizations that increasingly demand the promotion of a knowledge-based approach to productivity.

KNOWLEDGE MANAGEMENT THEORIES AND THEIR RELEVANCE IN CONTEMPORARY ORGANIZATIONS

As a result of a post-war economy there were significant structural and societal changes, from one based upon manufacturing to one based upon service. In the United States the service sector comprised a high percentage of the gross domestic product (GDP) and individuals became the center of production. This paradigm shift emphasizes the need to concentrate on identifying ways in which employees' knowledge can be retained, approaches for reduction of turnover can be identified, and an investment in knowledge acquisition by employees (training and capacitation) can be implemented. (Dornbusch et al., 1993; Collinge and Adreene, 2009). The year 1980 marked the expansion of Information and Communication Technology (ICT) and the internet and imposed an emergency in what Collinge and Adreene (2009) defined as knowledge-intensive business services, with a move to a knowledge-based economy which revolves around the ways that knowledge is created, transferred, used, and stored.

Knowledge Management (KM) is recognized as a "key resource for organizational success," (Oufki and Kasso, 2017, p. 1) and becomes a priority for organizations determined to optimize informational resources, increase profitability, promote innovation, and minimize deviant behaviors that impact operations and productivity. Being intrinsically connected with organizational performance, KM creates a demand to answer questions concerning the design, implementation, and evaluation of key performance indicator (KPI) metrics as relevant measures of tangible outcomes and methods for the successful design of business roadmaps, guidelines, and strategies, as well as the management of individuals and technological resources. Aligned with that perspective, Sarvary (1999) advocates that: "It is important to realize that there is much more to knowledge management than technology alone. Knowledge management is a business process. It is the process through which firms create and use their institutional or collective knowledge." (p. 95), making the process of using tangible knowledge a critical subject of discussion in organizations.

A seminal study by Nonaka & Takeuchi (1994) examines how knowledge is produced, used, and diffused within organizations and how much knowledge contributes to innovation. While some regard knowledge as identical to information, many researchers and practitioners understand that knowledge includes a contextual experience: the know-how, know-what, comprehension, and individuals' values, for example. Skyrme (2011) defines knowledge management as "the explicit and systematic management of vital knowledge - and its associated processes of creation, organization, diffusion, use and exploitation - in pursuit of business objectives." (p. 32). While methods of management evolve as the social, technological, and economic ecosystem changes, the sciences of business management remain the same, where "emerging concepts and paradigms (models, behaviors patterns, theories, and methodologies) are introduced and applied to organizational life using specific programs." (Mašić et al., 2017, 128). KM as a field of management connecting individuals and computer systems technologies promotes the capture of organizational information assets; thereby representing a critical factor in aligning organizational strategies in response to an increasingly evolving data driven society.

Wiig (1997) advocates that knowledge management allows organizations to: "understand, focus and manage systematic, explicit and deliberate knowledge building, renewal and application," (p. 1) which facilitates the maximization of organizational knowledge-related effectiveness and connects innovation management and organizational learning (McElroy, 2010). Therefore, it is defended that knowledge management success in organizations is strictly correlated to the organizational ability to focus on the effective management of information and knowledge assets through the establishment of clear policies about the retrieval and use of knowledge by individuals in all levels and roles in the organization (Davenport and Prusak, 2000).

The impact of KM practices on organizational performance is unquestionable as businesses become increasingly data driven and knowledge-based, from operations and processes improvement, to creating data governance roadmaps and competitive business strategies, to the adoption and implementation of computer systems and new technologies and the innovation of products and approaches, to services that more efficiently attend to the demands of the market remain a priority. Expanding studies in the field of KM and information technologies indicate that an integrative approach to the KM strategy will affect organizational performance in a significant way, to which Ahmed, Fiaz, and Shoaib (2015) evaluate: "is a persistent subject in the majority of management branches and there is an apprehension toward both instructive persons and additionally rehearsing supervisors." (p. 150).

In their studies, Ahmed et al. (2015) identifies knowledge management practices as the mixture of knowledge acquisition, knowledge conversion, knowledge application, and knowledge protection, concluding that this combination is necessary for organizational survival, and that high employee turnover critically affects knowledge management activities in organizations. One of the difficulties in designing and evaluating knowledge management metrics resides in the nature of knowledge itself and the challenges in creating an environment and the motivation for individuals to want to share knowledge.

ENABLING KNOWLEDGE MANAGEMENT SUCCESS THROUGH KNOWLEDGE MANAGEMENT SYSTEMS (KMS): INTEGRATING CULTURE AND TECHNOLOGY

Very often in organizations value is attributed to metrics as a way to measure effectiveness, procedures, policies, and even processes (Cruz and Cruz, 2018); nonetheless, with knowledge assets at the center of discussions about production, the traditional approach shifts to the measurement of knowledge resources and the many ways in which it might represent a challenge, particularly in specific organizational cultures where learning and innovation are not the core of the business nor is the value attributed to knowledge workers. Minonne and Tuner (2009) approach performance metrics through a dynamic and integrative perspective compromised of four forms of integration: 1. cultural, 2. organizational, 3. procedural, and 4. methodical; corresponding to the 1. Organizational culture and the culture of encouraging community practice; 2. The integration of skills and document management systems that will ensure high quality performance, higher productivity, and innovation; 3. Improvement of procedures in an organic, sustainable, and simplified manner, so that there will be better time management and a reduction of redundancies; 4. The consolidation of a knowledge base that focuses on revenue, costs, profitability, and investments through management imperatives that include responsibility, centralization, and decentralization.

In investigating those four approaches for KM integration, authors Minonne and Tuner (2009) reveal that obstacles were identified in the KM strategy which were attributed to the lack of integration with the measurable targets to appropriately determine the KPIs, whether qualitative or (ideally) quantitative. The integrative approach the authors introduce includes at the center of the organizational KM initiative the four aspects of culture, organization, methods, and processes. In reference to the principles of Kaplan and Norton (1996), the authors highlight the importance of balanced scorecard concepts (BSC), considered "essential in the effective measurement of KM performance" (Minonne and Tuner, 2009, p. 585).

Considered by many authors as a revolutionary year, 1930 marks the beginning of computer systems networking that dramatically changed the ways in which data and information are managed, imposing new ways of communication, access, storage, and retrieval of data and information, impacting individuals and organizations worldwide (Barachini and Stary, 2022). The introduction of innovative capabilities in network connection characterizes the first phase of the world wide web, Web 1.0, then unimaginably defining the beginning of a future belonging to those individuals and organizations with the skills and capability of understanding and managing data in a digital format. The phenomenon of advanced digitalization in data processing is defined by Barachini and Stary (2022) as "The connectivity of the web and the availability of nearly unlimited storage result in data oceans which cannot be controlled by humans exclusively." (p. 3), and the quickly evolving production and access to data and the use of artificial intelligence solutions, some would argue, is threatening to a workforce that often questions whether machines will replace humans in organizations in the near future.

Advances in digitalization and operating systems resulted in the expansion of both hardware and software capable of managing large datasets and the creation of machine learning (ML) that creates new organizational paradigms in artificial intelligence, and the beginning of the Web 4.0. The increase in the number and complexity of intelligent machines used in manufacturing, healthcare, energy, transportation, education, and cloud computing goes beyond conventional data management conditions and parameters, enacting a series of dramatic approaches to solve problems "of optimization, filtration, image recognition, prediction, etc." (Taymanow and Sapozhnikova, 2021, p. 2) which describes and justifies artificial intelligence.

KMS is defined by repositories and directories, both of which are used to manage knowledge in organizations by building data warehouse infrastructures for the preservation of organizational memories and past experiences, and support knowledge conversion from implicit to explicit. Knowledge, as defined by Huerta et al. (2012) is defined in organizations as: "the input by employees who transform their implicit knowledge into explicit knowledge, thus making it accessible to other employees." (p. 95). KMS are the information systems (IS) deployed by organizations to facilitate the creation, distribution, and utilization of knowledge that will enhance organizational competitiveness (Alavi and Leidner, 2006). The success of KMS in enhancing organizational processes and performance depends on the methodically designed and implemented business strategy, information systems design, and the holistic approach to KM that contemplates its complexity and a multitude of factors affecting the sharing of organizational knowledge. Technology alone will not resolve knowledge sharing issues in organizations. Investigations conducted by Young, Kuo, and Myers (2012) assert that up to 70% of KMS fail to meet organizational objectives, leading to problems with KMS deployment, use, and overall organizational performance and metrics.

Further corroborating with the notion that KMS is part of the information technology approach to KM implementation, Jonsson (2015), in research about practices of knowledge management sharing, found that the real motivation for workers is the learning and development of professionals as well as their ability to contribute to the development of the business through organizational spaces for knowledge sharing.

PRINCIPLES IN DESIGNING, IMPLEMENTING, AND EVALUATING KEY PERFORMANCE INDICATORS IN A KNOWLEDGE-BASED MODEL: THE BALANCED SCORECARD APPROACH

The seminal study of Kaplan and Norton (1992) evaluates measurements that drive performance, stating that: "senior executives understand that their organization's measurement system strongly affects the behavior of managers and employees." (p. 71). The authors discuss how the traditional financial performance measures worked well for an industrial based economy but wouldn't work for the type of skills and competencies that companies are trying to measure today. The argument made by the authors is that financial measurements are inadequate and that current performance measurements systems should focus on operations improvement, and that financial measures will follow (Kaplan, Norton, 1992).

Realizing that "no single measure can provide clear performance target or focus attention on the critical areas of the business. Managers want a balanced scorecard presentation of both financial and operational measures." (Kaplan and Norton, 1992, p. 71). The authors defend that the BSC construct is a management tool that, when correctly understood and properly implemented, will:

1. clearly communicate the organization's strategy to its employees.
2. allow employees to see how they contribute to the organization's strategic goals by translating these goals into specific, measurable activities.
3. increase employees' motivation by attaching well thought-out objectives and targets to performance measures and then pay incentives when reached

4. enhance employees' learning and accountability by measuring and providing feedback on their actions; and
5. enable managers to monitor and update their organization's strategies as their environments change. (Kalagnanam, Sheehan, and Vaidyanathan, 2010, p. 689).

The balanced scorecard is designed to allow managers a new perspective on the business approach, seeking to answer questions about customers' expectations, the potential for business improvements, and how the stakeholders perceive the business (Kaplan and Norton, 1996).

Pineno and Cristini (2003) assert that the balanced scorecard "translates the vision, mission, and strategies into four or five basic categories that cannot be conflicting: financial, customer, internal business process, employee (learning and knowledge), and/or innovation" (p. 35-36) with missions attached to each category. According to the authors, the establishment of scorecards accomplishes seven main objectives in the business environment:

1. Translates the vision, mission, and strategies
2. Defines and aligns objectives and measures
3. Communicates the objects and measures
4. Aligns strategic initiatives
5. Aligns people
6. Aligns compensation with performance
7. Provides feedback on strategy

Concurring with that approach, the studies of Kureshi (2014) discuss the effectiveness of the balanced scorecard, with the author attributing its success to a combination of factors in the organization, defending that: "While analyzing the success, it also needs to be kept in view that most Balanced Scorecard initiatives do not come alone. They accompany several other performance improvement initiatives, together attributable to the status quo dis-satisfaction and dynamism of top management" (p. 33). The survey conducted by Bain & Company in 2018 presents usage satisfaction among respondents as the defining factor, with a significant result in the stable level of satisfaction between 1996 and 2017, where the following categories were evaluated: **financial performance** (revenue, earnings, return of capital cash flow), **customer value performance** (market share, customer satisfaction measures, customer loyalty), **internal business process performance** (percentage of revenue from new products, employee suggestions, rate of improvement index), and **employee performance** (morale, knowledge, turnover, use of best demonstrated practices). (Brain & Company, 2018).

The BSC, as a broader concept for measurement of performance, was designed with the goal of enhancing business processes and overall performance based on core competencies. Consequently, it must be aligned with the strategy and vision of the organization, contemplating the best strategy to assess and measure intangible assets. An investigation conducted by Jelenic (2011) measuring the BSC in KM discussed the three BSC perspectives: financial, customer, and business processes. Results indicated "a large gap between the ability of people, processes, and systems" (p. 38). In his study Jelenic (2011) emphasized that the creation of a business infrastructure that focuses on people and processes is a decisive approach to long-term value creation, learning, and growth. The author advocates that learning and growth: "defines the core competencies and skills, technology and corporate culture necessary to support the strategy." (p. 38). The learning and growth perspective that defines intangible assets are based on three core competencies: strategic competencies (skills and knowledge of employees), strategic technologies (the information systems, databases, and methods), and the organizational climate (organizational response to cultural change, motivation and authority delegation) of the business strategy.

Measuring KPIs in a Knowledge-Based Business Strategy

The IEEE (1990) defines metric as a quantitative measure of the degree to which a system, entity, or process possesses a given attribute, and in knowledge management it is mostly associated with aspects of KMS, which in many instances are underutilized in organizations due to behavioral issues related to staff capacitation and/or poor leadership, resulting from an organizational culture that challenges knowledge workers. Defining metrics in a business is essential for its survival, and in an age of knowledge as an asset, companies must cope with the challenge of managing the complexities of intangible and tangible knowledge. Accepting knowledge as the core of the business is no longer a question, but rather an undeniable and irrevocable part of business competitiveness. For practitioners "metrics are a way of learning what works and what does not" (Kankanhalli and Tan, 2005, p. 2).

Based on those theories it is reasonable to conclude that there are important criteria for KM implementation and metrics evaluation, and that factors for successfully designing, implementing, and measuring KPIs in organizations will depend on a variety of variables, which should be aligned with the business strategies and management commitment to making KM part of the organizational culture. Overall, the successful design of KPIs for KM, in a simplified, but integrated, manner, should rely on five basic factors: **1**. Feedback from key players on the team, allowing that the data collected is a realistic reflection of the dynamic that individuals face when performing their roles on a daily basis. That assessment will encourage alignment with the business strategies and objectives of the organization; **2**. A clear timeline designed to establish goals and dates for implementation of the performance indicator; **3**. Active management involvement to ensure that the measurement tool is properly implemented, and continuously measured and re-assessed; **4.** Keep the process unbiased and based on analytics and metrics by adopting an effective knowledge base system and/or business intelligence tool that will provide reliable data and metrics. **5.** Consistently and periodically track output of system metrics, so that management initiatives will be aligned with the established goals. Some aspects to consider in designing the KPIs:

1. Consider the industry and competitors.
2. Have a clear understanding of the business goals.
3. Consider the company's requirement and Information Technology, Infrastructure Library (ITIL) best practices.
4. Consider organizational structure.
5. Consider the KMS available.
6. Consider the Business Intelligence tools and strategies.
7. Set targets and thresholds.
8. Describe the intended results and appropriate measures for each objective.
9. Determine the audience (executives in leadership, stakeholders, department managers, specific groups).

KMS, which is heavily supported by information and communication technologies (ICTs), provides tools for the codification and de-codification of explicit knowledge in an information ecosystem that benefits from intelligence gathering, data governance policies, document management, data mining and warehousing, and artificial intelligence. This externalization of knowledge allows for the easy measurement of metrics and performance based on quantitative components. Additional critical factors that include human capital, leadership, and the complexity of the human and computer interaction represent a second aspect of KMS in terms of measurements, which refer to the qualitative elements and tacit knowledge.

Minonne and Tuner (2009) advocate that KPIs will allow organizations to focus on the real needs of the organization and the measurement of outcomes related to the technological development, innovation, employees' experiences, trainings, learning, and turnover, which are believed to better reflect effectiveness. In a discussion about whether efficiency or efficacy are to be prioritized in the KM measurement process the authors present five stages on KM maturity, analyzing the level of KM implementation in relation to the KM control; the five levels that determine the assessment of KM maturity, the KM3 Model include:

1. Stage 1 – Existing awareness for KM – No KM control established: Some level of comprehension about KM and the difference between IT and information management with no established KPIs and the possibility of some level of qualitative assessment in managing knowledge assets.
2. Stage 2 – KM topic addressed – KM control topic addressed: Intermediate level of cultural and organizational integration with no meaningful methodological incorporation and a few qualitative metrics as part of the strategy.
3. Stage 3 – Individual practices implemented – KM control partially established: An advanced level of cultural and organizational integration achieved, still with no meaningful procedural integration and mostly qualitative, but some quantitative KPIs developed.
4. Stage 4 – Policy & Methods standardized – Control largely established: Marked by an advanced level of cultural and organizational integration with an intermediate level of procedural and methodological integration achieved and both qualitative and quantitative KPIs implemented to be monitored and assessed as part of the KM strategy.
5. Stage 5 - Policy & Methods fully standardized – KM control fully established: This is the most advanced level with cultural, organizational, procedural, and methodological integrations achieved and both qualitative and quantitative KPIs in place.

The success of the design and implementation of KPIs is strongly linked with the alignment between organizational strategies and business goals and objectives in response to internal and external factors. In their study, Minonne and Tuner (2009) assess that KPIs "assess the progress of organizations in this compelling strategic activity of integrative KM need to be aligned with one or another of those forms of integration" (p. 589) which are the evaluation of the objectives, targets, initiatives, and measures in a KM strategy that must be integrated in the four forms: cultural, organizational, methodical, and procedural.

Leadership Impacting and Defining KM Implementation and Performance Effectiveness: Empowering Knowledge Workers

Numerous investigations in the field of management, leadership, and knowledge management have revealed that only 5% (five percent) of knowledge in organizations is explicit, while 95% is tacit knowledge, including experiences, thinking processes, competence, commitment, etc. The conversion of knowledge remains a challenge to organizations and leaders seeking to promote an innovative, engaging, and productive workplace. The biggest challenge in empowering individuals to share knowledge and to want to share knowledge are the barriers in an organizational culture that is not favorable toward participation and learning, which attracts individuals who are unwilling to share knowledge.

Leadership style has a significant influence on Information Technology use (Gençer & Samur, 2016) and the level of engagement between individuals and computer systems. Studies by Yang (2007) found that there is a significantly positive relationship between the effectiveness of knowledge sharing and a collaborative culture. That perspective is corroborated by the study of Hutagalung et al. (2021) where the authors defend that leadership style plays an important role in knowledge creation because it affects how members learn, acquire, and share knowledge. On the other hand, leadership style can also be seen as a model of organizational behavior by members of the organization who share a complex set of beliefs and expectations.

The role and responsibilities of leadership in enabling and assessing KM and KPIs is critical in KM implementation because KM is a challenging process of identifying and leveraging individual and collective organizational knowledge in such a way that organizations can compete more effectively over time. Denford and Chan (2011) and Schiuma (2012) defend that: KM strategy serves as a roadmap to guide organizations toward more effective KM by managing workgroup knowledge processes, extending knowledge capabilities, and recommending solutions to KM problems. Leaders and executives must be responsible for creating a knowledge management process framework that is part of the organizational culture where all resources, including human, are aligned and working effectively, from the knowledge system adoption and implementation to the support for knowledge creation and sharing.

Hawryszkiewycz (2010) supports that "leadership in forward thinking businesses must therefore focus on using technologies to develop human capital" (p. 28). The main goal of organizations with a thriving knowledge management system is to create an environment that will allow the identification of knowledge resources and the discovery of data and information and distinguish value in internal and external knowledge assets. Shahbazi (2006) investigated the relationship of knowledge management with the innovation of information and communication technology and their roles in the improvement of efficiency of processes. Shahbazi found that making a commitment to organizational insight between management levels and personnel reinforces the organization's efficiency and enables group work as one of the major grounds of innovation.

The key approach to the decision-making process in organizations is to: "bring people to work together in productive ways to the benefit of all" (Hawryszkiewycz, 2010, p. 76), developing intellectual and social capital creating a culture of trust among individuals that are appointed to work towards a common business goal. The roles and responsibilities of leaders in organizations today are decisive in the consolidation of a workplace that values and encourages knowledge workers to thrive because: "the companies-leaders, which care about their high business performance, have realized that the market value of their property increases with greater participation of "intangibles" (intellectual) resources in relation to tangible property." (Jalenic, 2011, p. 34).

The level of productivity of employees reflects in their skills, morale, innovation, and the improvement of customer satisfaction and: "Through managing employees within this perspective, managers at the company realize what employees need to learn, improve and innovate to meet their goals. Thus, much of this perspective is related to the staff, which meets the other goals such as development of new products, continuous improvement, technological leadership and product diversification." (Jalenic, 2011, p. 39). Kaplan and Norton (1996) list some key indicators for analysis of learning and growth within a BSC system, which is based on: employee satisfaction, retention and productivity. Therefore, leaders have a critical responsibility to foster a workplace that is structurally and culturally ready for ideas to flourish, where participation is encouraged, and learning and growth are at the center of the business strategy priorities, eliminating deviant behaviors and issues in communication that prevent knowledge sharing, allowing knowledge workers to feel empowered and motivated to work towards innovation and collaboration.

Effective leadership will work to ensure that the work dynamic is conducive to a productive workplace, where individuals will feel supported and motivated to engage with each other, customers, and stakeholders with purpose, through strategically defined goals that promote a fluid process. Some behaviors to be encouraged should target the following objectives:

1. Ensuring consistent and transparent communication.
2. Eliminating misinformation by promoting clear and concise guidelines and setting expectations.
3. Encouraging knowledge sharing by creating rewards programs (material, financial or non-financial) which promote group interaction, brainstorming, and means to enhance individuals' contributions and performances.
4. Defining roles and responsibilities and ensuring that individuals are supported in work processes.
5. Providing feedback and showing interest in helping and supporting career growth and performance excellence.
6. Discouraging deviant behaviors.
7. Preventing information overload and the practice of overloading individuals that overachieve as workers.
8. Creating an environment where the withholding of information is not a practice of control and power.
9. Creating and enabling an environment for workers to feel safe expressing opinions, accepting failures, and asking questions.

Proactive and effective leaders will maximize the availability of resources (including human resources) to accomplish the goals of the business and maximize the practice of teamwork through a dynamic, trusting collaboration. Those behaviors benefit the organization by promoting a leadership style that will help with:

1. Reduction of costs and effective process improvement
2. Practicing full transparency
3. Increasing in employee participation
4. Increasing trust in leadership and the company
5. Raising morale
6. Increasing motivation
7. Increasing the level of productivity and innovation
8. A positive work culture
9. The promotion of a culture of learning and growth
10. Excellence in customer service through higher job satisfaction
11. Reduction in reluctance to adopt new technologies
12. Superior business intelligence practices
13. Improved investment, and return on investment, in trainings and skills development
14. Higher employee retention

While knowledge sharing is more feasible now thanks to technological advances, the investment in training and competencies development is at the core of KM sharing success, where individuals are the main agent and leaders take on a critical, defining role. Knowledge sharing is a process between people resulting from relationships, where motivation, communication, and skills are vital aspects. Knowledge sharing is part of organizational learning that is defined by leaders, mainly focusing on how members of the organization learn and practice organizational values and share knowledge. (Jonsson, 2015).

THE KNOWLEDGE WORKER AND INFORMATION SHARING

The literature about the knowledge worker conveys multiples concepts, since the term was first used by Peter Drucker in 1954, when Drucker defined the knowledge worker as "the person who has knowledge important for the organization and often is the only person who has it." (Mládková, 2012, p. 244). Drucker's seminal work seems to imply a tolerance for withholding knowledge, where individuals might not be encouraged to share knowledge because it makes them feel more valuable or indispensable to the organization. It also reflects a period of time when manual labor was often the main means of production. With the cultural and social shift and the technological evolution since 1954 there has been a promotion of less centralized data and information access in the workplace, however there are still companies today, perhaps, due to high competitiveness, that experience and suffer from individuals that are unwilling to be part of a collaborative organizational culture and team dynamic. These workers may refuse to share information and knowledge or actively and productively participate in communities of learning as way to feel indispensable.

Based on that understanding, the concepts of knowledge workers presented by contemporary authors are beneficial to innovative organizations, particularly referring to KM strategies and practices, such as the definition presented by Davenport (2005), who defended that "the primary purpose of knowledge workers' job involves the creation, distribution, or application of knowledge and that knowledge workers think for a living." (Mládková, 2012, p. 245).

Nonaka and Takeuchi (1995) promote that organizational investment in knowledge workers facilitates learning and an environment for shared experiences, resulting in the enhancement of teamwork and the development of competencies. The authors defend that by developing and retaining knowledge workers and therefore, creating a "knowledge-creating" environment, companies are better prepared to consolidate a problem-solving culture that will allow business to more effectively respond to changes both internally and externally. The seminal work of Nonaka and Takeuchi (1995) introduces the four models of knowledge conversion: socialization, externalization, combination, and internalization to explain the human knowledge process of information and the ways in which information and knowledge is transferred with an emphasis on externalization and combination, where individuals communicate, interconnect, and convert tacit knowledge into explicit knowledge.

Most studies in KM debate the challenge of externalization of knowledge with claims that successful explicit knowledge sharing in organizations must adhere to a few criteria that involve the following: articulation, awareness, access, and guidance; respectively, user's ability to define needs, awareness about knowledge availability, access to knowledge, and finally the role played by knowledge managers in ensuring that knowledge is based on a shareable implemented system. (Bukowitz and Williams, 1999; Davenport & Prusak 2000, Gamble & Blackwell 2001).

In the study of Lee et al. it is asserted that "knowledge internalization was measured by three constructs-capability to internalize task-related knowledge, education opportunity, level of organization learning. Capability to internalize task-related knowledge was operationalized by four items – 1. I have a unique know-how for tasks, 2. I can learn knowledge necessary for new tasks, 3. I can use the internet to obtain knowledge for tasks, 4. I can refer to best practices and apply them to my tasks. Education opportunity was operationalized by two items,

5. Employees are given education opportunity to improve adaptability to new tasks, 6. University administered education is offered to enhance employees' ability to perform tasks. Level of organization learning was operationalized by three items, 7. Professional knowledge such as customer knowledge and demand forecasting are managed systematically, 8. Organization-wide standards for information resources are built, 9. Organization-wide knowledge and information are updated regularly and maintained well." (Lee et al., 2005, p. 475).

Polanyi introduced the concept of tacit dimension in 1966, arguing that information is the result of personal experiences, cultural beliefs, skills, expertise, capabilities, and context. The author supports that tacit knowledge is a central part of knowledge in general defending an epistemological approach that individuals can know more than they can express, drawing the concept of knowledge based on indwelling. Polanyi (1966) defends that: "the process of formalizing all knowledge to the exclusion of any tacit knowledge is self-defeating" (p. xi). A question worth asking relates to enabling knowledge transfer to benefit organizations. In a study surveying 306 knowledge workers conducted by Oyefolahan and Dominic (2013) the authors investigated the factors inherent in organizational practices and KMS that lead to innovation, finding a strong correlation between KMS and innovative norms among knowledge workers. The authors defend that the usage of KMS prompts significant development of competencies among knowledge workers.

IMPACT OF WEB 4.0 IN DESIGNING BUSINESS REQUIREMENTS AND BSC METRICS FOR A KNOWLEDGE MANAGEMENT APPROACH: PROPOSING A LEARNING-CENTRIC FRAMEWORK

In 1989 Tim Burners-Lee introduced the new information construct of Web that has progressed over the past decades, with advances and more extensive use of information and communication technologies, allowing users increase the possibilities for interaction and build content; from Web 1.0 of cognition and access, Web 2.0 of communication and interaction, Web 3.0 of co-operation, and the current advent of Web 4.0, bringing integration. Web 4.0 is defined by Patil and Yogesh (2018) as:

...Underground idea in progress and there is no exact definition of how it would be. Web 4.0 is also known as symbiotic web. The dream behind of the symbiotic web is interaction between humans and machines in symbiosis. It is feasible to build more powerful interfaces such as mind-controlled interfaces using web 4.0. In simple words, machines would be clever on reading the contents of the web, and react in

the form of executing and deciding what to execute first to load the websites fast with superior quality and performance and build more commanding interfaces. (p. 814).

The capabilities introduced by the new generation of Web 4.0 are still unclear but its impact on the IT infrastructure (software, extranet, internet, etc.) defines the knowledge management system that is the basis of the data management process, costs, databases, repositories, and business requirements and strategies. BABOK (2005) describes business requirements as a schema, classification, and clear statement of business goals, objectives, and outcomes, which normally focus on the market share, level of production, customer relationship growth, and assess aspects of waste of resources and optimization. The importance of a well-defined and consistent business requirement will stem from the business' vision and mission and define the business model, policies, infrastructure, and culture, where knowledge management and metrics lie.

The presented study aligns with the investigation conveyed by Mbassegue and Gardoni (2017) who reported on the measurement of knowledge management projects based on balanced scorecard in an engineering and manufacturing environment, concluding that although it is still challenging to identify the scope of benefits introduced by knowledge management projects it was evident that organizational knowledge can be measured upon examining different cases studies in an exploratory methodological approach. The three aspects the authors identified as difficult to assess knowledge initiatives are: human resources, processes, and infrastructure. The authors claim that the combination of the three aspects generates positive impacts in organizations.

Publications that concentrate on information technology and knowledge management more frequently adopt a chronological approach for the use of information technology for profitability in organizations. Nevertheless, as evidenced in the study of Mbassegue and Gardoni (2017), access to information and the sharing of knowledge are controlled by individuals (the knowledge workers) whose commitment to transform data into decision is pivotal, so that new techniques and the improvement of artificial intelligence tools are applied to the discovery of new opportunities and the practice of science in an Industry 4.0 era (Taymanov et al., 2021).

As this study demonstrates, in designing, implementing, and measuring knowledge management in organizations, it is important that managers consider as critical factors the business mission, values, vision, value proposition, and the consolidation of an organizational culture favorable to knowledge creation and sharing, which will not only permit but inspire the individual knowledge process to flow: from tacit to explicit and vice-versa. This type of collaboration between individuals in all levels of organizations impacts the motivation and satisfaction of employees using technologies and improving job performance.

The BSC framework placing emphasis on the four dimensions of the business (customer, finance, internal processes, and learning and growth) allows the use of both quantitative and qualitative metrics, with an emphasis on return of investment in measuring results. Adapting from the BSC framework, the BSC model focused on KM processes means to establish clear business strategies for the development of the learning and growth of employees first and foremost, so that internal processes would be optimized and both internal and external customers would experience a high level of satisfaction with services, products, and processes, and have superior financial outcomes as result. See BSC adapted **Figure 1-** Designing a learning-centric BSC as key to KM success initiatives below:

Figure 1. Designing a learning-centric BSC as a key to KM success. Adapted from BSC model from Kaplan and North (1996).

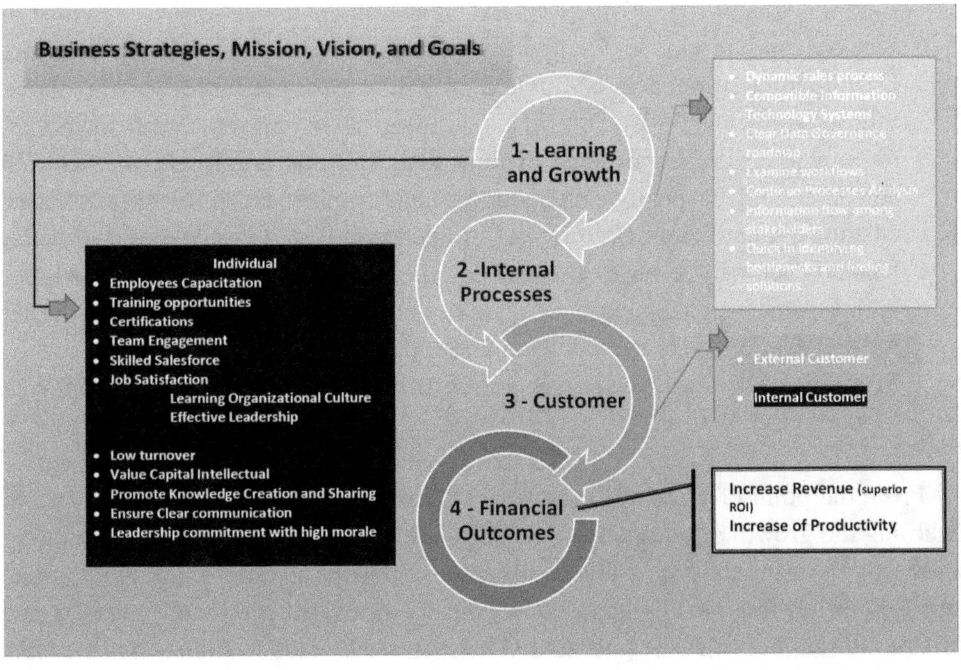

The adapted BSC for KM diagram introduces a concept that is based on the business strategy, mission, vision, and goals, and follows a numerically organized flow of the four original dimensions of BSC by their order of importance, as described below:

1. **Learning and Growth:** Focus on the hiring of skilled knowledge workers.
2. For individuals the focus should be on: capacitation, training opportunities, certifications, team engagement, the consolidation of a skilled salesforce; and job satisfaction. In terms of a learning organizational culture and effective leadership: low turnover, appreciation of intellectual capital, promotion of knowledge creation and sharing (meetings, workshops, communities of practice, etc.), ensure clear and honest communication, and a commitment to high morale represent top objectives and goals to be pursued by members.
3. **Internal Processes:** Dynamic sales process; Capable information technology systems; Successful sales process; Compatible information technology systems; Clear Data Governance roadmap; Examination of workflows; Continuous processes analysis and improvement; Information flow among stakeholders; Quick to identify bottlenecks and find solutions.
4. Customer:
   External Customer Satisfaction: Excellence in customer service; Quality of services and products; Competitive prices; Product/Services satisfaction, Customer retention, acquisition and growth of customer base.
   Internal Customer Satisfaction: This sub-dimension is introduced as an attempt to emphasize the importance of understanding that employees are internal customers and that positive interaction among employees is reflected in external customer satisfaction. Having well trained, motivated employees with solid business acumen, a sense of teamwork, the willingness to share knowledge, a high sense of engagement, and a desire to learn and grow is related to higher job satisfaction, as is evident throughout this study.
5. **Financial Outcomes:** Increase in profitability, revenue, and employee productivity.

From the point of view of Learning and Growth, leaders play a critical role in enabling the growth of competence among individuals. The benefits of promoting knowledge workers and their intellectual capital allows the business to hire, encourage, and rely on professionals whose knowledge is translated into best practices and diffused throughout the organization. That approach leads to higher productivity and innovation, resulting in reduction of costs, optimization of resources (from physical and technological to human), and ultimately the increase of profitability, as evidenced in the study of Mbassegué and Gardoni (2017), which investigated the success of knowledge management and evaluation in organizations, concluding that it depends on the employees as a decisive factor.

The emphasis on employee satisfaction and learning proposed in Diagram 1 contemplates the business mission, vision, and overall strategies, and focuses on superior processes, products and services; therefore, the creation of mechanisms to enhance and mitigate opportunities for a proactive resolution of internal and external issues, and better interaction with stakeholders. It also concentrates on the proposal that the adequate use of business resources prevents issues from escalating. The goal of a BSC that is learning centric is to provide the framework to align and optimize employees' training and capacitation with the leadership ability to engage employees and keep the motivation at a satisfactory level, so that knowledge workers will feel empowered to collaborate, innovate, and share in the workplace. The presented argument that BSC in KM initiatives should focus on learning and growth first and foremost is based on the principle that individuals are the main factor that permit knowledge creation either as independent users and contributors in the organizational ecosystem or as designers of and decision-makers for information systems that will determine, program, and make intelligent systems available to users.

An organizational culture that provides systematic documentation of how knowledge systems and knowledge workers interact results in the simplification of processes and practices for data and information transfer in organizations, leading to a better team interaction and understanding about the factors and dimensions affecting the long-term survival rates of organizations. Studies on performance evaluation have shown that leadership and technological systems are responsible for enabling creativity, including the creation of steps to develop, implement, and the improve the design and evaluation of performance metrics. Transparent and easily understandable performance indicators and measurements by knowledge workers is reflected in the overall organizational performance and team and leadership effectiveness.

Explaining the significance of the impact of Web 4.0 to knowledge management and measurements tools, Yıkılmaz (2020) claims that: "Web4.0 offers a future beyond previous technological advancement (people to people or machine to machine) where everything can be integrated and enable knowledge sharing and interaction." (p. 532), because knowledge transfer is supported by the communication between intelligent agents that will help create, reuse, and retrieve the exact knowledge on the exact time and in the exact form (Nath and Iswary, 2015).

A learning-centric organizational culture is shown in the generation and or improvement of metrics that include revenue for new products and services, analysis results of employee satisfaction and individual KPIs, increase in the sharing of ideas, an increase in innovation, and, most importantly, the managerial ability to track and assess resources allocation and performance progress in relation to lower organizational waste. In discussing performance indicators, Moreira (1999) listed three aspects: countenance, operational nature, and significance; respectively, the sharing of individual' information in the public domain; the ability to evaluate quantitative and qualitative contributions in a tangible way; and the clear significance of information to organizations over time.

While tangible and intangible assets are equally important in organizations, more emphasis on outcomes indicate that the KM process measures the rate in which knowledge is used in organizations, identifies and assesses gaps in opportunities for KM sharing, identifies problem areas in management and employee motivation and engagement, and assesses perceived knowledge relevance within the organizational culture. Petersen, Dahl, and Seim (2021) advocate that organizational learning enables the use of information and knowledge for organizational improvement, defending that crowdsourcing is an effective method to help promote problem-solving and the efficiency of individuals' contributions in organizations.

CONCLUSION

This chapter analyzed some aspects of business strategies in key performance indicators in organizations arguing that successful knowledge management initiatives must rely on the capital intellectual and knowledge workers. It presented and discussed the importance of clear KPIs and the balanced scorecard framework, presenting an adapted BSC model that emphasizes learning and growth as critical dimension for productivity.

Recent investigation on knowledge management has provided a more complete understanding of the increasing impact of data, information, and knowledge in organizations during an era of fast technological advances and high competitiveness in a global market. The organizational willingness and determination to learn, adapt, change, and reinvent processes and products in a fast-paced environment becomes critical to its survival. Evidence from research indicate that technological preparedness, human capital, and organizational culture play a decisive role in organizational performance, processes optimization, the ability to innovate, and ultimately generate higher profitability. Notwithstanding the fact that data management and the importance of knowledge workers have become central topics in discussions around the effective use of knowledge and profitability, the relationship between those factors and how to measure knowledge in an organization is still a topic of debate with some skeptics alleging that knowledge cannot be measured while defenders of knowledge workers advocate for more efforts directed at the creation of a workplace that encourages individuals to share knowledge and actively engage in business processes. Those emphasizing the importance of a culture that value knowledge workers advocate for an organizational culture that will enable the flourishment of a superior human-computer interaction, effective leadership that will encourage and value individual participation, and the adoption of information systems that will serve the business purpose and customer's needs. Because it is difficult to measure the intrinsic knowledge of a particular individual, research in that area serves as an inspiration to encourage explicit knowledge to occur between individuals in all levels of the organization, consequently, creating a culture that will allow metrics to be clearly communicated and measured.

Knowledge metrics will allow the implementation of a knowledge base/count with a better comprehension of the numbers, employees' contributions, and top performance indicators, including in some cases the numbers of best practices received and replicated, the percentage of replication, the percentage of employees' engagement in knowledge management projects and initiatives, tracking of users' views to trends- seasonal demands or periodical demands, and overall, more decentralized information access. Within the BSC model, the learning and growth dimension, is significant to KM and KMS as it allows new ways to assess humans as assets in organizations, under the understanding that in a knowledge-based economy individuals' knowledge and ability to constantly learn has a financial impact on organizations, recognizing that knowledge workers are a critical factor in the business strategy and the KM sharing and systems success.

The performance evaluation metric provides measurable procedures for the achievement of business and individual goals, allowing progress tracking, the identification of issues permitting companies and individuals to be proactive in preventing issues from escalating, and making sure that efforts are directed at a determined goal or set of goals. It gives meaning to the organizational existence and serves as key factor in evaluating profitability. Throughout the KM design, implementation, and assessment project, knowledge-based performance metrics must be aligned with the business strategic goals that is learning and growth centric. Following the BSC conceptual framework described in Diagram 1 place emphasizes in the enablement of a more effective team operations dynamic and higher cooperation, and the improvement of organizational resources management, so that employees' time, skills, and competences are valuable part of the business strategy that allows the organization to thrive.

Future empirical studies investigating the prioritization of learning and growth dimension proposed on Diagram 1 approach to knowledge management should provide detailed quantitative and qualitative indicators in how business strategies, operations, and outcomes are affected, and to what extent business benefits from individuals' increase in cooperation and knowledge sharing. Such investigation should validate the claims that knowledge workers and an organizational learning centric culture leads to higher productivity and successful knowledge management initiatives, as argued in this study.

REFERENCES

Aghaei, S., Nematbakhsh, M. A., & Farsani, H. K. (2012). Evolution of the World Wide Web: From Web 1.0 to Web 4.0. *International Journal of Web & Semantic Technology.*, *3*(1), 1–10. Advance online publication. doi:10.5121/ijwest.2012.3101

Alavi, K., Kayworth, T. R., & Leidner, D. (2006). An empirical examination of the influence of organizational culture on knowledge management practices. *Journal of Management Information Systems*, *23*(3), 191–224. doi:10.2753/MIS0742-1222220307

Almeida, F. (2017). Concept and Dimensions of Web 4.0. *International Journal of Computers and Technology. 16*(7). Retrieved from: Web4.0-with-cover-page-v2. pdfd1wqtxts1xzle7.cloudfront.net

Barachini, F., & Stary, C. (2022). *From digital twins to digital selves and beyond.* Springer. doi:10.1007/978-3-030-96412-2

Brain and Company. (2018). *Balanced.* Retrieved from: https://www.bain.com/insights/management-tools-balanced-scorecard/

Bukowitz, W., & Williams, R. (1999). *The Knowledge Management Fieldbook.* Financial Times/Prentice Hall.

Carchedi, G. (2005). On the production of knowledge. *Research in Political Economy*, *22*, 261–298. doi:10.1016/S0161-7230(04)22010-7

Collinge, C., & Adreene, S. (2009). Rethinking the knowledge-based economy. *Building and Environment*, *35*(2), 165–172. Advance online publication. doi:10.2148/benv.35.2.165

Davenport, T. (2005). *Thinking for Living*. HVB School Publishing.

Davenport, T. H., & Prusak, L. (2000). *Working Knowledge: How Organizations Manage What They Know*. Harvard Business School Press.

Drucker, P. F. (1954). *Landmarks of Tomorrow, A Report on the New 'Post-Modern' World.* Transaction Publisher London.

Gamble, P. R., & Blackwell, J. (2001). *Knowledge Management: A State of the Art Guide*. Kogan Page Ltd.

Gençer, M. S., & Samur, Y. (2016). Leadership styles and technology: Leadership competency level of educational leaders. *Procedia: Social and Behavioral Sciences*, *229*, 226–233. doi:10.1016/j.sbspro.2016.07.132

Housel, T., & Bell, A. (2001). *Measuring and Managing Knowledge*. Dudley Knox Library., Available https://www.nps.edu/library

Huerta, E., Salter, S., Lewis, P., & Yeow, P. (2012). Motivating employees to share their failures in knowledge management systems: Anonymity and culture. *Journal of Information Systems*, *26*(2), 93–117. doi:10.2308/isys-50214

Hutagalung, D., Admiral, A., Nuryanti, Y., Asbari, M., & Novitasari, D. (2021). Managing Tacit Knowledge Sharing: From Charismatic Leadership to Psychological Safety Climate. Inovbiz. *Jurnal Inovasi Bisnis*, *9*(1), 108–119. doi:10.35314/inovbiz.v9i1.1888

IEEE. (1990). IEEE Standard Glossary of Software Engineering Terminology. IEEE Std 610.12-1990. doi:10.1109/IEEESTD.1990.101064

International Institute of Business Analysis. (2005). *A Guide to the Business Analysis Body of Knowledge (BABOK Guide Ver 2.0)*. International Institute of Business Analysis.

Jelenic, S. (2011). The importance of knowledge management in organizations-with emphasis on the balanced scorecard learning and growth perspective. *Management Knowledge and Learning International Conference.* Retrieved from: http://issbs.si/press/ISBN/978-961-92486-3-8/papers/ML11-1.pdf

Jonsson, A. (2015). Beyond knowledge management-understanding how to share knowledge through logic and practice. *Knowledge Management Research and Practice*, *13*(1), 45–58. doi:10.1057/kmrp.2013.28

Kankanhalli, A., & Tan, B. (2005). Knowledge Management Metrics: A Review and Directions for Future Research. *International Journal of Knowledge Management*. Retrieved from: https://www.researchgate.net/publication/270092694

Kaplan, R., & Norton, D. (1992). The Balanced Scorecard-Measures that drive performance. *Harvard Business Review*. Retrieved from: https://www.steinbeis-bi.de/images/artikel/hbr_1992.pdf

Kaplan, R. S., & Norton, D. P. (1996). *The Balanced Scorecard*. Harvard Business School Press.

Kaplan, R. S., & Norton, D. P. (2001). The Strategy-focused Organization. Harvard Business School Press.

Karakilic, E. (2020). Why Do Humans Remain Central to the Knowledge Work in the Age of Robots? Marx's Fragment on Machines and Beyond. *SAGE Journals*, *36*(1), 179–189. doi:10.1177/0950017020958901

Kureshi, N. (2014). To balanced scorecard or not balanced scorecard, That is the question. *Journal of Strategy & Performance Management*, *2*(1), 31–38.

Lee, K., Lee, S., & Kang, I. (2005). KMPI: Measuring knowledge management performance. *Information & Management*, *42*(3), 469–482. doi:10.1016/j.im.2004.02.003

Masic, B., Nesic, S., Nikolic, D., & Dzeletovic, M. (2017). Evolution of knowledge management. *Industrija*, *45*(2), 127–147. doi:10.5937/industrija45-13201

Mbassegue, P. G., & Gardoni, M. (2017). Measuring the Performance of Knowledge Management Projects based on Balanced Scorecard in an Engineering and Manufacturing Environment. *International Journal of Engineering Research & Technology, IJERT.*, *6*(5), 1029–1035.

McElroy, M. W. (2010). *The New Knowledge Management*. Routledge. doi:10.4324/9780080512655

Mládková, L. (2012). Leadership in management of knowledge workers. *Social and Behavioral Sciences.*, *41*, 243–250.

Moreira, M. A. (1999). *Meaningful Learning* [Aprendizagem Significativa]. Brasília: UnB.

Nath, K., & Iswary, R. (2015). What comes after Web 3.0? Web 4.0 and the Future. *Proceedings of the International Conference and Communication System (I3CS'15)*, 337-341.

Nonaka, I. (1994). A Dynamic theory of organizational knowledge creation. *Organization Science*, *5*(1), 14–37. doi:10.1287/orsc.5.1.14

Nonaka, I., & Takeuchi, H. (1995). The Theory of Organizational Knowledge Creation. *International Journal of Technology Management*, *11*(7/8), 1996.

Oyefolahan, I. O. (2013). Knowledge management systems use and competency development among knowledge workers. *VINE Journal of Information and Knowledge Management Systems*, *43*(4), 482–500. doi:10.1108/VINE-07-2012-0023

Patil, H., & Surwade, Y. (2018). Web Technologies from Web 2.0 to Web 4.0. *IJSART*, *4*(4), 810–814.

Petersen, S. A., Dahl, T. L., & Seim, E. A. (2021). *Enhancing Learning and Collaboration in Organisations through In-house Crowdsourcing* (Paper presentation). NOKOBIT Norsk konferanse for organisasjoners bruk av IT, Conference 2021, Norway. https://www.researchgate.net/publication/356536415_Enhancing_Learning_and_Collaboration_in_Organisations_through_In-house_Crowdsourcing

Pettersen, L. (2018). Why Artificial Intelligence Will Not Outsmart Complex Knowledge Work. *SAGE Journals, 33*(6), 1058-1067. doi:10.1177/0950017018817489

Pineno, C., & Cristini, C. (2003). The balances scorecard: A vision report card. *Management Accounting Quarterly, 4*(4). https://www.imanet.org/-/media/8269bca77c3749fbab7e4936a960d41d.ashx

Polanyi, M. (1966). *The Tacit Dimension*. The University of Chicago Press.

Rifkin, J. (1995). *The End of Work: The Decline of the Global Work-Force and the Dawn of the Post-Market Era*. Penguin.

Sarvary, M. (1999). Knowledge management and competition in the consulting industry. *California Management Review, 41*(2), 95–107. doi:10.2307/41165988

Skillman, G. L. (1996). *The Role of Production Relations in Marx's Theory of Capitalist Exploitation*. Marxian Economics session of the History of Economics Society annual conference, Vancouver, Canada. Retrieved from: http://gskillman.web.wesleyan.edu/research/histmat2.pdf

Skyrme, D. (2011). *A Knowledge-Enriching Culture*. Available at http://www.skyrme.com/kmroadmap/culture.htm

Soderberg, M., Kalagnanam, S., Sheehan, N. T., & Vaidyanathan, G. (2011). Kalagnanam, Suresh; Sheehan, Norman; Vaidyanathan, Ganesh (2010). When is a balanced scorecard a balanced scorecard? *International Journal of Productivity and Performance Management, 60*(7), 688–708. doi:10.1108/17410401111167780

Taymanov, R., Sapozhnikova, K., & Prokopchina, S. (2021). What is immeasurable make measurable with artificial intelligence (measurements & artificial intelligence). Measurement. *Sensors (Basel), 18*, 100316. doi:10.1016/j.measen.2021.100316

Wiig, K. M. (1997). Knowledge Management: Where Did it Come From and Where Will It Go? *Expert Systems with Applications, 13*(1), 1–14. doi:10.1016/S0957-4174(97)00018-3

Yıkılmaz, I. (2020). The future of knowledge management: Web 4.0. In Data, Information and Knowledge Management. Nobel Bilimsel Eserler Sertifika.

Young, M.-L., Kuo, F.-Y., & Myers, M. (2012). To share or not to share: A critical research perspective on knowledge management. *European Journal of Information Systems, 21*(5), 496–511. doi:10.1057/ejis.2012.10

Compilation of References

Abdallah, A. (2021). Has the Lack of a Unified Halal Standard Led to a Rise in Organised Crime in the Halal Certification Sector? *Forensic Science*, *1*(3), 181–193. doi:10.3390/forensicsci1030016

Abeng, T. (1997). Business Ethics in Islamic Context: Perspectives of a Muslim Business Leader. *Business Ethics Quarterly*, *7*(3), 47–54. doi:10.2307/3857312

Abomhara, M., & Køien, G. (2015). Cyber Security and the Internet of Things: Vulnerabilities, Threats, Intruders and Attacks. *Journal of Cyber Security.*, *4*, 65–88. doi:10.13052/jcsm2245-1439.414

Ackoff, R. (1989). From Data to Wisdom. *Journal of Applied Systems Analysis*, *16*, 3–9.

Ackoff, R. L. (1989). From data to wisdom. *Journal of Applied Systems Analysis*, *16*(1), 3–9.

Agarwal, N., & Agarwal, R. (2016). Why communities of practice (CoP) are 'still' relevant for the organizations? *Studies in Asian Social Science*, *3*(2), 17–25. doi:10.5430ass.v3n2p17

Aghaei, S., Nematbakhsh, M. A., & Farsani, H. K. (2012). Evolution of the World Wide Web: From Web 1.0 to Web 4.0. *International Journal of Web & Semantic Technology.*, *3*(1), 1–10. Advance online publication. doi:10.5121/ijwest.2012.3101

Ahmad, A., Burgoyne, J., & Weir, D. (2010). The Learning Organization from an Islamic Perspective: A Case Study in Islamic Organization. *8th International Academy of Management and Business (IAMB 2010)*, 1–9.

Ajzen, I. (1991). The theory of planned behavior. *Organizational Behavior and Human Decision Processes*, *50*(2), 179–211. doi:10.1016/0749-5978(91)90020-T

Al-Alawi, A. I., Al-Marzooqi, N. Y., & Mohammed, Y. F. (2007). Organizational culture and knowledge sharing: Critical success factors. *Journal of Knowledge Management*.

Alavi, K., Kayworth, T. R., & Leidner, D. (2006). An empirical examination of the influence of organizational culture on knowledge management practices. *Journal of Management Information Systems*, *23*(3), 191–224. doi:10.2753/MIS0742-1222220307

Alavi, M., & Leidner, D. E. (2001). Knowledge management and knowledge management systems: Conceptual foundations and research issues. *Management Information Systems Quarterly*, *25*(1), 107–136. doi:10.2307/3250961

Alberto Ferraris, A. M. (2019). Big data analytics capabilities and knowledge management: Impact on firm performance. *Management Decision*, *57*(8), 1923–1936. doi:10.1108/MD-07-2018-0825

Al-Hawamdeh, S. (2002). Knowledge management: Re-thinking information management and facing the challenge of managing tacit knowledge. *Information Research*, *8*(1), 8–1.

Ali, I. M., Pascoe, C., & Warne, L. (2002). Interactions of organizational culture and collaboration in working and learning. *Journal of Educational Technology & Society*, *5*(2), 60–68.

Allee, V. (1997). 12 principles of knowledge management. *Training and Development Journal*, *51*(11), 71–74.

Allen, J. (2022). *Fostering Wisdom at Work*. Rutledge Taylor & Francis Group., doi:10.4324/9781003018759

Allen, J., Bracey, P., Aguilar, M., & Zimmerman, T. (2020). Supporting Workforce Wisdom in a Global Economy. In C. Hughes (Ed.), *Strategies for Attracting, Maintaining and Balancing a Mature Workforce*. IGI Global. doi:10.4018/978-1-7998-2277-6.ch007

Allessie, D., Sobolewski, M., & Vaccari, L. (2019). Blockchain for digital government. EUR 29677 EN, Publications Office of the European Union.

Almeida, F. (2017). Concept and Dimensions of Web 4.0. *International Journal of Computers and Technology*. *16*(7). Retrieved from: Web4.0-with-cover-page-v2.pdfd1wqtxts1xzle7.cloudfront.net

Alqahtani, F. N. K. (2016). *Identifying the Critical Factors that Impact on The Development of Electronic Government using TOE Framework in Saudi E-Government Context : A Thematic Analysis*. Academic Press.

Alsharo, M., Gregg, D., & Ramirez, R. (2017). Virtual Team Effectiveness: The Role of Knowledge Sharing and Trust. *Information & Management*, *54*(4), 479–490. doi:10.1016/j.im.2016.10.005

Alshurideh, M., & Alhadid, A. (2015). The effect of internal marketing on organizational citizenship behavior an applicable study on the University of Jordan employees. *Int. J. Mark. Stud.*, *7*(1), 138. doi:10.5539/ijms.v7n1p138

Alvarenga, A., Matos, F., Godina, R., Joao, C., & Matias, M. (2020). Digital Transformation and Knowledge Managementin the Public Sector. *Sustainability*, *12*, 5824. doi:10.3390u12145824

Amankwah-Amoah, J., Khan, Z., Wood, G., & Knight, G. (2021). COVID-19 and digitalization: The great acceleration. *Journal of Business Research*, *136*, 602–611. doi:10.1016/j.jbusres.2021.08.011 PMID:34538980

Amayah, A. T. (2013). Determinants of knowledge sharing in a public sector organization. *Journal of Knowledge Management*, *17*(3), 454–471. doi:10.1108/JKM-11-2012-0369

Ambira, C., & Kemoni, H. (2011). Records management and risk management at Kenya Commercial Bank Limited, Nairobi. *South Africa Journal of Information Management, 13*(1).

Anderson, M., & Jefferson, M. (2018). Transforming Organizations: Engaging the 4Cs for Powerful Organizational Learning and Change. Bloomsbury Publishing.

Annas, J. (2010). The structure of virtue. In *Intellectual virtue: Perspectives from ethics and epistemology*. Oxford University Press.

Ardelt, M., Pridgen, S., & Nutter-Pridgen, K. (2018). The relationship between age and three-dimensional wisdom: Variations by wisdom dimensions and education. *The Journals of Gerontology. Series B, Psychological Sciences and Social Sciences, 73*(8), 1339–1349. doi:10.1093/geronb/gbx182 PMID:29401232

Arne Isaksen, M. T. (2021). Digital transformation of regional industries through asset modification. *Competitiveness Review, 31*(1), 130–144. doi:10.1108/CR-12-2019-0140

Asrar-ul-Haq, M., & Anwar, S. (2016). A Systematic Review of Knowledge Management and Knowledge Sharing: Trends, Issues, and Challenges. *Cogent Business & Management, 3*(1), 1127744. Advance online publication. doi:10.1080/23311975.2015.1127744

Association of Flight Attendants-CWA. (n.d.). *About AFA*. https://www.afacwa.org/about_afa

AvrahamiH. (2021). Retrieved from https://www.kmslh.com/blog/how-to-support-hybrid-work-with-enterprise-knowledge-management/

Ayer, A. J., & Marić, S. (1956). *The problem of knowledge*. Penguin books.

Azizan, N., Alahoul, M. R., Alwi, N. H., & Mohd Zarif, M. M. (2016). Islamic Knowledge: Factors Effective Islamic Knowledge Transfer for Visually Impaired Users via Malaysia e-Learning Websites. *Seminar Perpustakaan Islam Serantau*, 1–19.

Baker, C. R. (1979). Defining and measuring affiliation motivation. *European Journal of Social Psychology, 9*(1), 97–99. doi:10.1002/ejsp.2420090108

Bakker, M., Leenders, R. T. A., Gabbay, S. M., Kratzer, J., & Van Engelen, J. M. (2006). Is trust really social capital? Knowledge sharing in product development projects. *The Learning Organization, 13*(6), 594–605. doi:10.1108/09696470610705479

Balaid, A., Rozan, M. Z. A., & Abdullah, S. N. (2014). Conceptual Model for Examining Knowledge Maps Adoption in Software Development Organizations. *Asian Social Science, 10*(15), 118–132. doi:10.5539/ass.v10n15p118

Ball, H. (2020). Retrieved from neo4j.com: https://neo4j.com/blog/building-enterprise-knowledge-graph/

Ballard, T., Romito, P., Lauria, L., Vigiliano, V., Caldora, M., & Mazzanti, C. (2006). Self-perceived health and mental health among women flight attendants. *Occupational and Environmental Medicine, 63*(1), 33–38. doi:10.1136/oem.2004.018812 PMID:16361403

Barachini, F., & Stary, C. (2022). *From digital twins to digital selves and beyond.* Springer. doi:10.1007/978-3-030-96412-2

Barbaroux, P., Attour, A., & Schenk, E. (2016). *Knowledge management and innovation: Interaction, collaboration, openness* (Vol. 6). John Wiley & Sons. doi:10.1002/9781119330134

Batelle for Kids. (2019). *21st century framework for learning*. Retrieved from http://www.battelleforkids.org

Bawden, D., & Robinson, L. (2009). The dark side of information: Overload, anxiety and other paradoxes and pathologies. *Journal of Information Science, 35*(2), 180–191. doi:10.1177/0165551508095781

Bayuk, J., Healey, J., Rohmeyer, P., Sachs, M., Schmidt, J., & Weiss, J. (2012). *Cyber Security Policy Guidebook.* Cyber Security Policy Guidebook., doi:10.1002/9781118241530

Baz, M., Alhakami, H., Agrawal, A., Baz, A., & Khan, R. A. (2021). Impact of covid-19 pandemic: a cybersecurity perspective. Intelligent Automation & Soft Computing, 27(3).

Beekun, R. I., & Badawi, J. A. (2005). Balancing ethical responsibility among multiple organizational stakeholders: The Islamic perspective. *Journal of Business Ethics, 60*(2), 131–145. doi:10.100710551-004-8204-5

Bergsma, A., & Ardelt, M. (2012). Self-reported wisdom and happiness: An empirical investigation. *Journal of Happiness Studies, 13*(3), 481–499. doi:10.100710902-011-9275-5

Bettiol, M., Di Maria, E., & Micelli, S. (2020). *Industry 4.0 and Knowledge Management: An Introduction*. Building Digital Government Strategies Principles and Practices. doi:10.1007/978-3-030-43589-9

Bharati, P., Zhang, W., & Chaudhury, A. (2015). Better knowledge with social media? Exploring the roles of social capital and organizational knowledge management. *Journal of Knowledge Management, 19*(3), 456–475. doi:10.1108/JKM-11-2014-0467

Birzniece, I. (2011). *Artificial Intelligence in Knowledge Management:Overview and Trends. Scientific Journal of Riga Technical University Computer Science.*

Bock, G. W., & Kim, Y. G. (2002). Breaking the myths of rewards: An exploratory study of attitudes about knowledge sharing. *Information Resources Management Journal, 15*(2), 14–21. doi:10.4018/irmj.2002040102

Bock, G. W., Zmud, R. W., Kim, Y. G., & Lee, J. N. (2005). Behavioral intention formation in knowledge sharing: Examining the roles of extrinsic motivators, social-psychological factors, and organizational climate. *Management Information Systems Quarterly, 29*(1), 87–111. doi:10.2307/25148669

Bogers, M., Chesbrough, H., & Moedas, C. (2018). Open Innovation: Research, Practices, and Policies. *California Management Review, 60*(2), 5–16. doi:10.1177/0008125617745086

Bolisani, E., & Scarso, E. (2014). The place of communities of practice in knowledge management studies: A critical review. *Journal of Knowledge Management*, *18*(2), 366–381. doi:10.1108/JKM-07-2013-0277

Boong, K. C., Woon-Dong, Y., & Dong, K. W. (2018). The implication of ANT (Actor-Network-Theory) methodology for R&D policy in open innovation paradigm. *Knowledge Management Research and Practice*, *16*(3), 315–326. Advance online publication. doi:10.1080/14778238.2018.1471329

Bowman, B., Grupe, F. H., Lund, D., & Moore, W. (1993). An examination of sources of support preferred by end-user computing personnel. *Journal of End User Computing*, *5*(4), 4–11. doi:10.4018/joeuc.1993100101

Brain and Company. (2018). *Balanced.* Retrieved from: https://www.bain.com/insights/management-tools-balanced-scorecard/

Brezočnik, L., & Majer, Č. (2016). *Comparison of agile methods: Scrum.* Kanban, and Scrumban.

Brous, P., Janssen, M., & Herder, P. (2020). The dual effects of the Internet of Things (IoT): A systematic review of the benefits and risks of IoT adoption by organizations. *International Journal of Information Management*, *51*, 51. doi:10.1016/j.ijinfomgt.2019.05.008

Brown, J. S., & Duguid, P. (1998). Organizing knowledge. *California Management Review*, *40*(3), 90–111. doi:10.2307/41165945

Brunges, M., & Foley-Brinza, C. (2014). Projects for increasing job satisfaction and creating a healthy work environment. *AORN Journal*, *100*(6), 670–681. doi:10.1016/j.aorn.2014.01.029 PMID:25453685

Brunswicker, S., & Chesbrough, H. (2018). The Adoption of Open Innovation in Large Firms: Practices, Measures, and Risks A survey of large firms examines how firms approach open innovation strategically and manage knowledge flows at the project level. *Research Technology Management*, *61*(1), 35–45. doi:10.1080/08956308.2018.1399022

Buchanan, J., & Kock, N. (2001). Information overload: A decision making perspective. In *Multiple criteria decision making in the new millennium* (pp. 49–58). Springer. doi:10.1007/978-3-642-56680-6_4

Buckland, M. K. (1991). Information as thing. *Journal of the American Society for Information Science*, *42*(5), 351–360. doi:10.1002/(SICI)1097-4571(199106)42:5<351::AID-ASI5>3.0.CO;2-3

Bukowitz, W., & Williams, R. (1999). *The Knowledge Management Fieldbook*. Financial Times/Prentice Hall.

Bulkley, N., & Alstyne, M. (2004). *Why information should influence productivity*. Center for eBusiness @ MIT. Retrieved from: http://citeseerx.ist.psu.edu/viewdoc/download?doi=10.1.1.295.7563&rep=rep1&type=pdf

Bumblauskas, D., Nold, H., Bumblauskas, P., & Igou, A. (2017). Big data analytics: Transforming data to action. *Business Process Management Journal, 23*(3), 703–720. doi:10.1108/BPMJ-03-2016-0056

Burchardt, C., & Maisch, B. (2019). Digitalization needs a cultural change – examples of applying Agility and Open Innovation to drive the digital transformation. *Procedia CIRP, 84*, 112–117. doi:10.1016/j.procir.2019.05.009

Burger, N. P. (2015). *The role of Management Information Systems in Measuring Organisational Performance in the Kwazulu- Natal Department of Arts & Culture*. Stellenbosch University.

Cabrera, A., Collins, W. C., & Salgado, J. F. (2006). Determinants of individual engagement in knowledge sharing. *International Journal of Human Resource Management, 17*(2), 245–264. doi:10.1080/09585190500404614

Cabrera, E. F., & Cabrera, A. (2005). Fostering knowledge sharing through people management practices. *International Journal of Human Resource Management, 16*(5), 720–735. doi:10.1080/09585190500083020

Carchedi, G. (2005). On the production of knowledge. *Research in Political Economy, 22*, 261–298. doi:10.1016/S0161-7230(04)22010-7

Casimir, G., Lee, K., & Loon, M. (2012). Knowledge sharing: Influences of trust, commitment and cost. *Journal of Knowledge Management, 16*(5), 740–753. doi:10.1108/13673271211262781

Castro Laszlo, K., & Laszlo, A. (2002). Evolving knowledge for development: The role of knowledge management in a changing world. *Journal of Knowledge Management, 6*(4), 400–412. doi:10.1108/13673270210440893

Chang, C., & Tung-Ching, L. (2015). The role of organizational culture in the knowledge management process. *Journal of Knowledge Management, 19*(3), 433–455. doi:10.1108/JKM-08-2014-0353

Chang, H. H., & Chuang, S. S. (2011). Social capital and individual motivations on knowledge sharing: Participant involvement as a moderator. *Information & Management, 48*(1), 9–18. doi:10.1016/j.im.2010.11.001

Chanzanagh, H. E., & Akbarnejad, M. (2011). The Meaning and Dimensions of Islamic Work Ethic: Initial Validation of a Multidimensional IWE in Iranian Society. *Procedia: Social and Behavioral Sciences, 30*, 916–924. doi:10.1016/j.sbspro.2011.10.178

Chau, P. Y., & Hu, P. J. H. (2001). Information technology acceptance by individual professionals: A model comparison approach. *Decision Sciences, 32*(4), 699–719. doi:10.1111/j.1540-5915.2001.tb00978.x

Chen, C. F., & Kao, Y. L. (2012). Investigating the antecedents and consequences of burnout and isolation among flight attendants. *Tourism Management, 33*(4), 868–874. doi:10.1016/j.tourman.2011.09.008

Chen, C. J., & Huang, J. W. (2007). How organizational climate and structure affect knowledge management—The social interaction perspective. *International Journal of Information Management, 27*(2), 104–118. doi:10.1016/j.ijinfomgt.2006.11.001

Chen, C., & Chen, C. (2012). Burnout and work engagement among cabin crew: Antecedents and consequences. *The International Journal of Aviation Psychology, 22*(1), 41–58. doi:10.1080/10508414.2012.635125

Chen, C., & Chen, C. (2014). Investigating the effects of job demands and job resources on cabin crew safety behaviors. *Tourism Management, 41*(4), 45–52. doi:10.1016/j.tourman.2013.08.009

Chen, D. N., & Liang, T. P. (2016). Knowledge diversity and firm performance: An ecological view. *Journal of Knowledge Management, 20*(4), 671–686. doi:10.1108/JKM-10-2015-0377

Chen, M. (2018). Improving website structure through reducing information overload. *Decision Support Systems, 110*, 84–94. doi:10.1016/j.dss.2018.03.009

Chennamaneni, A. (2007). *Determinants of knowledge sharing behaviors: Developing and testing an integrated theoretical model* (Doctoral dissertation). The University of Texas at Arlington.

Chennamaneni, A., Teng, J. T., & Raja, M. K. (2012). A unified model of knowledge sharing behaviours: Theoretical development and empirical test. *Behaviour & Information Technology, 31*(11), 1097–1115. doi:10.1080/0144929X.2011.624637

Chesalin, A., Grodzenskiy, S., Nilov, M., & Pham, V. (2020). Intelligent quality management tools for digital production and knowledge management system for their application. *IOP Conference Series. Materials Science and Engineering, 862*(4), 042032. doi:10.1088/1757-899X/862/4/042032

Chesbrough, H., & Bogers, M. (2014). Explicating Open Innovation: Clarifying an Emerging Paradigm for Understanding Innovation. In *New Frontiers in Open Innovation.* Oxford University Press. https://www.forbes.com/sites/oracle/2015/04/20/digital-disruption-its-not-what-you-think/?sh=68f3a14a9e06

Chesbrough, H. (2010). Business Model Innovation: Opportunities and Barriers. *Long Range Planning, 43*(2-3), 354–363. doi:10.1016/j.lrp.2009.07.010

Chetty, L. (2017). *Enhancing the effectiveness of a knowledge management toolkit in a professional services firm.* Academic Press.

Chiu, C. M., Hsu, M. H., & Wang, E. T. (2006). Understanding knowledge sharing in virtual communities: An integration of social capital and social cognitive theories. *Decision Support Systems, 42*(3), 1872–1888. doi:10.1016/j.dss.2006.04.001

Choi, B., & Lee, H. (2002). Knowledge management strategy and its link to knowledge creation process. *Expert Systems with Applications, 23*(3), 173–187. doi:10.1016/S0957-4174(02)00038-6

Choi, S. Y., Lee, H., & Yoo, Y. (2010). The impact of information technology and transactive memory systems on knowledge sharing, application, and team performance: A field study. *Management Information Systems Quarterly, 34*(4), 855–870. doi:10.2307/25750708

Chowdhury, S. (2005). The role of affect-and cognition-based trust in complex knowledge sharing. *Journal of Managerial Issues*, 310–326.

Chow, W. S., & Chan, L. S. (2008). Social network, social trust and shared goals in organizational knowledge sharing. *Information & Management*, *45*(7), 458–465. doi:10.1016/j.im.2008.06.007

Christensen, P. N., Rothgerber, H., Wood, W., & Matz, D. C. (2004). Social norms and identity relevance: A motivational approach to normative behavior. *Personality and Social Psychology Bulletin*, *30*(10), 1295–1309. doi:10.1177/0146167204264480 PMID:15466602

Chun, W. (2013). Information culture and organizational effectiveness. *International Journal of Information Management*, *33*(4), 775–779. doi:10.1016/j.ijinfomgt.2013.05.009

Collinge, C., & Adreene, S. (2009). Rethinking the knowledge-based economy. *Building and Environment*, *35*(2), 165–172. Advance online publication. doi:10.2148/benv.35.2.165

Connelly, C. E., & Kevin Kelloway, E. (2003). Predictors of employees' perceptions of knowledge sharing cultures. *Leadership and Organization Development Journal*, *24*(5), 294–301. doi:10.1108/01437730310485815

Cook, J., & Wall, T. (1980). New work attitude measures of trust, organizational commitment and personal need non-fulfilment. *Journal of Occupational Psychology*, *53*(1), 39–52. doi:10.1111/j.2044-8325.1980.tb00005.x

Cox, A. (2005). What are communities of practice? A comparative review of four seminal works. *Journal of Information Science*, *31*(6), 527–540. doi:10.1177/0165551505057016

Dalkir, K. (2017). *Knowledge management in theory and practice*. The MIT Press.

Daniele Giampaoli, F. S. (2021). Integrating knowledge management with intellectual capital to drive strategy: A focus on Italian SMEs. *VINE Journal of Information and Knowledge Management Systems*.

Dasgupta, A., Poco, J., Wei, Y., Cook, R., Bertini, E., & Silva, C. T. (2015). Bridging theory with practice: An exploratory study of visualization use and design for climate model comparison. *IEEE Transactions on Visualization and Computer Graphics*, *21*(9), 996–1014. doi:10.1109/TVCG.2015.2413774 PMID:26357283

DaSilvaA. (2021). Retrieved from https://www.poolparty.biz/what-is-customer-360-in-enterprise-360/

Davenport, T. (2005). *Thinking for Living*. HVB School Publishing.

Davenport, T. H. (1997). *Information ecology: Mastering the information and knowledge environment*. Oxford University Press on Demand.

Davenport, T. H., Barth, P., & Bean, R. (2012, Fall). How Big Data is Different? *Sloan Management Review*, *54*.

Davenport, T. H., & Prusak, L. (1998). *Working knowledge: How organizations manage what they know*. Harvard Business Press.

Davenport, T. H., & Prusak, L. (2000). *Working Knowledge: How Organizations Manage What They Know*. Harvard Business School Press.

Davenport, T. M. (1994). Saving IT's soul: Human-centered information management. *Harvard Business Review, 72*(2), 119–131.

Davenport, T., De Long, D., & Beers, M. (1998). Successful Knowledge Management Projects. *Sloan Management Review, 39*(2), 43–57.

Davis, F. D. (1989). Perceived usefulness, perceived ease of use, and user acceptance of information technology. *Management Information Systems Quarterly, 13*(3), 319–340. doi:10.2307/249008

Davison, R. M., Ou, C. X., & Martinsons, M. G. (2013). Information technology to support informal knowledge sharing. *Information Systems Journal, 23*(1), 89–109. doi:10.1111/j.1365-2575.2012.00400.x

De Long, D. W., & Fahey, L. (2000). Diagnosing cultural barriers to knowledge management. *The Academy of Management Perspectives, 14*(4), 113–127. doi:10.5465/ame.2000.3979820

De Rouw, S. (2019). *The importance of a work tribe and how to find yours*. Medium. https://medium.com/joingoodcompany/the-importance-of-a-work-tribe-and-how-to-find-yours-544d3ba1614c

De Vries, R. E., Bakker-Pieper, A., & Oostenveld, W. (2010). Leadership= communication? The relations of leaders' communication styles with leadership styles, knowledge sharing and leadership outcomes. *Journal of Business and Psychology, 25*(3), 367–380. doi:10.100710869-009-9140-2 PMID:20700375

De Vries, R. E., Van den Hooff, B., & de Ridder, J. A. (2006). Explaining knowledge sharing: The role of team communication styles, job satisfaction, and performance beliefs. *Communication Research, 33*(2), 115–135. doi:10.1177/0093650205285366

Denning, S. (2018). *The Age of Agile: How Smart Companies Are Transforming the Way Work Gets Done*. AMACOM.

Derrick McIver, D. A. (2017). Effects of knowledge management on unit performance: Examining the moderating role of tacitness and learnability. *Journal of Knowledge Management*.

Deslauriers, M. (2002). How to distinguish Aristotle's virtues. *Phronesis (Barcelona, Spain), 47*(2), 101–126.

Dessein, W., & Santos, T. (2006). Adaptive Organizations. *Journal of Political Economy, 114*(5), 956–995. doi:10.1086/508031

Di Vaio, A., Palladino, R., Pzzi, A., & Kalisz, D. E. (2021). The Role of Digital Innovation In Knowledge Management Systems: A Systematic Literature Review. *Journal of Business Research, 123*, 220–231. doi:10.1016/j.jbusres.2020.09.042

Dijksterhuis, A., & Bargh, J. A. (2001). The perception-behavior expressway: Automatic effects of social perception on social behavior. In Advances in experimental social psychology (Vol. 33, pp. 1–40). Academic Press. doi:10.1016/S0065-2601(01)80003-4

Dillon, S., Stahl, F., Vossen, G., & Rastrick, K. (2013). A Contemporary Approach to Coping with Modern Information Overload. *Communications of the ICISA, 14*(1), 1–24.

Dilworth, R. L. (2010). Explaining traditional action learning: concepts and beliefs. In *Action Learning* (pp. 3–28). Palgrave Macmillan. doi:10.1057/9780230250734_1

Dima, A. M., Begu, L., Vasilescu, M. D., & Maassen, M. A. (2018). The relationship between the knowledge economy and global competitiveness in the European Union. *Sustainability, 10*(6), 1706. doi:10.3390u10061706

Diogenes, Y., & Ozkaya, E. (2018). *Cybersecurity Attack and Defense Strategies.* Packt Publishing.

Drucker, P. (1994, November). The age of social transformation. *Atlantic Monthly*, 53–80.

Drucker, P. (2000). Knowledge work. *Executive Excellence, 17*(4), 11–11.

Drucker, P. (2012). *Managing in a time of great change.* Routledge. doi:10.4324/9780080938752

Drucker, P. F. (1954). *Landmarks of Tomorrow, A Report on the New 'Post-Modern' World.* Transaction Publisher London.

Drucker, P. F. (1993). The rise of the knowledge society. *The Wilson Quarterly, 17*(2), 52–72.

Duma, G. M. N. (2020). Assessment of records management practices among the senior managers in a South African Municipality. Master in Business Administration. North-West University. Potchefstroom, South Africa.

Dunn, A. (2021). *Monitoring and Evaluation of Public Libraries: A Case of Public Libraries in Namibia*. Wiley Library.

Edmunds, A., & Morris, A. (2000). The problem of information overload in business organisations: A review of the literature. *International Journal of Information Management, 20*(1), 17–28. doi:10.1016/S0268-4012(99)00051-1

EducationI. C. (2021). Retrieved from https://www.ibm.com/cloud/learn/knowledge-graph#:~:text=A%20knowledge%20graph%2C%20also%20known,the%20term%20knowledge%20%E2%80%9Cgraph.%E2%80%9D

Egan, T. M., Yang, B., & Bartlett, K. R. (2004). The Effects of Organizational Learning Culture and Job Satisfaction on Motivation to Transfer Learning and Turnover Intention. *Human Resource Development Quarterly, 15*(3), 279–301. doi:10.1002/hrdq.1104

Eggers, W. D., & Bellman, J. (2015). *The journey to government's digital transformation.* Deloitte University Press. https://www2.deloitte.com/content/dam/insights/us/articles/digital-transformation-in-government/DUP_1081_Journey-to-govt-digital-future_MASTER.pdf

Eisenhauer, T. (2021). Retrieved from axerosolutions.com: https://axerosolutions.com/blog/17-hot-knowledge-management-trends-for-2021

Eliasson, G. (2000). *The role of knowledge in economic growth*. Royal Institute of Technology.

Ertan, A., Crossland, G., Heath,C., Denny, D.& Jensen, R. (2020). *Cyber Security Behaviors in Organizations*. Academic Press.

Faraj, S., Renno, W., & Bhardwaj, A. (2021). Unto the breach: What the COVID-19 pandemic exposes about digitalization. *Information and Organization*, *31*(1), 100337. doi:10.1016/j.infoandorg.2021.100337

Ferdinand J. (2015) Building organizational cyber resilience: A strategic knowledge-based view of cyber security management. *J Bus Contin Emer Plan*, *9*(2), 185-95.

Ferguson, M. J., & Bargh, J. A. (2004). How social perception can automatically influence behavior. *Trends in Cognitive Sciences*, *8*(1), 33–39. doi:10.1016/j.tics.2003.11.004 PMID:14697401

Fernie, S., Green, S. D., Weller, S. J., & Newcombe, R. (2003). Knowledge sharing: Context, confusion and controversy. *International Journal of Project Management*, *21*(3), 177–187. doi:10.1016/S0263-7863(02)00092-3

Ford, D. P., & Chan, Y. E. (2003). Knowledge sharing in a multi-cultural setting: A case study. *Knowledge Management Research and Practice*, *1*(1), 11–27. doi:10.1057/palgrave.kmrp.8499999

Fourkas, V. (2004). What is 'cyberspace'? *Media Development*.

Frick'e, M. (2019). The Knowledge Pyramid: The DIKW Hierarchy. *Knowledge Organization*, *46*(1), 33–46. doi:10.5771/0943-7444-2019-1-33

Frické, M. (2009). The knowledge pyramid: A critique of the DIKW hierarchy. *Journal of Information Science*, *35*(2), 131–142. doi:10.1177/0165551508094050

Friesl, M., Sackmann, S. A., & Kremser, S. (2011). Knowledge sharing in new organizational entities: The impact of hierarchy, organizational context, micro-politics and suspicion. *Cross Cultural Management*, *18*(1), 71–86. doi:10.1108/13527601111104304

Fuller, S. (2017). Prolegomena to a Deep History of "Information Overload.". *Journal of Information Ethics*, *26*(1), 81–92. http://search.ebscohost.com/login.aspx?direct=true&db=lls&AN=123908416&scope=site

Fullwood, R., Rowley, J., & Delbridge, R. (2013). Knowledge sharing amongst academics in UK universities. *Journal of Knowledge Management*, *17*(1), 123–136. doi:10.1108/13673271311300831

Gamble, P. R., & Blackwell, J. (2001). *Knowledge Management: A State of the Art Guide*. Kogan Page Ltd.

Gangwar, H., Date, H., & Ramaswamy, R. (2015). Understanding Determinants of Cloud Computing Adoption Using an Integrated TAM-TOE Model. *Journal of Enterprise Information Management*, *28*(1), 107–130. doi:10.1108/JEIM-08-2013-0065

Gardner, H. (1983). *Frames of mind: The theory of multiple intelligences*. Basic Books.

Gartner. (2021). Data Virtualization. *Gartner Peer Insights.*

Garvin, D. A. (2003). *Learning in action: A guide to putting the learning organization to work*. Harvard Business Review Press.

Gençer, M. S., & Samur, Y. (2016). Leadership styles and technology: Leadership competency level of educational leaders. *Procedia: Social and Behavioral Sciences*, *229*, 226–233. doi:10.1016/j.sbspro.2016.07.132

Ghafar, A., Don, H. J., & Awang, J. (2009). Knowledge Management and its Impact on Islamic Da ' wah : A Historical Perspective. *Journal of Islamic and Arabic Education*, *1*(2), 61–68.

Godin, S. (2008). *Tribes: We Need You to Lead Us*. Portfolio/Penguin.

Gold, A., Malhotra, A., & Segars, A. (2001). Knowledge management: An organizational capabilities perspective. *Journal of Management Information Systems*, *18*(1), 185–214. doi:10.1080/07421222.2001.11045669

Goleman, D. (1995). *Emotional intelligence*. Bantam Books.

Gopalakrishnan, S., & Santoro, M. D. (2004). Distinguishing between knowledge transfer and technology transfer activities: The role of key organizational factors. *IEEE Transactions on Engineering Management*, *51*(1), 57–69. doi:10.1109/TEM.2003.822461

Gourlay, S. (2001). Knowledge management and HRD. *Human Resource Development International*, *4*(1), 27–46. doi:10.1080/13678860121778

Graham, W. (2017). Developing organizations: A system of enquiry, action and learning. *Development and Learning in Organizations*, *31*(1), 12–14. doi:10.1108/DLO-03-2016-0023

Grajewski, B., Whelan, E., Nguyen, M., Kwan, L., & Cole, R. (2016). Sleep disturbance in female flight attendants and teachers. *Aerospace Medicine and Human Performance*, *87*(7), 638–645. doi:10.3357/AMHP.4512.2016 PMID:27503044

Grant, D., Mergen, E., & Wildrick, S. (2007). A Comparative Analysis of Quality Management in US and International Universities. *Total Quality Management & Business Excellence*, *15*(4), 423–438.

Greenberg, J. R., & Greenberg, P. J. (1991). *Oedipus and beyond: A clinical theory*. Harvard University Press.

Griffiths, R., & Powell, D. (2012). The occupational health and safety of flight attendants. *Aviation, Space, and Environmental Medicine*, *83*(5), 514–521. doi:10.3357/ASEM.3186.2012 PMID:22606869

Grimard, J. (2004). Program Evaluation and Archives: "Appraising" Archival Work and Achievements, Counterpoint. *Archivaria*, *57*, 69–87.

Gupta, M., & George, J. F. (2016). Toward the development of a big data analytics capability. *Information & Management, 53*(8), 1049–1064. doi:10.1016/j.im.2016.07.004

Haldorai, K., Kim, W. G., Phetvaroon, K., & Li, J. J. (2020). Left out of the office "tribe": The influence of workplace ostracism on employee work engagement. *International Journal of Contemporary Hospitality Management, 32*(8), 2717–2735. doi:10.1108/IJCHM-04-2020-0285

Han, B. M., & Anantatmula, V. S. (2007). Knowledge sharing in large IT organizations: A case study. *Vine, 37*(4), 421–439. doi:10.1108/03055720710838506

Hanson, K. (n.d.). *Integrating Knowledge Management and E-Learningto Enhance Knowledge Creation and Conversion for Competitive Advantage*. Academic Press.

Harald Vacik, C. T. (2013). *The role of knowledge management tools in supporting sustainable forest management*. Academic Press.

HarrinsonE. (2021). Retrieved from https://www.kminstitute.org/blog/learn-top-5-knowledge-management-trends-2021

Hartmann, R. S.-d. (2008). The use of tacit knowledge within innovative companies: Knowledge management in innovative enterprises. *Journal of Knowledge Management*, 14.

Hassani, H., Huand, X., & Silva, E. (2021). The Human Digitalisation Journey: Technology First at the Expense of Humans? *Information (Basel), 2021*(12), 267. doi:10.3390/info12070267

Hendriks, P. (1999). Why share knowledge? The influence of ICT on the motivation for knowledge sharing. *Knowledge and Process Management, 6*(2), 91–100. doi:10.1002/(SICI)1099-1441(199906)6:2<91::AID-KPM54>3.0.CO;2-M

Herbane, B. (2019). Rethinking organizational resilience and strategic renewal in SMEs. *Entrepreneurship and Regional Development, 31*(5-6), 476–495. doi:10.1080/08985626.2018.1541594

Hess, T., Matt, C., Benlian, A., & Wiesbock, F. (2016). Options for Formulating a Digital "Transformation Strategy. *MIS Quarterly Executive, 15*(2), 123–139.

Hiltz, S. R., & Turoff, M. (1985). Structuring computer-mediated communication systems to avoid information overload. *Communications of the ACM, 28*(7), 680–689. doi:10.1145/3894.3895

Hoegl, M., & Gemuenden, H. G. (2001). Teamwork quality and the success of innovative projects: A theoretical concept and empirical evidence. *Organization Science, 12*(4), 435–449. doi:10.1287/orsc.12.4.435.10635

Hogg, M., & Terry, D. (2000). Social identity and self-categorization processes in organizational contexts. *Academy of Management Review, 25*(1), 121–140. doi:10.5465/amr.2000.2791606

Holste, J. S., & Fields, D. (2010). Trust and tacit knowledge sharing and use. *Journal of Knowledge Management, 14*(1), 128–140. doi:10.1108/13673271011015615

Housel, T., & Bell, A. (2001). *Measuring and Managing Knowledge*. Dudley Knox Library., Available https://www.nps.edu/library

Hsu, F-M., & Chen, T-Y., & Wang. (2009). Efficiency and Satisfaction of electronic records management systems in e-government in Taiwan. *The Electronic Library*, *27*(3), 461–473.

Hsu, M. H., & Chang, C. M. (2014). Examining interpersonal trust as a facilitator and uncertainty as an inhibitor of intra-organisational knowledge sharing. *Information Systems Journal*, *24*(2), 119–142. doi:10.1111/isj.12000

Huang, C. (2009). Knowledge sharing and group cohesiveness on performance: An empirical study of technology R&D teams in Taiwan. *Technovation*, *29*(11), 786–797. doi:10.1016/j.technovation.2009.04.003

Huang, Q., Davison, R. M., & Gu, J. (2008). Impact of personal and cultural factors on knowledge sharing in China. *Asia Pacific Journal of Management*, *25*(3), 451–471. doi:10.100710490-008-9095-2

Huerta, E., Salter, S., Lewis, P., & Yeow, P. (2012). Motivating employees to share their failures in knowledge management systems: Anonymity and culture. *Journal of Information Systems*, *26*(2), 93–117. doi:10.2308/isys-50214

Hussain Alsayed, M., Mohamed Dahlan, H., & Che Hussin, A. R. (2012). Knowledge Sharing in Collaborative Research Activities. *Journal of Information Systems Research and Innovation*, *2*, 1–8.

Hussain, S., Al-Hudawi, V., Musah, M. B., & Hamdan, A. R. (2014). Islamic Worldview on Knowledge Management: Implication for Muslim Education System. *World Journal of Islamic History and Civilization*, *4*(2), 66–74. doi:10.5829/idosi.wjihc.2014.4.2.185

Husserl, E. (1970). *The Crisis of European Sciences and Transcendental Phenomenology: An Introduction to Phenomenological Philosophy*. Northwestern University Press. doi:10.100713398-014-0173-7.2

Hutagalung, D., Admiral, A., Nuryanti, Y., Asbari, M., & Novitasari, D. (2021). Managing Tacit Knowledge Sharing: From Charismatic Leadership to Psychological Safety Climate. Inovbiz. *Jurnal Inovasi Bisnis*, *9*(1), 108–119. doi:10.35314/inovbiz.v9i1.1888

Huysman, M., & Wulf, V. (2006). IT to support knowledge sharing in communities, towards a social capital analysis. *Journal of Information Technology*, *21*(1), 40–51. doi:10.1057/palgrave.jit.2000053

Iansiti, M., & Lakhani, K. (2021). *Competing in the Age of AI: Strategy and Leadership When Algorithms and Networks Run the World. Harvard Business Review Press.*

Ibrahim, A. (2015). *The Fast Food Consumption Experiences and Identity Construction of British Muslims : A Phenomenological Study*. Issue March.

IEEE. (1990). IEEE Standard Glossary of Software Engineering Terminology. IEEE Std 610.12-1990. doi:10.1109/IEEESTD.1990.101064

Inkpen, A. C., & Tsang, E. W. (2005). Social capital, networks, and knowledge transfer. *Academy of Management Review*, *30*(1), 146–165. doi:10.5465/amr.2005.15281445

International Institute of Business Analysis. (2005). *A Guide to the Business Analysis Body of Knowledge (BABOK Guide Ver 2.0)*. International Institute of Business Analysis.

Iqbal, A., Latif, F., Marimon, F., Umar, F. S., & Hussain, S. (2019). From knowledge management to organizational performance: Modelling the mediating role of innovation and intellectual capital in higher education. *Journal of Enterprise Information Management*, *32*(1), 36–59. doi:10.1108/JEIM-04-2018-0083

Isaksen, S. G., & Tidd, J. (2007). *Meeting the Innovation Challenge: Leadership for Transformation and Growth.* Wiley.

Jackson, T. W., & Farzaneh, P. (2012). Theory-based model of factors affecting information overload. *International Journal of Information Management*, *32*(6), 523–532. doi:10.1016/j.ijinfomgt.2012.04.006

Jacoby, J. (1984). Perspectives on information overload. *The Journal of Consumer Research*, *10*(4), 432–435. doi:10.1086/208981

Jain, K. K., Sandhu, M. S., & Goh, S. K. (2015). Organizational climate, trust and knowledge sharing: Insights from Malaysia. *Journal of Asia Business Studies*, *9*(1), 54–77. doi:10.1108/JABS-07-2013-0040

Janssen, M., & Voort, H. (2016). Adaptive governance: Towards a stable, accountable and responsive government. *Government Information Quarterly*, *33*(1), 1–5. doi:10.1016/j.giq.2016.02.003

Janus, S. S. (2016). *Becoming a Knowledge Sharing Organization: A Handbook for Scaling Up Solutions through Knowledge Capturing and Sharing*. World Bank Group. doi:10.1596/978-1-4648-0943-9

Jelenic, S. (2011). The importance of knowledge management in organizations-with emphasis on the balanced scorecard learning and growth perspective. *Management Knowledge and Learning International Conference.* Retrieved from: http://issbs.si/press/ISBN/978-961-92486-3-8/papers/ML11-1.pdf

Jennex, M. (2007). *What is Knowledge Management?* doi:10.4018/9781599042619.ch001

Jeon, A. (2016). The effect of pre-flight attendants' emotional intelligence, emotional labor, and emotional exhaustion on commitment to customer service. *Service Business*, *10*(2), 345–367. doi:10.100711628-015-0273-2

Jeon, S., Kim, Y. G., & Koh, J. (2011). An integrative model for knowledge sharing in communities-of-practice. *Journal of Knowledge Management*, *15*(2), 251–269. doi:10.1108/13673271111119682

Jeste, D., & Lee, E. (2019). The Emerging Empirical Science of Wisdom: Definition, Measurement, Neurobiology, Longevity, and Interventions. *Harvard Review of Psychiatry*, *27*(3), 127–140. doi:10.1097/HRP.0000000000000205 PMID:31082991

Jin, Z., Zhangwen, W., & Naichen, N. (2019). Helping consumers to overcome information overload with a diversified online review subset. *Frontiers of Business Research in China*, *13*(1), 1–25. doi:10.118611782-019-0062-1

John Lannon, J. N. (2020). Paradoxes and partnerships: A study of knowledge exploration and exploitation in international development programmes. *Journal of Knowledge Management*, 8–31.

Joia, L. A., & Lemos, B. (2010). Relevant factors for tacit knowledge transfer within organisations. *Journal of Knowledge Management*, *14*(3), 410–427. doi:10.1108/13673271011050139

Jolaee, A., Nor, K. M., Khani, N., & Yusoff, R. M. (2014). Factors affecting knowledge sharing intention among academic staff. *International Journal of Educational Management*, *28*(4), 413–431. doi:10.1108/IJEM-03-2013-0041

Jones, M. C., Cline, M., & Ryan, S. (2006). Exploring knowledge sharing in ERP implementation: An organizational culture framework. *Decision Support Systems*, *41*(2), 411–434. doi:10.1016/j.dss.2004.06.017

Jonsson, A. (2015). Beyond knowledge management-understanding how to share knowledge through logic and practice. *Knowledge Management Research and Practice*, *13*(1), 45–58. doi:10.1057/kmrp.2013.28

Kader Jilani, M. M. A., Fan, L., Islam, M. T., & Uddin, M. A. (2020). The influence of knowledge sharing on sustainable performance: A moderated mediation study. *Sustainability (Switzerland)*, *12*(3), 1–18. doi:10.3390u12030908

Kaehler, B. & Grundei, J. (2018). *HR Governance: A Theoretical Introduction*. doi:10.1007/978-3-319-94526-2

Kane, A., Argote, L., & Levine, J. (2005). Knowledge transfer between groups via personnel rotation: Effects of social identity and knowledge quality. *Organizational Behavior and Human Decision Processes*, *96*(1), 56–71. doi:10.1016/j.obhdp.2004.09.002

Kankanhalli, A., & Tan, B. (2005). Knowledge Management Metrics: A Review and Directions for Future Research. *International Journal of Knowledge Management*. Retrieved from: https://www.researchgate.net/publication/270092694

Kankanhalli, A., Tan, B. C., & Wei, K. K. (2005). Contributing knowledge to electronic knowledge repositories: An empirical investigation. *Management Information Systems Quarterly*, *29*(1), 113. doi:10.2307/25148670

Kaplan, R. S., & Norton, D. P. (2001). The Strategy-focused Organization. Harvard Business School Press.

Kaplan, R., & Norton, D. (1992). The Balanced Scorecard-Measures that drive performance. *Harvard Business Review*. Retrieved from: https://www.steinbeis-bi.de/images/artikel/hbr_1992.pdf

Kaplan, R. S., & Norton, D. P. (1996). *The Balanced Scorecard*. Harvard Business School Press.

Karakilic, E. (2020). Why Do Humans Remain Central to the Knowledge Work in the Age of Robots? Marx's Fragment on Machines and Beyond. *SAGE Journals*, *36*(1), 179–189. doi:10.1177/0950017020958901

Karatepe, O. M., & Vatankhah, S. (2015). High-performance work practices, career satisfaction, and service recovery performance: A study of flight attendants. *Tourism Review*, *70*(1), 56–71. doi:10.1108/TR-01-2014-0004

Karr-Wisniewski, P., & Lu, Y. (2010). When more is too much: Operationalizing technology overload and exploring its impact on knowledge worker productivity. *Computers in Human Behavior, 26*(5), 1061-1072. doi:10.1016/j.chb.2010.03.008

KentE. (2021). Retrieved from https://blog.coveo.com/4-steps-to-knowledge-management-in-hybrid-offices/

Killingsworth, B., Xue, Y., & Liu, Y. (2016). Factors influencing knowledge sharing among global virtual teams. *Team Performance Management*, *22*(5/6), 284–300. doi:10.1108/TPM-10-2015-0042

Kimmerle, J., Wodzicki, K., & Cress, U. (2008). The social psychology of knowledge management. *Team Performance Management*, *14*(7), 381–401. doi:10.1108/13527590810912340

Kim, S., & Lee, H. (2006). The impact of organizational context and information technology on employee knowledge-sharing capabilities. *Public Administration Review*, *66*(3), 370–385. doi:10.1111/j.1540-6210.2006.00595.x

Klaus, N., Maier, R., & Haas, O. (2018). Knowledge Management in Digital Change. In *Progress in IS*. Springer.

Kloos, C. D. (2021). Towards a Cloud-Based University Accelerated by the Pandemic. *IEEE Global Engineering Education Conference (EDUCON)*, 1642-1649. 10.1109/EDUCON46332.2021.9453967

Koike, O. (2013). Institutionalizing performance management in Asia: Looking East or West? *International Journal of Public Sector Management*, *25*(5), 347–360.

Koltay, T. (2017). The bright side of information: Ways of mitigating information overload. *The Journal of Documentation*, *73*(4), 767–775. doi:10.1108/JD-09-2016-0107

Kuhn, T. S. (1962). *The structure of scientific revolutions*. University of Chicago Press.

Kureshi, N. (2014). To balanced scorecard or not balanced scorecard, That is the question. *Journal of Strategy & Performance Management*, *2*(1), 31–38.

Kwon, B. C., Kim, S. H., Duket, T., Catalán, A., & Yi, J. S. (2015). Do people really experience information overload while reading online reviews? *International Journal of Human-Computer Interaction*, *31*(12), 959–973. doi:10.1080/10447318.2015.1072785

Lalli, H. S., S., L. A., Nurse, J. R. C., Erola, A., Epiphaniou, G., Maple, C., & Bellekens, X. (2021). CyberSecurity in the Age of COVID-19: A Timeline and Analysis of Cyber-Crime and Cyber-Attacks during the Pandemic. Computers & Security, 105.

Lam, A., & Lambermont-Ford, J. P. (2010). Knowledge sharing in organisational contexts: A motivation-based perspective. *Journal of Knowledge Management, 14*(1), 51–66. doi:10.1108/13673271011015561

Larose, D. T. (2014). *Discovering knowledge in data: An introduction to data mining*. John Wiley & Sons.

LawesT. (2021). Retrieved from https://www.symphonysummit.com/itil/automating-your-knowledge-management/

Lee, H., Reid, E., & Kim, W. G. (2012). Understanding knowledge sharing in online travel communities: Antecedents and the moderating effects of interaction modes. *Journal of Hospitality & Tourism Research (Washington, D.C.), 38*(2), 222–242. doi:10.1177/1096348012451454

Lee, J. H., & Kim, Y. G. (2001). A stage model of organizational knowledge management: A latent content analysis. *Expert Systems with Applications, 20*(4), 299–311. doi:10.1016/S0957-4174(01)00015-X

Lee, J. H., Kim, Y. G., & Kim, M. Y. (2006). Effects of managerial drivers and climate maturity on knowledge-management performance: Empirical validation. *Information Resources Management Journal, 19*(3), 48–60. doi:10.4018/irmj.2006070104

Lee, K., Lee, S., & Kang, I. (2005). KMPI: Measuring knowledge management performance. *Information & Management, 42*(3), 469–482. doi:10.1016/j.im.2004.02.003

Lee, K.-W., Lanting, M. C. L., & Rojdamrongratana, M. (2017). Managing customer life cycle through knowledge management capability: A contextual role of information technology. *Total Quality Management & Business Excellence, 28*(13–14), 1559–1583. doi:10.1080/14783363.2016.1150779

Lee, M., Yun, J., Pyka, A., Won, D., Kodama, F., Schiuma, G., Park, H., Jeon, J., Park, K., Id, K., Jung, K., Yan, M., Lee, S., & Zhao, X. (2018). How to Respond to the Fourth Industrial Revolution, or the Second Information Technology Revolution? Dynamic New Combinations between Technology, Market, and Society through Open Innovation. *Journal of Open Innovation, 4*(3), 21. Advance online publication. doi:10.3390/joitmc4030021

Lee, S., Gon Kim, B., & Kim, H. (2012). An integrated view of knowledge management for performance. *Journal of Knowledge Management, 16*(2), 183–203. doi:10.1108/13673271211218807

Leitão, J. (2019). *Open Innovation Business Modeling Gamification and Design Thinking Applications*. Academic Press.

Leonard, S., & Niskala, R. (2021). *Do Quality Assessment Matter in an Academic Library? A case study of the University of Namibia Library*. Academic Press.

Levin, D. Z., & Cross, R. (2004). The strength of weak ties you can trust: The mediating role of trust in effective knowledge transfer. *Management Science*, *59*(11), 1477–1490. doi:10.1287/mnsc.1030.0136

Levin, D. Z., Cross, R., Abrams, L. C., & Lesser, E. L. (2002). Trust and knowledge sharing: A critical combination. *IBM Institute for Knowledge-Based Organizations*, *19*, 1–9.

Liao, S. S., Chen, C. C., Hu, D. C., Chung, Y. C., & Liu, C. L. (2017). Assessing the influence of leadership style, organizational learning and organizational innovation. *Leadership and Organization Development Journal*, *38*(5), 590–609. Advance online publication. doi:10.1108/LODJ-11-2015-0261

Liebowitz, J., & Beckman, T. (2020). *Knowledge organizations: What every manager should know*. CRC press. doi:10.4324/9781003076001

Li, L., Lin, J., Ouyang, Y., & Luo, X. R. (2022). Evaluating the impact of big data analytics usage on the decision-making quality of organizations. *Technological Forecasting and Social Change*, *175*, 121355. doi:10.1016/j.techfore.2021.121355

Lin, H. F. (2007). Knowledge sharing and firm innovation capability: An empirical study. *International Journal of Manpower*, *28*(3/4), 315–332. doi:10.1108/01437720710755272

Lin, H. F., & Lee, G. G. (2004). Perceptions of senior managers toward knowledge-sharing behaviour. *Management Decision*, *42*(1), 108–125. doi:10.1108/00251740410510181

Lin, W. B. (2008). The effect of knowledge sharing model. *Expert Systems with Applications*, *34*(2), 1508–1521. doi:10.1016/j.eswa.2007.01.015

Liu, F., Wu, J., Huang, X., & Fong, P. S. W. (2020). Impact of intra-group coopetitive incentives on the performance outcomes of knowledge sharing: Evidence from a randomized experiment. *Journal of Knowledge Management*, *24*(2), 346–368. doi:10.1108/JKM-05-2019-0256

Logan, D., & Fischer-Wright, H. (2008). *The five stages of work "tribes."* Gallup. https://news.gallup.com/businessjournal/106903/five-stages-workplace-tribes.aspx

Lopes, C., Scavarda, A., Hofmeister, L., Thomé, A. M., & Vaccaro, G. (2016). An analysis of the interplay between organizational sustainability, knowledge management, and open innovation. *Journal of Cleaner Production*, *142*, 476–488. doi:10.1016/j.jclepro.2016.10.083

Lutchyn, Y. (2016). Email Duration, Batching and Self-interruption: Patterns of Email Use on Productivity and Stress. *CHI '16: Proceedings of the 2016. CHI Conference on Human Factors in Computing Systems*, 1717–1728. 10.1145/2858036.2858262

Luthar, S., Crossman, E., & Small, P. (2015). *Resilience and Adversity. Handbook of Child Psychology and Developmental Science* (7th ed.). Wiley. doi:10.1002/9781118963418.childpsy307

Maes, P. (1995). Agents that reduce work and information overload. In *Readings in human–computer interaction* (pp. 811–821). Morgan Kaufmann. doi:10.1016/B978-0-08-051574-8.50084-4

Mahdi, O. R., & Nassar, I. A. (2021). The Business Model of Sustainable Competitive Advantage through Strategic Leadership Capabilities and Knowledge Management Processes to Overcome COVID-19 Pandemic. *Sustainability, 13*(17), 9891. doi:10.3390u13179891

Maizza, A., Fait, M., Scorrano, P., & Iazzi, A. (2019). How Knowledge Sharing Culture Can Become a Facilitator of the Sustainable Development in the Agrifood Sector. *Sustainability (Switzerland), 11*(4), 952. Advance online publication. doi:10.3390u11040952

Mallasi, H., & Ainin, S. (2015). Investigating Knowledge Sharing Behaviour in Academic Environment. *Journal of Organizational Knowledge Management*, 1–19. 10.5171/2015.643253

Malviya, A., & Malmgren, M. (2019). *Big Data for Managers: Creating Value*. Academic Press.

Market Information. (2013). *Halal Knowledge Centre*. http://www.hdcglobal.com/publisher/hkc_market_information#overview

Marques, J. P. (2014). Closed versus Open Innovation: Evolution or Combination? *International Journal of Business and Management, 9*(3). Advance online publication. doi:10.5539/ijbm.v9n3p196

Marr, B. (2018, July 6). *The 7 Best Data Visualization Tools Available Today*. Retrieved from https://www.forbes.com/sites/bernardmarr/2017/07/20/the-7-best-data-visualization-tools-in-2017

Marwick, A. D. (2001). Knowledge management technology. *IBM Systems Journal, 40*(4), 814–830. doi:10.1147j.404.0814

Masic, B., Nesic, S., Nikolic, D., & Dzeletovic, M. (2017). Evolution of knowledge management. *Industrija, 45*(2), 127–147. doi:10.5937/industrija45-13201

Matangira, V. (2016). Recordkeeping in Zimbabwe in Colonial and Post –Independence Contexts. *ESARBICA Journal, 35*, 67–88.

Maurer, I., Bartsch, V., & Ebers, M. (2011). The value of intra-organizational social capital: How it fosters knowledge transfer, innovation performance, and growth. *Organization Studies, 32*(2), 157–185. doi:10.1177/0170840610394301

Mbassegue, P. G., & Gardoni, M. (2017). Measuring the Performance of Knowledge Management Projects based on Balanced Scorecard in an Engineering and Manufacturing Environment. *International Journal of Engineering Research & Technology, IJERT., 6*(5), 1029–1035.

McAfee, A., Brynjolfsson, E., Davenport, T. H., Patil, D. J., & Barton, D. (2012). Big data. The management revolution. *Harvard Business Review, 90*(10), 61–67. PMID:23074865

McAllister, D. J. (1995). Affect-and cognition-based trust as foundations for interpersonal cooperation in organizations. *Academy of Management Journal, 38*(1), 24–59.

McDermott, R. (1999). Why information technology inspired but cannot deliver knowledge management. *California Management Review, 41*(4), 103–117. doi:10.2307/41166012

McElroy, M. W. (2010). *The New Knowledge Management*. Routledge. doi:10.4324/9780080512655

McGivern, G., Dopson, S., Ferlie, E., Bennett, C., Fischer, M., Fitzgerald, L., & Ledger, J. (2016). "Epistemic fit" and the mobilisation of management knowledge in health care. *Mobilizing Knowledge in Health Care: Challenges for Management and Organization*, 23.

McLeod, J., Childs, S., & Heaford, S. (2007). Records management capacity and compliance toolkits: A critical assessment. *Records Management Journal, 17*(3), 216–232.

McNeely, E., Gale, S., Tager, I., Kincl, L., Bradley, J., Coull, B., & Hecker, S. (2014). The self-reported health of U.S. flight attendants compared to the general population. *Environmental Health, 13*(1), 1–11. doi:10.1186/1476-069X-13-13 PMID:24612632

McNeely, E., Mordukhovich, I., Tideman, S., Gale, S., & Coull, B. (2018). Estimating the health consequences of flight attendant work: Comparing flight attendant health to the general population in a cross-sectional study. *BMC Public Health, 18*(1), 346–358. doi:10.118612889-018-5221-3 PMID:29566648

Meenu Dave, Y. S. (2013). Cloud Computing and Knowledge Management as a Service: A Collaborative Approach to Harness and Manage the Plethora of Knowledge. BVICAM's International Journal of Information Technology Bharati Vidyapeeth's Institute of Computer Applications and Management, 619-622.

Metaxiotis, K., Ergazakis, K., Samouilidis, E., & Psarras, J. (2003). Decision support through knowledge management: The role of the artificial intelligence. *Information Management & Computer Security*.

Mládková, L. (2012). Leadership in management of knowledge workers. *Social and Behavioral Sciences., 41*, 243–250.

Mogole, E. (2014). *A South African Retail Bank's Readiness for Knowledge Management Implementation*. Academic Press.

Mohanta, G. C., Kannan, V., & Thooyamani, K. P. (2006). Strategies for improving productivity of knowledge workers-An overview. *Strength Based Strategies*, 77-84.

Mojapelo, M., & Ngoepe, M. (2021). Contribution of Auditor-General South Africa to Records Management in the Public Sector in South Africa. *New Review of Information Networking, 26*, 1–2.

Mooradian, T., Renzl, B., & Matzler, K. (2006). Who trusts? Personality, trust and knowledge sharing. *Management Learning, 37*(4), 523–540. doi:10.1177/1350507606073424

Moore, J. (2017). Data Visualization in Support of Executive Decision Making. *Interdisciplinary Journal of Information, Knowledge & Management, 12*, 125–138. doi:10.28945/3687

Moore, J. (2017). Data Visualization in support of executive decision making. *Interdisciplinary Journal of Information, Knowledge, and Management, 12*, 126–134. doi:10.28945/3687

Moreira, M. A. (1999). *Meaningful Learning* [Aprendizagem Significativa]. Brasília: UnB.

Mosimege, B.S & Masiya, T (2021). Assessing audit outcomes of pre-determined objectives in a public institution (South Africa). *International Journal of Productivity and Performance Management.* https://doi.org/ doi:10.1108/uppm-02-2021-0091

Muhammad Rafiq, A. B. (2016). Innovative Trends in Knowledge Management: A Cloud Computing Perspective. ME14 DUBAI Conference.

Mujeye, D. (2016). *Investigating The Effectiveness Of Concept Maps In Facilitating Tacit Knowledge Conversion During Requirements Elicitation: A Quantitative Evaluative Study.* Academic Press.

Mukred, M., Yusof, M. Z., Alotaibi, M. F., Mokhtar, A. U., & Fauzi, F. (2019). The Key Factors in Adopting an Electronic Records Management System (ERMS) in Educational Sector: A UTAUT-Based Framework. IEEE, 7, 35963-35980.

Mura, M., Lettieri, E., Radaelli, G., & Spiller, N. (2013). Promoting professionals' innovative behaviour through knowledge sharing: The moderating role of social capital. *Journal of Knowledge Management, 17*(4), 527–544. doi:10.1108/JKM-03-2013-0105

Murayama, K., Blake, A. B., Kerr, T., & Castel, A. D. (2016). When enough is not enough: Information overload and metacognitive decisions to stop studying information. *Journal of Experimental Psychology. Learning, Memory, and Cognition, 42*(6), 914–924. doi:10.1037/xlm0000213 PMID:26595067

Murphy, S. (2019). *Work Tribes: The Surprising Secret to Breakthrough Performance, Astonishing Results, and Keeping Teams Together.* Harper Collins Leadership.

Nahapiet, J., & Ghoshal, S. (1998). Social capital, intellectual capital, and the organizational advantage. *Academy of Management Review, 23*(2), 242–266. doi:10.5465/amr.1998.533225

Nath, K., & Iswary, R. (2015). What comes after Web 3.0? Web 4.0 and the Future. *Proceedings of the International Conference and Communication System (I3CS'15),* 337-341.

Netshakhuma, N. S. (2019). The Blurry Line between archives and records management at the universities in South Africa. *Journal of the South African Society of Archivists, 52*, 62–78.

Nevo, D. (2003). *Developing Effective Knowledge Management Systems.* Academic Press.

Newell, S. (2009). Managing knowledge work and innovation. (2nd ed.). Palgrave: Hampshire. doi:10.1007/978-0-230-36641-1

Ngoepe, M., & Ngulube, P. (2014). The need for Records Management in the Auditing Process in the Public Sector in South Africa. *African Journal of Library Archives and Information Science, 24*(2), 136–150.

Nonaka, I. (1994). A dynamic theory of organizational knowledge creation. *Organization Science, 5*(1), 14–37. doi:10.1287/orsc.5.1.14

Nonaka, I. (1995). *The Knowledge-Creating Company. How Japanese Companies Create the Dynamics of Innovation.* Harvard Business Review Classics.

Nonaka, I., & Takeuchi, H. (1995). The Theory of Organizational Knowledge Creation. *International Journal of Technology Management, 11*(7/8), 1996.

North, K.,Maier, R. & Haas, O. (2018). *Knowledge Management in Digital Change New Findings and Practical Cases: New Findings and Practical Cases.* . doi:10.1007/978-3-319-73546-7

Nuottila, J., Aaltonen, K., & Kujala, J. (2016). Challenges of adopting agile methods in a public organization. *International Journal of Information Systems and Project Management.*

O'Neill, B. S., & Adya, M. (2007). Knowledge sharing and the psychological contract: Managing knowledge workers across different stages of employment. *Journal of Managerial Psychology, 22*(4), 411–436. doi:10.1108/02683940710745969

Obitade, P. (2019). Big data analytics: A link between knowledge management capabilities and superior cyber protection. *Journal of Big Data, 6*(1), 71. Advance online publication. doi:10.1186/s40537-019-0229-9

Oliver, S., & Kandadi, K. R. (2006). How to develop knowledge culture in organizations? A multiple case study of large distributed organizations. *Journal of Knowledge Management, 10*(4), 6–24. doi:10.1108/13673270610679336

Olofsson, L.& Farr, R. (2006). *Business Model Tools and Definition - a Literature Review.* Academic Press.

Orlikowski, W. J. (2000). Using technology and constituting structures: A practice lens for studying technology in organizations. *Organization Science, 11*(4), 404–428. doi:10.1287/orsc.11.4.404.14600

Oyefolahan, I. O. (2013). Knowledge management systems use and competency development among knowledge workers. *VINE Journal of Information and Knowledge Management Systems, 43*(4), 482–500. doi:10.1108/VINE-07-2012-0023

Pablos, P. O., & Lytras, M. (2018). Knowledge Management, Innovation and Big Data: Implications for Sustainability, Policy Making and Competitiveness. *Sustainability, 10*(6), 2073. doi:10.3390u10062073

Panahi, S., Watson, J., & Partridge, H. (2013). Towards tacit knowledge sharing over social web tools. *Journal of Knowledge Management, 17*(3), 379–397. doi:10.1108/JKM-11-2012-0364

Pangil, F., & Moi Chan, J. (2014). The mediating effect of knowledge sharing on the relationship between trust and virtual team effectiveness. *Journal of Knowledge Management, 18*(1), 92–106. doi:10.1108/JKM-09-2013-0341

Pan, S. L., & Leidner, D. E. (2003). Bridging communities of practice with information technology in pursuit of global knowledge sharing. *The Journal of Strategic Information Systems, 12*(1), 71–88. doi:10.1016/S0963-8687(02)00023-9

Pan, S. L., & Scarbrough, H. (1998). A socio-technical view of knowledge sharing at Buckman Laboratories. *Journal of Knowledge Management, 2*(1), 55–66. doi:10.1108/EUM0000000004607

Patil, H., & Surwade, Y. (2018). Web Technologies from Web 2.0 to Web 4.0. *IJSART*, *4*(4), 810–814.

Pereira, R. (2018). Assessing the implementation of the National Archives and Records Services Act at Eduardo Mondlane University in Mozambique. *ESARBICA Journal*, *37*, 221–239.

Peter Sharp, A. E. (2003). *Visual Tools within Make- A Knowledge Management Method.* Academic Press.

Petersen, S. A., Dahl, T. L., & Seim, E. A. (2021). *Enhancing Learning and Collaboration in Organisations through In-house Crowdsourcing* (Paper presentation). NOKOBIT Norsk konferanse for organisasjoners bruk av IT, Conference 2021, Norway. https://www.researchgate.net/publication/356536415_Enhancing_Learning_and_Collaboration_in_Organisations_through_In-house_Crowdsourcing

Petros Belsis, S. K. (2005). Information systems security from a knowledge management perspective. *Information Management & Computer Security*, *13*(3), 189–202. doi:10.1108/09685220510602013

Pettersen, L. (2018). Why Artificial Intelligence Will Not Outsmart Complex Knowledge Work. *SAGE Journals, 33*(6), 1058-1067. doi:10.1177/0950017018817489

Pham, X., & Stack, M. (2018). How data analytics is transforming agriculture. *Business Horizons*, *61*(1), 125–133. doi:10.1016/j.bushor.2017.09.011

Phusavat, K. (2013). *Productivity Management in an organization: measurement and analysis.* Bangkok: ToKnoPress.

Pineno, C., & Cristini, C. (2003). The balances scorecard: A vision report card. *Management Accounting Quarterly*, *4*(4). https://www.imanet.org/-/media/8269bca77c3749fbab7e4936a960d41d.ashx

Polanyi, M. (1966). *The Tacit Dimension.* University of Chicago Press.

Politis, J. D. (2003). The connection between trust and knowledge management: What are its implications for team performance. *Journal of Knowledge Management*, *7*(5), 55–66. doi:10.1108/13673270310505386

Ponzi, L., & Koenig, M. (2002). Knowledge management: Another management fad. *Information Research*, *8*(1), 8–1.

Porter, L. W., & McLaughlin, G. B. (2006). Leadership and the organizational context: Like the weather? *The Leadership Quarterly*, *17*(6), 559–576. doi:10.1016/j.leaqua.2006.10.002

Priyono, A., Moin, A., & Putri, V. N. A. O. (2020). Identifying Digital Transformation Paths in the Business Model of SMEs during the COVID-19 Pandemic. *Journal of Open Innovation*, *6*(4), 104. doi:10.3390/joitmc6040104

PWC. (2016). *Blockchain – an opportunity for energy producers and consumers?* https://www.pwc.com/gx/en/industries/assets/pwc-blockchain-opportunity-for-energy-producers-and-consumers.pdf

Qin, C., Zhao, P., Mou, J., & Zhang, J. (2018). Construction of personal knowledge maps for a peer-to-peer information-sharing environment. *The Electronic Library*, *36*(3), 394–413. doi:10.1108/EL-03-2017-0071

Raimo, N., De Turi, I., Ricciardelli, A., & Vitolla, F. (2021). Digitalization in the cultural industry: Evidence from Italian museums. *International Journal of Entrepreneurial Behaviour & Research*, 1355–2554. doi:10.1108/IJEBR-01-2021-0082

Randeree, E. (2006). Knowledge management: Securing the future. *Journal of Knowledge Management*, *10*(4), 145–156. doi:10.1108/13673270610679435

Randhawa, K., Wilden, R., & Hohberger, J. (2017). A Bibliometric Review of Open Innovation: Setting a Research Agenda. *Journal of Product Innovation Management*, *33*(6), 750–772.

Rapert, M. I., & Wren, B. M. (1998). Reconsidering organizational structure: A dual perspective of frameworks and processes. *Journal of Managerial Issues*, 287–302.

Rayman, R. (2002). Cabin air quality: An overview. *Aviation, Space, and Environmental Medicine*, *73*(3), 211–215. PMID:11908887

Reagans, R., & McEvily, B. (2003). Network structure and knowledge transfer: The effects of cohesion and range. *Administrative Science Quarterly*, *48*(2), 240–267. https://doiorg.libproxy.library.unt.edu/10.2307/3556658. doi:10.2307/3556658

Refsdal, A., Solhaug, B., & Stølen, K. (2015). Cyber- *Risk Management*. Advance online publication. doi:10.1007/978-3-319-23570-7

Reis, J., Amorim, M., Melao, N., Cohen, Y., & Rodriguez, M. (2020). Digitalization: A Literature Review and Research Agenda. *Proceedings on 25th International Joint Conference on Industrial Engineering and Operations Management*, 443-456. 10.1007/978-3-030-43616-2_47

Renzl, B. (2008). Trust in management and knowledge sharing: The mediating effects of fear and knowledge documentation. *Omega*, *36*(2), 206–220. doi:10.1016/j.omega.2006.06.005

Rice, G. (1999). Islamic Ethics and the Implications for Business. *Journal of Business Ethics*, *18*(4), 345–358. doi:10.1023/A:1005711414306

Rifkin, J. (1995). *The End of Work: The Decline of the Global Work-Force and the Dawn of the Post-Market Era*. Penguin.

Robinson, F. (1992). Knowledge, its Transmission and The Making of Muslim Societies. In *The Cambridge Illustrated History of the Islamic World*. Cambridge University Press. https://pure.royalholloway.ac.uk/portal/en/publications/knowledge-its-transmission-and-the-making-of-muslim-societies(13bfabeb-c589-47ec-ad86-21757eb52983).html

Robinson, R. (1971). The concept of knowledge. *Mind, 80*(317), 17–28. doi:10.1093/mind/LXXX.317.17

Roetzel, P. G. (2019). Information overload in the information age: a review of the literature from business administration, business psychology, and related disciplines with a bibliometric approach and framework development. *Business Research, 12*(2), 479-522.

Roetzel, P. G. (2018). *Information overload in the information age: A review of the literature from business administration, business psychology, and related disciplines with a bibliometric approach and framework development.* Business Research. doi:10.100740685-018-0069-z

Rohman, A., Eliyana, A., Purwana, D., & Hamidah, H. (2020). Individual and Organizational Factors' Effect on Knowledge Sharing Behavior. *Entrepreneurship and Sustainability Issues, 8*(1), 38–48. doi:10.9770/jesi.2020.8.1(3)

Rowley, J. (2007). The wisdom hierarchy: Representations of the DIKW hierarchy. *Journal of Information Science, 33*(2), 163–180. doi:10.1177/0165551506070706

Roy, M. C., Roy, M. J., & Bouchard, L. (2017). Improving Board Knowledge with Information and Communication Technologies. *Electronic Journal of Knowledge Management, 15*(4), 215–224. http://search.ebscohost.com/login.aspx?direct=true&db=lls&AN=126281196&scope=site

Rutten, W., Blaas-Franken, J., & Martin, H. (2016). The impact of (low) trust on knowledge sharing. *Journal of Knowledge Management, 20*(2), 199–214. doi:10.1108/JKM-10-2015-0391

Ryu, S., Ho, S. H., & Han, I. (2003). Knowledge sharing behavior of physicians in hospitals. *Expert Systems with Applications, 25*(1), 113–122. doi:10.1016/S0957-4174(03)00011-3

Sahar Hayaeian, R. H. (2021). The impact of knowledge management strategies on the relationship between intellectual capital and innovation: Evidence from SMEs. *Journal of Intellectual Capital.*

Sailer, P., Stutzman, B., & Kobold, L. (2019). *Successful Digital Transformation.* Siemens Advanta. https://www.siemensadvanta.com/system/files/202011/Successful%20digital%20transformation_whitepaper%20by%20SIEMENS%20Advanta.pdf

Salahudin, S. N., Baharuddin, S. S., Abdullah, M. S., & Osman, A. (2016). The Effect of Islamic Work Ethics on Organizational Commitment. *Procedia Economics and Finance, 35*, 582–590. doi:10.1016/S2212-5671(16)00071-X

Salis, S., & Williams, A. M. (2010). Knowledge sharing through face-to-face communication and labour productivity: Evidence from British workplaces. *British Journal of Industrial Relations, 48*(2), 436–459. doi:10.1111/j.1467-8543.2009.00762.x

Salloum, S. A., Al-Emran, M., & Shaalan, K. (2017). Mining text in news channels: A case study from facebook. *Int. J. Inf. Technol. Lang. Stud., 1*(1), 1–9.

Sandhu, M. S., Jain, K. K., & Ahmad, I. U. K. B. (2011). Knowledge Sharing Among Public Sector Employees: Evidence from Malaysia. *International Journal of Public Sector Management, 24*(3), 206–226. doi:10.1108/09513551111121347

Sankowska, A. (2013). Relationships between organizational trust, knowledge transfer, knowledge creation, and firm's innovativeness. *The Learning Organization*, *20*(1), 85–100. doi:10.1108/09696471311288546

Santoro, G., Vrontis, D., Thrassou, A., & Dezi, L. (2018). The Internet of Things: Building a knowledge management system for open innovation and knowledge management capacity. *Technological Forecasting and Social Change*, *136*, 347–354. doi:10.1016/j.techfore.2017.02.034

Sarvary, M. (1999). Knowledge management and competition in the consulting industry. *California Management Review*, *41*(2), 95–107. doi:10.2307/41165988

Saulais, P., & Ermine, J.L. (2019). *Understanding and Deploying a KM Plan within a Learning Organization*. Academic Press.

Saxena, D., & Lamest, M. (2018). Information overload and coping strategies in the big data context: Evidence from the hospitality sector. *Journal of Information Science*, *44*(3), 287–297. doi:10.1177/0165551517693712

Schnackenber, A., & Tomlinson, E. (2014). Organizational transparency: A new perspective on Managing trust in organization-stakeholder relationships. *Journal of Management*, *42*(7), 1784–1810. doi:10.1177/0149206314525202

Schutte, N., & Barkhuizen, N. (2015). Knowledge management and sharing in local government: A social identity theory perspective: EJKM. *Electronic Journal of Knowledge Management*, *13*(2), 130–141.

Seemma, P. S., Sundaresan, N., & Sowmiya, M. (2018). Overview of Cyber Security. *IJARCCE*, *7*, 125–128. doi:10.17148/IJARCCE.2018.71127

Senge, P. (1990). *The Fifth Discipline: The Art and Practice of the Learning Organization*. Doubleday/Currency.

Shackleton, C. (2006). *Developing Key Performance Indicators For Corporate Communication in the Information Technology Industry. MCOM in Communication Management*. The University of Pretoria.

Shahbandeh, M. (2018). *Market Value of Halal Foods Worldwide from 2017 to 2023*. https://www.statista.com/statistics/562857/market-value-of-halal-products-worldwide/

Shamim, S., Zeng, J., Khan, Z., & Zia, N. U. (2020). Big data analytics capability and decision making performance in emerging market firms: The role of contractual and relational governance mechanisms. *Technological Forecasting and Social Change*, *161*, 120315. doi:10.1016/j.techfore.2020.120315

Sharratt, M., & Usoro, A. (2003). Understanding knowledge-sharing in online communities of practice. *Electronic Journal of Knowledge Management*, *1*(2), 187–196.

Shuck, B. (2011). Integrative Literature Review: Four Emerging Perspectives of Employee Engagement: An Integrative Literature Review. *Human Resource Development Review*, *10*(3), 304–328. doi:10.1177/1534484311410840

Siegel, C. A., & Sweeney, M. (2020). Cyber Strategy: Risk-Driven Security and Resiliency. Auerbach Publications.

Siti-Nabiha, A. K., & Scapens, R. W. (2005). Institutional work and the implementation of performance measurement and management system in a developing country. *Journal of Accounting and Organisational Change. Accounting, Auditing & Accountability Journal*, *18*(1), 44–73.

Skillman, G. L. (1996). *The Role of Production Relations in Marx's Theory of Capitalist Exploitation.* Marxian Economics session of the History of Economics Society annual conference, Vancouver, Canada. Retrieved from: http://gskillman.web.wesleyan.edu/research/histmat2.pdf

Skyrme, D. (2011). *A Knowledge-Enriching Culture*. Available at http://www.skyrme.com/kmroadmap/culture.htm

Smith, R. (1991). Where is the wisdom...? *BMJ (Clinical Research Ed.)*, *303*(6806), 798–799. doi:10.1136/bmj.303.6806.798 PMID:1932964

Snell, J. (2019). *Text Analytics and Natural Language Processing: Knowledge Management's Next Frontier*. Academic Press.

Soderberg, M., Kalagnanam, S., Sheehan, N. T., & Vaidyanathan, G. (2011). Kalagnanam, Suresh; Sheehan, Norman; Vaidyanathan, Ganesh (2010). When is a balanced scorecard a balanced scorecard? *International Journal of Productivity and Performance Management*, *60*(7), 688–708. doi:10.1108/17410401111167780

Sousa, M., & Rocha, Á. (2019). Strategic Knowledge Management in the Digital Age. *Journal of Business Research*, *91*, 223–226. doi:10.1016/j.jbusres.2018.10.016

Sousa, R., Miranda, R., Moreira, A., Alves, C., Lori, N., & Machado, J. (2021). Software Tools for Conducting Real-Time Information Processing and Visualization in Industry: An Up-to-Date Review. *Applied Sciences (Basel, Switzerland)*, *2021*(11), 4800. doi:10.3390/app11114800

Sousa, W. G., Melo, E. R. P., Bermejo, P. H. D., Farias, R. A. S., & Gomes, A. O. (2019). How and where is artificial intelligence in the public sector going? A literature review and research agenda. *Government Information Quarterly*, *36*(4), 36. doi:10.1016/j.giq.2019.07.004

Sowell, T. (2022). *Knowledge and decisions*. Basic Books.

Srinivas, J., Kumar, D. A., & Neeraj, K. (2018). Government regulations in cyber security: Framework, standards and recommendations. *Future Generation Computer Systems*, *92*, 178–188. Advance online publication. doi:10.1016/j.future.2018.09.063

Staples, D. S., & Webster, J. (2008). Exploring the effects of trust, task interdependence and virtualness on knowledge sharing in teams. *Information Systems Journal*, *18*(6), 617–640. doi:10.1111/j.1365-2575.2007.00244.x

Staudinger, U. (2010). Older and wiser? Integrated results on the relationship between age and wisdom-related performance. *International Journal of Behavioral Development*, *23*(3), 641–664. doi:10.1080/016502599383739

Stronen, F., Ronning, V. H., & Breunig, K. J. (2019). Innovation Capabilities in Banking: The Case of Norwegian Mobile Payment. *Proceedings of the 20th European Conference On Knowledge Management (ECKM 2019)*, 998-1005.

Sulaiman, M., Sabian, N. A. A., & Othman, A. K. (2013). The Understanding of Islamic Management Practices among Muslim Managers in Malaysia. *Asian Social Science*, *10*(1), 189–199. doi:10.5539/ass.v10n1p189

Sutton, D. C. (2001). What is knowledge and can it be managed? *European Journal of Information Systems*, *10*(2), 80–88. doi:10.1057/palgrave.ejis.3000397

Sveiby, K. E. (1990). *Kunskapsledning: 101 råd till ledare i kunskapsintensiva organisationer*. Affärsvärlden.

Sveiby, K. E. (1997). *The new organizational wealth: Managing & measuring knowledge-based assets*. Berrett-Koehler Publishers.

Swan, J., Newell, S., & Nicolini, D. (Eds.). (2016). *Mobilizing knowledge in health care: challenges for management and organization*. Oxford University Press. doi:10.1093/acprof:oso/9780198738237.001.0001

Swift, P. E., & Hwang, A. (2013). The impact of affective and cognitive trust on knowledge sharing and organizational learning. *The Learning Organization*, *20*(1), 20–37. doi:10.1108/09696471311288500

Tajfel, H., Billig, M. G., Bundy, R. P., & Flament, C. (1971). Social categorization and intergroup behaviour. *European Journal of Social Psychology*, *1*(2), 149–178. doi:10.1002/ejsp.2420010202

Talab, A. H., Scholten, V., & van Beers, C. (2018). Knowledge Sharing and Open Innovation. In Open Innovation and Knowledge Management in Small and Medium Enterprises (pp. 117-140). doi:10.1142/9789813233591_0007

Tamjidyamcholo, A., Baba, M. S. B., Tamjid, H., & Gholipour, R. (2013). Information security–Professional perceptions of knowledge-sharing intention under self-efficacy, trust, reciprocity, and shared-language. *Computers & Education*, *68*, 223–232. doi:10.1016/j.compedu.2013.05.010

Tammaro, A. M. (2008). *Performance indicators in Library and Information Science (LIS) education: towards cross-border quality assurance in Europe*. Conference paper presented at the Universita Di Parma.

Tawalbeh, L., Muheidat, F., Tawalbeh, M., & Quwaider, M. (2020). IoT Privacy and Security: Challenges and Solutions. *Applied Sciences (Basel, Switzerland)*, *10*(12), 4102. doi:10.3390/app10124102

Taymanov, R., Sapozhnikova, K., & Prokopchina, S. (2021). What is immeasurable make measurable with artificial intelligence (measurements & artificial intelligence). Measurement. *Sensors (Basel)*, *18*, 100316. doi:10.1016/j.measen.2021.100316

Teece, D., Peteraf, M., & Leih, S. (2016). Dynamic capabilities and organizational agility: Risk, uncertainty, and strategy in the innovation economy. *California Management Review*, *58*(4), 13–35. doi:10.1525/cmr.2016.58.4.13

Tohidinia, Z., & Mosakhani, M. (2010). Knowledge sharing behaviour and its predictors. *Industrial Management & Data Systems*, *110*(4), 611–631. doi:10.1108/02635571011039052

Tomé, E., & Gromova, E. (2021). Development of emergent knowledge strategies and new dynamic capabilities for business education in a time of crisis. *Sustainability*, *13*(8), 4518. doi:10.3390u13084518

Torabi, F., & El-Den, J. (2017). The impact of Knowledge Management on Organizational Productivity: case study on Koosar Bank of Iran. *Procedia Computer Science, International Conference, ISICO*, 300-310. 10.1016/j.procs.2017.12.159

Tortorella, G., Narayanamurthy, G., & Staines, J. (2021). COVID-19 Implications on the Relationship between Organizational Learning and Performance. *Knowledge Management Research and Practice*, *19*(4), 551–564. Advance online publication. doi:10.1080/14778238.2021.1909430

Tosey, P., Visser, M., & Saunders, M. N. (2012). The origins and conceptualizations of 'triple-loop 'learning: A critical review. *Management Learning*, *43*(3), 291–307. doi:10.1177/1350507611426239

TreesL. (2019). Retrieved from https://www.apqc.org/blog/5-reasons-why-knowledge-management-moving-cloud

Tsai, M. T., & Cheng, N. C. (2010). Programmer perceptions of knowledge-sharing behavior under social cognitive theory. *Expert Systems with Applications*, *37*(12), 8479–8485. doi:10.1016/j.eswa.2010.05.029

Tsai, W. (2002). Social structure of "coopetition" within a multiunit organization: Coordination, competition, and intraorganizational knowledge sharing. *Organization Science*, *13*(2), 179–190. doi:10.1287/orsc.13.2.179.536

Tumuhairwe, R., & Ahimbisibwe, A. (2016). Procurement records compliance, effective risk management and records management performance. Evidence from Ugandan public procuring and disposing entities. *Records Management Journal*, *26*(1), 83–101.

Turner, J. C. (1982). Towards a cognitive redefinition of the social group. In H. Tajfel (Ed.), *Social identity and intergroup relations* (pp. 15–40). Cambridge University Press.

U.S. Bureau of Labor and Statistics. (2021, September 8). *Flight attendants.* https://www.bls.gov/ooh/transportation-and-material-moving/flight-attendants.htm

Udin, U., Dananjoyo, R., Shaikh, M., & Vio Linarta, D. (2022). Islamic Work Ethics, Affective Commitment, and Employee's Performance in Family Business: Testing Their Relationships. *SAGE Open*, *12*(1), 1–12. doi:10.1177/21582440221085263

Umar Farooq Sahibzada, C. J. (2020). Fueling knowledge management processes in Chinese higher education institutes (HEIs): The neglected mediating role of knowledge worker satisfaction. *Journal of Enterprise Information Management*, *33*(6), 1395–1417. doi:10.1108/JEIM-07-2019-0197

Umar Farooq Sahibzada, J. C. (2020). Knowledge management processes, knowledge worker satisfaction, and organizational performance: Symmetric and asymmetrical analysis. *Aslib Journal of Information Management*, 112–129.

Umar, H. (2019). Records Management and Accountable Governance in two tertiary institutions of learning in Taraba State. *Bakundi Journal of Technology, Agriculture and Entrepreneurship*, *1*(1), 1–8.

Valle-Cruz, D., Ruvalcaba-Gomez, E. A., Sandoval-Almazan, R., & Criado, J. I. (2019). A Review of Artificial Intelligence in Government and its Potential from a Public Policy Perspective. *20th Annual International Conference on Digital Government Research.*

Van Den Hooff, B., & De Ridder, J. A. (2004). Knowledge sharing in context: The influence of organizational commitment, communication climate and CMC use on knowledge sharing. *Journal of Knowledge Management*, *8*(6), 117–130. doi:10.1108/13673270410567675

Van Wijk, R., Jansen, J. J., & Lyles, M. A. (2008). Inter-and intra-organizational knowledge transfer: A meta-analytic review and assessment of its antecedents and consequences. *Journal of Management Studies*, *45*(4), 830–853. doi:10.1111/j.1467-6486.2008.00771.x

Van Wyk, C., & Moeng, B. G. (2014). The Design and Implementation of a Strategic Plan in Primary School. *International Business & Economics Research Journal*, *13*(1), 137–143.

Voelpel, S. C., & Han, Z. (2005). Managing knowledge sharing in China: The case of Siemens ShareNet. *Journal of Knowledge Management*, *9*(3), 51–63. doi:10.1108/13673270510602764

Wallace, D. P. (2007). *Knowledge Management-Historical and Cross-Disciplinary Themes.* Academic Press.

Wang, C. (2018). *Integrating Data Analytics & Knowledge Management: A Conceptual Model.* Academic Press.

Wang, S., & Noe, R. A. (2010). Knowledge sharing: A review and directions for future research. *Human Resource Management Review*, *20*(2), 115–131. doi:10.1016/j.hrmr.2009.10.001

Wasko, M. M., & Faraj, S. (2000). "It is what one does": Why people participate and help others in electronic communities of practice. *The Journal of Strategic Information Systems*, *9*(2-3), 155–173. doi:10.1016/S0963-8687(00)00045-7

Wasko, M. M., & Faraj, S. (2005). Why should I share? Examining social capital and knowledge contribution in electronic networks of practice. *Management Information Systems Quarterly, 29*(1), 35–57. doi:10.2307/25148667

Watkins, K. E., & Marsick, V. J. (1996). *In action: creating the learning organization*. American Society for Training and Development.

Watkins, K. E., & Marsick, V. J. (Eds.). (2003). Make learning count! Diagnosing the learning culture in organizations. *Advances in Developing Human Resources, 5*(2), 132–151. doi:10.1177/1523422303251341

Weick, K. E. (1995). *Sensemaking in organizations* (Vol. 3). Sage.

Weinberger, D. (2010). The problem with the data-information-knowledge-wisdom hierarchy. *Harvard Business Review*, 2.

West & Bogers. (n.d.). Open Innovation: Current Status and Research Opportunities. *Innovation. Organization & Management, 19*(1), 43–50.

West, J., Salter, A., Vanhaverbeke, W., & Chesbrough, H. (2014). Open Innovation: The Next Decade. *Research Policy, 43*(5), 805–811. doi:10.1016/j.respol.2014.03.001

Whittaker, S., Bellotti, V., & Gwizdka, J. (2006). Email in personal information management. *Communications of the ACM, 49*(1), 68–73. doi:10.1145/1107458.1107494

Wickman, D. (2009). Measuring performance or performing measurements? Measuring the impact and sustainability of the PARBICA Recordkeeping For Good Governance Toolkit. *Archives and Manuscript, 37*(2), 114–126.

Widén-Wulff, G., & Ginman, M. (2004). Explaining knowledge sharing in organizations through the dimensions of social capital. *Journal of Information Science, 30*(5), 448–458. doi:10.1177/0165551504046997

Wiig, K. M. (1997). Knowledge Management: Where Did it Come From and Where Will It Go? *Expert Systems with Applications, 13*(1), 1–14. doi:10.1016/S0957-4174(97)00018-3

Wiig, K. M. (1999). What future knowledge management users may expect. *Journal of Knowledge Management, 3*(2), 155–166. doi:10.1108/13673279910275611

Willem, A., & Buelens, M. (2009). Knowledge sharing in inter-unit cooperative episodes: The impact of organizational structure dimensions. *International Journal of Information Management, 29*(2), 151–160. doi:10.1016/j.ijinfomgt.2008.06.004

Williams, C. (2003). Sky service: The demands of emotional labour in the airline industry. *Gender, Work and Organization, 10*(5), 513–550. doi:10.1111/1468-0432.00210

Wilson, T.D. (2002). The nonsense of 'knowledge management'. *Information Research*, 8(1). Available at http://InformationR.net/ir/8-1/paper144.html]

Wilson, E. (1998). *Consilience: The Unity of Knowledge*. Vintage Books.

Wirtz, B. W., Weyerer, J. C., & Schichtel, F. T. (2019). An integrative public IoT framework for smart government. *Government Information Quarterly, 36*(2), 333–345. doi:10.1016/j.giq.2018.07.001

Wolfert, S., Ge, L., Verdouw, C., & Bogaardt, M.-J. (2017). Big data in smart farming – A review. *Agricultural Systems, 153*, 69–80. doi:10.1016/j.agsy.2017.01.023

Wu, W. L., Lin, C. H., Hsu, B. F., & Yeh, R. S. (2009). Interpersonal trust and knowledge sharing: Moderating effects of individual altruism and a social interaction environment. *Social Behavior and Personality, 37*(1), 83–93. doi:10.2224bp.2009.37.1.83

Wu, W. Y., & Sukoco, B. M. (2010). Why should I share? Examining consumers' motives and trust on knowledge sharing. *Journal of Computer Information Systems, 50*(4), 11–19.

Wu, Y., & Zhu, W. (2012). An integrated theoretical model for determinants of knowledge sharing behaviours. *Kybernetes, 41*(10), 1462–1482. doi:10.1108/03684921211276675

Xanthopoulou, D., Bakker, A., Demerouti, E., & Scjaufeli, W. (2007). The role of personal resources in the job demands-resources model. *International Journal of Stress Management, 14*(2), 121–141. doi:10.1037/1072-5245.14.2.121

Xue, Y., Bradley, J., & Liang, H. (2011). Team climate, empowering leadership, and knowledge sharing. *Journal of Knowledge Management, 15*(2), 299–312. doi:10.1108/13673271111119709

Yaakub. (2011). Islamic Conceptualisation of Knowledge Management. *American Journal of Economics and Business Administration, 3*(2), 363–369. doi:10.3844/ajebasp.2011.363.369

Yadav, R. (2021). Cyber Security Threats During Covid-19 Pandemic. *International Transaction Journal of Engineering Management & Applied Sciences & Technologies, 12*(3).

Yıkılmaz, I. (2020). The future of knowledge management: Web 4.0. In Data, Information and Knowledge Management. Nobel Bilimsel Eserler Sertifika.

Yilmaz, A. A., & Tuzlukaya, S. E. (2022). Competency Trap in Organizational Learning: Turkish E-Government Gateway Application During the COVID-19 Pandemic. *International Journal of Electronic Government Research, 18*(1), 1–13. doi:10.4018/IJEGR.288068

Young, M.-L., Kuo, F.-Y., & Myers, M. (2012). To share or not to share: A critical research perspective on knowledge management. *European Journal of Information Systems, 21*(5), 496–511. doi:10.1057/ejis.2012.10

Yuan, Y. C., Zhao, X., Liao, Q., & Chi, C. (2013). The use of different information and communication technologies to support knowledge sharing in organizations: From e-mail to micro-blogging. *Journal of the American Society for Information Science and Technology, 64*(8), 1659–1670. doi:10.1002/asi.22863

Yu, T. K., Lu, L. C., & Liu, T. F. (2010). Exploring factors that influence knowledge sharing behavior via weblogs. *Computers in Human Behavior, 26*(1), 32–41. doi:10.1016/j.chb.2009.08.002

Zagzebski, L. (2017). What is knowledge? *The Blackwell guide to epistemology*, 92-116.

Zarraga, C., & Bonache, J. (2005). The impact of team atmosphere on knowledge outcomes in self-managed teams. *Organization Studies 26*(5), 661-681. https://doi-org.libproxy.library.unt.edu/10.1177/0170840605051820

Zboralski, K. (2009). Antecedents of knowledge sharing in communities of practice. *Journal of Knowledge Management, 13*(3), 90–101. doi:10.1108/13673270910962897

Zeggelink, E. (1994). Dynamics of structure: An individual oriented approach. *Social Networks, 16*(4), 295–333. doi:10.1016/0378-8733(94)90014-0

Zheng, W., Yang, G., & McLean, G. (2010). Linking organizational culture, structure, strategy, and organizational effectiveness: Mediating role of knowledge management. *Journal of Business Research, 63*(7), 763–771. doi:10.1016/j.jbusres.2009.06.005

Zhou, J., Li, X., Zhao, X., & Wang, L. (2021). Driving performance grading and analytics; learning internal indicators and external factors from multi-source data. Driving performance grading. *Industrial Management & Data System*. https://www.emerald.com/insight/0263-5577.htm

Related References

To continue our tradition of advancing information science and technology research, we have compiled a list of recommended IGI Global readings. These references will provide additional information and guidance to further enrich your knowledge and assist you with your own research and future publications.

Abdul Razak, R., & Mansor, N. A. (2021). Instagram Influencers in Social Media-Induced Tourism: Rethinking Tourist Trust Towards Tourism Destination. In M. Dinis, L. Bonixe, S. Lamy, & Z. Breda (Eds.), *Impact of New Media in Tourism* (pp. 135-144). IGI Global. https://doi.org/10.4018/978-1-7998-7095-1.ch009

Abir, T., & Khan, M. Y. (2022). Importance of ICT Advancement and Culture of Adaptation in the Tourism and Hospitality Industry for Developing Countries. In C. Ramos, S. Quinteiro, & A. Gonçalves (Eds.), *ICT as Innovator Between Tourism and Culture* (pp. 30–41). IGI Global. https://doi.org/10.4018/978-1-7998-8165-0.ch003

Abir, T., & Khan, M. Y. (2022). Importance of ICT Advancement and Culture of Adaptation in the Tourism and Hospitality Industry for Developing Countries. In C. Ramos, S. Quinteiro, & A. Gonçalves (Eds.), *ICT as Innovator Between Tourism and Culture* (pp. 30–41). IGI Global. https://doi.org/10.4018/978-1-7998-8165-0.ch003

Abtahi, M. S., Behboudi, L., & Hasanabad, H. M. (2017). Factors Affecting Internet Advertising Adoption in Ad Agencies. *International Journal of Innovation in the Digital Economy*, *8*(4), 18–29. doi:10.4018/IJIDE.2017100102

Afenyo-Agbe, E., & Mensah, I. (2022). Principles, Benefits, and Barriers to Community-Based Tourism: Implications for Management. In I. Mensah & E. Afenyo-Agbe (Eds.), *Prospects and Challenges of Community-Based Tourism and Changing Demographics* (pp. 1–29). IGI Global. doi:10.4018/978-1-7998-7335-8.ch001

Agbo, V. M. (2022). Distributive Justice Issues in Community-Based Tourism. In I. Mensah & E. Afenyo-Agbe (Eds.), *Prospects and Challenges of Community-Based Tourism and Changing Demographics* (pp. 107–129). IGI Global. https://doi.org/10.4018/978-1-7998-7335-8.ch005

Agrawal, S. (2017). The Impact of Emerging Technologies and Social Media on Different Business(es): Marketing and Management. In O. Rishi & A. Sharma (Eds.), *Maximizing Business Performance and Efficiency Through Intelligent Systems* (pp. 37–49). Hershey, PA: IGI Global. doi:10.4018/978-1-5225-2234-8.ch002

Ahmad, A., & Johari, S. (2022). Georgetown as a Gastronomy Tourism Destination: Visitor Awareness Towards Revisit Intention of Nasi Kandar Restaurant. In M. Valeri (Ed.), *New Governance and Management in Touristic Destinations* (pp. 71–83). IGI Global. https://doi.org/10.4018/978-1-6684-3889-3.ch005

Alkhatib, G., & Bayouq, S. T. (2021). A TAM-Based Model of Technological Factors Affecting Use of E-Tourism. *International Journal of Tourism and Hospitality Management in the Digital Age*, *5*(2), 50–67. https://doi.org/10.4018/IJTHMDA.20210701.oa1

Altinay Ozdemir, M. (2021). Virtual Reality (VR) and Augmented Reality (AR) Technologies for Accessibility and Marketing in the Tourism Industry. In C. Eusébio, L. Teixeira, & M. Carneiro (Eds.), *ICT Tools and Applications for Accessible Tourism* (pp. 277-301). IGI Global. https://doi.org/10.4018/978-1-7998-6428-8.ch013

Anantharaman, R. N., Rajeswari, K. S., Angusamy, A., & Kuppusamy, J. (2017). Role of Self-Efficacy and Collective Efficacy as Moderators of Occupational Stress Among Software Development Professionals. *International Journal of Human Capital and Information Technology Professionals*, *8*(2), 45–58. doi:10.4018/IJHCITP.2017040103

Aninze, F., El-Gohary, H., & Hussain, J. (2018). The Role of Microfinance to Empower Women: The Case of Developing Countries. *International Journal of Customer Relationship Marketing and Management*, *9*(1), 54–78. doi:10.4018/IJCRMM.2018010104

Antosova, G., Sabogal-Salamanca, M., & Krizova, E. (2021). Human Capital in Tourism: A Practical Model of Endogenous and Exogenous Territorial Tourism Planning in Bahía Solano, Colombia. In V. Costa, A. Moura, & M. Mira (Eds.), *Handbook of Research on Human Capital and People Management in the Tourism Industry* (pp. 282–302). IGI Global. https://doi.org/10.4018/978-1-7998-4318-4.ch014

Arsenijević, O. M., Orčić, D., & Kastratović, E. (2017). Development of an Optimization Tool for Intangibles in SMEs: A Case Study from Serbia with a Pilot Research in the Prestige by Milka Company. In M. Vemić (Ed.), *Optimal Management Strategies in Small and Medium Enterprises* (pp. 320–347). Hershey, PA: IGI Global. doi:10.4018/978-1-5225-1949-2.ch015

Aryanto, V. D., Wismantoro, Y., & Widyatmoko, K. (2018). Implementing Eco-Innovation by Utilizing the Internet to Enhance Firm's Marketing Performance: Study of Green Batik Small and Medium Enterprises in Indonesia. *International Journal of E-Business Research, 14*(1), 21–36. doi:10.4018/IJEBR.2018010102

Asero, V., & Billi, S. (2022). New Perspective of Networking in the DMO Model. In M. Valeri (Ed.), *New Governance and Management in Touristic Destinations* (pp. 105–118). IGI Global. https://doi.org/10.4018/978-1-6684-3889-3.ch007

Atiku, S. O., & Fields, Z. (2017). Multicultural Orientations for 21st Century Global Leadership. In N. Baporikar (Ed.), *Management Education for Global Leadership* (pp. 28–51). Hershey, PA: IGI Global. doi:10.4018/978-1-5225-1013-0.ch002

Atiku, S. O., & Fields, Z. (2018). Organisational Learning Dimensions and Talent Retention Strategies for the Service Industries. In N. Baporikar (Ed.), *Global Practices in Knowledge Management for Societal and Organizational Development* (pp. 358–381). Hershey, PA: IGI Global. doi:10.4018/978-1-5225-3009-1.ch017

Atsa'am, D. D., & Kuset Bodur, E. (2021). Pattern Mining on How Organizational Tenure Affects the Psychological Capital of Employees Within the Hospitality and Tourism Industry: Linking Employees' Organizational Tenure With PsyCap. *International Journal of Tourism and Hospitality Management in the Digital Age, 5*(2), 17–28. https://doi.org/10.4018/IJTHMDA.2021070102

Ávila, L., & Teixeira, L. (2018). The Main Concepts Behind the Dematerialization of Business Processes. In M. Khosrow-Pour, D.B.A. (Ed.), Encyclopedia of Information Science and Technology, Fourth Edition (pp. 888-898). Hershey, PA: IGI Global. https://doi.org/ doi:10.4018/978-1-5225-2255-3.ch076

Ayorekire, J., Mugizi, F., Obua, J., & Ampaire, G. (2022). Community-Based Tourism and Local People's Perceptions Towards Conservation: The Case of Queen Elizabeth Conservation Area, Uganda. In I. Mensah & E. Afenyo-Agbe (Eds.), *Prospects and Challenges of Community-Based Tourism and Changing Demographics* (pp. 56–82). IGI Global. https://doi.org/10.4018/978-1-7998-7335-8.ch003

Baleiro, R. (2022). Tourist Literature and the Architecture of Travel in Olga Tokarczuk and Patti Smith. In R. Baleiro & R. Pereira (Eds.), *Global Perspectives on Literary Tourism and Film-Induced Tourism* (pp. 202-216). IGI Global. https://doi.org/10.4018/978-1-7998-8262-6.ch011

Barat, S. (2021). Looking at the Future of Medical Tourism in Asia. *International Journal of Tourism and Hospitality Management in the Digital Age*, *5*(1), 19–33. https://doi.org/10.4018/IJTHMDA.2021010102

Barbosa, C. A., Magalhães, M., & Nunes, M. R. (2021). Travel Instagramability: A Way of Choosing a Destination? In M. Dinis, L. Bonixe, S. Lamy, & Z. Breda (Eds.), *Impact of New Media in Tourism* (pp. 173-190). IGI Global. https://doi.org/10.4018/978-1-7998-7095-1.ch011

Bari, M. W., & Khan, Q. (2021). Pakistan as a Destination of Religious Tourism. In E. Alaverdov & M. Bari (Eds.), *Global Development of Religious Tourism* (pp. 1-10). IGI Global. https://doi.org/10.4018/978-1-7998-5792-1.ch001

Bartens, Y., Chunpir, H. I., Schulte, F., & Voß, S. (2017). Business/IT Alignment in Two-Sided Markets: A COBIT 5 Analysis for Media Streaming Business Models. In S. De Haes & W. Van Grembergen (Eds.), *Strategic IT Governance and Alignment in Business Settings* (pp. 82–111). Hershey, PA: IGI Global. doi:10.4018/978-1-5225-0861-8.ch004

Bashayreh, A. M. (2018). Organizational Culture and Organizational Performance. In W. Lee & F. Sabetzadeh (Eds.), *Contemporary Knowledge and Systems Science* (pp. 50–69). Hershey, PA: IGI Global. doi:10.4018/978-1-5225-5655-8.ch003

Bechthold, L., Lude, M., & Prügl, R. (2021). Crisis Favors the Prepared Firm: How Organizational Ambidexterity Relates to Perceptions of Organizational Resilience. In A. Zehrer, G. Glowka, K. Schwaiger, & V. Ranacher-Lackner (Eds.), *Resiliency Models and Addressing Future Risks for Family Firms in the Tourism Industry* (pp. 178–205). IGI Global. https://doi.org/10.4018/978-1-7998-7352-5.ch008

Bedford, D. A. (2018). Sustainable Knowledge Management Strategies: Aligning Business Capabilities and Knowledge Management Goals. In N. Baporikar (Ed.), *Global Practices in Knowledge Management for Societal and Organizational Development* (pp. 46–73). Hershey, PA: IGI Global. doi:10.4018/978-1-5225-3009-1.ch003

Bekjanov, D., & Matyusupov, B. (2021). Influence of Innovative Processes in the Competitiveness of Tourist Destination. In J. Soares (Ed.), *Innovation and Entrepreneurial Opportunities in Community Tourism* (pp. 243–263). IGI Global. https://doi.org/10.4018/978-1-7998-4855-4.ch014

Bharwani, S., & Musunuri, D. (2018). Reflection as a Process From Theory to Practice. In M. Khosrow-Pour, D.B.A. (Ed.), Encyclopedia of Information Science and Technology, Fourth Edition (pp. 1529-1539). Hershey, PA: IGI Global. doi:10.4018/978-1-5225-2255-3.ch132

Bhatt, G. D., Wang, Z., & Rodger, J. A. (2017). Information Systems Capabilities and Their Effects on Competitive Advantages: A Study of Chinese Companies. *Information Resources Management Journal*, *30*(3), 41–57. doi:10.4018/IRMJ.2017070103

Bhushan, M., & Yadav, A. (2017). Concept of Cloud Computing in ESB. In R. Bhadoria, N. Chaudhari, G. Tomar, & S. Singh (Eds.), *Exploring Enterprise Service Bus in the Service-Oriented Architecture Paradigm* (pp. 116–127). Hershey, PA: IGI Global. doi:10.4018/978-1-5225-2157-0.ch008

Bhushan, S. (2017). System Dynamics Base-Model of Humanitarian Supply Chain (HSCM) in Disaster Prone Eco-Communities of India: A Discussion on Simulation and Scenario Results. *International Journal of System Dynamics Applications*, *6*(3), 20–37. doi:10.4018/IJSDA.2017070102

Binder, D., & Miller, J. W. (2021). A Generations' Perspective on Employer Branding in Tourism. In V. Costa, A. Moura, & M. Mira (Eds.), *Handbook of Research on Human Capital and People Management in the Tourism Industry* (pp. 152–174). IGI Global. https://doi.org/10.4018/978-1-7998-4318-4.ch008

Birch Freeman, A. A., Mensah, I., & Antwi, K. B. (2022). Smiling vs. Frowning Faces: Community Participation for Sustainable Tourism in Ghanaian Communities. In I. Mensah & E. Afenyo-Agbe (Eds.), *Prospects and Challenges of Community-Based Tourism and Changing Demographics* (pp. 83–106). IGI Global. https://doi.org/10.4018/978-1-7998-7335-8.ch004

Biswas, A., & De, A. K. (2017). On Development of a Fuzzy Stochastic Programming Model with Its Application to Business Management. In S. Trivedi, S. Dey, A. Kumar, & T. Panda (Eds.), *Handbook of Research on Advanced Data Mining Techniques and Applications for Business Intelligence* (pp. 353–378). Hershey, PA: IGI Global. doi:10.4018/978-1-5225-2031-3.ch021

Boragnio, A., & Faracce Macia, C. (2021). "Taking Care of Yourself at Home": Use of E-Commerce About Food and Care During the COVID-19 Pandemic in the City of Buenos Aires. In M. Korstanje (Ed.), *Socio-Economic Effects and Recovery Efforts for the Rental Industry: Post-COVID-19 Strategies* (pp. 45–71). IGI Global. https://doi.org/10.4018/978-1-7998-7287-0.ch003

Borges, V. D. (2021). Happiness: The Basis for Public Policy in Tourism. In A. Perinotto, V. Mayer, & J. Soares (Eds.), *Rebuilding and Restructuring the Tourism Industry: Infusion of Happiness and Quality of Life* (pp. 1–25). IGI Global. https://doi.org/10.4018/978-1-7998-7239-9.ch001

Bücker, J., & Ernste, K. (2018). Use of Brand Heroes in Strategic Reputation Management: The Case of Bacardi, Adidas, and Daimler. In A. Erdemir (Ed.), *Reputation Management Techniques in Public Relations* (pp. 126–150). Hershey, PA: IGI Global. doi:10.4018/978-1-5225-3619-2.ch007

Buluk Eşitti, B. (2021). COVID-19 and Alternative Tourism: New Destinations and New Tourism Products. In M. Demir, A. Dalgıç, & F. Ergen (Eds.), *Handbook of Research on the Impacts and Implications of COVID-19 on the Tourism Industry* (pp. 786–805). IGI Global. https://doi.org/10.4018/978-1-7998-8231-2.ch038

Bureš, V. (2018). Industry 4.0 From the Systems Engineering Perspective: Alternative Holistic Framework Development. In R. Brunet-Thornton & F. Martinez (Eds.), *Analyzing the Impacts of Industry 4.0 in Modern Business Environments* (pp. 199–223). Hershey, PA: IGI Global. doi:10.4018/978-1-5225-3468-6.ch011

Buzady, Z. (2017). Resolving the Magic Cube of Effective Case Teaching: Benchmarking Case Teaching Practices in Emerging Markets – Insights from the Central European University Business School, Hungary. In D. Latusek (Ed.), *Case Studies as a Teaching Tool in Management Education* (pp. 79–103). Hershey, PA: IGI Global. doi:10.4018/978-1-5225-0770-3.ch005

Camillo, A. (2021). *Legal Matters, Risk Management, and Risk Prevention: From Forming a Business to Legal Representation*. IGI Global. doi:10.4018/978-1-7998-4342-9.ch004

Căpusneanu, S., & Topor, D. I. (2018). Business Ethics and Cost Management in SMEs: Theories of Business Ethics and Cost Management Ethos. In I. Oncioiu (Ed.), *Ethics and Decision-Making for Sustainable Business Practices* (pp. 109–127). Hershey, PA: IGI Global. doi:10.4018/978-1-5225-3773-1.ch007

Chan, R. L., Mo, P. L., & Moon, K. K. (2018). Strategic and Tactical Measures in Managing Enterprise Risks: A Study of the Textile and Apparel Industry. In K. Strang, M. Korstanje, & N. Vajjhala (Eds.), *Research, Practices, and Innovations in Global Risk and Contingency Management* (pp. 1–19). Hershey, PA: IGI Global. doi:10.4018/978-1-5225-4754-9.ch001

Charlier, S. D., Burke-Smalley, L. A., & Fisher, S. L. (2018). Undergraduate Programs in the U.S: A Contextual and Content-Based Analysis. In J. Mendy (Ed.), *Teaching Human Resources and Organizational Behavior at the College Level* (pp. 26–57). Hershey, PA: IGI Global. doi:10.4018/978-1-5225-2820-3.ch002

Chumillas, J., Güell, M., & Quer, P. (2022). The Use of ICT in Tourist and Educational Literary Routes: The Role of the Guide. In C. Ramos, S. Quinteiro, & A. Gonçalves (Eds.), *ICT as Innovator Between Tourism and Culture* (pp. 15–29). IGI Global. https://doi.org/10.4018/978-1-7998-8165-0.ch002

Dahlberg, T., Kivijärvi, H., & Saarinen, T. (2017). IT Investment Consistency and Other Factors Influencing the Success of IT Performance. In S. De Haes & W. Van Grembergen (Eds.), *Strategic IT Governance and Alignment in Business Settings* (pp. 176–208). Hershey, PA: IGI Global. doi:10.4018/978-1-5225-0861-8.ch007

Damnjanović, A. M. (2017). Knowledge Management Optimization through IT and E-Business Utilization: A Qualitative Study on Serbian SMEs. In M. Vemić (Ed.), *Optimal Management Strategies in Small and Medium Enterprises* (pp. 249–267). Hershey, PA: IGI Global. doi:10.4018/978-1-5225-1949-2.ch012

Daneshpour, H. (2017). Integrating Sustainable Development into Project Portfolio Management through Application of Open Innovation. In M. Vemić (Ed.), *Optimal Management Strategies in Small and Medium Enterprises* (pp. 370–387). Hershey, PA: IGI Global. doi:10.4018/978-1-5225-1949-2.ch017

Daniel, A. D., & Reis de Castro, V. (2018). Entrepreneurship Education: How to Measure the Impact on Nascent Entrepreneurs. In A. Carrizo Moreira, J. Guilherme Leitão Dantas, & F. Manuel Valente (Eds.), *Nascent Entrepreneurship and Successful New Venture Creation* (pp. 85–110). Hershey, PA: IGI Global. doi:10.4018/978-1-5225-2936-1.ch004

David, R., Swami, B. N., & Tangirala, S. (2018). Ethics Impact on Knowledge Management in Organizational Development: A Case Study. In N. Baporikar (Ed.), *Global Practices in Knowledge Management for Societal and Organizational Development* (pp. 19–45). Hershey, PA: IGI Global. doi:10.4018/978-1-5225-3009-1.ch002

De Uña-Álvarez, E., & Villarino-Pérez, M. (2022). Fostering Ecocultural Resources, Identity, and Tourism in Inland Territories (Galicia, NW Spain). In G. Fernandes (Ed.), *Challenges and New Opportunities for Tourism in Inland Territories: Ecocultural Resources and Sustainable Initiatives* (pp. 1-16). IGI Global. https://doi.org/10.4018/978-1-7998-7339-6.ch001

Delias, P., & Lakiotaki, K. (2018). Discovering Process Horizontal Boundaries to Facilitate Process Comprehension. *International Journal of Operations Research and Information Systems*, *9*(2), 1–31. doi:10.4018/IJORIS.2018040101

Denholm, J., & Lee-Davies, L. (2018). Success Factors for Games in Business and Project Management. In *Enhancing Education and Training Initiatives Through Serious Games* (pp. 34–68). Hershey, PA: IGI Global. doi:10.4018/978-1-5225-3689-5.ch002

Deshpande, M. (2017). Best Practices in Management Institutions for Global Leadership: Policy Aspects. In N. Baporikar (Ed.), *Management Education for Global Leadership* (pp. 1–27). Hershey, PA: IGI Global. doi:10.4018/978-1-5225-1013-0.ch001

Deshpande, M. (2018). Policy Perspectives for SMEs Knowledge Management. In N. Baporikar (Ed.), *Knowledge Integration Strategies for Entrepreneurship and Sustainability* (pp. 23–46). Hershey, PA: IGI Global. doi:10.4018/978-1-5225-5115-7.ch002

Dezdar, S. (2017). ERP Implementation Projects in Asian Countries: A Comparative Study on Iran and China. *International Journal of Information Technology Project Management*, *8*(3), 52–68. doi:10.4018/IJITPM.2017070104

Domingos, D., Respício, A., & Martinho, R. (2017). Reliability of IoT-Aware BPMN Healthcare Processes. In C. Reis & M. Maximiano (Eds.), *Internet of Things and Advanced Application in Healthcare* (pp. 214–248). Hershey, PA: IGI Global. doi:10.4018/978-1-5225-1820-4.ch008

Dosumu, O., Hussain, J., & El-Gohary, H. (2017). An Exploratory Study of the Impact of Government Policies on the Development of Small and Medium Enterprises in Developing Countries: The Case of Nigeria. *International Journal of Customer Relationship Marketing and Management*, *8*(4), 51–62. doi:10.4018/IJCRMM.2017100104

Durst, S., Bruns, G., & Edvardsson, I. R. (2017). Retaining Knowledge in Smaller Building and Construction Firms. *International Journal of Knowledge and Systems Science*, *8*(3), 1–12. doi:10.4018/IJKSS.2017070101

Edvardsson, I. R., & Durst, S. (2017). Outsourcing, Knowledge, and Learning: A Critical Review. *International Journal of Knowledge-Based Organizations*, *7*(2), 13–26. doi:10.4018/IJKBO.2017040102

Edwards, J. S. (2018). Integrating Knowledge Management and Business Processes. In M. Khosrow-Pour, D.B.A. (Ed.), Encyclopedia of Information Science and Technology, Fourth Edition (pp. 5046-5055). Hershey, PA: IGI Global. doi:10.4018/978-1-5225-2255-3.ch437

Eichelberger, S., & Peters, M. (2021). Family Firm Management in Turbulent Times: Opportunities for Responsible Tourism. In A. Zehrer, G. Glowka, K. Schwaiger, & V. Ranacher-Lackner (Eds.), *Resiliency Models and Addressing Future Risks for Family Firms in the Tourism Industry* (pp. 103–124). IGI Global. https://doi.org/10.4018/978-1-7998-7352-5.ch005

Eide, D., Hjalager, A., & Hansen, M. (2022). Innovative Certifications in Adventure Tourism: Attributes and Diffusion. In R. Augusto Costa, F. Brandão, Z. Breda, & C. Costa (Eds.), *Planning and Managing the Experience Economy in Tourism* (pp. 161-175). IGI Global. https://doi.org/10.4018/978-1-7998-8775-1.ch009

Ejiogu, A. O. (2018). Economics of Farm Management. In *Agricultural Finance and Opportunities for Investment and Expansion* (pp. 56–72). Hershey, PA: IGI Global. doi:10.4018/978-1-5225-3059-6.ch003

Ekanem, I., & Abiade, G. E. (2018). Factors Influencing the Use of E-Commerce by Small Enterprises in Nigeria. *International Journal of ICT Research in Africa and the Middle East*, *7*(1), 37–53. doi:10.4018/IJICTRAME.2018010103

Ekanem, I., & Alrossais, L. A. (2017). Succession Challenges Facing Family Businesses in Saudi Arabia. In P. Zgheib (Ed.), *Entrepreneurship and Business Innovation in the Middle East* (pp. 122–146). Hershey, PA: IGI Global. doi:10.4018/978-1-5225-2066-5.ch007

El Faquih, L., & Fredj, M. (2017). Ontology-Based Framework for Quality in Configurable Process Models. *Journal of Electronic Commerce in Organizations*, *15*(2), 48–60. doi:10.4018/JECO.2017040104

Faisal, M. N., & Talib, F. (2017). Building Ambidextrous Supply Chains in SMEs: How to Tackle the Barriers? *International Journal of Information Systems and Supply Chain Management*, *10*(4), 80–100. doi:10.4018/IJISSCM.2017100105

Fernandes, T. M., Gomes, J., & Romão, M. (2017). Investments in E-Government: A Benefit Management Case Study. *International Journal of Electronic Government Research*, *13*(3), 1–17. doi:10.4018/IJEGR.2017070101

Figueira, L. M., Honrado, G. R., & Dionísio, M. S. (2021). Human Capital Management in the Tourism Industry in Portugal. In V. Costa, A. Moura, & M. Mira (Eds.), *Handbook of Research on Human Capital and People Management in the Tourism Industry* (pp. 1–19). IGI Global. doi:10.4018/978-1-7998-4318-4.ch001

Gao, S. S., Oreal, S., & Zhang, J. (2018). Contemporary Financial Risk Management Perceptions and Practices of Small-Sized Chinese Businesses. In I. Management Association (Ed.), Global Business Expansion: Concepts, Methodologies, Tools, and Applications (pp. 917-931). Hershey, PA: IGI Global. doi:10.4018/978-1-5225-5481-3.ch041

Garg, R., & Berning, S. C. (2017). Indigenous Chinese Management Philosophies: Key Concepts and Relevance for Modern Chinese Firms. In B. Christiansen & G. Koc (Eds.), *Transcontinental Strategies for Industrial Development and Economic Growth* (pp. 43–57). Hershey, PA: IGI Global. doi:10.4018/978-1-5225-2160-0.ch003

Gencer, Y. G. (2017). Supply Chain Management in Retailing Business. In U. Akkucuk (Ed.), *Ethics and Sustainability in Global Supply Chain Management* (pp. 197–210). Hershey, PA: IGI Global. doi:10.4018/978-1-5225-2036-8.ch011

Gera, R., Arora, S., & Malik, S. (2021). Emotional Labor in the Tourism Industry: Strategies, Antecedents, and Outcomes. In V. Costa, A. Moura, & M. Mira (Eds.), *Handbook of Research on Human Capital and People Management in the Tourism Industry* (pp. 73–91). IGI Global. https://doi.org/10.4018/978-1-7998-4318-4.ch004

Giacosa, E. (2018). The Increasing of the Regional Development Thanks to the Luxury Business Innovation. In L. Carvalho (Ed.), *Handbook of Research on Entrepreneurial Ecosystems and Social Dynamics in a Globalized World* (pp. 260–273). Hershey, PA: IGI Global. doi:10.4018/978-1-5225-3525-6.ch011

Glowka, G., Tusch, M., & Zehrer, A. (2021). The Risk Perception of Family Business Owner-Manager in the Tourism Industry: A Qualitative Comparison of the Intra-Firm Senior and Junior Generation. In A. Zehrer, G. Glowka, K. Schwaiger, & V. Ranacher-Lackner (Eds.), *Resiliency Models and Addressing Future Risks for Family Firms in the Tourism Industry* (pp. 126–153). IGI Global. https://doi.org/10.4018/978-1-7998-7352-5.ch006

Glykas, M., & George, J. (2017). Quality and Process Management Systems in the UAE Maritime Industry. *International Journal of Productivity Management and Assessment Technologies*, *5*(1), 20–39. doi:10.4018/IJPMAT.2017010102

Glykas, M., Valiris, G., Kokkinaki, A., & Koutsoukou, Z. (2018). Banking Business Process Management Implementation. *International Journal of Productivity Management and Assessment Technologies*, *6*(1), 50–69. doi:10.4018/IJPMAT.2018010104

Gomes, J., & Romão, M. (2017). The Balanced Scorecard: Keeping Updated and Aligned with Today's Business Trends. *International Journal of Productivity Management and Assessment Technologies*, *5*(2), 1–15. doi:10.4018/IJPMAT.2017070101

Gomes, J., & Romão, M. (2017). Aligning Information Systems and Technology with Benefit Management and Balanced Scorecard. In S. De Haes & W. Van Grembergen (Eds.), *Strategic IT Governance and Alignment in Business Settings* (pp. 112–131). Hershey, PA: IGI Global. doi:10.4018/978-1-5225-0861-8.ch005

Goyal, A. (2021). Communicating and Building Destination Brands With New Media. In M. Dinis, L. Bonixe, S. Lamy, & Z. Breda (Eds.), *Impact of New Media in Tourism* (pp. 1-20). IGI Global. https://doi.org/10.4018/978-1-7998-7095-1.ch001

Grefen, P., & Turetken, O. (2017). Advanced Business Process Management in Networked E-Business Scenarios. *International Journal of E-Business Research*, *13*(4), 70–104. doi:10.4018/IJEBR.2017100105

Guasca, M., Van Broeck, A. M., & Vanneste, D. (2021). Tourism and the Social Reintegration of Colombian Ex-Combatants. In J. da Silva, Z. Breda, & F. Carbone (Eds.), *Role and Impact of Tourism in Peacebuilding and Conflict Transformation* (pp. 66-86). IGI Global. https://doi.org/10.4018/978-1-7998-5053-3.ch005

Haider, A., & Saetang, S. (2017). Strategic IT Alignment in Service Sector. In S. Rozenes & Y. Cohen (Eds.), *Handbook of Research on Strategic Alliances and Value Co-Creation in the Service Industry* (pp. 231–258). Hershey, PA: IGI Global. doi:10.4018/978-1-5225-2084-9.ch012

Hajilari, A. B., Ghadaksaz, M., & Fasghandis, G. S. (2017). Assessing Organizational Readiness for Implementing ERP System Using Fuzzy Expert System Approach. *International Journal of Enterprise Information Systems*, *13*(1), 67–85. doi:10.4018/IJEIS.2017010105

Haldorai, A., Ramu, A., & Murugan, S. (2018). Social Aware Cognitive Radio Networks: Effectiveness of Social Networks as a Strategic Tool for Organizational Business Management. In H. Bansal, G. Shrivastava, G. Nguyen, & L. Stanciu (Eds.), *Social Network Analytics for Contemporary Business Organizations* (pp. 188–202). Hershey, PA: IGI Global. doi:10.4018/978-1-5225-5097-6.ch010

Hall, O. P. Jr. (2017). Social Media Driven Management Education. *International Journal of Knowledge-Based Organizations*, *7*(2), 43–59. doi:10.4018/IJKBO.2017040104

Hanifah, H., Halim, H. A., Ahmad, N. H., & Vafaei-Zadeh, A. (2017). Innovation Culture as a Mediator Between Specific Human Capital and Innovation Performance Among Bumiputera SMEs in Malaysia. In N. Ahmad, T. Ramayah, H. Halim, & S. Rahman (Eds.), *Handbook of Research on Small and Medium Enterprises in Developing Countries* (pp. 261–279). Hershey, PA: IGI Global. doi:10.4018/978-1-5225-2165-5.ch012

Hartlieb, S., & Silvius, G. (2017). Handling Uncertainty in Project Management and Business Development: Similarities and Differences. In Y. Raydugin (Ed.), *Handbook of Research on Leveraging Risk and Uncertainties for Effective Project Management* (pp. 337–362). Hershey, PA: IGI Global. doi:10.4018/978-1-5225-1790-0.ch016

Hass, K. B. (2017). Living on the Edge: Managing Project Complexity. In Y. Raydugin (Ed.), *Handbook of Research on Leveraging Risk and Uncertainties for Effective Project Management* (pp. 177–201). Hershey, PA: IGI Global. doi:10.4018/978-1-5225-1790-0.ch009

Hawking, P., & Carmine Sellitto, C. (2017). Developing an Effective Strategy for Organizational Business Intelligence. In M. Tavana (Ed.), *Enterprise Information Systems and the Digitalization of Business Functions* (pp. 222–237). Hershey, PA: IGI Global. doi:10.4018/978-1-5225-2382-6.ch010

Hawking, P., & Sellitto, C. (2017). A Fast-Moving Consumer Goods Company and Business Intelligence Strategy Development. *International Journal of Enterprise Information Systems*, *13*(2), 22–33. doi:10.4018/IJEIS.2017040102

Hawking, P., & Sellitto, C. (2017). Business Intelligence Strategy: Two Case Studies. *International Journal of Business Intelligence Research*, *8*(2), 17–30. doi:10.4018/IJBIR.2017070102

Hee, W. J., Jalleh, G., Lai, H., & Lin, C. (2017). E-Commerce and IT Projects: Evaluation and Management Issues in Australian and Taiwanese Hospitals. *International Journal of Public Health Management and Ethics*, *2*(1), 69–90. doi:10.4018/IJPHME.2017010104

Hernandez, A. A. (2018). Exploring the Factors to Green IT Adoption of SMEs in the Philippines. *Journal of Cases on Information Technology*, *20*(2), 49–66. doi:10.4018/JCIT.2018040104

Hollman, A., Bickford, S., & Hollman, T. (2017). Cyber InSecurity: A Post-Mortem Attempt to Assess Cyber Problems from IT and Business Management Perspectives. *Journal of Cases on Information Technology, 19*(3), 42–70. doi:10.4018/JCIT.2017070104

Ibrahim, F., & Zainin, N. M. (2021). Exploring the Technological Impacts: The Case of Museums in Brunei Darussalam. *International Journal of Tourism and Hospitality Management in the Digital Age, 5*(1), 1–18. https://doi.org/10.4018/IJTHMDA.2021010101

Igbinakhase, I. (2017). Responsible and Sustainable Management Practices in Developing and Developed Business Environments. In Z. Fields (Ed.), *Collective Creativity for Responsible and Sustainable Business Practice* (pp. 180–207). Hershey, PA: IGI Global. doi:10.4018/978-1-5225-1823-5.ch010

Iwata, J. J., & Hoskins, R. G. (2017). Managing Indigenous Knowledge in Tanzania: A Business Perspective. In P. Jain & N. Mnjama (Eds.), *Managing Knowledge Resources and Records in Modern Organizations* (pp. 198–214). Hershey, PA: IGI Global. doi:10.4018/978-1-5225-1965-2.ch012

Jain, P. (2017). Ethical and Legal Issues in Knowledge Management Life-Cycle in Business. In P. Jain & N. Mnjama (Eds.), *Managing Knowledge Resources and Records in Modern Organizations* (pp. 82–101). Hershey, PA: IGI Global. doi:10.4018/978-1-5225-1965-2.ch006

James, S., & Hauli, E. (2017). Holistic Management Education at Tanzanian Rural Development Planning Institute. In N. Baporikar (Ed.), *Management Education for Global Leadership* (pp. 112–136). Hershey, PA: IGI Global. doi:10.4018/978-1-5225-1013-0.ch006

Janošková, M., Csikósová, A., & Čulková, K. (2018). Measurement of Company Performance as Part of Its Strategic Management. In R. Leon (Ed.), *Managerial Strategies for Business Sustainability During Turbulent Times* (pp. 309–335). Hershey, PA: IGI Global. doi:10.4018/978-1-5225-2716-9.ch017

Jean-Vasile, A., & Alecu, A. (2017). Theoretical and Practical Approaches in Understanding the Influences of Cost-Productivity-Profit Trinomial in Contemporary Enterprises. In A. Jean Vasile & D. Nicolò (Eds.), *Sustainable Entrepreneurship and Investments in the Green Economy* (pp. 28–62). Hershey, PA: IGI Global. doi:10.4018/978-1-5225-2075-7.ch002

Joia, L. A., & Correia, J. C. (2018). CIO Competencies From the IT Professional Perspective: Insights From Brazil. *Journal of Global Information Management, 26*(2), 74–103. doi:10.4018/JGIM.2018040104

Juma, A., & Mzera, N. (2017). Knowledge Management and Records Management and Competitive Advantage in Business. In P. Jain & N. Mnjama (Eds.), *Managing Knowledge Resources and Records in Modern Organizations* (pp. 15–28). Hershey, PA: IGI Global. doi:10.4018/978-1-5225-1965-2.ch002

K., I., & A, V. (2018). Monitoring and Auditing in the Cloud. In K. Munir (Ed.), *Cloud Computing Technologies for Green Enterprises* (pp. 318-350). Hershey, PA: IGI Global. https://doi.org/ doi:10.4018/978-1-5225-3038-1.ch013

Kabra, G., Ghosh, V., & Ramesh, A. (2018). Enterprise Integrated Business Process Management and Business Intelligence Framework for Business Process Sustainability. In A. Paul, D. Bhattacharyya, & S. Anand (Eds.), *Green Initiatives for Business Sustainability and Value Creation* (pp. 228–238). Hershey, PA: IGI Global. doi:10.4018/978-1-5225-2662-9.ch010

Kaoud, M. (2017). Investigation of Customer Knowledge Management: A Case Study Research. *International Journal of Service Science, Management, Engineering, and Technology*, *8*(2), 12–22. doi:10.4018/IJSSMET.2017040102

Katuu, S. (2018). A Comparative Assessment of Enterprise Content Management Maturity Models. In N. Gwangwava & M. Mutingi (Eds.), *E-Manufacturing and E-Service Strategies in Contemporary Organizations* (pp. 93–118). Hershey, PA: IGI Global. doi:10.4018/978-1-5225-3628-4.ch005

Khan, M. Y., & Abir, T. (2022). The Role of Social Media Marketing in the Tourism and Hospitality Industry: A Conceptual Study on Bangladesh. In C. Ramos, S. Quinteiro, & A. Gonçalves (Eds.), *ICT as Innovator Between Tourism and Culture* (pp. 213–229). IGI Global. https://doi.org/10.4018/978-1-7998-8165-0.ch013

Kinnunen, S., Ylä-Kujala, A., Marttonen-Arola, S., Kärri, T., & Baglee, D. (2018). Internet of Things in Asset Management: Insights from Industrial Professionals and Academia. *International Journal of Service Science, Management, Engineering, and Technology*, *9*(2), 104–119. doi:10.4018/IJSSMET.2018040105

Klein, A. Z., Sabino de Freitas, A., Machado, L., Freitas, J. C. Jr, Graziola, P. G. Jr, & Schlemmer, E. (2017). Virtual Worlds Applications for Management Education. In L. Tomei (Ed.), *Exploring the New Era of Technology-Infused Education* (pp. 279–299). Hershey, PA: IGI Global. doi:10.4018/978-1-5225-1709-2.ch017

Kővári, E., Saleh, M., & Steinbachné Hajmásy, G. (2022). The Impact of Corporate Digital Responsibility (CDR) on Internal Stakeholders' Satisfaction in Hungarian Upscale Hotels. In M. Valeri (Ed.), *New Governance and Management in Touristic Destinations* (pp. 35–51). IGI Global. https://doi.org/10.4018/978-1-6684-3889-3.ch003

Kożuch, B., & Jabłoński, A. (2017). Adopting the Concept of Business Models in Public Management. In M. Lewandowski & B. Kożuch (Eds.), *Public Sector Entrepreneurship and the Integration of Innovative Business Models* (pp. 10–46). Hershey, PA: IGI Global. doi:10.4018/978-1-5225-2215-7.ch002

Kumar, J., Adhikary, A., & Jha, A. (2017). Small Active Investors' Perceptions and Preferences Towards Tax Saving Mutual Fund Schemes in Eastern India: An Empirical Note. *International Journal of Asian Business and Information Management, 8*(2), 35–45. doi:10.4018/IJABIM.2017040103

Latusi, S., & Fissore, M. (2021). Pilgrimage Routes to Happiness: Comparing the Camino de Santiago and Via Francigena. In A. Perinotto, V. Mayer, & J. Soares (Eds.), *Rebuilding and Restructuring the Tourism Industry: Infusion of Happiness and Quality of Life* (pp. 157–182). IGI Global. https://doi.org/10.4018/978-1-7998-7239-9.ch008

Lavassani, K. M., & Movahedi, B. (2017). Applications Driven Information Systems: Beyond Networks toward Business Ecosystems. *International Journal of Innovation in the Digital Economy, 8*(1), 61–75. doi:10.4018/IJIDE.2017010104

Lazzareschi, V. H., & Brito, M. S. (2017). Strategic Information Management: Proposal of Business Project Model. In G. Jamil, A. Soares, & C. Pessoa (Eds.), *Handbook of Research on Information Management for Effective Logistics and Supply Chains* (pp. 59–88). Hershey, PA: IGI Global. doi:10.4018/978-1-5225-0973-8.ch004

Lechuga Sancho, M. P., & Martín Navarro, A. (2022). Evolution of the Literature on Social Responsibility in the Tourism Sector: A Systematic Literature Review. In G. Fernandes (Ed.), *Challenges and New Opportunities for Tourism in Inland Territories: Ecocultural Resources and Sustainable Initiatives* (pp. 169–186). IGI Global. https://doi.org/10.4018/978-1-7998-7339-6.ch010

Lederer, M., Kurz, M., & Lazarov, P. (2017). Usage and Suitability of Methods for Strategic Business Process Initiatives: A Multi Case Study Research. *International Journal of Productivity Management and Assessment Technologies, 5*(1), 40–51. doi:10.4018/IJPMAT.2017010103

Lee, I. (2017). A Social Enterprise Business Model and a Case Study of Pacific Community Ventures (PCV). In V. Potocan, M. Üngan, & Z. Nedelko (Eds.), *Handbook of Research on Managerial Solutions in Non-Profit Organizations* (pp. 182–204). Hershey, PA: IGI Global. doi:10.4018/978-1-5225-0731-4.ch009

Leon, L. A., Seal, K. C., Przasnyski, Z. H., & Wiedenman, I. (2017). Skills and Competencies Required for Jobs in Business Analytics: A Content Analysis of Job Advertisements Using Text Mining. *International Journal of Business Intelligence Research, 8*(1), 1–25. doi:10.4018/IJBIR.2017010101

Levy, C. L., & Elias, N. I. (2017). SOHO Users' Perceptions of Reliability and Continuity of Cloud-Based Services. In M. Moore (Ed.), *Cybersecurity Breaches and Issues Surrounding Online Threat Protection* (pp. 248–287). Hershey, PA: IGI Global. doi:10.4018/978-1-5225-1941-6.ch011

Levy, M. (2018). Change Management Serving Knowledge Management and Organizational Development: Reflections and Review. In N. Baporikar (Ed.), *Global Practices in Knowledge Management for Societal and Organizational Development* (pp. 256–270). Hershey, PA: IGI Global. doi:10.4018/978-1-5225-3009-1.ch012

Lewandowski, M. (2017). Public Organizations and Business Model Innovation: The Role of Public Service Design. In M. Lewandowski & B. Kożuch (Eds.), *Public Sector Entrepreneurship and the Integration of Innovative Business Models* (pp. 47–72). Hershey, PA: IGI Global. doi:10.4018/978-1-5225-2215-7.ch003

Lhannaoui, H., Kabbaj, M. I., & Bakkoury, Z. (2017). A Survey of Risk-Aware Business Process Modelling. *International Journal of Risk and Contingency Management, 6*(3), 14–26. doi:10.4018/IJRCM.2017070102

Li, J., Sun, W., Jiang, W., Yang, H., & Zhang, L. (2017). How the Nature of Exogenous Shocks and Crises Impact Company Performance?: The Effects of Industry Characteristics. *International Journal of Risk and Contingency Management, 6*(4), 40–55. doi:10.4018/IJRCM.2017100103

Lopez-Fernandez, M., Perez-Perez, M., Serrano-Bedia, A., & Cobo-Gonzalez, A. (2021). Small and Medium Tourism Enterprise Survival in Times of Crisis: "El Capricho de Gaudí. In D. Toubes & N. Araújo-Vila (Eds.), *Risk, Crisis, and Disaster Management in Small and Medium-Sized Tourism Enterprises* (pp. 103–129). IGI Global. doi:10.4018/978-1-7998-6996-2.ch005

Mahajan, A., Maidullah, S., & Hossain, M. R. (2022). Experience Toward Smart Tour Guide Apps in Travelling: An Analysis of Users' Reviews on Audio Odigos and Trip My Way. In R. Augusto Costa, F. Brandão, Z. Breda, & C. Costa (Eds.), *Planning and Managing the Experience Economy in Tourism* (pp. 255-273). IGI Global. https://doi.org/10.4018/978-1-7998-8775-1.ch014

Malega, P. (2017). Small and Medium Enterprises in the Slovak Republic: Status and Competitiveness of SMEs in the Global Markets and Possibilities of Optimization. In M. Vemić (Ed.), *Optimal Management Strategies in Small and Medium Enterprises* (pp. 102–124). Hershey, PA: IGI Global. doi:10.4018/978-1-5225-1949-2.ch006

Malewska, K. M. (2017). Intuition in Decision-Making on the Example of a Non-Profit Organization. In V. Potocan, M. Ünğan, & Z. Nedelko (Eds.), *Handbook of Research on Managerial Solutions in Non-Profit Organizations* (pp. 378–399). Hershey, PA: IGI Global. doi:10.4018/978-1-5225-0731-4.ch018

Maroofi, F. (2017). Entrepreneurial Orientation and Organizational Learning Ability Analysis for Innovation and Firm Performance. In N. Baporikar (Ed.), *Innovation and Shifting Perspectives in Management Education* (pp. 144–165). Hershey, PA: IGI Global. doi:10.4018/978-1-5225-1019-2.ch007

Marques, M., Moleiro, D., Brito, T. M., & Marques, T. (2021). Customer Relationship Management as an Important Relationship Marketing Tool: The Case of the Hospitality Industry in Estoril Coast. In M. Dinis, L. Bonixe, S. Lamy, & Z. Breda (Eds.), Impact of New Media in Tourism (pp. 39-56). IGI Global. https://doi.org/doi:10.4018/978-1-7998-7095-1.ch003

Martins, P. V., & Zacarias, M. (2017). A Web-based Tool for Business Process Improvement. *International Journal of Web Portals*, *9*(2), 68–84. doi:10.4018/IJWP.2017070104

Matthies, B., & Coners, A. (2017). Exploring the Conceptual Nature of e-Business Projects. *Journal of Electronic Commerce in Organizations*, *15*(3), 33–63. doi:10.4018/JECO.2017070103

Mayer, V. F., Fraga, C. C., & Silva, L. C. (2021). Contributions of Neurosciences to Studies of Well-Being in Tourism. In A. Perinotto, V. Mayer, & J. Soares (Eds.), *Rebuilding and Restructuring the Tourism Industry: Infusion of Happiness and Quality of Life* (pp. 108–128). IGI Global. https://doi.org/10.4018/978-1-7998-7239-9.ch006

McKee, J. (2018). Architecture as a Tool to Solve Business Planning Problems. In M. Khosrow-Pour, D.B.A. (Ed.), Encyclopedia of Information Science and Technology, Fourth Edition (pp. 573-586). Hershey, PA: IGI Global. doi:10.4018/978-1-5225-2255-3.ch050

McMurray, A. J., Cross, J., & Caponecchia, C. (2018). The Risk Management Profession in Australia: Business Continuity Plan Practices. In N. Bajgoric (Ed.), *Always-On Enterprise Information Systems for Modern Organizations* (pp. 112–129). Hershey, PA: IGI Global. doi:10.4018/978-1-5225-3704-5.ch006

Meddah, I. H., & Belkadi, K. (2018). Mining Patterns Using Business Process Management. In R. Hamou (Ed.), *Handbook of Research on Biomimicry in Information Retrieval and Knowledge Management* (pp. 78–89). Hershey, PA: IGI Global. doi:10.4018/978-1-5225-3004-6.ch005

Melian, A. G., & Camprubí, R. (2021). The Accessibility of Museum Websites: The Case of Barcelona. In C. Eusébio, L. Teixeira, & M. Carneiro (Eds.), *ICT Tools and Applications for Accessible Tourism* (pp. 234–255). IGI Global. https://doi.org/10.4018/978-1-7998-6428-8.ch011

Mendes, L. (2017). TQM and Knowledge Management: An Integrated Approach Towards Tacit Knowledge Management. In D. Jaziri-Bouagina & G. Jamil (Eds.), *Handbook of Research on Tacit Knowledge Management for Organizational Success* (pp. 236–263). Hershey, PA: IGI Global. doi:10.4018/978-1-5225-2394-9.ch009

Menezes, V. D., & Cavagnaro, E. (2021). Communicating Sustainable Initiatives in the Hotel Industry: The Case of the Hotel Jakarta Amsterdam. In F. Brandão, Z. Breda, R. Costa, & C. Costa (Eds.), *Handbook of Research on the Role of Tourism in Achieving Sustainable Development Goals* (pp. 224-234). IGI Global. https://doi.org/10.4018/978-1-7998-5691-7.ch013

Menezes, V. D., & Cavagnaro, E. (2021). Communicating Sustainable Initiatives in the Hotel Industry: The Case of the Hotel Jakarta Amsterdam. In F. Brandão, Z. Breda, R. Costa, & C. Costa (Eds.), *Handbook of Research on the Role of Tourism in Achieving Sustainable Development Goals* (pp. 224-234). IGI Global. https://doi.org/10.4018/978-1-7998-5691-7.ch013

Mitas, O., Bastiaansen, M., & Boode, W. (2022). If You're Happy, I'm Happy: Emotion Contagion at a Tourist Information Center. In R. Augusto Costa, F. Brandão, Z. Breda, & C. Costa (Eds.), *Planning and Managing the Experience Economy in Tourism* (pp. 122-140). IGI Global. https://doi.org/10.4018/978-1-7998-8775-1.ch007

Mnjama, N. M. (2017). Preservation of Recorded Information in Public and Private Sector Organizations. In P. Jain & N. Mnjama (Eds.), *Managing Knowledge Resources and Records in Modern Organizations* (pp. 149–167). Hershey, PA: IGI Global. doi:10.4018/978-1-5225-1965-2.ch009

Mokoqama, M., & Fields, Z. (2017). Principles of Responsible Management Education (PRME): Call for Responsible Management Education. In Z. Fields (Ed.), *Collective Creativity for Responsible and Sustainable Business Practice* (pp. 229–241). Hershey, PA: IGI Global. doi:10.4018/978-1-5225-1823-5.ch012

Monteiro, A., Lopes, S., & Carbone, F. (2021). Academic Mobility: Bridging Tourism and Peace Education. In J. da Silva, Z. Breda, & F. Carbone (Eds.), *Role and Impact of Tourism in Peacebuilding and Conflict Transformation* (pp. 275-301). IGI Global. https://doi.org/10.4018/978-1-7998-5053-3.ch016

Muniapan, B. (2017). Philosophy and Management: The Relevance of Vedanta in Management. In P. Ordóñez de Pablos (Ed.), *Managerial Strategies and Solutions for Business Success in Asia* (pp. 124–139). Hershey, PA: IGI Global. doi:10.4018/978-1-5225-1886-0.ch007

Murad, S. E., & Dowaji, S. (2017). Using Value-Based Approach for Managing Cloud-Based Services. In A. Turuk, B. Sahoo, & S. Addya (Eds.), *Resource Management and Efficiency in Cloud Computing Environments* (pp. 33–60). Hershey, PA: IGI Global. doi:10.4018/978-1-5225-1721-4.ch002

Mutahar, A. M., Daud, N. M., Thurasamy, R., Isaac, O., & Abdulsalam, R. (2018). The Mediating of Perceived Usefulness and Perceived Ease of Use: The Case of Mobile Banking in Yemen. *International Journal of Technology Diffusion*, *9*(2), 21–40. doi:10.4018/IJTD.2018040102

Naidoo, V. (2017). E-Learning and Management Education at African Universities. In N. Baporikar (Ed.), *Management Education for Global Leadership* (pp. 181–201). Hershey, PA: IGI Global. doi:10.4018/978-1-5225-1013-0.ch009

Naidoo, V., & Igbinakhase, I. (2018). Opportunities and Challenges of Knowledge Retention in SMEs. In N. Baporikar (Ed.), *Knowledge Integration Strategies for Entrepreneurship and Sustainability* (pp. 70–94). Hershey, PA: IGI Global. doi:10.4018/978-1-5225-5115-7.ch004

Naumov, N., & Costandachi, G. (2021). Creativity and Entrepreneurship: Gastronomic Tourism in Mexico. In J. Soares (Ed.), *Innovation and Entrepreneurial Opportunities in Community Tourism* (pp. 90–108). IGI Global. https://doi.org/10.4018/978-1-7998-4855-4.ch006

Nayak, S., & Prabhu, N. (2017). Paradigm Shift in Management Education: Need for a Cross Functional Perspective. In N. Baporikar (Ed.), *Management Education for Global Leadership* (pp. 241–255). Hershey, PA: IGI Global. doi:10.4018/978-1-5225-1013-0.ch012

Nedelko, Z., & Potocan, V. (2017). Management Solutions in Non-Profit Organizations: Case of Slovenia. In V. Potocan, M. Üngan, & Z. Nedelko (Eds.), *Handbook of Research on Managerial Solutions in Non-Profit Organizations* (pp. 1–22). Hershey, PA: IGI Global. doi:10.4018/978-1-5225-0731-4.ch001

Nedelko, Z., & Potocan, V. (2017). Priority of Management Tools Utilization among Managers: International Comparison. In V. Wang (Ed.), *Encyclopedia of Strategic Leadership and Management* (pp. 1083–1094). Hershey, PA: IGI Global. doi:10.4018/978-1-5225-1049-9.ch075

Nedelko, Z., Raudeliūnienė, J., & Črešnar, R. (2018). Knowledge Dynamics in Supply Chain Management. In N. Baporikar (Ed.), *Knowledge Integration Strategies for Entrepreneurship and Sustainability* (pp. 150–166). Hershey, PA: IGI Global. doi:10.4018/978-1-5225-5115-7.ch008

Nguyen, H. T., & Hipsher, S. A. (2018). Innovation and Creativity Used by Private Sector Firms in a Resources-Constrained Environment. In S. Hipsher (Ed.), *Examining the Private Sector's Role in Wealth Creation and Poverty Reduction* (pp. 219–238). Hershey, PA: IGI Global. doi:10.4018/978-1-5225-3117-3.ch010

Obicci, P. A. (2017). Risk Sharing in a Partnership. In *Risk Management Strategies in Public-Private Partnerships* (pp. 115–152). Hershey, PA: IGI Global. doi:10.4018/978-1-5225-2503-5.ch004

Obidallah, W. J., & Raahemi, B. (2017). Managing Changes in Service Oriented Virtual Organizations: A Structural and Procedural Framework to Facilitate the Process of Change. *Journal of Electronic Commerce in Organizations, 15*(1), 59–83. doi:10.4018/JECO.2017010104

Ojo, O. (2017). Impact of Innovation on the Entrepreneurial Success in Selected Business Enterprises in South-West Nigeria. *International Journal of Innovation in the Digital Economy, 8*(2), 29–38. doi:10.4018/IJIDE.2017040103

Okdinawati, L., Simatupang, T. M., & Sunitiyoso, Y. (2017). Multi-Agent Reinforcement Learning for Value Co-Creation of Collaborative Transportation Management (CTM). *International Journal of Information Systems and Supply Chain Management, 10*(3), 84–95. doi:10.4018/IJISSCM.2017070105

Olivera, V. A., & Carrillo, I. M. (2021). Organizational Culture: A Key Element for the Development of Mexican Micro and Small Tourist Companies. In J. Soares (Ed.), *Innovation and Entrepreneurial Opportunities in Community Tourism* (pp. 227–242). IGI Global. doi:10.4018/978-1-7998-4855-4.ch013

Ossorio, M. (2022). Corporate Museum Experiences in Enogastronomic Tourism. In R. Augusto Costa, F. Brandão, Z. Breda, & C. Costa (Eds.), Planning and Managing the Experience Economy in Tourism (pp. 107-121). IGI Global. https://doi.org/doi:10.4018/978-1-7998-8775-1.ch006

Ossorio, M. (2022). Enogastronomic Tourism in Times of Pandemic. In G. Fernandes (Ed.), *Challenges and New Opportunities for Tourism in Inland Territories: Ecocultural Resources and Sustainable Initiatives* (pp. 241–255). IGI Global. https://doi.org/10.4018/978-1-7998-7339-6.ch014

Özekici, Y. K. (2022). ICT as an Acculturative Agent and Its Role in the Tourism Context: Introduction, Acculturation Theory, Progress of the Acculturation Theory in Extant Literature. In C. Ramos, S. Quinteiro, & A. Gonçalves (Eds.), *ICT as Innovator Between Tourism and Culture* (pp. 42–66). IGI Global. https://doi.org/10.4018/978-1-7998-8165-0.ch004

Pal, K. (2018). Building High Quality Big Data-Based Applications in Supply Chains. In A. Kumar & S. Saurav (Eds.), *Supply Chain Management Strategies and Risk Assessment in Retail Environments* (pp. 1–24). Hershey, PA: IGI Global. doi:10.4018/978-1-5225-3056-5.ch001

Palos-Sanchez, P. R., & Correia, M. B. (2018). Perspectives of the Adoption of Cloud Computing in the Tourism Sector. In J. Rodrigues, C. Ramos, P. Cardoso, & C. Henriques (Eds.), *Handbook of Research on Technological Developments for Cultural Heritage and eTourism Applications* (pp. 377–400). Hershey, PA: IGI Global. doi:10.4018/978-1-5225-2927-9.ch018

Papadopoulou, G. (2021). Promoting Gender Equality and Women Empowerment in the Tourism Sector. In F. Brandão, Z. Breda, R. Costa, & C. Costa (Eds.), Handbook of Research on the Role of Tourism in Achieving Sustainable Development Goals (pp. 152-174). IGI Global. https://doi.org/ doi:10.4018/978-1-7998-5691-7.ch009

Papp-Váry, Á. F., & Tóth, T. Z. (2022). Analysis of Budapest as a Film Tourism Destination. In R. Baleiro & R. Pereira (Eds.), *Global Perspectives on Literary Tourism and Film-Induced Tourism* (pp. 257-279). IGI Global. https://doi.org/10.4018/978-1-7998-8262-6.ch014

Patiño, B. E. (2017). New Generation Management by Convergence and Individual Identity: A Systemic and Human-Oriented Approach. In N. Baporikar (Ed.), *Innovation and Shifting Perspectives in Management Education* (pp. 119–143). Hershey, PA: IGI Global. doi:10.4018/978-1-5225-1019-2.ch006

Patro, C. S. (2021). Digital Tourism: Influence of E-Marketing Technology. In M. Dinis, L. Bonixe, S. Lamy, & Z. Breda (Eds.), *Impact of New Media in Tourism* (pp. 234-254). IGI Global. https://doi.org/10.4018/978-1-7998-7095-1.ch014

Pawliczek, A., & Rössler, M. (2017). Knowledge of Management Tools and Systems in SMEs: Knowledge Transfer in Management. In A. Bencsik (Ed.), *Knowledge Management Initiatives and Strategies in Small and Medium Enterprises* (pp. 180–203). Hershey, PA: IGI Global. doi:10.4018/978-1-5225-1642-2.ch009

Pejic-Bach, M., Omazic, M. A., Aleksic, A., & Zoroja, J. (2018). Knowledge-Based Decision Making: A Multi-Case Analysis. In R. Leon (Ed.), *Managerial Strategies for Business Sustainability During Turbulent Times* (pp. 160–184). Hershey, PA: IGI Global. doi:10.4018/978-1-5225-2716-9.ch009

Perano, M., Hysa, X., & Calabrese, M. (2018). Strategic Planning, Cultural Context, and Business Continuity Management: Business Cases in the City of Shkoder. In A. Presenza & L. Sheehan (Eds.), *Geopolitics and Strategic Management in the Global Economy* (pp. 57–77). Hershey, PA: IGI Global. doi:10.4018/978-1-5225-2673-5.ch004

Pereira, R., Mira da Silva, M., & Lapão, L. V. (2017). IT Governance Maturity Patterns in Portuguese Healthcare. In S. De Haes & W. Van Grembergen (Eds.), *Strategic IT Governance and Alignment in Business Settings* (pp. 24–52). Hershey, PA: IGI Global. doi:10.4018/978-1-5225-0861-8.ch002

Pérez-Uribe, R. I., Torres, D. A., Jurado, S. P., & Prada, D. M. (2018). Cloud Tools for the Development of Project Management in SMEs. In R. Perez-Uribe, C. Salcedo-Perez, & D. Ocampo-Guzman (Eds.), *Handbook of Research on Intrapreneurship and Organizational Sustainability in SMEs* (pp. 95–120). Hershey, PA: IGI Global. doi:10.4018/978-1-5225-3543-0.ch005

Petrisor, I., & Cozmiuc, D. (2017). Global Supply Chain Management Organization at Siemens in the Advent of Industry 4.0. In L. Saglietto & C. Cezanne (Eds.), *Global Intermediation and Logistics Service Providers* (pp. 123–142). Hershey, PA: IGI Global. doi:10.4018/978-1-5225-2133-4.ch007

Pierce, J. M., Velliaris, D. M., & Edwards, J. (2017). A Living Case Study: A Journey Not a Destination. In N. Silton (Ed.), *Exploring the Benefits of Creativity in Education, Media, and the Arts* (pp. 158–178). Hershey, PA: IGI Global. doi:10.4018/978-1-5225-0504-4.ch008

Pipia, S., & Pipia, S. (2021). Challenges of Religious Tourism in the Conflict Region: An Example of Jerusalem. In E. Alaverdov & M. Bari (Eds.), *Global Development of Religious Tourism* (pp. 135-148). IGI Global. https://doi.org/10.4018/978-1-7998-5792-1.ch009

Poulaki, P., Kritikos, A., Vasilakis, N., & Valeri, M. (2022). The Contribution of Female Creativity to the Development of Gastronomic Tourism in Greece: The Case of the Island of Naxos in the South Aegean Region. In M. Valeri (Ed.), *New Governance and Management in Touristic Destinations* (pp. 246–258). IGI Global. https://doi.org/10.4018/978-1-6684-3889-3.ch015

Radosavljevic, M., & Andjelkovic, A. (2017). Multi-Criteria Decision Making Approach for Choosing Business Process for the Improvement: Upgrading of the Six Sigma Methodology. In J. Stanković, P. Delias, S. Marinković, & S. Rochhia (Eds.), *Tools and Techniques for Economic Decision Analysis* (pp. 225–247). Hershey, PA: IGI Global. doi:10.4018/978-1-5225-0959-2.ch011

Radovic, V. M. (2017). Corporate Sustainability and Responsibility and Disaster Risk Reduction: A Serbian Overview. In M. Camilleri (Ed.), *CSR 2.0 and the New Era of Corporate Citizenship* (pp. 147–164). Hershey, PA: IGI Global. doi:10.4018/978-1-5225-1842-6.ch008

Raghunath, K. M., Devi, S. L., & Patro, C. S. (2018). Impact of Risk Assessment Models on Risk Factors: A Holistic Outlook. In K. Strang, M. Korstanje, & N. Vajjhala (Eds.), *Research, Practices, and Innovations in Global Risk and Contingency Management* (pp. 134–153). Hershey, PA: IGI Global. doi:10.4018/978-1-5225-4754-9.ch008

Raman, A., & Goyal, D. P. (2017). Extending IMPLEMENT Framework for Enterprise Information Systems Implementation to Information System Innovation. In M. Tavana (Ed.), *Enterprise Information Systems and the Digitalization of Business Functions* (pp. 137–177). Hershey, PA: IGI Global. doi:10.4018/978-1-5225-2382-6.ch007

Rao, Y., & Zhang, Y. (2017). The Construction and Development of Academic Library Digital Special Subject Databases. In L. Ruan, Q. Zhu, & Y. Ye (Eds.), *Academic Library Development and Administration in China* (pp. 163–183). Hershey, PA: IGI Global. doi:10.4018/978-1-5225-0550-1.ch010

Ravasan, A. Z., Mohammadi, M. M., & Hamidi, H. (2018). An Investigation Into the Critical Success Factors of Implementing Information Technology Service Management Frameworks. In K. Jakobs (Ed.), *Corporate and Global Standardization Initiatives in Contemporary Society* (pp. 200–218). Hershey, PA: IGI Global. doi:10.4018/978-1-5225-5320-5.ch009

Rezaie, S., Mirabedini, S. J., & Abtahi, A. (2018). Designing a Model for Implementation of Business Intelligence in the Banking Industry. *International Journal of Enterprise Information Systems*, *14*(1), 77–103. doi:10.4018/IJEIS.2018010105

Richards, V., Matthews, N., Williams, O. J., & Khan, Z. (2021). The Challenges of Accessible Tourism Information Systems for Tourists With Vision Impairment: Sensory Communications Beyond the Screen. In C. Eusébio, L. Teixeira, & M. Carneiro (Eds.), *ICT Tools and Applications for Accessible Tourism* (pp. 26–54). IGI Global. https://doi.org/10.4018/978-1-7998-6428-8.ch002

Rodrigues de Souza Neto, V., & Marques, O. (2021). Rural Tourism Fostering Welfare Through Sustainable Development: A Conceptual Approach. In A. Perinotto, V. Mayer, & J. Soares (Eds.), *Rebuilding and Restructuring the Tourism Industry: Infusion of Happiness and Quality of Life* (pp. 38–57). IGI Global. https://doi.org/10.4018/978-1-7998-7239-9.ch003

Romano, L., Grimaldi, R., & Colasuonno, F. S. (2017). Demand Management as a Success Factor in Project Portfolio Management. In L. Romano (Ed.), *Project Portfolio Management Strategies for Effective Organizational Operations* (pp. 202–219). Hershey, PA: IGI Global. doi:10.4018/978-1-5225-2151-8.ch008

Rubio-Escuderos, L., & García-Andreu, H. (2021). Competitiveness Factors of Accessible Tourism E-Travel Agencies. In C. Eusébio, L. Teixeira, & M. Carneiro (Eds.), *ICT Tools and Applications for Accessible Tourism* (pp. 196–217). IGI Global. https://doi.org/10.4018/978-1-7998-6428-8.ch009

Rucci, A. C., Porto, N., Darcy, S., & Becka, L. (2021). Smart and Accessible Cities?: Not Always – The Case for Accessible Tourism Initiatives in Buenos Aries and Sydney. In C. Eusébio, L. Teixeira, & M. Carneiro (Eds.), *ICT Tools and Applications for Accessible Tourism* (pp. 115–145). IGI Global. https://doi.org/10.4018/978-1-7998-6428-8.ch006

Ruhi, U. (2018). Towards an Interdisciplinary Socio-Technical Definition of Virtual Communities. In M. Khosrow-Pour, D.B.A. (Ed.), Encyclopedia of Information Science and Technology, Fourth Edition (pp. 4278-4295). Hershey, PA: IGI Global. doi:10.4018/978-1-5225-2255-3.ch371

Ryan, L., Catena, M., Ros, P., & Stephens, S. (2021). Designing Entrepreneurial Ecosystems to Support Resource Management in the Tourism Industry. In V. Costa, A. Moura, & M. Mira (Eds.), *Handbook of Research on Human Capital and People Management in the Tourism Industry* (pp. 265–281). IGI Global. https://doi.org/10.4018/978-1-7998-4318-4.ch013

Sabuncu, I. (2021). Understanding Tourist Perceptions and Expectations During Pandemic Through Social Media Big Data. In M. Demir, A. Dalgıç, & F. Ergen (Eds.), *Handbook of Research on the Impacts and Implications of COVID-19 on the Tourism Industry* (pp. 330–350). IGI Global. https://doi.org/10.4018/978-1-7998-8231-2.ch016

Safari, M. R., & Jiang, Q. (2018). The Theory and Practice of IT Governance Maturity and Strategies Alignment: Evidence From Banking Industry. *Journal of Global Information Management, 26*(2), 127–146. doi:10.4018/JGIM.2018040106

Sahoo, J., Pati, B., & Mohanty, B. (2017). Knowledge Management as an Academic Discipline: An Assessment. In B. Gunjal (Ed.), *Managing Knowledge and Scholarly Assets in Academic Libraries* (pp. 99–126). Hershey, PA: IGI Global. doi:10.4018/978-1-5225-1741-2.ch005

Saini, D. (2017). Relevance of Teaching Values and Ethics in Management Education. In N. Baporikar (Ed.), *Management Education for Global Leadership* (pp. 90–111). Hershey, PA: IGI Global. doi:10.4018/978-1-5225-1013-0.ch005

Sambhanthan, A. (2017). Assessing and Benchmarking Sustainability in Organisations: An Integrated Conceptual Model. *International Journal of Systems and Service-Oriented Engineering, 7*(4), 22–43. doi:10.4018/IJSSOE.2017100102

Sambhanthan, A., & Potdar, V. (2017). A Study of the Parameters Impacting Sustainability in Information Technology Organizations. *International Journal of Knowledge-Based Organizations, 7*(3), 27–39. doi:10.4018/IJKBO.2017070103

Sánchez-Fernández, M. D., & Manríquez, M. R. (2018). The Entrepreneurial Spirit Based on Social Values: The Digital Generation. In P. Isaias & L. Carvalho (Eds.), *User Innovation and the Entrepreneurship Phenomenon in the Digital Economy* (pp. 173–193). Hershey, PA: IGI Global. doi:10.4018/978-1-5225-2826-5.ch009

Sanchez-Ruiz, L., & Blanco, B. (2017). Process Management for SMEs: Barriers, Enablers, and Benefits. In M. Vemić (Ed.), *Optimal Management Strategies in Small and Medium Enterprises* (pp. 293–319). Hershey, PA: IGI Global. doi:10.4018/978-1-5225-1949-2.ch014

Sanz, L. F., Gómez-Pérez, J., & Castillo-Martinez, A. (2018). Analysis of the European ICT Competence Frameworks. In V. Ahuja & S. Rathore (Eds.), *Multidisciplinary Perspectives on Human Capital and Information Technology Professionals* (pp. 225–245). Hershey, PA: IGI Global. doi:10.4018/978-1-5225-5297-0.ch012

Sarvepalli, A., & Godin, J. (2017). Business Process Management in the Classroom. *Journal of Cases on Information Technology, 19*(2), 17–28. doi:10.4018/JCIT.2017040102

Saxena, G. G., & Saxena, A. (2021). Host Community Role in Medical Tourism Development. In M. Singh & S. Kumaran (Eds.), *Growth of the Medical Tourism Industry and Its Impact on Society: Emerging Research and Opportunities* (pp. 105–127). IGI Global. https://doi.org/10.4018/978-1-7998-3427-4.ch006

Saygili, E. E., Ozturkoglu, Y., & Kocakulah, M. C. (2017). End Users' Perceptions of Critical Success Factors in ERP Applications. *International Journal of Enterprise Information Systems, 13*(4), 58–75. doi:10.4018/IJEIS.2017100104

Saygili, E. E., & Saygili, A. T. (2017). Contemporary Issues in Enterprise Information Systems: A Critical Review of CSFs in ERP Implementations. In M. Tavana (Ed.), *Enterprise Information Systems and the Digitalization of Business Functions* (pp. 120–136). Hershey, PA: IGI Global. doi:10.4018/978-1-5225-2382-6.ch006

Schwaiger, K. M., & Zehrer, A. (2021). The COVID-19 Pandemic and Organizational Resilience in Hospitality Family Firms: A Qualitative Approach. In A. Zehrer, G. Glowka, K. Schwaiger, & V. Ranacher-Lackner (Eds.), *Resiliency Models and Addressing Future Risks for Family Firms in the Tourism Industry* (pp. 32–49). IGI Global. https://doi.org/10.4018/978-1-7998-7352-5.ch002

Scott, N., & Campos, A. C. (2022). Cognitive Science of Tourism Experiences. In R. Augusto Costa, F. Brandão, Z. Breda, & C. Costa (Eds.), Planning and Managing the Experience Economy in Tourism (pp. 1-21). IGI Global. https://doi.org/ doi:10.4018/978-1-7998-8775-1.ch001

Seidenstricker, S., & Antonino, A. (2018). Business Model Innovation-Oriented Technology Management for Emergent Technologies. In M. Khosrow-Pour, D.B.A. (Ed.), Encyclopedia of Information Science and Technology, Fourth Edition (pp. 4560-4569). Hershey, PA: IGI Global. doi:10.4018/978-1-5225-2255-3.ch396

Selvi, M. S. (2021). Changes in Tourism Sales and Marketing Post COVID-19. In M. Demir, A. Dalgıç, & F. Ergen (Eds.), *Handbook of Research on the Impacts and Implications of COVID-19 on the Tourism Industry* (pp. 437–460). IGI Global. doi:10.4018/978-1-7998-8231-2.ch021

Senaratne, S., & Gunarathne, A. D. (2017). Excellence Perspective for Management Education from a Global Accountants' Hub in Asia. In N. Baporikar (Ed.), *Management Education for Global Leadership* (pp. 158–180). Hershey, PA: IGI Global. doi:10.4018/978-1-5225-1013-0.ch008

Sensuse, D. I., & Cahyaningsih, E. (2018). Knowledge Management Models: A Summative Review. *International Journal of Information Systems in the Service Sector, 10*(1), 71–100. doi:10.4018/IJISSS.2018010105

Seth, M., Goyal, D., & Kiran, R. (2017). Diminution of Impediments in Implementation of Supply Chain Management Information System for Enhancing its Effectiveness in Indian Automobile Industry. *Journal of Global Information Management, 25*(3), 1–20. doi:10.4018/JGIM.2017070101

Seyal, A. H., & Rahman, M. N. (2017). Investigating Impact of Inter-Organizational Factors in Measuring ERP Systems Success: Bruneian Perspectives. In M. Tavana (Ed.), *Enterprise Information Systems and the Digitalization of Business Functions* (pp. 178–204). Hershey, PA: IGI Global. doi:10.4018/978-1-5225-2382-6.ch008

Shaqrah, A. A. (2018). Analyzing Business Intelligence Systems Based on 7s Model of McKinsey. *International Journal of Business Intelligence Research, 9*(1), 53–63. doi:10.4018/IJBIR.2018010104

Sharma, A. J. (2017). Enhancing Sustainability through Experiential Learning in Management Education. In N. Baporikar (Ed.), *Management Education for Global Leadership* (pp. 256–274). Hershey, PA: IGI Global. doi:10.4018/978-1-5225-1013-0.ch013

Shetty, K. P. (2017). Responsible Global Leadership: Ethical Challenges in Management Education. In N. Baporikar (Ed.), *Innovation and Shifting Perspectives in Management Education* (pp. 194–223). Hershey, PA: IGI Global. doi:10.4018/978-1-5225-1019-2.ch009

Sinthupundaja, J., & Kohda, Y. (2017). Effects of Corporate Social Responsibility and Creating Shared Value on Sustainability. *International Journal of Sustainable Entrepreneurship and Corporate Social Responsibility, 2*(1), 27–38. doi:10.4018/IJSECSR.2017010103

Škarica, I., & Hrgović, A. V. (2018). Implementation of Total Quality Management Principles in Public Health Institutes in the Republic of Croatia. *International Journal of Productivity Management and Assessment Technologies, 6*(1), 1–16. doi:10.4018/IJPMAT.2018010101

Skokic, V. (2021). How Small Hotel Owners Practice Resilience: Longitudinal Study Among Small Family Hotels in Croatia. In A. Zehrer, G. Glowka, K. Schwaiger, & V. Ranacher-Lackner (Eds.), *Resiliency Models and Addressing Future Risks for Family Firms in the Tourism Industry* (pp. 50–73). IGI Global. doi:10.4018/978-1-7998-7352-5.ch003

Smuts, H., Kotzé, P., Van der Merwe, A., & Loock, M. (2017). Framework for Managing Shared Knowledge in an Information Systems Outsourcing Context. *International Journal of Knowledge Management, 13*(4), 1–30. doi:10.4018/IJKM.2017100101

Sousa, M. J., Cruz, R., Dias, I., & Caracol, C. (2017). Information Management Systems in the Supply Chain. In G. Jamil, A. Soares, & C. Pessoa (Eds.), *Handbook of Research on Information Management for Effective Logistics and Supply Chains* (pp. 469–485). Hershey, PA: IGI Global. doi:10.4018/978-1-5225-0973-8.ch025

Spremic, M., Turulja, L., & Bajgoric, N. (2018). Two Approaches in Assessing Business Continuity Management Attitudes in the Organizational Context. In N. Bajgoric (Ed.), *Always-On Enterprise Information Systems for Modern Organizations* (pp. 159–183). Hershey, PA: IGI Global. doi:10.4018/978-1-5225-3704-5.ch008

Steenkamp, A. L. (2018). Some Insights in Computer Science and Information Technology. In *Examining the Changing Role of Supervision in Doctoral Research Projects: Emerging Research and Opportunities* (pp. 113–133). Hershey, PA: IGI Global. doi:10.4018/978-1-5225-2610-0.ch005

Stipanović, C., Rudan, E., & Zubović, V. (2022). Reaching the New Tourist Through Creativity: Sustainable Development Challenges in Croatian Coastal Towns. In M. Valeri (Ed.), *New Governance and Management in Touristic Destinations* (pp. 231–245). IGI Global. https://doi.org/10.4018/978-1-6684-3889-3.ch014

Tabach, A., & Croteau, A. (2017). Configurations of Information Technology Governance Practices and Business Unit Performance. *International Journal of IT/Business Alignment and Governance, 8*(2), 1–27. doi:10.4018/IJITBAG.2017070101

Talaue, G. M., & Iqbal, T. (2017). Assessment of e-Business Mode of Selected Private Universities in the Philippines and Pakistan. *International Journal of Online Marketing, 7*(4), 63–77. doi:10.4018/IJOM.2017100105

Tam, G. C. (2017). Project Manager Sustainability Competence. In *Managerial Strategies and Green Solutions for Project Sustainability* (pp. 178–207). Hershey, PA: IGI Global. doi:10.4018/978-1-5225-2371-0.ch008

Tambo, T. (2018). Fashion Retail Innovation: About Context, Antecedents, and Outcome in Technological Change Projects. In I. Management Association (Ed.), Fashion and Textiles: Breakthroughs in Research and Practice (pp. 233-260). Hershey, PA: IGI Global. https://doi.org/ doi:10.4018/978-1-5225-3432-7.ch010

Tantau, A. D., & Frăţilă, L. C. (2018). Information and Management System for Renewable Energy Business. In *Entrepreneurship and Business Development in the Renewable Energy Sector* (pp. 200–244). Hershey, PA: IGI Global. doi:10.4018/978-1-5225-3625-3.ch006

Teixeira, N., Pardal, P. N., & Rafael, B. G. (2018). Internationalization, Financial Performance, and Organizational Challenges: A Success Case in Portugal. In L. Carvalho (Ed.), *Handbook of Research on Entrepreneurial Ecosystems and Social Dynamics in a Globalized World* (pp. 379–423). Hershey, PA: IGI Global. doi:10.4018/978-1-5225-3525-6.ch017

Teixeira, P., Teixeira, L., Eusébio, C., Silva, S., & Teixeira, A. (2021). The Impact of ICTs on Accessible Tourism: Evidence Based on a Systematic Literature Review. In C. Eusébio, L. Teixeira, & M. Carneiro (Eds.), *ICT Tools and Applications for Accessible Tourism* (pp. 1–25). IGI Global. doi:10.4018/978-1-7998-6428-8.ch001

Trad, A., & Kalpić, D. (2018). The Business Transformation Framework, Agile Project and Change Management. In M. Khosrow-Pour, D.B.A. (Ed.), Encyclopedia of Information Science and Technology, Fourth Edition (pp. 620-635). Hershey, PA: IGI Global. https://doi.org/ doi:10.4018/978-1-5225-2255-3.ch054

Trad, A., & Kalpić, D. (2018). The Business Transformation and Enterprise Architecture Framework: The Financial Engineering E-Risk Management and E-Law Integration. In B. Sergi, F. Fidanoski, M. Ziolo, & V. Naumovski (Eds.), *Regaining Global Stability After the Financial Crisis* (pp. 46–65). Hershey, PA: IGI Global. doi:10.4018/978-1-5225-4026-7.ch003

Trengereid, V. (2022). Conditions of Network Engagement: The Quest for a Common Good. In R. Augusto Costa, F. Brandão, Z. Breda, & C. Costa (Eds.), *Planning and Managing the Experience Economy in Tourism* (pp. 69-84). IGI Global. https://doi.org/10.4018/978-1-7998-8775-1.ch004

Turulja, L., & Bajgoric, N. (2018). Business Continuity and Information Systems: A Systematic Literature Review. In N. Bajgoric (Ed.), *Always-On Enterprise Information Systems for Modern Organizations* (pp. 60–87). Hershey, PA: IGI Global. doi:10.4018/978-1-5225-3704-5.ch004

Vargas-Hernández, J. G. (2017). Professional Integrity in Business Management Education. In N. Baporikar (Ed.), *Management Education for Global Leadership* (pp. 70–89). Hershey, PA: IGI Global. doi:10.4018/978-1-5225-1013-0.ch004

Varnacı Uzun, F. (2021). The Destination Preferences of Foreign Tourists During the COVID-19 Pandemic and Attitudes Towards: Marmaris, Turkey. In M. Demir, A. Dalgıç, & F. Ergen (Eds.), *Handbook of Research on the Impacts and Implications of COVID-19 on the Tourism Industry* (pp. 285–306). IGI Global. https://doi.org/10.4018/978-1-7998-8231-2.ch014

Vasista, T. G., & AlAbdullatif, A. M. (2017). Role of Electronic Customer Relationship Management in Demand Chain Management: A Predictive Analytic Approach. *International Journal of Information Systems and Supply Chain Management, 10*(1), 53–67. doi:10.4018/IJISSCM.2017010104

Vieru, D., & Bourdeau, S. (2017). Survival in the Digital Era: A Digital Competence-Based Multi-Case Study in the Canadian SME Clothing Industry. *International Journal of Social and Organizational Dynamics in IT, 6*(1), 17–34. doi:10.4018/IJSODIT.2017010102

Vijayan, G., & Kamarulzaman, N. H. (2017). An Introduction to Sustainable Supply Chain Management and Business Implications. In M. Khan, M. Hussain, & M. Ajmal (Eds.), *Green Supply Chain Management for Sustainable Business Practice* (pp. 27–50). Hershey, PA: IGI Global. doi:10.4018/978-1-5225-0635-5.ch002

Vlachvei, A., & Notta, O. (2017). Firm Competitiveness: Theories, Evidence, and Measurement. In A. Vlachvei, O. Notta, K. Karantininis, & N. Tsounis (Eds.), *Factors Affecting Firm Competitiveness and Performance in the Modern Business World* (pp. 1–42). Hershey, PA: IGI Global. doi:10.4018/978-1-5225-0843-4.ch001

Wang, C., Schofield, M., Li, X., & Ou, X. (2017). Do Chinese Students in Public and Private Higher Education Institutes Perform at Different Level in One of the Leadership Skills: Critical Thinking?: An Exploratory Comparison. In V. Wang (Ed.), *Encyclopedia of Strategic Leadership and Management* (pp. 160–181). Hershey, PA: IGI Global. doi:10.4018/978-1-5225-1049-9.ch013

Wang, J. (2017). Multi-Agent based Production Management Decision System Modelling for the Textile Enterprise. *Journal of Global Information Management, 25*(4), 1–15. doi:10.4018/JGIM.2017100101

Wiedemann, A., & Gewald, H. (2017). Examining Cross-Domain Alignment: The Correlation of Business Strategy, IT Management, and IT Business Value. *International Journal of IT/Business Alignment and Governance, 8*(1), 17–31. doi:10.4018/IJITBAG.2017010102

Wolf, R., & Thiel, M. (2018). Advancing Global Business Ethics in China: Reducing Poverty Through Human and Social Welfare. In S. Hipsher (Ed.), *Examining the Private Sector's Role in Wealth Creation and Poverty Reduction* (pp. 67–84). Hershey, PA: IGI Global. doi:10.4018/978-1-5225-3117-3.ch004

Yablonsky, S. (2018). Innovation Platforms: Data and Analytics Platforms. In *Multi-Sided Platforms (MSPs) and Sharing Strategies in the Digital Economy: Emerging Research and Opportunities* (pp. 72–95). Hershey, PA: IGI Global. doi:10.4018/978-1-5225-5457-8.ch003

Yaşar, B. (2021). The Impact of COVID-19 on Volatility of Tourism Stocks: Evidence From BIST Tourism Index. In M. Demir, A. Dalgıç, & F. Ergen (Eds.), *Handbook of Research on the Impacts and Implications of COVID-19 on the Tourism Industry* (pp. 23–44). IGI Global. https://doi.org/10.4018/978-1-7998-8231-2.ch002

Yusoff, A., Ahmad, N. H., & Halim, H. A. (2017). Agropreneurship among Gen Y in Malaysia: The Role of Academic Institutions. In N. Ahmad, T. Ramayah, H. Halim, & S. Rahman (Eds.), *Handbook of Research on Small and Medium Enterprises in Developing Countries* (pp. 23–47). Hershey, PA: IGI Global. doi:10.4018/978-1-5225-2165-5.ch002

Zacher, D., & Pechlaner, H. (2021). Resilience as an Opportunity Approach: Challenges and Perspectives for Private Sector Participation on a Community Level. In A. Zehrer, G. Glowka, K. Schwaiger, & V. Ranacher-Lackner (Eds.), *Resiliency Models and Addressing Future Risks for Family Firms in the Tourism Industry* (pp. 75–102). IGI Global. https://doi.org/10.4018/978-1-7998-7352-5.ch004

Zanin, F., Comuzzi, E., & Costantini, A. (2018). The Effect of Business Strategy and Stock Market Listing on the Use of Risk Assessment Tools. In *Management Control Systems in Complex Settings: Emerging Research and Opportunities* (pp. 145–168). Hershey, PA: IGI Global. doi:10.4018/978-1-5225-3987-2.ch007

Zgheib, P. W. (2017). Corporate Innovation and Intrapreneurship in the Middle East. In P. Zgheib (Ed.), *Entrepreneurship and Business Innovation in the Middle East* (pp. 37–56). Hershey, PA: IGI Global. doi:10.4018/978-1-5225-2066-5.ch003

About the Contributors

Tereza Raquel Merlo is a researcher, professor, and practitioner working for the University of North Texas where she teaches courses in Knowledge Management Tools and Technologies. She is an avid investigator focused on Knowledge Management Systems and their impact on organizational operations and strategies. Her professional interests include business development and operations improvement processes, sales strategies, knowledge management, business intelligence, machine learning, artificial intelligence, and leadership. She received her Ph.D in Organizational Management with a minor in Information Technologies, and holds two Masters in Information Sciences from the Federal University of Bahia (UFBa) and University of North Texas. Dr. Merlo has been the recipient of multiple awards for leadership, data and records management, information literacy, diversity and inclusion, and business development. She was also the recipient of multiple scholarships, including Coordenacão de Aperfeiçoamento de Pessoal de Nível Superior (CAPES), and Fundação de Amparo à pesquisa do estado da Bahia (Fapesb) for research focusing on digital repositories in a post graduate program at UNIFACS University in Salvador, Bahia, Brazil. Dr. Merlo is part of scientific committees for Knowledge and Performance Management, Knowledge-Based System, and the Journal of Information and Knowledge Management journals, among others. Dr. Merlo serves on the international advisory board for the International Conference on Knowledge Management (ICKM), having served as co-chair, organizing the 15th annual ICKM Conference. Dr. Merlo was the keynote speaker for the 15th Annual ICKM Conference at the University of Santa Catarina, Brazil in 2019. In addition, she has a background as a consultant and professional in the field of library management and has built several information units, including libraries and archives. She worked for the City of Austin, Texas for 10 years as a librarian, where she chaired the Culture and Diversity Committee for several years and had an active role serving as chair for the Texas Library Association. Dr. Merlo was the recipient of the Junior Guild Award in 2015 for best project and leadership on diversity and inclusion in public libraries in the state of Texas. Dr. Merlo's research interests include Knowledge Management Systems (tools, technologies, governance, and processes), information systems, artificial intelligence and machine learning, business intelligence, data analytics and governance, leadership, and cloud computing. Her professional experience in the private sector includes work at multiple Fortune 100 companies. She is the editor of the book Understanding, Implementing, and Evaluating Knowledge Management in Business Settings by IGI-Global.

* * *

Jeff M. Allen is an internationally recognized scholar in the area of workforce innovation for the knowledge economy. He serves as a Regents Professor of Information Science at the University of North Texas. Together with his colleagues, he prepares students for jobs that are not yet created. At the national level, he has provided executive leadership in numerous professional organizations including the Academy of Human Resource Development, Knowledge & Information Professional Association, and University Council for Workforce and Human Resource Education. In addition, he has served as Founding-Editor of Learning and Performance Quarterly, Editor-in-Chief of Performance Improvement Quarterly, Editor of Career and Technical Education Research and Founding Director of the Center for Knowledge Solutions.

Mustafa Hafizoglu is Program Director at SDT Space and Defence Tech. with over 23 years of project/program management experience in software and hardware R&D projects in the aerospace and defense industry. He's a Ph.D. candidate at the Department of Management, Atılım University, and his main research areas are project management, social network, benefit realization management, digital and agile transformation, and knowledge management. He is teaching classes in project management and leadership development.

Suliman Hawamdeh is a professor in the Department of Information Science, College of Information, University of North Texas. He is a leading authority in the field of knowledge management and information science. Dr. Hawamdeh founded and directed several academic programs including the Master of Science in Knowledge Management in Asia in the School of Communication and Information at Nanyang Technological University in Singapore and the Master of Science in Data Science. He served as department chair and director of the interdisciplinary PhD program in Information Science at University of North Texas. Dr. Hawamdeh is the editor in chief of the Journal of Information and Knowledge Management (JIKM) and the editor of the book series on Innovation of Knowledge Management Published by World Scientific. He has authored and edited several books in the areas of knowledge management, information science, data analytics and cybersecurity. He is the founding chair of the International Conference on Knowledge Management (ICKM). In 2020, he received the ALISE Award for Professional Contribution to Library and Information Science Education.

Adil İbin obtained a bachelor's degree from Çanakkale Onsekiz Mart University, Department of Business Administration in 2012. He holds his Ph.D. degree (2022) in Management and Organization from Çukurova University. He works currently at Mersin University, Faculty of Economics and Administrative Sciences, Department of Marketing & Advertising as a lecturer. İbin delivers marketing courses at the undergraduate level. As the research area, he focuses on strategic management and has aimed to contribute to this specific area.

Malak Khader is a Ph.D. Candidate at the University of North Texas, where her field of study is broadly Information literacy, in collaboration with cultural and religious literacies. She has also done research with Information Behavior, Information Seeking, and Data Ethics.

Siti Zakiah Bt. Melatu Samsi is a lecturer in Knowledge Management and Quantitative Analysis (KMEQA) Department, Faculty of Business (FOB), Multimedia University, Malaysia. Most of her research contributions are in the area of Knowledge Management, E-Marketing, entrepreneurship education and Islamic e-Tourism.

Millicent (Milly) Njeri is currently pursuing her Ph.D., at the University of North Texas, in Information Science with a concentration in Consumer Behavior and Experience Management and minor in Research, Measurement and Statistics. Her research interests include smart tourism, data analytics, consumer experience and behavior management, and marketing. She has been, and still is, involved in various research projects, with one of the projects winning the Best Paper Award at the 8th World Tourism Conference & 22nd International Joint World Cultural Tourism Conference. She also passionate about teaching and has taught several courses in Hospitality and Tourism.

Yakkala B. V. L. Pratyusha is currently Marketing and Product Development Head of an Ed tech Start-up called Infelearn, Bangalore. Currently, she is researching on academics and life skills simultaneously to enhance student personality through engaging media content. Working on new product ideas where current generation of children in a way that they can monetize their skills in any environment.

Amy Rosellini is a knowledge management strategist currently working as Chief People Officer for a national investment real estate group. She received her PhD in Information Science with the University of North Texas. Her research focuses primarily on knowledge management systems, corporate culture and knowledge measurement.

Musa Şanal obtained a bachelor's degree from Çukurova University, Department of Economics in 2003. He holds his Ph.D. degree (2011) in Management and Organization from the same university. He works currently at Çukurova University, Faculty of Economics and Administrative Sciences, Department of Business Administration as an Associate Professor. Şanal delivers courses in the field of organizational behavior at the undergraduate and graduate levels. As the research area, he focuses on organizational behavior and has published many quality national & international manuscripts in this area. Besides journal articles, he published books & book chapters, and proceedings to contribute to the literature.

Şule Erdem Tuzlukaya is Assoc. Prof. at the Faculty of Management, Department of Management, Atılım University. Her research focuses on social networks, social capital and complex systems. Her major publications include writings of book chapters and articles in management and organization fields. Dr. TUZLUKAYA received her MSc from the University of Northampton in Management Science, and Ph.D. in Management and Organization from the Başkent University. She teaches classes in organization theory and organizational behavior.

Umut Uyan obtained a bachelor's degree from Çukurova University, Department of Business Administration in 2013. He holds his Ph.D. degree (2021) in Management and Organization from the same university. He works currently at Munzur University, Faculty of Economics and Administrative Sciences, Department of Business Administration as a lecturer. Uyan delivers courses in the field of organizational behavior at the undergraduate and graduate levels. As the research area, he focuses on knowledge management and has aimed to contribute to this area.

Bindi Varghese is a Doctorate in Commerce, specializing in tourism. As an academician and tourism professional, she has over 19 years of academic and Industrial experience. Currently, she is affiliated with Christ University, as an Associate Professor. Her research interest is towards Destination Marketing and Impact assessment studies.

Ayşe Aslı Yilmaz received her MS in Management and Organization from Inonu University in 2009. In 2011 she was assigned as the course director and instructor on Peace Support Operations(PSO), Cultural awareness in Multinational Environments, Strategic Communication, Civil Military Cooperation and Gender Awareness in PSOs in Partnership for Peace Training Center as well as different UN and NATO affiliated agencies and training centers. She is currently studying Ph.D. in Business Administration (English prg.), Social Sciences Institute at Atılım University. She is teaching classes on Airport Master Planning and International Aviation Law.

Index

www.ingramcontent.com/pod-product-compliance
Lightning Source LLC
LaVergne TN
LVHW061548290926
849162LV00004B/947